THE UNDERGROUND WAR
AGAINST REVOLUTIONARY FRANCE

William Wickham. From the portrait by Füger

THE
UNDERGROUND WAR AGAINST
REVOLUTIONARY FRANCE

The Missions of
William Wickham 1794–1800

HARVEY MITCHELL
University of Alberta, Calgary

CLARENDON PRESS · OXFORD
1965

Oxford University Press, Amen House, London E.C.4

GLASGOW   NEW YORK   TORONTO   MELBOURNE   WELLINGTON
BOMBAY   CALCUTTA   MADRAS   KARACHI   LAHORE   DACCA
CAPE TOWN   SALISBURY   NAIROBI   IBADAN   ACCRA
KUALA LUMPUR   HONG KONG

Printed in Great Britain by Butler and Tanner Ltd.
Frome and London

CONTENTS

PREFACE

THIS volume owes a debt to many people, but most of all to Professor Alfred Cobban in whose remarkable seminar at the Institute of Historical Research in the University of London I was able to meet with a number of others whose chief interest was the discussion of various problems in the history of modern France. It was there that some of my ideas were first tested; it was under the wise guidance of Professor Cobban that they took shape; and further reflection provided a broader frame of reference for the assumptions and conclusions of this study. At first dimly-conceived, the frame became clearer as I set myself the task of writing this book.

There are others whose assistance I am glad to acknowledge. For helping me to find my way through the printed and manuscript sources, I wish to record my thanks to the librarians and archivists of the Public Record Office, the British Museum, the Archives Nationales, the Archives des Affaires Étrangères, the Institute of Historical Research, the University of London, and University College. For the opportunity to consult the archival collections in Paris, I am indebted to the Central Research Fund of the University of London; for a year's stay in London, uninterrupted by teaching duties, I am most grateful to the Nuffield Foundation's generous support; and for free time in which to re-examine sources, I am happy to express my thanks to the Canada Council. For permission to reproduce the substance of my article, 'Francis Drake and the comte d'Antraigues: a Study of the Dropmore Bulletins, 1793–1796', which appeared in the *Bulletin of the Institute of Historical Research,* thanks are due to its Editor and the Institute; thanks are also owing to the Editor of the *Journal of Modern History* for allowing me to reprint certain portions of my article, 'Vendémiaire, a Revaluation', University of Chicago Press, (copyright 1958 by the University of Chicago). The kindness of Lady Charlotte Bonham-Carter is responsible for the inclusion in this book of the Füger portrait of William Wickham. To the Universities of Saskatchewan and Alberta, I wish to express my gratitude for their generous provision of secretarial assistance. Finally, it is largely because of my wife's encouragement, sound advice and patience that this book came to be written.

I

INTRODUCTION

THE history of Great Britain's involvement with the French royalists has largely been neglected by historians. It is explored in the following pages in the expectation that it will provide one of the keys to the meaning and importance of the counter-revolution, not only as it affected Anglo-royalist relations but the French Revolution itself.

The indifferent treatment of the counter-revolution has blurred the outlines of one of the great revolutionary struggles of modern times. If historians continue to confine their investigations to the thoughts, policies and activities of the men and groups who made the Revolution to the exclusion of the ideas and actions of the men who resisted it, their quest for some measure of historical objectivity will surely fail.[1] Furthermore, the success of the Revolution in overcoming the dangers to its existence must not blind us to their reality. To be sure, few historians have ignored all the forces ranged against revolutionary France, but they have invariably stressed the conventional military threats. They have devoted little attention to the rather formidable menace from the counter-revolutionary forces in all their bewildering complexity. It should also be remembered that the failure of the counter-revolution in the 'decade of revolution' and in the period of Napoleon's ascendancy was transformed into temporary success under the Restoration. Of even greater significance was the

---

[1] Although Professor E. H. Carr (*What is History* (London, 1961), p. 120) argues that history is a record of success, he concedes that 'the historian must not underestimate the opposition; he must not represent the victory as a walk-over if it was touch and go'. Professor A. B. Cobban, some time before this, was much more persuasive on this same point: 'Long ago it was pointed out that by writing the history of one side in the struggle without that of the other, the policies of the revolutionaries were reduced on occasion to the appearance of maniacal gestures in the air, like the actions of a duellist if those of his opponent were rubbed out of the picture.' ('The French Revolution', *Times Literary Supplement*, 6 January 1956.) For a stimulating rebuttal of Professor Carr's view that history is 'inevitably a success story', see Professor H. R. Trevor-Roper's article, 'E. H. Carr's Success Story', *Encounter*, xviii (May 1962), 69–77.

persistence of counter-revolutionary ideology and action in the nineteenth and twentieth centuries. That the counter-revolution is a subject worthy of major consideration is therefore beyond dispute. It will not do to permit its history to fall into the hands of the 'historian' whose *genre* is properly the spy-thriller; nor the historian whose chief purpose is the rejuvenation of the counter-revolutionary myths that have fed the enemies of the Revolution since 1789. A deeper and more enduring understanding of the revolutionary period will only be developed when more serious thought is given to the problem of the counter-revolution.

This is not meant as a slur on the valuable studies that have been published over the years. Even the first large-scale work on the subject by Antoine,[1] written during the Restoration, is useful, though excessively partisan. Blanc, while living in London, in exile from the France of Napoleon III, was the first historian to reveal the riches of British sources to future investigators.[2] It was not until the Third Republic, however, that the first standard works on the counter-revolution appeared. Thureau-Dangin's book[3] was an important landmark. The acrimonious but futile struggles between contending monarchist factions in the post-1870 period gave him a special insight into the equally sterile arguments that divided the pure and constitutional royalists of the revolutionary period. Then, within a few years of one another, Forneron[4] and Daudet[5] each produced three-volume studies. Based on original sources, their value is greatly attenuated by a curious clutter of the significant and the trivial; and Daudet's treatment is marred by excessive hostility to British intentions and by a reluctance to assess the appeal of royalism to the French people. These defects were absent in Vingtrinier's work[6] which was published after the first World War. Had he lived to complete his projected study, it would have been possible to test his claim

[1] A. Antoine (de Saint-Gervais), *Histoire des émigrés français depuis 1789 jusqu'en 1828* (3 vols., Paris, 1828).
[2] L. Blanc, *Histoire de la Révolution française* (Docks edition, 2 vols., Paris, n.d.). The first edition is dated 1847–62.
[3] P. Thureau-Dangin, *Royalistes et Républicains* (Paris, 1874).
[4] H. Forneron, *Histoire générale des émigrés pendant la Révolution française* (3 vols., Paris, 1884–90).
[5] E. Daudet, *Histoire de l'émigration pendant la Révolution française* (3 vols., Paris, 1904–7).
[6] E. Vingtrinier, *La Contre-Révolution: Première période 1789–91* (2 vols., Paris, 1924–5).

that the earliest royalist plans were the prototype of all those that were to follow. Madelin's study,[1] published in the 1930's, failed as a major contribution, because it was a thinly-disguised denigration of the Revolution and added nothing to our understanding of the counter-revolution.

Among the historians at the Sorbonne who dealt with the counter-revolution it is fair to say that Alphonse Aulard,[2] staunch defender of Republican virtue, was inclined to brush aside all royalist manifestations as momentary diversions which interfered with the great and inevitable sweep of the Revolution. Mathiez,[3] his successor, devoted more attention to royalism, but he, too, found it distasteful. Lefebvre brought to the subject a greater objectivity but, like his predecessors, he surveyed the counter-revolution from the vantage point of the revolutionaries.[4] The field of vision of all three '*universitaires*' was thus restricted to an examination of how the Revolution defended itself from its enemies. It is unfortunate that Lefebvre, having clarified the significance of the aristocratic revolution, did not expand this theme further to show the links between the *révolte nobiliaire*[5] and the counter-revolution, which after all did possess a momentum

[1] L. Madelin, *La Contre-Révolution sous la Révolution* (Paris, 1935).

[2] This is most apparent in his *Histoire politique de la Révolution française 1789-1804* (Paris, 1901).

[3] A. Mathiez, *La Révolution française* (3 vols., Paris, 1922-7). Two of his more specialized studies, *La Révolution et les étrangers* (Paris, 1918) and *La Conspiration et l'étranger* (Paris, 1918), delve more deeply into the counter-revolution. He began a more intensive study of the subject in *La Réaction Thermidorienne* (Paris, 1929) and *Le Directoire* (Paris, 1934), the latter completed by J. Godechot.

[4] G. Lefebvre, *La Révolution française* (Paris, 2nd edition, 1956). He, of course, has contributed a great deal to our understanding in *Les Thermidoriens* (Paris, 1937), *Le Directoire* (Paris, 1946), in other studies, and particularly in the book reviews and *glanes* that appeared in the *Annales historiques de la Révolution française*.

[5] P. Sagnac had already paid some attention to the problem in *La Fin de l'ancien régime et la Révolution américaine (1763-1789)* (Paris, 3rd edition, 1952). Lefebvre himself gives a good short statement in *Quatre-vingt-neuf* (Paris, 1939), Eng. tr. by R. R. Palmer, *The Coming of the French Revolution* (Princeton, 1947); and, in his course of lectures at the Sorbonne, dactylographed as *La Révolution aristocratique* (Paris, 1946), he developed fully the nature of the aristocratic revolt.   J. Egret has perhaps added most to our knowledge of this problem in a number of books and articles, the most important being *Le Parlement du Dauphiné et les affaires publiques dans la seconde moitié du XVIIIe siècle* (2 vols., Grenoble, 1942), *La Révolution des notables: Mounier et les monarchiens, (1789)* (Paris, 1950), and 'L'Aristocratie parlementaire à la fin de l'ancien régime', *Revue historique*, ccvii (1952), 1-14. He brought the results of some twenty years of work into full focus with the publication of his *La Pre-Révolution française (1787-1788)* (Paris, 1962). Still useful is H. Carré's older work, *La Fin des parlements, 1788-90* (Paris, 1912).

of its own. Such an approach, however, is evident in Professor Palmer's first volume of his projected study of the *Age of the Democratic Revolution*,[1] and is implicit in Godechot's work[2] on the counter-revolution, which might have been even better had he brought the two aspects of doctrine and action together.

A number of special studies, not all of which can be mentioned here, have served to fill the gaps. In the area of counter-revolutionary ideology, nothing has yet superseded Baldensperger's superb investigation of the ideas thrown up by the emigration.[3] He reveals with great skill how the *émigrés*, at first clinging to their previous contexts of culture and thought, were gradually forced by the necessities of distress to discover their individual capacities and to develop new theories in explanation of the débâcle. Some became prophets of the past and embraced the idyllic time of the Middle Ages; others looked to the future, trying to discover the basis of the state; and from this ferment of ideas, there emerged a significant influence on the Romantic movement. Written some thirty years later, Beik's examination[4] of the ideas of the important and not-so important thinkers of the counter-revolution is more restricted in scope but is a worthy addition to the field. Individual ideologues of the counter-revolution have not been neglected and, in this connection, no account, however brief, should omit to mention the works on Burke and Mallet du Pan, both of whom, in their vastly different ways, did so much to influence the thought of the counter-revolution. Outstanding in its subtle appreciation of Burke's political thought is Professor Cobban's book,[5] while the Italian scholar, Matteucci, has given us a careful and lively account of Mallet du Pan.[6] While hardly as important

<hr/>

[1] R. R. Palmer, *The Age of the Democratic Revolution*, vol. 1: *The Challenge* (Princeton, 1959). Vol. II: *The Struggle* (Princeton, 1964) appeared while this study was in the press.

[2] J. Godechot, *La Contre-Révolution, doctrine et action 1789-1804* (Paris, 1961).

[3] F. Baldensperger, *Le Mouvement des idées dans l'émigration française 1789-1815* (2 vols., Paris, 1924).

[4] P. H. Beik, *The French Revolution Seen from the Right* (Philadelphia, 1956).

[5] A. B. Cobban, *Edmund Burke and the Revolt against the Eighteenth Century* (London, 2nd edition, 1960). It is difficult to select other studies from the large number that have been written. Nevertheless, the following cannot be omitted from even a brief survey: J. MacCunn, *The Political Philosophy of Burke* (London, 1913); P. Magnus, *Edmund Burke* (London, 1939); P. J. Stanlis, *Edmund Burke and the Natural Law* (Ann Arbor, 1958).

[6] N. Matteucci, *Jacques Mallet du Pan* (Naples, 1957). Also see the works by B. Mallet, *Mallet du Pan and the French Revolution* (London, 1902) and F. Descostes, *La Révolution française vue de l'étranger 1789-99* (Tours, 1897).

an original thinker as either Burke or Mallet du Pan, the comte d'Antraigues received special attention some time ago from Pingaud in a work whose chief importance is biographical.[1] De Maistre,[2] Bonald,[3] and Chateaubriand[4] have, of course, been the subjects of many studies, and minor thinkers, like Maury,[5] Montlosier,[6] and Rivarol[7] have also had their views explored.

Godechot's study,[8] which is more interesting for its analysis of the active side of the counter-revolution than for its rather inchoate and drastically brief measure of counter-revolutionary ideas, must for the present be regarded as the only book that brings together the various foyers of counter-revolution, not only in France, but elsewhere. He has, in his work of synthesis, relied upon his own investigations[9] and upon a number of studies of special areas, particularly of the Vendée and the Midi.

Because the Vendée was the most dramatic stronghold of royalism, it has inspired a flood of books. During the early nineteenth century, the memory of the Vendée's struggles stimulated a battle of words between former officers of the armies

[1] L. Pingaud, *Un Agent secret sous la Révolution et l'Empire, le comte d'Antraigues* (Paris, 2nd edition, 1894).

[2] Of the literature on de Maistre, the three studies mentioned here are a good introduction: G. Cogordan, *Joseph de Maistre* (Paris, 1894); F. Descostes, *Joseph de Maistre pendant la Révolution* (Tours, 1895); H. J. Laski, *Studies in the Problems of Sovereignty* (New Haven, 1917), ch. v.

[3] Four works on Bonald should be cited: R. Mauduit, *Les Conceptions politiques et sociales de Bonald* (Paris, 1913); H. Moulinié, *De Bonald* (Paris, 1915); H. J. Laski, *Authority in the Modern State* (New Haven, 1919), ch. ii; A. Koyré, 'Bonald', *Journal of the History of Ideas*, vii (1946), 56–73.

[4] The best works on Chateaubriand are: A. Cassagne, *La Vie politique de François de Chateaubriand* (Paris, 1911); E. Beau de Loménie, *La Carrière politique de Chateaubriand de 1814 à 1830* (2 vols., Paris, 1929); H. Gillot, *Chateaubriand, ses idees—son action—son œuvre* (Paris, 1934).

[5] On Maury see J. J. F. Poujoulat, *Le cardinal Maury; sa vie et ses œuvres* (Paris, 1855).

[6] J. Brugerette, *Le comte de Montlosier et son temps (1755–1838)* (Aurillac, 1931).

[7] A. Le Breton, *Rivarol, sa vie, ses idées, son talent, d'après des documents nouveaux* (Paris, 1895). A more recent study can be found in A. V. Roche, *Les Idées traditionalistes en France de Rivarol à Charles Maurras* (Urbana, Illinois, 1937).

[8] Godechot, op. cit.

[9] Godechot's most important works in this area are: 'Moreau et les papiers de Klinglin', *Annales historiques de la Révolution française*, ix (1932), 309–24; 'Les Insurrections militaires sous le Directoire', ibid., x (1933), 129–52, 193–221; 'Le Directoire vu de Londres', ibid., xxi (1949), 311–36; xxii (1950), 1–27.

of the Republic and surviving leaders of the royalist legions. Later, works were written to support the claims of this or that party, to glorify a leader, to support a particular thesis, and especially to allocate responsibility. Republicans and royalists accused one another of having caused the civil war, and the royalists bandied charges among themselves for the defeats they had suffered. The studies of Chassin,[1] Gabory,[2] Dubreuil,[3] and Walter[4] should be singled out as typical contributions to the study of the western rebellions. A significant departure from this traditional approach has been initiated by Paul Bois.[5] Not content with exploration of insurgent motivation and responsibility, he has posed new questions and found that the accepted orthodoxies are no longer wholly valid. As a result, we can no longer be certain of the alliance between rural isolation and counter-revolutionary mentality. Of equal moment are a number of stimulating articles by Charles Tilly.[6] Moving away from the conventional sources, he has begun an intensive analysis of vital statistics, voters' lists, population registers and interrogation records. He argues that the sociologist's tools can be of immense help in defining the social distinctions between revolutionary and counter-revolutionary, in discovering what effect the changing social situation from 1789 to 1793 had in the development of opposition to the Revolution, and in singling out the regions of

[1] C. L. Chassin has rendered historians a great service by gathering together a formidable collection of documents on the Vendée: *Etudes documentaires sur la Révolution française: La Préparation de la guerre de Vendée, 1789–93* (3 vols., Paris, 1892); *La Vendée patriote, 1793–1800* (4 vols., Paris, 1893–5); *Les Pacifications de l'Ouest, 1794–1800* (3 vols., Paris, 1896–9). It should be noted, however, that Chassin's documentation is of the usual kind used by historians of the Vendée; it was intended primarily to provide illustrations of motives and responsibility.
[2] E. Gabory, *La Révolution et la Vendée* (3 vols., Paris, 1925–8); *L'Angleterre et la Vendée* (2 vols., Paris, 1930–1).
[3] L. Dubreuil, *Histoire des insurrections de l'Ouest* (2 vols., Paris, 1929–30).
[4] G. Walter, *La Guerre de Vendée, sociologie d'une contre-révolution* (Paris, 1953).
[5] Bois's pioneering works are: *Paysans de l'Ouest* (Le Mans, 1960); *Cahier de doléances du tiers état de la Sénéchaussée de Château-du-Loir pour les Etats généraux de 1789* (Gap, 1960); 'Réflexions sur les survivances de la Révolution dans l'Ouest', *Annales historiques de la Révolution française*, xxxiii (1961), 177–86.
[6] See 'Civil Constitution and Counter-Revolution in Southern Anjou', *French Historical Studies*, i (1959), 172–99; 'Local Conflicts in the Vendée before the Rebellion of 1793', ibid., ii (1961), 209–31; 'Some Problems in the History of the Vendée', *American Historical Review*, lxvii (1961), 19–33; and 'The Analysis of a Counter-Revolution', *History and Theory*, iii (1963), 30–58. His study on *The Vendée* (Cambridge, Mass., 1964) was published while this book was in the press.

counter-revolution from those that remained loyal to the Revolution. Meanwhile the British historians, Cobban, Goodwin and Hutt are extending our knowledge of Britain's concerns in the west of France during this troubled period.[1] As a result, historians are beginning to appreciate Britain's rôle in the vicissitudes of the counter-revolution.

The Midi and the south-western regions of France have also been chosen for investigation. Examinations of Pichegru's treason were popular at the beginning of the century, with Daudet[2] and Caudrillier[3] and the British historian, Hall,[4] sharing the limelight. Caudrillier's book was the most impartial and is still the best source, since it also deals with the royalist insurrections in the Midi, but Hall's study has the advantage of bringing the story down to Pichegru's death. Caudrillier's additional study of counter-revolutionary activities at Bordeaux during the second coalition is a valuable collection of documents but hardly an analysis.[5] Lebon, writing before the others, attempted a study of Britain's relations with the Midi royalists, but his exclusive reliance on British sources puts the story out of focus.[6] Other works vary in importance; Barruol's on the counter-revolution

---

[1] See, for example, A. Goodwin, 'Counter-Revolution in Brittany: The Royalist Conspiracy of the Marquis de la Rouërie, 1791–1793', *Bulletin of the John Rylands Library*, xxxix (1957), 326–55; A. B. Cobban, 'The Beginnings of the Channel Isles Correspondence', *English Historical Review*, lxxvii (1962), 38–52; M. Hutt, 'The British Government's Responsibility for the *divided command* of the Expedition to Quiberon', ibid., lxxvi (1961), 479–89; 'Spies in France 1793–1808', *History Today*, xii (1962), 158–67. (Mr. Hutt is preparing a study of the comte de Puisaye.) Three doctoral dissertations at the University of London must also be mentioned as evidence of the interest in the problem of the counter-revolution. The first is by A. King, 'The Relations of the British Government with the Emigrés and Royalists of Western France, 1793–95' (1931). (Under her married name of Williamson, Miss King has published 'Jersey, centre d'espionnage au début de la période révolutionnaire', *Revue d'histoire moderne*, ix (1934), 423–34.) N. F. Richards' 'British Policy and the Problem of Monarchy in France, 1789–1802' (1954), the second doctoral study, is good but makes the error of confusing the aims of the Paris agency with those of the constitutionalists. The third of these studies is by J. A. Johnson, 'Calonne and the Counter-Revolution, 1787–92' (1955).

[2] E. Daudet, *La Conjuration de Pichegru et les complots royalistes du Midi et de l'est, 1795–97* (Paris, 1901).

[3] G. Caudrillier, *La Trahison de Pichegru et les intrigues royalistes dans l'est avant fructidor* (Paris, 1908).

[4] J. Hall, *General Pichegru's Treason* (London, 1915).

[5] G. Caudrillier, *L'Association royaliste de l'Institut philanthropique à Bordeaux et la conspiration anglaise en France pendant la seconde coalition* (Paris, 1908).

[6] A. Lebon, *L'Angleterre et l'émigration française de 1794 à 1801* (Paris, 1882).

in Provence is badly-proportioned, the period of major interest being given the least space;[1] Lacouture's, on the other hand, is a conscientious attempt to trace the beginnings and explain the nature of the royalist movement in the south-west.[2] The history of the resistance of Lyons to the republic has been treated well in a number of studies,[3] as has the royalist reaction after 1794 in the south-east.[4] As one may expect, Lyons occupies the centre of attention, because of its massive struggles against the Jacobin dictatorship and the violence of its reaction after Thermidor. Two of the leading figures in the Lyons insurrections, Précy[5] and Imbert-Colomès,[6] have been the subjects of biographies.

A few historians have tried to evaluate the manner in which the decisions of the revolutionary government impinged upon the various problems of administration at the local level and with the growth of an indigenous counter-revolutionary movement in specific areas. Sauzay's encyclopaedic ten-volume work[7] is a good example of the first kind of study, and though particularly concerned with the persecutions endured by the church in the department of the Doubs, it is useful as a source of information on secular matters. The book on public opinion in Vienne by Doucet[8] underlines the progress of royalist agitation in its several guises from Thermidor to the *coup d'état* of Fructidor. Works on the state of public opinion in the departments of

---

[1] J. Barruol, *La Contre-Révolution en Provence et dans le Comtat* (Cavaillon, 1928).

[2] J. Lacouture, *Le Mouvement royaliste dans le sud-ouest 1797–1800* (Hossegor, 1932).

[3] E. Herriot's full-scale study, *Lyon n'est plus* (4 vols., Paris, 1937–40), can be supplemented both by earlier and later works. For example, C. Riffaterre, *Le Mouvement anti-jacobin et anti-parisien à Lyon et dans le Rhône-et-Loire en 1793* (2 vols., Lyons, 1912, 1928); L. Dubois and F. Dutacq, *Histoire de Lyon 1595 à 1814* (Lyons, 1948), vol. ii of A. J. Kleinclausz, *Histoire de Lyon* (3 vols., Lyons, 1939–in progress); R. Fuoc, *La Réaction thermidorienne à Lyon* (Lyons, 1957).

[4] Consult P. Vaillandet, 'Les Débuts de la Terreur blanche en Vaucluse', *Annales historiques de la Révolution française*, v (1928), 109–27 and 'Le Procès des juges de la commission populaire d'Orange', ibid., vi (1929), 137–63; E. Courcelle, 'La Réaction thermidorienne dans le district de Melun', ibid., vii (1930), 112–28, 252–61, 329–50, 443–53.

[5] R. du Lac, *Le Général comte de Précy* (Paris, 1908).

[6] R. Poidebard, *La Vie agitée d'Imbert-Colomès* (Lyons, 1942).

[7] J. Sauzay, *Histoire de la persecution révolutionnaire dans le département de Doubs de 1789 à 1801* (10 vols., Bescançon, 1871).

[8] R. Doucet, *L'Esprit public dans les départements de la Vienne pendant la Révolution* (Poitiers, 1909).

Côtes-du-Nord,[1] Ardèche,[2] Haute-Loire,[3] and Nord[4] follow rather closely the lines of inquiry which Doucet initiated, but only Reinhard's book on conditions in the Sarthe under the Directory can be considered comprehensive and a model for future studies.[5] Thus far perhaps the most fruitful inquiries have been those concerned with an examination of the statistics of emigration.[6] D. Greer, some ten years ago, performed an invaluable service by publishing his findings on the volume, social incidence, average length, and motivation of the emigration.[7] Though he believed that his statistical method could not claim complete exactitude because all the necessary sources for a complete tabulation were not available, it would appear that researchers in France and elsewhere are now endeavouring to provide a more accurate assessment.[8]

This rapid and necessarily incomplete survey of the historiography of the counter-revolution is proof that there exists an abundance of topics for further serious study. The point that bears repetition is that works of this kind are a relatively new phenomenon and have by no means found a secure niche in the larger study of the Revolution. In the past the major contributions to the history of the Revolution were the works of men who had a fundamental sympathy for its ideals; those who chose

[1] H. Pommeret, *L'Esprit public dans le département des Côtes-du-Nord pendant la Révolution 1789–1799* (Saint-Brieuc, 1921).

[2] C. Jolivet, *L'Agitation contre-révolutionnaire dans l'Ardèche sous le Directoire* (Lyons, 1930).

[3] E. Delcambre, *La Vie dans la Haute-Loire sous le Directoire* (Rodez, 1943).

[4] L. Jacob, 'L'Esprit public dans le Nord au début du Directoire', *Revue du Nord*, xvii (1944), 33–45.

[5] M. Reinhard, *Le Département de la Sarthe sous le régime Directorial* (Saint-Brieuc, 1936).

[6] An aid in locating the literature on this subject is to be found in D. Greer, 'A Guide to Source Material on the Emigrés of the French Revolution', *Journal of Modern History*, xv (1943), 39–46. Two of the more outstanding works will be listed here: A. Gain, *Liste des émigrés, déportés et condamnés pour cause révolutionnaire du département de la Moselle* (2 vols., Metz, 1925–32); M. Bouloiseau, *Liste des émigrés, déportés et condamnés pour cause révolutionnaire dans le district de Rouen* (Paris, 1937). G. Sangnier's *Les Émigrés du Pas-de-Calais pendant la Révolution* (Blangermont, 1959) is workmanlike but antiquarian.

[7] D. Greer, *The Incidence of the Emigration during the French Revolution* (Cambridge, Mass., 1951).

[8] Marc Bouloiseau has opened new lines of inquiry and has suggested others in his article, 'L'Émigration et les milieux populaires. Émigrations, paniques, embauchages (1791–1794)', *Annales historiques de la Révolution française*, xxxi (1959), 110–26.

to study the counter-revolution were invariably men whose chief purpose was criticism of the Revolution. Indeed the conspiracy view of revolution can still find a public.[1] There obviously still remains a vested interest in the proposition that the Revolution was avoidable, unnecessary and disastrous. Moreover, the French predilection to identify the battles of the present in terms of the past has seriously hampered the study of one of the Revolution's most important aspects. This psychological curiosity has had the effect of alienating the school of pro-Revolution students and, until quite recently, has allowed the anti-Revolutionary romantics and the modern Right to make a captive of the counter-revolution. Fortunately the bitter quarrels of the past are being dissipated and we may yet see equal attention being given to the study of the counter-revolution by historians who can bring to it the same qualities of scholarship that have inspired the great and enduring works of Revolutionary history.

It may also be that the counter-revolution has rarely been given serious consideration because students have not always realized the significant rôle that Great Britain assumed in its destinies. Indeed, the counter-revolution studied without reference to its most powerful protector—and surely its most sympathetic—would be a study of a movement in a vacuum. It is the object of this book to show that the counter-revolution in France could never have posed the danger it did had it not been for the objectives of the British government. This fact has been forgotten or minimized, because historians have not traced the process by which Britain hoped and tried to restore the balance of power in Europe. It is quite clear, as this study aims to show, that while Britain wavered from time to time, she acted on the premise that peace would be achieved only with the re-establishment of some form of monarchy in France. This was not her attitude from the very beginning of the Revolution. Until virtually Britain's entry into the war, her ministers tried to avoid being drawn into the maelstrom. When they finally took the fatal step, their reasons were to prevent French expansion into the Austrian Netherlands and to halt the spread of revolutionary principles. Only later did they develop a kind of counter-revolutionary mentality, that is, the view that the restoration of a reformed monarchy in France was essential to peace. It is the intention

[1] B. Fay, *La Grande Révolution* (Paris, 1959).

of this investigation to reveal the development of this attitude, with its attendant consequences on the course of the counter-revolutionary movement in and outside France.

Thus this study will try to assess the causes for Britain's involvement with the royalists and what she hoped to achieve by it. It will try to answer the question of how seriously the British government committed itself to the success of the counter-revolution and why its efforts failed. It will look at these efforts as an integral part of the counter-revolutionary movement itself, for just as that movement cannot be evaluated in isolation from the actions of the British government, the policies of the latter cannot be studied apart from the movement it hoped to influence. The missions of William Wickham to Switzerland bring to light one of the most significant features of the counter-revolution. While Wickham is commonly believed to have been the British government's firmest advocate of counter-revolution, his efforts were not, as many French historians have assumed, his own private venture, but were evolved in consultation with Lord Grenville, foreign secretary in the Pitt cabinet. French historians have also tended to consider British collaboration with the royalists as marked by unbroken and harmonious agreement. This assumption must be examined in the first place, by treating in detail the organization, objectives, and methods of the royalists; and secondly, by discovering on what questions the latter and the British were in agreement and on what points they differed.

Accounts have hitherto stressed the inefficiency of royalist organization and the petty rivalries which weakened it with the result that its crude and amateurish features are impressions that have commanded acceptance. This study will suggest that although these characteristics should not be overlooked, the activities of the *émigré* royalist groups and the royalists within France were pursued with deadly earnestness. The remarkable growth of the *Institut philanthropique*, which was of tremendous importance to royalist success in the crucial elections of 1797, would not have been possible if the protagonists of royalism had constantly been at each other's throats. An attempt will also be made to discover why the period after the elections was marked by increasing divisions between the majority of the royalist deputies who were sympathetic to the monarchy but were reluctant to depart from parliamentary methods, and a small minority who, in the final stages of the struggle with the Directory, insisted that force alone would decide the issue.

The men who shaped the Revolution worked towards the realization of various goals; some of them were achieved; others were not. In almost every case, they have been the subject of serious study. The key figures of the counter-revolution also had goals, and their frustration must also be studied if we are to understand the history of the Revolution more fully. My effort to examine Britain's part in the counter-revolution forms the underlying theme of this study. It does not claim to throw a powerful searchlight on the broader problems of the counter-revolution, but will, I hope, help to restore the balance in the field of revolutionary studies.

2

RELUCTANT ALBION

T HE chancelleries of Europe had good cause to envy the position of Great Britain in the year of the great Revolution. Only six years after the loss of her American colonies, she had made a remarkable recovery. The dark cloud which had hung over British fortunes in 1783 had lifted. Exports to her former colonies, instead of diminishing, had increased. Her alliance with the United Provinces assured an entry for trade with the Continent by means of the river Scheldt, and as Prussia's ally, she was able to exploit her trade with the German states. As Russia's best customer, her influence in the North Sea and Baltic was unchallenged. In the Mediterranean, she held Spain in fetters through her possession of Gibraltar and her protection of Portugal; while, as guarantor of the dominions of the Ottoman Empire, she maintained factors there for her trade with the Far East. Her commercial ascendancy was crowned by the Commercial Treaty of 1786 with France, giving her manufactures a most lucrative market.

The rush of events that disturbed France in the spring and summer of 1789 hardly broke the surface of complacency in Britain. It was as if the French had temporarily taken leave of their senses and had adjourned to another planet. The utter incredulity of British public men was perhaps best expressed by young William Wyndham Grenville who, in later years, as foreign secretary, was to adopt a crusading spirit in the war against France. For him the Constituent Assembly's elevation of the ephemeral rights of mankind above the prerogatives of Louis XVI was a totally misguided exercise and, he hoped, a momentary aberration; he quickly accepted the news of the Bastille's capture as marking the end of the Revolution.[1] The more seasoned diplomat William Eden who was returning to Britain via France

[1] Grenville to Buckingham, 14, 20 July 1789, Historical Manuscripts Commission, *Report on the Manuscripts of J. B. Fortescue, Preserved at Dropmore* (10 vols., London, 1892–1927), i. 484, 485. Hereafter cited as *Dropmore Papers*.

from his post at Madrid was less certain that the last curtain had descended.[1] By the end of July, the duke of Leeds, the foreign secretary, set the tone for British official opinion with the statement that 'the French have done infinitely better for us hitherto, than we could possibly have done'.[2] By giving themselves up to idle theorizing about a Constitution, the French were assuring Britain's future peace and prosperity.[3] France had ceased to be 'an object of alarm' and would, for a long time to come, be 'of little importance with respect to its external politics'.[4]

As the Revolution continued to unfold, it was bound to create problems not only for France but for her neighbours. In response to them, Britain clung tenaciously to a posture of strict neutrality, which she believed was the only way to preserve her unprecedented prosperity and to ensure herself against futile entanglements in Europe. Economic expansion based on peace was the desideratum of British policy. In spite of this, Britain was drawn into the struggle engendered by the Revolution, and later became the spearhead of opposition to Revolutionary France. It is not possible to understand Britain in this rôle without examining the successive challenges to her neutrality. At first these challenges failed to make any impact upon her policy of non-intervention; however, as the war progressed, they set in motion the germs of ideas which were to form the basis of British support for the restoration of the French monarchy.

The first challenge came from the émigré princes. Under the leadership of the comte d'Artois, Louis XVI's younger brother, they settled in Piedmont and, after the October days, hopefully laid the basis for counter-revolution. That the overthrow of the Revolution could only be achieved with the aid of the sovereigns of Europe seemed to them axiomatic. Only a few years before, foreign intervention had decisively put an end to revolution in Geneva and Holland. High expectations were therefore aroused by the possibility of applying external pressure upon the new masters of France. Moreover, in a period of revolutionary

---

[1] Eden to Morton Eden, 30 July 1789, Auckland Papers, Brit. Mus. (Add. MSS.) 34429.
[2] Leeds to Fitzgerald, 31 July 1789, Leeds Papers, Brit. Mus. (Add. MSS.) 28064.
[3] Grenville to Buckingham, 14 September 1789, Duke of Buckingham and Chandos, *Memoirs of the Court and Cabinets of George the Third* (4 vols., London, 1853–5), ii. 165.
[4] Eden to Morton Eden, 29 September, 20 October 1789, Add. MSS., 34429.

upheaval, widely believed to be the result of conspiracies, few questioned the probable success of using similar means to effect a counter-revolution.[1] Hence Artois appealed to the rulers of Spain, Austria and Piedmont for assistance.[2] In December, he asked Calonne, the former French controller-general of finances,[3] to present a similar request to the British ministry. Calonne insisted that Artois was interested only in restoring Louis XVI to his ancient prerogatives and so terminate the disturbances that were convulsing France and that failure to halt the revolutionaries would involve all of Europe in commercial ruin. He invited the British government to support Artois' plan to lead a counter-revolutionary force to France. Once success had crowned his efforts, the restored monarchy would willingly surrender an unspecified number of French colonies to Britain. Calonne further suggested that an alliance of France, Britain and Prussia would serve the interests of Europe better than the 'unnatural' Franco-Austrian Treaty of 1756.[4]

The diplomatic situation made nonsense of Calonne's proposal to bring France and Prussia closer together. Prussia was doing all in her power to embarrass Austria and win Poland as an ally. Moreover, Prussia's encouragement of the revolution in Brabant in the summer of 1789 threatened British as well as Austrian interests. As Pitt put it, a successful revolution in Brabant would lead to the union of the Austrian Netherlands with France, and to prevent this rupture in the balance of power he was prepared to go to war.[5] Neither would he countenance Prussia's policy of subversion in the other Habsburg territories: Austria must be given every opportunity to extricate herself honourably from her war with Turkey and to bring the Belgian revolt to a conclusion. The accession of the more practical Leopold II to the Habsburg

[1] For a lively discussion of foreign intervention in Holland, see A. B. Cobban, *Ambassadors and Secret Agents* (London, 1954). Palmer considers the implications of the Dutch, Belgian and Genevan revolutions and the revolutionary and counter-revolutionary patterns they established in his *Age of the Democratic Revolution*, pp. 323–70, esp. pp. 364–70.

[2] Vingtrinier, op. cit., i. 76–82, 126.

[3] See A. Goodwin ('Calonne, the Assembly of French Notables and the Origins of the Révolte Nobiliaire', *English Historical Review*, lxi (1946), 202–34, 329–77) for a sympathetic account of Calonne's pre-Revolutionary reform programme.

[4] Mémoire secrète, 14 December 1789, Add. MSS., 28068.

[5] A. W. Ward and G. P. Gooch (eds.), *The Cambridge History of British Foreign Policy 1783–1919* (3 vols., Cambridge, 1922–3), i. 186–8.

throne and his profession of friendship for Britain were to cul-
minate in the achievement of Pitt's goals.

The dispute, early in 1790, between Britain and Spain over
Nootka Sound hardly simplified the diplomatic tangle. Under
the Family Compact of 1761, France was committed to support
Spain in the event of war. It was highly unlikely that the British
government would support the *émigré* scheme to bolster Louis'
sinking fortunes, since the French monarchy, facing a crisis at
home, could neither offer much assistance to Spain nor opposition
to Britain. To George III, who studied Calonne's memoir, a
peaceful end to the Nootka Sound affair was a necessary prelude
to any declaration supporting the restoration of Louis XVI's
full powers.[1] A less negative reply to the *émigrés* could be made,
George III implied, after the settlement of the Nootka Sound
impasse; and the solution of the latter would preferably render
any pro-royalist statement rather innocuous. Thus at this juncture,
Pitt put off Calonne with a polite but firm refusal and denied the
imputation that Britain was responsible for the chaos in France.[2]
For the time being Calonne remained silent but in May he
renewed his request for a forthright declaration on behalf of
Louis XVI.[3] This time he received no acknowledgement whatever and, soon after, informed Artois of his failure to make any
impression on the British government.

The Nootka Sound dispute was to loom ever larger during
1790. In May, Lord Robert Stephen Fitzgerald, the secretary of
the British embassy at Paris, deputizing for ambassador Dorset,

[1] George III to Pitt, 28 March 1790, Public Record Office, Chatham Papers,
[PRO 30] /8/103.
[2] Pitt to Calonne, 6 April 1790, Public Record Office, Privy Council Papers, [P.C.]
1/126. This is clearly the letter which J. Holland Rose (*Life of William Pitt* (2 vols.,
London, 1923), 1. 550) was unable to discover. Calonne's allusion to Britain's
subversion of order in France doubtless irritated the ministry, for, at the height
of the revolutionary agitation in the summer of 1789, Leeds had assured Luzerne,
the French ambassador, that there was absolutely no substance to the charges.
Nevertheless Montmorin, the French foreign secretary, pressed Luzerne to seek
evidence of British machinations. See A. Sorel, *L'Europe et la Révolution française*
(8 vols. 21st edition, Paris, 1927), ii. 30. While Holland Rose (op. cit., i. 550)
gives to the *émigrés* the honour of first place among those who spoke of 'Pitt's gold',
it is clear, from the above, that the French government was equally convinced of
Pitt's 'nefarious' plots. A. Cobban finally disposes of the myth in his article, 'British
Secret Service in France, 1784–1792', *English Historical Review*, lxix (1954), 226–61.
[3] Calonne to Pitt, 9 April 1790, P.C. 1/126; Calonne to Pitt, 15 May 1790, PRO
30/8/119.

assured the French that his government desired to preserve harmony and understanding between their two countries.[1] The advocates of war, Fitzgerald found, were the 'aristocratical party':

[They] pretend that it is incumbent on the head of the Bourbon family to protect the Spanish branch and to be faithful to the Compact. But in this they have other views than those of fidelity to the Treaty, and the glimmering hopes of Counter-Revolution, I do conceive, to be again raised within them; they see the necessity there will be of investing the King with some degree of power and hope themselves to gain strength from the reflecting rays. They pretend that we have sought the cause of the quarrel with the Spaniards in the hopes of involving France in a war and thereby making to ourselves a pretext to fall upon the French Colonies and dismember their enfeebled Empire. In short, I do believe that from despair they wish for war, and in that case . . . no artifice will be left untried to bring about a favourable change in the people and exasperate them against their Leaders and the British Nation which is the source, as they pretend to say, of all their evils and the chief fomenter, by the means of money, of the late Revolution.[2]

That the aristocrats were in the vanguard of the war party was confirmed to the British ministry by additional intelligence from Paris. In August and September, Dorset's successor at Paris, Lord Gower, informed the foreign office that the 'aristocratical party has little to hope from peace and shews evident signs of wishing to profit by the confusion which a war would certainly occasion'.[3] The outbreak of counter-revolutionary violence in the Vivarais at the Château de Jalès, he felt, was a serious threat to peace; the counter-revolutionaries were counting on it to precipitate a general war.[4]

Here was proof enough to convince the British ministry that the counter-revolutionaries' chief aim was to embroil Britain in a war with France. Moreover, it now appeared certain that they had circulated the fantastic charge that Britain was spending huge

---

[1] Fitzgerald to Leeds, 14 May 1790, O. Browning (ed.), *Despatches from Paris, 1784–1790* (2 vols., London, 1909–10), ii. 311.

[2] Fitzgerald to Leeds, 14 May 1790, ibid., 314. On the basis of this excerpt from Fitzgerald's despatch, it would seem that Holland Rose (op. cit., ii. 546) is mistaken in claiming that Fitzgerald 'longed for the political reaction . . .'

[3] Gower to Leeds, 29 August 1790, O. Browning (ed.), *Despatches of Earl Gower* (Cambridge, 1885), p. 29.

[4] Gower to Leeds, 10 September 1790, ibid., p. 32. On the various Jalès camps, see Godechot, *La Contre-Révolution*, pp. 249–53.

sums to foment disturbances in France. War with France was far from the minds of the British. In October, Pitt sent Hugh Elliott and William Augustus Miles on a special mission to dissuade the Diplomatic Committee of the Constituent Assembly from supporting Spain in the Nootka Sound affair.[1] Their instructions reveal Britain's pacific intentions:

Under the present circumstances, the utmost care is necessary to use no language which can lead to an expectation of our taking measures to forward the internal views of any political party, or of our being ripe to form any alliance between the two countries, which—even if such a thing should be really wished in France—various events might make it impossible for us to accede to, and which would, in any case, require great consideration.[2]

As the year ended, James Bland Burges, under-secretary at the Foreign Office, surveyed the situation with his habitual frankness and clarity:

. . . It is surely our Interest, and there can be no doubt of its being our Plan to preserve a strict neutrality. . . . We have felt too strongly the immense advantages to be derived by this Country from such a state of anarchy and weakness as France is at present plunged in, to be so mad as to interfere in any measure, which, may, even remotely, tend to put France into the situation, where a long and sensible Experience has taught us she had the power to injure us. When she had the power, . . . she never wanted the will.[3]

Undeterred by the blank refusal with which his previous representations had been greeted, Calonne returned to the attack in April 1791, some months after Spain had submitted to British pressure. The course of the Revolution, he pleaded, was growing more dangerous.[4] The provinces were, however, straining to break with Paris, and would succeed if the powers of Europe crossed the borders into France. The uncertainty with which British intentions were viewed in the courts of Europe could be removed by Britain's renewal of her statement of April 1790 that she would like to see French dissensions ended quickly.

---

[1] For an account of this episode, see Holland Rose, op. cit., i. 578–81 and Cobban, loc. cit., 255–7.
[2] Pitt to Elliott and Miles, 25 October 1790, PRO 30/8/102.
[3] Burges to Auckland, 28 December 1790, Add. MSS., 34434.
[4] Calonne to Pitt, 29 April 1791, P.C. 1/126.

Pitt's reply intimates that British policy had not wavered.[1] Indeed, his refusal to allow Calonne to use his letter of the previous April as a propaganda weapon in the courts of Europe was an even firmer declaration of Britain's determination to refrain from all adventures in Europe.

If the British ministry turned a deaf ear to the appeals of the *émigrés*, it was not oblivious of the dangers to peace in the event that the Continental powers should give the princes a kinder reception. In May, Lord Grenville, who had succeeded Leeds at the Foreign Office, asked Eden (now Lord Auckland) at the Hague whether the Austrian government in the Netherlands was encouraging the desperate *démarches* of the *émigrés*.[2] Auckland, predicting the bankruptcy of the French government, thought it probable that Leopold was planning to intervene in France.[3] A few weeks later, he disposed of the evidence of Austrian preparations for assisting the *émigrés* as too vague, but gave some weight to Leopold's desire to 'relieve an unhappy sister . . . and also to re-establish a monarchy which may again form a counter-balance to England'.[4] As for the *émigrés*, he dismissed them with the words: 'A contre-révolution must be composed of sterner stuff.' The concluding passage of his letter is revealing in its proof of Britain's unswerving belief that so long as the new ideas held sway across the channel, France was no danger, and that continued isolation from Europe was the best guarantee of peace:

I heartily detest and abjure the whole system of the Democrates [*sic*] abstractedly consider'd; but I am not sure that the continued course of their struggles to maintain a disjointed and inefficient Government would not be beneficial to our political interests, and the best security to the permanence of our prosperity.

At any rate, the whole is involved within the womb of Time in so much obscurity, that it would surely be the part of Wisdom for us and for this Republic [Holland], to connect ourselves both ostensibly and really closer than ever, and at the same time to withdraw as well as we can from the Tourbillon of Continental Politics; and to watch the result of circumstances and events.

---

[1] Pitt to Calonne, 3 June 1791, ibid.
[2] Grenville to Auckland, 24 May 1791, *Dropmore Papers*, ii. 80.
[3] Auckland to Grenville, 27 May 1791, ibid., 85.
[4] Auckland to Grenville, 13 June 1791, ibid., 96–7.

There is a note of ironic detachment in Grenville's observation that Leopold would betray the hopes of the princes.[1] The consequences of the flight to Varennes, however, dispelled his notion that the danger of intervention had passed. The prince of Orange had apparently good grounds for believing in Austria's preparations to march with the princes. Both Gower and Auckland considered foreign intervention the height of folly. According to Gower, every opportunity ought to be given the French to 'fritter [their government] away into a nondescript metaphysical permanent anarchy, or rather ochlocracy', and they would be sure of doing so unless intervention forced them to form a powerful instrument of state both against Louis and Europe.[2] Auckland echoed these sentiments; he believed that the pressure of financial chaos would intensify 'the French Calamities [and] . . . afford the best lesson against the Abstractions of Politics, . . .[3]

Leopold's Padua Circular of 6 July, inviting the Powers 'to vindicate the liberty and honour of the Most Christian King and his family, and to limit the dangerous extremes of the French Revolution',[4] failed to elicit from Britain the expected concurrence. Conclusion of the war between Austria and Turkey remained Britain's chief diplomatic aim, for so long as they continued at loggerheads Britain could not relax her defences. Once it had been realized, there could be no objection to Austrian intervention in France.[5] Almost simultaneously, Calonne, who had journeyed to London to renew his supplications to the British government,[6] encountered a hostility which had become Britain's frozen response in her relations with the princes. 'I have an extremely bad opinion', observed Grenville, 'of any scheme the success of which is in any the smallest degree to depend on the exertions, or prudence, or means of the French Aristocrates'[7] [sic].

The news of the Treaty of Sistova of 5 August, which liquidated the war between Austria and Turkey, reached Grenville on 17 August. Even before peace was a reality, Grenville and his envoys, particularly Auckland and Gower, were turning their

[1] Grenville to Auckland, 14 June 1791, ibid., 98.
[2] Gower to Grenville, 1 July 1791, ibid., 117.
[3] Auckland to Grenville, 9 July 1791, Add. MSS., 34438.
[4] Leopold II to George III, 6 July 1791, ibid.
[5] George III to Leopold II, 23 July 1791; Grenville to Ewart, 26 July 1791, ibid.
[6] Mémoire de M. de Calonne au roi d'Angleterre, 13 July 1791, P.C. 1/127.
[7] Grenville to Auckland, 22 July 1791, Dropmore Papers, ii. 136.

thoughts to the related problems of Louis' position *vis-à-vis* the new Constitution and of Leopold's intentions towards France. Should Austria and Prussia move against France, they would proceed, Auckland believed, on the principle of restoring Louis to his full authority; they would certainly not 'become the armed mediators of a free Constitution or moderated monarchy'.[1] In Paris, Gower, tormented by the question of how Louis would be able to accept the Constitution, was consoled by the known divisions of the *émigrés* at Coblentz.[2] From Brussels, colonel William Gardiner, the government's special envoy in Belgium, reported that Louis and the National Assembly were endeavouring to make the Constitution as palatable as possible to the monarchy, and that consequently the French court was appealing to Leopold to suspend his plans to intervene.[3]

Speculation continued at a high level during those febrile days of August. Auckland enlisted Clio's aid to prove that 'offensive Leagues against a particular People have seldom succeeded; and for this obvious reason that the Party attack'd immediately acquire an union of Interests'. To strengthen the cause of peace, he suggested that the time was ripe for a British declaration of neutrality and non-intervention.[4] This course of action had been anticipated in Whitehall, for, with the conclusion of the Turkish war, the British ministry could avow its 'determination of the most scrupulous neutrality'. 'No acquisition', Grenville wrote,

is worth the expense of conquering and maintaining it. If while they [Austria and Prussia] are gaining this experience they will leave Great Britain and Holland to the undisturbed enjoyment of their external and internal tranquillity I know not what more we can wish. Our only danger (to either of us) is at home, and for averting that danger peace and œconomy are our best resources: and with them I flatter myself we have not, and I hope Holland has not, much to fear.[5]

Although Grenville ended his observations on this note of confidence, the influence of 'democratical' ideas in the Austrian

---

[1] Auckland to Grenville, 8 August 1791, ibid.
[2] Gower to Auckland, 11 August 1791, Add. MSS., 34439; Gower to Grenville, 12 August 1791, Browning, *Despatches of Earl Gower*, pp. 114-15.
[3] Gardiner to Auckland, 14 August 1791, Add. MSS., 34439.
[4] Auckland to Grenville, 16 August 1791, *Dropmore Papers*, ii. 167.
[5] Grenville to Auckland, 23 August 1791, ibid., 171-2.

Netherlands made him uneasy. His greatest source of worry was the potential union of revolutionary forces in the Netherlands and France the moment Austria decided to wage war.[1] It would be very difficult to prevent the 'flame from spreading to Holland; we must [then] interfere, and what a scene does that open?'[2] The fear that the armies, invading France ostensibly 'to prevent the infection from spreading, [would] catch it themselves, and circulate it all over Europe',[3] was an additional reason for doing everything to maintain 'that invaluable tranquillity which we are now enjoying'.[4]

The scales, Auckland believed, were tilted against intervention. While he did not minimize it as a distinct possibility, he suspected that the 'crusade' would 'halt grievously in the execution'; moreover, winter, the great 'Trucemaker', was approaching.[5] His assessment of the situation proved sound. On 27 August, Leopold and Frederick William of Prussia issued the Declaration of Pillnitz, revealing that they were not ready to intervene unless the other powers and Great Britain joined them. Auckland was content, confident that France would now 'find . . . a corrective for its own folly' and serve as a warning 'to Mankind to abstain from mad Democracies, and from the folly of attempting to establish a great Government on an abstract theory'.[6] Grenville was equally relieved; Austria and Prussia would surely remain quiescent in the face of British opposition to active intervention.[7] Within the next week, Louis' acceptance of the Constitution seemed to remove all sense of urgency.

This turn of events was little short of disastrous for the princes. The immediate aftermath of Pillnitz was the frustration of Artois' plan to seek funds and soldiers.[8] Without questioning the motives of the Pillnitz Declaration, the princes tried to persuade the British to withdraw their opposition to Leopold's use of his troops in the Netherlands against France.[9] To this

[1] Grenville to Auckland, 23 August 1791, ibid., 171–2.
[2] Grenville to Auckland, 26 August 1791, ibid., 177.
[3] Grenville to Lord St. Helens, 26 August 1791, ibid., 176.
[4] Grenville to Gower, 31 August 1791, ibid., 181.
[5] Auckland to Grenville, 27 August 1791, ibid., 177–8.
[6] Auckland to Eden, 6 September 1791, Add. MSS., 34439.
[7] Grenville to Dundas, 14 September 1791, *Dropmore Papers*, ii. 192.
[8] Jackson to Grenville, 15 September 1791, ibid., 194.
[9] De la Bintinaye to Grenville, 19 September 1791, Public Record Office, Foreign Office [F.O.] 27/37; De la Bintinaye to Dundas, 19 September 1791, F.O. 95/2.

request, came the reply that the British policy of neutrality applied 'not only to the taking no part either in supporting or opposing measures which the Powers may adopt, but also to the not influencing in any manner their determination in that respect'.[1]

Only Edmund Burke was eager to support the princes. But his influence in the inner circles of government was negligible. While most public men paid service to the eloquence and enduring qualities of his *Reflections*,[2] Huskisson, the future president of the Board of Trade in the Liverpool Cabinet, perhaps expressed best the views of the ministry by attacking Burke's 'romantic doctrines' and 'incorrectness of imagination'.[3] Because of his unyielding belief that only armed intervention could turn back the tide of Revolution, Burke was the princes' obvious candidate as intermediary with the British ministry to reverse its hands-off, 'watch and see' policy. At Calonne's request, and with the approval of the British ministry, Burke had sent his son, Richard, to Coblentz in July as an observer. The princes were at that time trying to wrest from Austria and Prussia a firm declaration favouring the restoration of the *status quo* in France.[4] As we have seen, the Pillnitz Declaration did not embody their views. Richard Burke wrote despairingly to his father of Austrian and Prussian hesitancy,[5] and sent a long memoir to Henry Dundas, secretary of war, with details of the conferences between the princes, the emperor and the king of Prussia.[6] Burke's intervention had the effect of clarifying British motives. Pitt and Grenville expressed to him their confidence in Britain's power to absorb the shock of revolutionary ideas from France. They were equally certain that the imminent bankruptcy of the French government, rather than armed intervention, would bring down the Revolution.[7]

---

[1] Grenville to Aust, 20 September 1791, F.O. 27/37.
[2] See, for example, the reactions of Bland Burges and George Rose: Burges to Auckland, 2 November 1790; Rose to Auckland, early November 1790, Add. MSS., 34434.
[3] Huskisson to his father, 18 February 1791, Huskisson Papers, Brit. Mus. (Add. MSS.) 38734.
[4] E. Burke to R. Burke Jr., 5, 9, 16 August 1791, Charles William, Earl Fitzwilliam and Sir Richard Bourke (eds.), *The Correspondence of the Right Hon. Edmund Burke* (4 vols., London, 1844), iii. 224-8, 231-3, 265-80.
[5] R. Burke to E. Burke, 10 September 1791, ibid., 314-30.
[6] Dundas to Grenville, 13 September 1791, *Dropmore Papers*, ii. 192.
[7] Burke to R. Burke Jr., 26 September 1791, ibid., 341-9.

Since Burke was unable to sway Pitt and Grenville, it is hardly surprising that comte Edouard Dillon failed as had Calonne before him.[1] Dillon's own account is worthy of being reproduced:

Upon taking my leave of Pitt, I asked him if it was necessary to inscribe on the door of his chamber the words that appear on the gates of Hell: 'Here ends all hope.' And he told me: 'My answer will be as candid as your question—yes, for anyone who looks towards a change in our system and our pledge of neutrality.'

At the beginning of 1792, Grenville assured his brother, the marquis of Buckingham, that, with few exceptions, the French wished to avoid war.[2] Neutrality was proving to be the wisest course. There was indeed no departure from it, as may be seen in the ministry's attitude towards Talleyrand's missions to London that year. As spokesman for the French constitutionalists, Talleyrand was instructed to approach the British with a suggestion for a Franco-British alliance. Though this was the essential object of his conferences with Grenville, Talleyrand was also told to request a loan of three to four million pounds and to press for the renewal of the 1786 Treaty on more favourable terms.[3]

That the constitutional royalists should have an entrée to Whitehall was nothing short of catastrophic for the princes. Would the British ministry succumb to the blandishments of the cabal at Paris? Calonne, in desperation, warned Pitt that the sole object of Talleyrand's mission was to disseminate revolutionary ideas and plant sedition. Moreover, the offer to revise the 1786 Treaty would be unproductive so long as France was the scene of interminable disorder.[4] From another source, the princes learned that the British government would not deviate from her neutrality but could not, without earning the disapproval of the Opposition, refuse to discuss commercial arrangements with the French. And from Burke, they discovered that the British ministry would do nothing to oppose Austrian and Prussian intervention, pro-

---

[1] Calonne to Pitt, 5 October 1791, PRO 30/8/119; Calonne's instructions to Dillon, same date, P.C. 1/127.
[2] Grenville to Buckingham, 6 January 1792, *Memoirs of the Court and Cabinets*, ii. 201.
[3] The only study of Talleyrand's mission in London is by G. Pallain, *La mission de Talleyrand à Londres en 1792* (Paris, 1889).
[4] Calonne to Pitt, 28 January 1792, P.C. 1/125.

vided that Frederick William did not upset the *status quo* in the Netherlands.[1]

Calonne's anxieties over Talleyrand's mission were without foundation. In two long interviews with Grenville, Talleyrand broached the subject of a Franco-British defensive alliance, asked for British neutrality in the event of war in Europe, and claimed that if hostilities did occur, the French invasion of the Netherlands would be an essentially defensive operation. Grenville refused to consider such an alliance but earnestly confirmed Britain's resolve to maintain good relations with France.[2] An alliance was out of the question, as it would wreck relations with Prussia and the United Provinces. It would also imply British approval of the Constitution, a risky venture in the light of the progress of the parliamentary reformers at home. Consequently Talleyrand returned to Paris empty-handed. He was no more successful in his second attempt, made after the French declaration of war against Austria. Even Louis' appeal to George III for an alliance received no more than a perfunctory assurance of Britain's good-will towards France.[3] A week later, Britain announced formally her intention to remain neutral in the struggle.

The outbreak of war did nothing to shatter Britain's confidence in neutrality as a safeguard against the turmoil in Europe. Indeed, as Auckland noted, had the Revolution taken its own course, mankind would have been happier.[4] There was nothing worth fighting for; there seemed to be no threat to the old 'Bugbear of the Balance of Europe'; above all, British prosperity demanded peace. Then, too, the establishment of a new government in France was difficult; perhaps it would be insuperable; it might even lead to further chaos which could turn to Britain's advantage.[5] Grenville, on the other hand, predicted French defeat and contemplated the possibility that Britain would be called upon to act as mediator between the belligerents and thus be in a position to bring good government to France.[6]

[1] Ferrand to Calonne, 3 February 1792, ibid.
[2] Pallain, op. cit., pp. 98–109, 136–41.
[3] Ibid., pp. 215–18, 282.
[4] Auckland to Grenville, 1 June 1792, Add. MSS., 34443.
[5] Auckland to Eden, 10 June 1792; see also, Auckland to Elliott, 12 June 1792, ibid.
[6] Grenville to Auckland, 19 June 1792, *Dropmore Papers*, ii. 281.

Throughout July and the first half of August, the themes of British prosperity, impending French defeat, and the future form of the French government were sounded again and again.[1]

While the fall of the French monarchy on 10 August did not alter British policy, it evoked a shrill note of alarm from British ministers. Two Cabinets were held and it was decided to recall Gower from Paris. Before departing, he was instructed to re-assert Britain's neutral position and to express deep concern for the safety of Louis and his family.[2] The immediate hope of the ministry and its friends was the rapid annihilation of the revolutionary forces. 'If no mercy is shown to places found a second time in a state of military array, it may be possible to restore order to that mad and profligate country.'[3] Thus wrote Auckland, who on the eve of Valmy prayed for the destruction of Paris at the hands of the duke of Brunswick whom he dubbed the 'scourge of Providence'.[4] Without indulging in such apocalyptic visions, Dundas intimated that Britain wished to have a hand in the re-establishment of 'such a government in France as would protect other powers from the spirit of restlessness and intrigue and would secure to the Executive Government a degree of energy as might enable it to extirpate anarchy and misrule'.[5]

Such attitudes infuriated Burke for whom a more active British policy to halt the aggressive *élan* of the Revolution seemed essential. He ridiculed the ministry's notion that the ideas of the Revolution could not cross the Channel. 'These principles', he declared, 'considering their *quality* and the *means* by which they are supported, cannot possibly be realized in practice in France, without an *absolute certainty*, and that at no remote period, of overturning the whole fabric of the British Constitution.[6] By mid-October, when it became evident that Brunswick's progress

---

[1] See, for example, Auckland to Eden, 10, 17 July 1792, Add. MSS., 34443; Auckland to Grenville, 3 July, 14 August 1792; Grenville to Gower, 13, 19 July 1792, *Dropmore Papers*, ii. 286, 291, 294, 300; Grenville to Auckland, 4 August 1792, Bishop of Bath and Wells (ed.), *Journal and Correspondence of William, Lord Auckland* (4 vols., London, 1861-2), ii. 425-6.

[2] Burges to Auckland, 17 August 1792, *Journal and Correspondence of Auckland*, ii. 433-5; Rose to Auckland, 20 August 1792, Add. MSS., 34444.

[3] Auckland to Burges, 28 August 1792, Add. MSS., 34444.

[4] Auckland to Eden, 11 September 1792, ibid.

[5] Dundas to Murray, 12 September 1792, *Dropmore Papers*, ii. 313.

[6] Burke to Grenville, 19 September 1792, ibid., iii. 466-7.

was being checked by the French, Burke noted that the military might of Europe had fled before a troop of 'strolling-players', while Britain did nothing but add to the inanity of Austria and Prussia.[1]

The ministry was indeed determined to remain aloof. The disasters suffered by the invaders were for Grenville a conclusive demonstration of British wisdom. Doubtless referring to Burke's strictures, he conceded that Britain's attitude appeared indifferent; but had not the invasion of France accomplished precisely what it had set out to prevent? Had not the Revolution been strengthened? Would France become a Republic? Perhaps. Would Britain recognize her? Yes—if a republican form of government took firm root.[2] Every day of peace was a blessing: it would preserve the Constitution and improve the conditions of the 'lower orders'.[3] At The Hague, Auckland subscribed to Grenville's ultimate plans to recognize the Republic on the principle of the *status quo*.[4] At the same time the rapid advance of the French in the Netherlands might force the United Provinces to seek the support and protection of Britain.[5] Grenville, for whom these observations were meant, noted that the ministry would not hesitate to come to the assistance of the Dutch Republic;[6] and he did not conceal his belief that the French conquest of Flanders would likely precipitate matters.[7] Pitt was of the same mind. It was 'absolutely impossible to hesitate as to supporting our ally in case of necessity . . .'[8]

[1] Burke to R. Burke Jr., 17 October 1792, *Correspondence of Edmund Burke*, iv. 19–24.

[2] Grenville to Auckland, 6 November 1792, *Journal and Correspondence of Auckland*, ii. 464–7.

[3] Grenville to Buckingham, 7 November 1792, *Memoirs of the Court and Cabinets*, ii. 221–5.

[4] Auckland to Grenville, 9 November 1792, *Dropmore Papers*, ii. 329; Auckland to Eden, 10 November 1792, Add. MSS., 34445.

[5] Auckland to Grenville, 9 November 1792, ibid.

[6] Grenville to Auckland, 13 November 1792, ibid.

[7] Grenville to Buckingham, 14 November 1792, *Memoirs of the Court and Cabinets*, ii. 226–8.

[8] Pitt to Stafford, 13 November 1792, L. V. Harcourt (ed.), *Diaries and Correspondence of the Right Hon. George Rose* (2 vols., London, 1860), i. 114–16. Burges believed that the march of French troops could be halted by starving France of supplies of wheat and flour, which were in short supply due to the disastrous French harvest. Why not encourage the Dutch government to purchase all supplies and thus deprive France of them? Burges to Auckland, 13 November 1792, Add. MSS., 34445.

The remainder of the year and the first month of 1793 were spent in trying to avoid catastrophe. The government's endeavours to reach a *modus vivendi* with France were unproductive. French designs on the Scheldt, their threats to the United Provinces, and their pledge to help all peoples gain freedom from oppression[1] hardly created a favourable atmosphere for negotiation. Until the news of the Scheldt decree reached Grenville, he was prepared to second Auckland's secret efforts[2] to reach a settlement with Paris through an agent ostensibly acting on behalf of Dumouriez. On 25 November, he confided to Auckland that it seemed 'unquestionably to be right that every method should be tried which affords a reasonable hope of extinguishing a flame now brought so near to us that if it continues we must suffer by it'.[3] Accordingly, with George III's reluctant approval, Auckland was given authority to continue his secret negotiations.[4] Within twenty-four hours, the news of the Scheldt Decree transformed Grenville's hopes: he now wrote of a 'concerted plan to drive us to extremities', and asked to be informed at once if Dumouriez intended to demand from the Dutch access to the Scheldt for French ships.[5]

Unprepared for war, the Dutch gave way. Auckland maintained that as the channel of the Scheldt had long been unsuitable for navigation, the importance of the Decree had been exaggerated.[6] On 2 December, Pitt's conference with the French envoys in London appeared so promising[7] that Auckland was asked to send an official communication of the progress of his negotiations with Dumouriez's agent.[8] Grenville differed both with Pitt and Auckland: the time had come for firmness and resistance to French

---

[1] By the decree of 16 November, the Convention declared open the navigation of the Scheldt and the Meuse, in violation of the Treaty of Westphalia (1648), which guaranteed to the Dutch Republic control of that navigation within its borders. By the decree of 19 November, the Convention declared its intention to support all the peoples of Europe who were desirous of overthrowing their rulers.

[2] For the details of the proposed negotiations, see Auckland to Grenville, 19, 20, 23 November 1792, Add. MSS., 34445.

[3] Grenville to Auckland, 25 November 1792, ibid.

[4] Grenville to George III, 25 November 1792; George III to Grenville, same date, *Dropmore Papers*, ii. 339.

[5] Grenville to Auckland, 26, 27 November 1792, ibid. 341, 344.

[6] Auckland to Grenville, 28 November 1792, *Dropmore Papers*, ii. 346.

[7] Pitt's memorandum on his conference with Maret, 3 December 1792, Add. MSS., 34446.

[8] Grenville to Auckland, 2 December 1792, *Dropmore Papers*, ii. 350.

pretensions.[1] The French Decree of 15 December, which announced the sequestration of noble and ecclesiastical property, the abolition of feudal dues, the suppression of the existing governments, the introduction of French paper currency and the forcible dissemination of revolutionary doctrines, drove home to the British the nature of the new France. Grenville was now convinced that war was inevitable and urged the Dutch to prepare for it.[2] By 20 January, Pitt, too, concluded that war was imminent.[3] Louis' execution provided the occasion; the French diplomats were handed their passports on 24 January, and on 1 February, the Convention declared war upon Britain and the United Provinces.

[1] Grenville to Auckland, 4 December 1792, ibid., 351-2.
[2] Grenville to Auckland, 29 December 1792, 1 January 1793, ibid., 361, 362.
[3] *Diaries and Correspondence of James Harris, first Earl of Malmesbury* (4 vols., London, 1844), ii. 501-2.

3

'ENGLAND WILL NEVER
CONSENT . . .'

ALTHOUGH the impact of revolutionary doctrines had not
been discounted by the British ministry, its hope that isolation
from the European struggle would be the most effective guarantee against them could not be sustained in the face of French
expansion. 'It is most manifest', Pitt said, of the revolutionaries in France, in his address to the House of Commons on
1 February,

> they mean to carry their principles into every nation, without exception,
> subvert and destroy every government, and to plant on their ruins their
> sacred tree of liberty. . . . England will never consent that France shall
> arrogate the power of annulling at her pleasure, and under the pretence
> of a natural right of which she makes herself the only judge, the political
> system of Europe, established by solemn treaties, and guaranteed by
> the consent of all the powers.[1]

Grenville concurred: the peace of Europe could never be secure
until France abandoned her conquests and refrained from inter-
fering in the affairs of other countries.[2]

Until the autumn of 1793, French military reverses and civil
war seemed to be fulfilling the conditions for peace. With few
exceptions, the powers of Europe had banded together and surrounded France, and by the end of June more than sixty departments were in revolt against the Convention. The Vendée[3] had
been the first to take up arms against the Republic. Brittany saw

---

[1] William Cobbett, *Parliamentary History of England* (36 vols., London, 1806–20),
xxx. 278–83.

[2] Grenville to Eden, 5 February 1793, *Cambridge History of British Foreign Policy*,
i. 549–50.

[3] 'Vendée' is the name of the department in the west which included parts of the
old provinces of Poitou and Anjou. The Vendée, as it will be used in this study,
included large parts of four departments: Loire-Inférieure; Maine-et-Loire; Deux-
Sèvres; and Vendée proper. Its boundary on the north was the Loire, it extended as
far south as the road connecting the port of Les Sables d'Olonne with Fontenay and
Niort, its western boundary was the Atlantic, and the towns of Saumur, Thouars and
Parthenay were the region's eastern limits.

similar uprisings. While the ministry made sporadic and half-hearted attempts to learn the extent of the western revolt, it was so certain of immediate military success that it blithely agreed with the continental powers to 'a great and solid dismemberment of France'.[1] Auckland, now back in Britain, told the maréchal de Castries, who pressed for British recognition of the comte de Provence as Regent of France, that this would be incompatible with the ministry's aim to seek French territory at the close of the war.[2] In Brussels, Quintin Craufurd expressed the aims of British policy even more frankly: 'to repel aggression, defend the Constitution, preserve our commercial interest, restore order and tranquillity, and establish the balance of Europe. Though the monarchy may be restored, still restoration can never be held out as a motive for the war.'[3] To Dundas at the War Office, for whom the war against France was a mere revival of the traditional rivalry, success in the West and East Indies was 'of infinite moment, both in the view of humbling the power of France, and with the view of enlarging our national wealth and security'. The ministry would therefore not be justified in altering these plans 'for the purpose of keeping a force collected to act on the coast of France'.[4]

The ministry's conception of the war and, by implication, of the Revolution came under attack from two quarters. The first of these were the counter-revolutionaries whose most dedicated spokesman in Britain was Burke. Burke, who would have been at home among the ultra-royalists of the Restoration, saw the war as an ideological struggle. Jacobinism could be destroyed only 'by putting everything, without exception, as nearly as possible, upon its former basis'.[5] The opportunities for over-throwing the Republic lay in France herself, 'if you can get to grapple with her internally'.[6] Burke was adverting to the revolt

[1] Auckland to Grenville, 17 May 1793, *Journal and Correspondence of Auckland*, iii. 60–1. The allies discussed plans for a dismemberment of France for the first time in April; Britain did not demur.

[2] Auckland to Grenville, 18 May 1793, ibid., 62–4.

[3] Craufurd to Auckland, 23 May 1793, ibid., 64–8.

[4] C. Matheson, *Life of Henry Dundas, first Viscount Melville, 1742–1811* (London, 1933), p. 182.

[5] Burke to Mercy-Argenteau, [?] August 1793, *Correspondence of Edmund Burke*, iv. 136–50.

[6] Burke to Windham, 18 August 1793, J. P. Gilson (ed.), *Correspondence of Edmund Burke and William Windham* (Cambridge, 1910), p. 49.

in the Vendée, ascribing to it more importance than to the battle-front in Flanders. When Toulon capitulated to Lord Hood at the end of August, he also questioned the wisdom of the admiral's declarations in favour of the Constitution of 1791: 'That pretended Constitution, was, in truth, the very cause of all the evils which at this moment afflict Europe; and if even it could be set up again . . . by our arms and politics, be assured . . . that things would move on again in the very same circle.'[1]

Quite another diagnosis of the struggle was entertained by the constitutional royalists, among whom the most important figures were Mallet du Pan, the celebrated Swiss publicist; Malouet, an intendant of the navy under the old regime; and Mounier, the former anglophile president of the Constituent Assembly. Malouet, in response to Mallet's urgent appeals for an allied offensive in support of the Lyons uprising,[2] complained that however enlightened the British government was, it was 'shackled by circumstances and national prejudices which leave it little advantage over other ministries'. His analysis of British aims and fears is acute:

I firmly believe that the sole interest of England is to preserve what she has, and remain as she is; but the development of power presented by France, in its actual state of disorganization, excites a sort of terror as to what she might do with a good government, as if a good government would not inevitably conduce to the order, the tranquillity, the happiness even of other nations. These erroneous ideas have prevailed everywhere and over all considerations.[3]

In two trenchant reports written for Lord Elgin, the British ambassador at Brussels, Mallet revealed the extent to which he differed from Burke. Those who were directing the revolt in the Vendée were tragically mistaken. Their hasty proclamation of a counter-revolution had strengthened the Convention, not weakened it. The Convention's opponents in the Midi, on the other hand, were acting more prudently by deliberately deferring discussion of the future form of government. If their efforts were

[1] Burke to Elliot, 22 September 1793, *Correspondence of Edmund Burke*, iv. 150–7. The other two commissioners were admiral Hood and general O'Hara.

[2] Mallet du Pan to Malouet, 16 August 1793, *Dropmore Papers*, iii. 484–5. Lyons had been in revolt against the Convention since the late spring of 1793. It fell to Republican forces on 8 October.

[3] Malouet to Mallet du Pan, 26 August 1793, A. Sayous (ed.), *Memoirs and Correspondence of Mallet du Pan* (2 vols., London, 1852), i. 383–5.

not supported by the allies, the Midi would succumb to the Convention.[1] In a second memoir, Mallet, without referring once to Burke's *Reflections*, was plainly critical of them. The Revolution, he insisted, did not find its origins in philosophy and irreligion. Neither was it a conspiracy. A revolution is a dislocation of power, which must necessarily take place whenever those in power lose the strength to protect the commonwealth. From the moment Louis XVI convoked the Estates-General, the dislocation of power occurred. The Revolution was the product of financial disorder, ministerial malversation, half-baked government measures, and successive conflicts between the sovereign and the *Parlements*. Once power had slipped from the king's hands, a struggle was bound to ensue between various groups for control of the state. The struggle was not yet over.[2]

The reactions of the British ministry to the representations of the pure and the constitutional royalists are not easily discernible because no firm agreement existed between Grenville, on the one hand, and Pitt and Dundas, on the other. Toulon provided the ministry with the occasion for issuing a declaration of Britain's ultimate war aims. Some hint of its contents was already available to prescient observers when Grenville decided to send Mounier to Switzerland, 'with a view to second and support the operations in the southern provinces of France. . . . If affairs go on well, he may be of material advantage in the arrangement of affairs in France'.[3] The constitutionalists obviously had some influence with Grenville.

The foreign secretary, however, was not uncritical of Mounier and his friends. This emerges from a consideration of the process by which the instructions to the three British Commissioners appointed to administer Toulon were drawn up. Grenville wished to include with the instructions a manifesto outlining the nature of the government which Britain was prepared to support in France. He gave much thought to the problem and his letter to Pitt concerning it throws light on his attitude to the contending royalist factions.[4] If the Constitution of 1791 were re-established purely and simply, the question of a Regency was

[1] Mallet du Pan to Elgin, 29 August 1793, Liverpool Papers, Brit. Mus. (Add. MSS.) 38352.
[2] Mallet du Pan to Elgin, 20 November 1793, Sayous, op. cit., i. 406–31.
[3] Grenville to Fitzgerald, 26 September 1793, *Dropmore Papers*, ii. 427.
[4] Grenville to Pitt, 4 October 1793, PRO 30/8/140.

not urgent because it was elective under that instrument. If, however, the hereditary monarchy were restored in the person of a minor and captive king, the problem of a Regency became immediate; it would become even more pressing if a royalist army were formed and succeeded in overthrowing the Convention. Under those circumstances the Regency would automatically fall into the hands of the young king's uncle. Of greater importance was whether to support a re-assembling of the Estates-General or to back some form of written constitution with provision in it for a representative assembly. It would be wiser still to convene an Assembly of Notables, 'or some Convention expressly differing from all Legislative bodies than to go back to all the ancient uncertainties'. Discussion with Mounier on these points apparently convinced Grenville 'how little these theorists have profited by experience, and how much danger there is in committing ourselves hastily to any distinct line . . .'

In the final instance it was Pitt who decided. He vetoed Grenville's idea of publishing a manifesto. He argued, instead, to defer it until an army was in readiness to march overland to effect a junction with Hood's naval forces. As for the vexing question of the monarchy, he thought 'a more pointed recommendation of monarchical government with proper limitations' should be the desired goal.[1] The final instructions of 19 October to the Toulon Commissioners stated 'His Majesty's conviction that the acknowledgement of an hereditary monarchy and of Louis XVII as lawful sovereign, affords the only probable ground for restoring regular government in France'. The inclusion of the word 'probable' was doubtless a concession to Grenville's fears of a hasty decision. Yet his demand for consideration of the problem of the Regency was passed over.

On 27 October, Burke asked permission to present his views on the manifesto,[2] but he was too late to prevent it from being gazetted two days later. The key passages declared that Britain did not wish to impose any form of government upon France. Instead the French people were entreated to 'join the standard of an hereditary Monarchy, not for the purpose of deciding, in this Moment of Disorder, Calamity, and Public Danger, on all the Modifications of which this Form of Government may hereafter

---

[1] Pitt to Grenville, 5 October 1793, *Dropmore Papers*, ii. 438.
[2] Burke to Dundas, 27 October 1793, ibid., 450–1.

be susceptible, but in order to unite themselves once more under the Empire of Law, of Morality, and of Religion. . . .'[1] The clear implication was that the monarchy would be reformed. With equal emphasis, the manifesto declared Britain's intention to seek territorial indemnities for herself and her allies.

Burke and his chief disciple, William Windham, were disappointed. Windham questioned the logic of the ministry's refusal to interfere in the affairs of France. Would not Britain ultimately be forced to do so?[2] Burke welcomed the ministry's decision to prosecute the war against Jacobinism and not against France, but damned it for its stupid allusions to indemnification. What roused his anger even more was the inconsistency between Britain's avowed preference for an hereditary monarchy and her refusal to recognize Louis XVII, the young king, or to aid the rebels in the Vendée.[3] A similar protest was voiced by one of the Toulon commissioners, Sir Gilbert Elliot, who believed that it was high time for his government to take action:

The interests of the Monarchy, which (although H.M. is not ultimately pledged to that principle) we have in the meanwhile avowedly espoused . . . would surely be much promoted by the presence of an ostensible and legitimate representation of the royal authority. I am persuaded it would detach from us no support on which we can depend, and it would add great accession of numbers and zeal in the service. The white cockade is universal, and 'Mon Roi' in every mouth.[4]

The ministry had, however, previously decided not to bestow its recognition on the comte de Provence as Regent. Although it was not until November that Provence informed George III of his intention to proceed to Toulon,[5] the ministry had been aware of the possibility for some time. It had known, for example, that Spain was encouraging Provence to assert his rights and

---

[1] *The London Gazette*, 1793, 947–50, cited in A. B. Cobban, *The Debate on the French Revolution* (London, 1950), pp. 460–2.

[2] Windham to Burke, 7 November 1793, Gilson, op. cit., pp. 77–8.

[3] Burke to Windham, about 8 November 1793, ibid., pp. 79–80.

[4] Elliot to Dundas, end November 1793, Countess of Minto (ed.), *Life and Letters of Sir Gilbert Elliot, first Earl of Minto from 1751 to 1806* (3 vols., London, 1874), ii. 189. In 1797 Elliot wrote: 'From the time of my arrival at Toulon nothing was heard there but the purest royalism, and I strongly solicited Government to send for the Princes and put them at the head of the counter-revolution at Toulon and in the South.' Ibid., 403.

[5] Provence to George III, 9 November 1793, *Dropmore Papers*, iii. 487.

believed that she was doing so as a means of increasing her influence in Toulon. Fear of Spain and suspicion of Provence prompted Grenville to instruct his envoys at Madrid and Genoa to dissuade the prince from carrying out his plans.[1] He also asked the government's most accomplished envoy, Malmesbury, who was on his way to Berlin, to urge the comte de Provence to abandon 'his foolish project on Toulon, which will expose him to a public affront, and oblige us to cast a slur upon him at the very moment when our interests lead us to try to raise his character, and to use him as an instrument of effecting the important objects we have in view'.[2] But before Provence could reach Toulon, it fell to the Convention.

Determined though the ministry was to withhold public recognition from the comte de Provence, it cannot be accused of neglecting entirely the question of extending assistance to the Vendée. George III would not approve of any scheme to send British troops but was not opposed to the despatch of an *émigré* corps led by Lord Moira to the coast of Brittany.[3] There was, surprisingly enough, no divergence in the views of Burke and Auckland—whose conceptions of the war were otherwise opposed—on the need to assist the Vendée. Like Burke, who felt that Dundas's West Indies strategy was shortsighted,[4] Auckland begged Grenville to consider that the overseas islands were bound to fall if Britain fought the war against the Convention in the Vendée.[5] Grenville refused to abandon the West Indies expedition; at the same time, he intimated that the ministry was thinking of a small expedition to the western coast of France.[6] Such a plan was in line with Pitt's conviction that the rout of the royalists in the Vendée had strengthened the Convention.[7] The Vendée disaster provoked Burke to caustic indignation: 'What can the meaning be of their [the British] having done so little there? Is it want of activity? Of address? Or was relief impracticable? One can't help suspecting selfishness—and that they

[1] P. Cottin, *Toulon et les Anglais en 1793* (Paris, 1898), pp. 425, 428.

[2] Grenville to Malmesbury, 9 December 1793, *Dropmore Papers*, ii. 476.

[3] Pitt to Grenville, [?] September 1793, ibid., 431.

[4] Burke to Dundas, 7 October 1793, *Correspondence of Edmund Burke*, iv. 159-61.

[5] Auckland to Grenville, 7 November 1793, *Journal and Correspondence of Auckland*, iii. 137.

[6] Grenville to Auckland, 11 November 1793, ibid., 141-3.

[7] Spencer to Windham, 11 November 1793, Gilson, op. cit., p. 82.

haven't been equally active where success was to produce no immediate credit.'[1]

Burke's accusations were, in part, justified. The ministry lacked sufficient information from the Vendée to make a considered decision on the feasibility of supporting Artois' appeal[2] to be allowed to join Moira's expedition. The Cabinet was also averse to committing itself to Artois until he and the comte de Provence consented to the principle of indemnities and to the establishment of a reformed monarchy.[3] In any case the original plan to land an expedition on the Ile de Noirmoutier was out of the question because the royalists had been cut off from the coast.[4] Nevertheless, the ministry decided to despatch Moira's expedition to another point on the French coast. The decision was also a desperate gamble, for the Cabinet already knew that the rebels had failed to take Granville, the point at which Moira was to disembark his force. Thus Moira's signals off the coast remained unanswered: the rebels had retreated towards the Loire.[5] As late as 12 December, Grenville was still mildly hopeful that the rebels would regain the offensive and march towards the coast.[6] A few days later the worst news was confirmed: Moira had failed to establish contact and had fallen back on Guernsey. The ministry had acted too late, and the rebels were left to be massacred at Le Mans and Savenay.

The first year of the war was about to close not only with the defeat of the Vendée but with the allies expelled or held in check on all frontiers. There was now no reason to defer the West Indies expedition; at the same time every effort would be made to reactivate the eastern front by pouring additional subsidies into the coffers of Berlin. As Dundas was to say later, the conquest of France's possessions overseas would contribute mightily to French reverses in Europe, because the enemy's resources depended on its colonial empire.[7] Little consideration was therefore given to the urgings of the Vendée lobby—the royalists and their

---

[1] Burke to Windham, 14 November 1793, ibid., pp. 87–9.
[2] Artois to Harcourt, 10 October 1793, F.O. 27/42.
[3] Grenville to Harcourt, 15 November 1793, ibid.
[4] Artois to Grenville, 19 November 1793, *Dropmore Papers*, ii. 469.
[5] Gabory, *L'Angleterre et la Vendée*, i. 109–10.
[6] Grenville to Buckingham, 12 December 1793, *Memoirs of the Court and Cabinets*, ii. 248–9.
[7] Matheson, op. cit., p. 198.

friends, the Portland Whigs. Yet the representations of both did not cease.

Not all of the Portland Whigs were totally disinterested lovers of the *ancien régime* for its own sake. The future secretary to the lord lieutenant of Ireland, Thomas Pelham, for example, who kept a diary of the events of this crucial period, saw in ministerial support for the monarchy an opportunity for Britain to increase her influence in Europe:

. . . It seems advisable that we should try, as far as may be consistent with our engagements to our allies, to make the Princes and nobility of France feel that their restoration is principally owing to us; by which we shall justly gain such an influence in the councils of the future government of France as will enable us to take a lead in arranging a general pacification. . . . It seems no country will be more benefited in restoring Europe to its former situation or less protected by any dismemberment of France than Great Britain . . . If this system is a good one, the capture of San Domingo, Pondicherry, or any possession of France is prejudicial . . . A dismemberment of France is a thing that every Frenchman, Aristocrate [*sic*] and Democrate [*sic*] equally revolts at . . .[1]

Given access to the secret correspondence from France, Pelham alleged that the ministry had been adequately informed of the insurrections and discontents in France; another campaign might have been avoided had the government taken prompt action.[2] Portland was equally at a loss to understand why the ministry continued to cold-shoulder the 'true royalists'.[3] '. . . Neither the capture of Martinico nor all of the French Possessions in the West Indies', he wrote, 'will have any effect here, or do one hundredth part of the Service which the Common Cause would derive from the real French army in the Vendée.'[4]

Through Francis Drake, Britain's minister at Genoa, the comte d'Antraigues was also endeavouring to convince the ministry of the expediency and moral duty to recognize the princes and launch an offensive in the Vendée. The *émigré* comte, attached to the Spanish embassy in Venice, had become the most virile

[1] Entry for 20 December 1793, Diary of 2nd Earl of Chichester, Brit. Mus. (Add. MSS.) 33629.
[2] Entry for 2 February 1794, Add. MSS., 33630.
[3] Portland to Windham, 23 March 1794, Windham Papers, Brit. Mus. (Add. MSS.) 37845.
[4] Portland to Windham, 16 April 1794, ibid.

propagandist of pure royalism. What more obvious way to influence the course of the war than to win Britain's support? This d'Antraigues endeavoured to do in a remarkable series of purportedly authentic news bulletins, which had as their motive the two great objectives of the pure royalists: recognition of a Regency and support for the Vendée. Another point, to which he alluded more than once, was the folly of a war of indemnities which was striking fear in the hearts of *all* Frenchmen, irrespective of their political views. Arch-conspirator himself, he credited the anti-royalist policy of the British ministry to the subtle intrigues of the constitutionalists at Whitehall.[1] D'Antraigues' failure to move the ministry in the first half of 1794, as well as in succeeding months and years, was not for lack of trying. However, for the time being the Vendée was dismissed as a viable theatre of war.[2]

The transformation of the military and diplomatic situation, the inclusion of the Portland Whigs in the ministry, and changes in France herself brought the government closer to a counter-revolutionary policy, albeit on lines which were not to be entirely acceptable to the pure royalists. Although Britain was victorious in the West Indies and on the seas, her land forces, together with those of Austria, sustained defeats in Belgium; and the Austrians decided to abandon Belgium to turn their attention eastwards to the final partition of Poland. The ministerial changes were a signal, however, for greater exertion, and two of the Portland Whigs, Grenville's brother, Thomas Grenville, and Earl Spencer were sent to urge Thugut, the Austrian foreign secretary, to reactivate the Flemish front. Windham, now secretary at war, was sent to Flanders for the same purpose; and Pitt considered the feasibility of recruiting an *émigré* regiment for service in Brittany and the recognition of Louis XVII and the Regent 'as soon as any footing shall be gained in the interior of France'.[3] His calculations depended on the success of the Windham and Spencer-Grenville missions; for he was thinking of a diversion in Brittany to coincide with an Austrian offensive in the east and

[1] For a fuller discussion of d'Antraigues' activities, see below, pp. 73–83, 89–92, 106–7, 187–90.
[2] Artois to Harcourt, 3 February 1794; Grenville to Harcourt, 20 March 1794, F.O. 27/43.
[3] Minute of Pitt in reference to military operations against France, 15 July 1794, *Dropmore Papers*, ii. 589.

a royalist rising in the area of Lyons.[1] When the Austrians refused to resume offensive operations, the ministry had to defer its plans. With an eye to the beginning of a fresh campaign in the spring of 1795, Grenville wrote: 'We have . . . for the present, renounced the idea of doing more than barely trying to throw in arms and supplies [to the Vendée]; and we reserve our attack for the spring, when, if our present expectations do not deceive us, we shall have the means of disposing of a very large force, independent of *émigrés*, etc.'[2]

The significance of Robespierre's fall did not go unnoticed. Thermidor was to have far-reaching consequences not only in France, but also in Britain, where the government's interpretation of its meaning was to affect her policy towards the counter-revolution. Malmesbury had no doubts that Robespierre's successors would themselves be overthrown in what had become a perpetual struggle for power.[3] He also attached great weight to the suppression of the Jacobin clubs following the attempted assassination of Tallien, one of the leaders of the anti-Robespierrist faction.[4] Grenville, himself, rejoiced because he believed that Robespierre's successors would be forced to 'lower the despotism of the Revolutionary Government'. The establishment of a number of committees challenging the powers of the great Committee of Public Safety seemed to him sufficient proof of this thesis.[5] He despaired nevertheless that military and diplomatic circumstances prevented Britain from delivering a knockout blow.[6] It was therefore essential to persevere in the struggle and not to give way.[7]

The unmistakable signs of the disintegration of the First Coalition were, however, to challenge the ministry's determination to continue the war. The constitutionalists had their own ideas on the best means of effecting a counter-revolution. In June Theodore de Lameth approached Mallet du Pan in Berne

[1] Pitt to Grenville, 24 July 1794, ibid., 604.
[2] Grenville to Thomas Grenville, 15 September 1794, *Memoirs of the Court and Cabinets*, ii. 301–2.
[3] Malmesbury to Thomas Grenville, 7 August 1794, *Diaries and Correspondence of . . . Malmesbury*, iii. 124–5.
[4] Malmesbury to Grenville, 20 September 1794, ibid., 139–40.
[5] Grenville to Buckingham, 26 August 1794, *Memoirs of the Court and Cabinets*, ii. 271–2.
[6] Grenville to Thomas Grenville, 15 September 1794, ibid., 301–2.
[7] Grenville to Buckingham, 27 September 1794, ibid., 304–7.

with a plan which he had devised in conjunction with his colleagues, Mathieu Dumas, Lafayette's former aide-de-camp, and
Brémond, who had been secretary to Terrier de Monciel when
the latter was minister of the interior in 1792. They proposed
joint action by the Thermidorians and the moderates in the
royalist camp against the Convention as soon as the allies had
penetrated France. Because of their extreme views, the princes
would not be asked to participate in the undertaking. In return
for their promise to bring an end to the war, the constitutionalists demanded that Austria free Lafayette, Alexandre de Lameth,
the duc d'Aiguillon, Duport, Bordieu and Chollet. They also
requested funds to finance their negotiations in France.[1]

In August, without revealing that these overtures had been
made to him, Mallet sent Lord Elgin at Brussels his reading of the
events that had culminated in Thermidor. The Thermidorians,
according to Mallet, were the real counter-revolutionaries. What
they had accomplished, probably with the aid of the constitutionalists and the federalists, would tend to the restoration of
the constitutional monarchy of 1791. They were consequently
opposed to a counter-revolution inspired by the devotées of the
ancien régime. In any case, such an attempt was bound to fail; the
only counter-revolution that stood any chance of succeeding
was one entrusted to men who had come to terms with the
achievements of 1789 and 1791; and Britain could be of immense help especially if she abandoned the chimerical Vendée
plans.[2]

On 24 September, Lord Fitzgerald, minister at Berne, forwarded to the Foreign Office another three of Mallet's memoirs.
In the first of these,[3] Mallet argued that recognition of the king
would rally to the Convention all shades of opinion and was
therefore to be avoided. In the Convention there were still some
170 members who had not voted for the death of Louis XVI;
some of them were already making known their approval of the
measures taken by the Thermidorians to dismantle the revolutionary government. The aristocratic party was an apparition
and no good would come from chasing after shadows. It was
otherwise with the constitutionalists. Once freedom of expression

[1] Sayous, op. cit., ii. 96–105.
[2] Mallet du Pan to Elgin, 3 August 1794, *Dropmore Papers*, ii. 616–17.
[3] Mémoire of Mallet du Pan, 16 September 1794, F.O. 74/4.

prevailed, their influence would outweigh that of the Thermidorians not only in Paris, but also in the departments and in the army.

Mallet chose the second of his memoirs[1] to disclose that overtures had been made to him to forge a union between the constitutionalists and the moderates. He added that it was conditional upon British financial support and the release of Lafayette. The constitutionalists were, it was intimated, in touch with the moderates in the Convention and would instruct them to form a league with the non-regicides and win over others to form a majority. Once assured of a majority, they would move for the release and reinstatement of the Girondins, legislate for the freedom of the press, and suppress the revolutionary committees. Would the British government, on the basis of this plan, send an agent to Switzerland to begin discussions?

In his final memoir,[2] Mallet gave the Foreign Office his views on the nature of the restoration he favoured. In the first place, it was imperative to unite all the royalist factions: the pure royalists who wished to restore the monarchy responsible to the nation through the Estates-General in three distinct orders; the *monarchiens* who desired to see the monarchy limited by a form of national representation based on heavy property qualifications, with a balance of power between the king and a bicameral legislature; and the constitutionalists who were advocates of the 1791 Constitution. Such a coalition could restore Louis XVII and recognize Monsieur as Regent. A provisional assembly of the most capable and objective men in the kingdom would then be requested to draft a constitution on the basis of the *cahiers*, the social, economic and religious reforms outlined in the decrees of August 1789, and Louis XVI's criticisms of the Constitution of 1791 on the eve of his flight to Varennes. Representation in the assembly established by the new constitution would be limited to property holders, with electors also having to fulfill property qualifications. The clergy would be re-established in all their functions but would be required to abide by an oath to the Constitution, subject to modfication through convocation. They would also be asked to confirm the alienation of clerical property, save for a capital fund which would be used to maintain the church

---

[1] Mémoire of Mallet du Pan, 19 September 1794, ibid.
[2] Mémoire of Mallet du Pan, 22 September 1794, ibid.

and its servants. The nobility would recover its property but renounce forever all personal feudal privileges.

The despatch bags containing Mallet's memoirs reached Downing Street on the night of 4 October, and the following day Grenville, after conferring with Pitt and Portland, informed George III of their eagerness to go ahead with the plan: 'We agree that, supposing this overture really to come from the prevailing party at Paris, considerable use might be made of it to accomplish the great object on which the safety of Europe seems to depend, that of restoring a government in France capable of giving protection to the inhabitants of that country and security to the other nations of Europe.'[1] He suggested therefore that a secret agent be sent to make use of the opening. The king doubted the efficacy of the plan, but agreed that it should be explored.[2]

The person whom Grenville chose for the mission to Switzerland was William Wickham, a relatively obscure government official in the Home Office where he had been in charge of the aliens division since the summer. Wickham left London for the continent on 15 October on what was to be one of the most important British missions of the war.

[1] Grenville to George III, 5 October 1794, *Dropmore Papers*, ii. 637–8.
[2] George III to Grenville, 6 October 1794, ibid., 638.

4

WICKHAM'S YEAR OF HOPE AND DISAPPOINTMENT

WILLIAM WICKHAM's place in history has been rashly under-estimated by historians of the Revolution. With one or two exceptions,[1] British historians have given Wickham only passing mention as being engaged in some dark deeds in France; they seem to have deliberately consigned him to oblivion, in a conscious or perhaps subconscious attempt to dismiss a rather unorthodox aspect of British diplomacy. The neglect, which he has suffered at the hands of his countrymen, has not been entirely matched by French historians who have linked his name with every conspiracy conceived by the 'diabolical' British. The result is that a caricature rather than a true picture of him has emerged. Typical of this sort of treatment is that by Sorel.[2] This reputable French scholar, while acknowledging the extensive nature of Wickham's counter-revolutionary projects, held him in low esteem. He condemns him as a petty conspirator, indiscriminate, impetuous, impressionable, and, above all, lacking in mature judgement. His unqualified dislike amounts to a national prejudice: what true republican could think indulgently or kindly of a man whose main aim was the subversion of a nation fighting for its life against the combined might of Europe?

William Wickham[3] was especially suited for the secret mission which Grenville asked him to undertake. They had met as students at Christ Church, Oxford. From Oxford, Wickham went, at the age of twenty-one, to Switzerland in 1782 to study civil law at the University of Geneva, where he obtained his master

[1] The chief exception is Hall's study, op. cit., in which there will be found an account of Wickham's relations with Pichegru. The military historian Colonel Ramsay W. Phipps (*The Armies of the First French Republic* (5 vols., London, 1926–1939), ii. 262–6, 269–71) pays Wickham the compliment of possessing 'great good sense which seems to have characterized him', but seems to have thought of him only as a secret service agent, ibid., ii. 262, 265.

[2] Sorel, op. cit., iv. 209–12.

[3] *Dictionary of National Biography*, xxi. 177–8.

of arts degree four years later. His connections with Geneva were strengthened in 1788 when he married Eléonore Madeleine, the daughter of Louis Bertrand, a professor of mathematics at the Academy. Bertrand was one of the two members of the privileged groups to win election to the Revolutionary Committee that replaced the old government in 1792.[1] Wickham's marriage into the Bertrand family made him a cousin of one of the most venerable men in Geneva, the ex-syndic, Pierre Rigaud; he was thus in a position to gain an intimate knowledge of Genevan politics. His friendship with Grenville and his knowledge of Switzerland brought him into the public service. His abilities as a secret agent were tested in Switzerland and Savoy even before the Revolution, and later, at the Foreign Office, he assumed responsibility for a secret foreign correspondence,[2] supervising it even after he was appointed as superintendent of aliens in the Home Office in the summer of 1794. His experience with the various *émigré* groups was an obvious qualification for the confidential mission to Switzerland. He was discreet, informed, and his convictions were in perfect accord with ministerial policy.

The instructions,[3] which Wickham carried with him as he sailed from Harwich in mid-October, contained contradictions and difficulties that were to defy easy reconciliation. On the one hand, Grenville stated firmly that a legitimate principle of government had to be restored in the person of Louis XVII. In conformity with this view, he declared that the ministry had always regarded the Constitution of 1791 as 'vicious and destructive; containing in itself the seeds of its own ruin and having led by a natural progression to all that has since happened'. Yet, while revealing thereby the extent to which Burke's horror of the French constitutional royalists had penetrated the counsels of the ministry, Grenville was prepared to negotiate with a government founded on the basis of the 1791 Constitution, provided that it did not threaten the security of its neighbours. Political expediency would, it seemed, have precedence over principle, especially as it was both impossible and undesirable to work out in advance the

[1] J. Bénétruy (ed.), E. Dumont, *Souvenirs sur Mirabeau et sur les deux premières assemblées législatives* (Paris, 1951), pp. 246-7, 313. The other was the celebrated naturalist Saussure.

[2] *Correspondence of William Wickham* (2 vols., London, 1870). Documentary confirmation of this phase of his career is lacking.

[3] Instructions to Wickham, 15 October 1794, F.O. 74/4.

political principles best suited to meet French needs. What would work was Grenville's chief guide in policy making. He consequently found it easy to accept at its face value the princes' pledge that they would pursue a policy of conciliation and moderation 'conformable to the representations which have been made from hence'. Overlooking the serious divisions between the pure and constitutional royalists, Grenville naïvely expected them to bury their picayune differences in a sudden glow of friendship. He never dreamt that disputes concerning the ultimate shape of the monarchy would loom so large and prevent, during a critical period, the mutual trust so necessary to success. The legacy of Grenville's wishful thinking was left to Wickham to work out.

Upon reaching Berne on 1 November, Wickham set out to verify the authenticity of the overtures from Paris for a restoration and peace. Even before leaving Britain, Wickham anticipated that Dumas, Lameth and Brémond would insist on the liberation of Lafayette and his fellow-prisoners as the condition of negotiation. His fears materialized. What he did not expect was that far from having received assurances from Paris, they had drawn a blank. After careful and persistent questioning they confessed that the so-called overtures from Paris had really never taken place![1] Although the affair was a ruse, it had succeeded in arousing British interest and, while the object of Wickham's mission was completed, Grenville instructed him to remain in Switzerland as chargé d'affaires in succession to Fitzgerald.[2]

Although Wickham was given no formal instructions, his mission was to involve him in a number of activities extending from the maintenance of good relations with the Cantons to the recruiting of men for the British army. His mission, perhaps the most difficult in the diplomatic service, had two main purposes. In the first place, the gathering of intelligence was deemed an essential service in Britain's efforts to decipher the motives behind the tempestuous changes in revolutionary France. As a neutral, Switzerland was one of the few remaining listening posts in Europe. Its value as a centre of communication with France would depend on Wickham's judgement, skill and tact, qualities that Barthélemy, the French ambassador in Switzerland, recognized

---

[1] Wickham to Grenville, 15 November 1794, F.O. 74/4.
[2] George III to Grenville, 4 December 1794, *Dropmore Papers*, ii. 649; Grenville to Wickham, 9 December 1794, *Correspondence of William Wickham*, i. 17-18.

in the new British envoy. In the second place, Wickham had to find means of communicating with the different factions within and outside France who wished to overthrow the Republic. Success in this required an ability to silence the squabbles between the various *émigré* groups, each of which was convinced of its charismatic powers in solving the problems of France. Wickham wanted to unite the royalist factions in a tightly-knit organization, as he believed that their continued dissension would prove suicidal. While recognizing the mutual hatred and suspicion which coloured royalist thought, he was ready to do everything within his power to reconcile the disputing parties.

With this as his objective Wickham maintained his connections with the constitutionalists. In the event that they gained power in France some measure of agreement with them was necessary.[2] Grenville neither encouraged nor dissuaded him from this course; he stressed only that it was essential to treat with any group that could provide information.[3] But Wickham reasoned that the positive co-operation of the constitutionalists was of primary importance. On condition that they would end their intrigues against Britain and take on the semblance of an organized group, he was prepared to share his confidence with them through the well-disposed Terrier de Monciel.[4] At the same time, he urged that a representative of the princes be given semi-official status to allay their suspicions of British intentions. Grenville complied with Wickham's request and sent Monciel to Switzerland.[5] Meanwhile Wickham sounded out La Champagne who had joined the standards of the prince de Condé, one of the first princes of the blood to emigrate in 1789.[6] Guessing that Monciel's purpose was the union of all the opponents of the Revolution, La Champagne was prepared to support it if the constitutionalists would agree to the restoration of the Bourbons. He admitted difficulties —and this was what Wickham had foreseen; without Condé's consent, the royalists would sabotage the plan. This was the

[1] Barthélemy to Committee of Public Safety, 7 January 1795, J. Kaulek (ed.), *Papiers de Barthélemy 1792–1797* (5 vols., Paris, 1886–94), iv. 540.

[2] Wickham to Grenville, 12 January 1795, F.O. 74/5; Fitzgerald to Grenville, 13 January 1795, *Dropmore Papers*, iii. 6–7.

[3] Grenville to Wickham, 24 February 1795, F.O. 74/5.

[4] Wickham to Grenville, 28 March 1795, ibid.

[5] Grenville to Wickham, 5 May 1795, F.O. 74/6.

[6] Wickham to Grenville, 25 May 1795, F.O. 74/7.

crucial point in the negotiations, for Monciel was eager to arrange a truce. The great obstacle he foresaw was that the blind hatred of the royalists for the constitutionalists would render trust improbable.[1] The royalists demanded complete submission. The constitutionalists were willing to sacrifice some of their demands if their opponents promised to liberalize their programme. Wickham refused to despair. He sought and gained an interview with Condé at his headquarters in Mulheim. Condé would not budge. He was convinced that the constitutionalists were laying the basis of a counter-revolution totally divorced from true royalist principles. He was, moreover, absolutely certain that they were supporters of the Orléanists and demanded nothing less than a public avowal of loyalty to the comte de Provence from the duc d'Orléans.[2] This was a condition which the constitutionalists could not meet in as much as they did not regard support for Orléans as central to their political programme.

Wickham's efforts were thus bedevilled at the outset. He had not only to harmonize the prejudices of an arch-royalist like Condé and the slightly less doctrinaire views of the prince's critics, but he also sought to prevent the possibility of their reconciliation without his mediation and against the interests of Britain.[3] At this time (June 1795) the constitutionalists were causing him the greatest anxiety; they were potentially the most powerful group both among the *émigrés* and inside France itself. Their anti-British bias seemed more virulent than the royalists'; Wickham even credited them with secret plans against Britain. British strategy should therefore be aimed at winning over some of the less intransigent constitutionalists and getting them to submit to the princes. Agreement between Monciel and Condé would be the first step. Monciel pleaded for an end to the bitterness, but Condé refused to acquiesce unless deferential apologies were forthcoming.[4] He persisted in his refusal even when a leading Lyons constitutionalist indicated his readiness for a *rapprochement*.[5] Whichever way Wickham turned, his patience and common sense were tried by the selfish and short-sighted tactics of the very groups with whom he had to work.

[1] Monciel to Wickham, 19 May 1795, F.O. 74/7.
[2] Wickham to Grenville, 25 May 1795, ibid.
[3] Wickham to Grenville, 6 June 1795, F.O. 74/8.
[4] Wickham to Grenville, 5 January 1796, F.O. 74/14.
[5] Wickham to Eden, 6 August 1795, F.O. 74/11.

The acerbity and suspicions which separated the constitutionalists from the royalists dated from the very beginning of the Revolution. The royalists regarded the constitutionalists as having been the first to undermine the king's authority. Their first, faltering, mistaken decisions had led to the bloodier events of 1792–4. It was they who had challenged the royal prerogative; it was their artless, perhaps Machiavellian dissemination of the pernicious ideas of the *philosophes*[1] which had fatally weakened the monarchy; it was their advocacy of a constitutional monarchy responsible to an elected assembly which had destroyed the work of centuries. These seditious doctrines were at the root of the Revolution and until they were repudiated any accommodation was unthinkable. To the constitutionalists, on the other hand, pure royalism was the embodiment of obsolete and dangerous ideas. To insist on their preservation was sheer folly. There could be no return to the untarnished 'ancient constitution',[2] for such a political instrument existed only in the minds of a handful of theorists who, when challenged, were unable to define, elucidate or elaborate its meaning. The revival of the *ancien régime* minus the abuses of centuries was an illusion. The restoration of the unreformed monarchy, responsible to no one and to nothing but to its enlightened good sense, was a dream. Refusal to recognize the valuable and necessary changes of the first two or three years of the Revolution would not attract popular support.

These were the arguments with which Wickham had to contend: on the one side were the royalists unwilling to accept a settlement except of their own choosing; on the other stood the constitutionalists, a little more willing to delay the question of the nature of the monarchy until success was achieved but afraid that their political beliefs and ambitions would be sacrificed. To confound the confusion, the royalists suspected that the British, by refusing to recognize Louis XVII and the comte de Provence as his Regent, were the instruments of the constitutionalists. Any

[1] The view that the *philosophes* were responsible for the débâcle is to be found in the writings of such early critics of the Revolution as the abbé Barruel. See Beik, op. cit., pp. 20–2.

[2] According to the constitutionalist, Montlosier, the pure royalists meant by the ancient constitution 'The France of Clovis and the Champs-de-Mars; ... the France of Philip the Fair and the Estates-General; ... the France of Louis XIV.' See Cte. de Larouzière-Montlosier and E. d'Hauterive (eds.) *Souvenirs d'un émigré 1791–1798* (Paris, 1951), pp. 232–3.

manœuvre which did not take account of their susceptibilities was attributed to this supposed unholy alliance of British and constitutionalist interests.

Wickham's colleague, John Trevor, minister at Turin, summed up his dilemma succinctly: 'He is necessarily obliged to put his trust in Princes and in emigrants—and he is to be pitied, perhaps as much as blamed, in this respect.'[1]

Even while Wickham was trying to unite the two parties, he was engaged in secret negotiations with a group of agents in Paris who had no connection with either the royalists or the constitutionalists and from whom he expected positive results. His rather ingenuous hope of winning over a substantial number of deputies was shattered only after months of futile negotiation; had the plan materialized, however, he had been prepared to make an outlay of £20,000.[2] His abortive attempt throws a certain amount of light on his concept of counter-revolution. He considered that success was dependent on two broad factors: an external military attack to be held in check until the intensity of internal dissension had reached a point of saturation. Thus, his insistence on the need to attract and confide in the critics of the Revolution, in this case the obviously disaffected politicians. At the same time, because the backbone of the Revolution was the army, he held that the fall of the Republic would be hastened by promoting the defection of its top military personnel. His analysis of the political temper of France proved faulty. The opponents of the Revolution were eternally hopeful and some of their unjustified optimism infected him. The military and diplomatic situation was, after all, heavily in France's favour; the first coalition had fallen apart by July. Mistaken though he was, his efforts reveal for us his intention to work with a group in France without informing either of the *émigré* groups. If he had been successful, if in fact a government had been set up in France which was ready not only to accept some form of a modified monarchy but also to settle for peace terms with Britain,[3] he had intended to present his achievement to the *émigrés* as a *fait accompli*, certain that they would have had to accept a counter-revolution not of their own making or resign themselves to permanent exile.

[1] Trevor to Drake, 18 November 1795, Drake Papers, Brit. Mus. (Add. MSS.) 46825.
[2] Wickham to Grenville, 29 April 1795, F.O. 74/6.
[3] Wickham to Grenville, 20 May 1795, F.O. 74/7.

II

As the Paris *démarche* tottered to its grave, Wickham's imagination
was captured by a plan to precipitate a series of insurrections in
the Midi, particularly in Lyons and its environs, by an invasion
of Franche-Comté. The project was first mooted in February by
Grenville who instructed Wickham to act with the Austrians in
supporting the prince de Condé's efforts to ensure his participation in a forthcoming allied offensive on the eastern borders in
the region of Franche-Comté.[1] As it was necessary to ascertain
Vienna's attitude to the plan, inquiries were made through Sir
Morton Eden, the British ambassador. While awaiting an answer
from Vienna, Grenville advised Wickham to set the scene for
insurrection in Franche-Comté and the Jura; to estimate the extent of Condé's needs and to furnish him with £30,000 if Austria
refused the necessary funds.[2] Wickham at once began to investi-
gate the feasibility of applying the first of these recommendations.

The occasion for exploiting the causes of discontent in the
eastern and southern provinces was opportune. The Thermidorian Reaction had spread from Paris to the provinces. The Convention had authorized the return of various categories of *émigrés*
and had deprived of their position of trust all those who had been
active in the revolutionary government. In the south-east, royalist
groups, arrogantly calling themselves 'Companies of Jesus' or
'Companies of the Sun', attacked known and alleged Jacobins, purchasers of national property, constitutional priests, and
'patriots of 1789'. In Lyons the first massacre of 2 February 1795
marked the beginning of the White Terror.[3] Similar orgies of
vengeance and reprisal took place at Lons-le-Saunier, Bourg,
Montbrison, Saint Etienne, Aix, Marseilles, Nîmes and Tarascon.
Either because of intimidation suffered during the prolonged
period of revolutionary zeal or because pent-up passions were
now finding long-sought release, the population of the south-
eastern provinces seemed ripe for change. This was true of Lyons
especially. The electors of Lyons had always chosen moderates

---

[1] Grenville to Wickham, 24 February 1795, *Correspondence of William Wickham*,
i. 23–5.

[2] Grenville to Wickham, 9 March 1795, ibid., 27–30.

[3] Lefebvre, *La Révolution française*, p. 423.

as their deputies in the national elections, and in 1792 had returned men who had joined the Girondin faction in Paris. In 1793 the Convention's firm but brutal suppression of the massive Lyons revolt had almost tipped the scales against the Republic. These causes, together with the industrial crises occasioned by the loss of international trade, made Lyons the most counter-revolutionary city in France.[1]

For Wickham the reports from the Midi confirmed his belief that opinion favoured a return to the pre-revolutionary forms of religion and to the monarchy. He was in touch with the comte de Précy who had taken refuge in Turin and had joined the Sardinian service after leading the terrible retreat from Lyons in 1793.[2] Together they undertook to arrange the return of *émigré* priests to France, and to put them under the supervision of a member of the higher clergy in exile at Fribourg. They then planned to instruct colonel Roland, the commander-in-chief of the Bernese troops, to take up residence at Salins in Franche-Comté, midway between Lyons and Belfort. The Salins post would be utilized as a convenient centre for the reception and transmission of intelligence from and to Paris.[3] Intrigued by the counter-revolutionary resources at hand, Wickham went on to unveil a more grandiose scheme than that first proposed by Grenville. Why not make Lyons the centre of counter-revolutionary activity in France? This could be achieved once the Austrian army penetrated Franche-Comté and the Piedmontese forces carried out successful offensive measures through Mont Cenis, the fifty-mile Alpine pass, separating Italy and France.[4]

Subsequently Wickham sent one of his agents, the chevalier d'Artéz, to urge Précy to lead the projected Lyons insurrection and to ascertain whether the Sardinian court was giving serious consideration to general De Vins' further operations in Savoy.[5] Meanwhile his Salins operations ended abruptly when the French discovered the nature of colonel Roland's activities. This, together with the succession of atrocities in Lyons and Franche-

---

[1] A good analysis of the causes of royalist resurgence in Lyons is to be found in Fuoc, op. cit., chs. ii and iii.

[2] For this part of Précy's career, see du Lac's biography, op. cit. On the retreat from Lyons, see Dubois and Dutacq, op. cit., pp. 343–4.

[3] Wickham to Grenville, 28 March 1795, F. O. 74/5.

[4] Wickham to Grenville, 28 March 1795, separate from above, ibid.

[5] D'Artéz to Grenville, 16 April 1795, ibid.

Comté, which Wickham attributed to the rash and premature actions of returning *émigré* priests and royalists, raised the possibility of punitive measures by the Convention—an eventuality which he dreaded.[1]

These unfavourable developments were offset by the news that the court at Turin had sanctioned a military expedition under De Vins who was instructed to synchronize his movements with the uprising in Lyons.[2] The situation in Lyons, Wickham now saw through the eyes of Louis Bayard, a young engineer who brought him a glowing report of the state of opinion in Lyons following the general massacres on 4 May. The instigators of the slaughter were the young men in the 'Companies of Jesus' and of the 'Sun' who had united the majority of the people in favour of royalism. They awaited only a leader, preferably Précy,[3] to convince the merchants and shopkeepers of the feasibility of acting against the army. The general insurrection in Lyons appeared so imminent that Wickham urged Grenville in the strongest terms to approve the use of funds for a volunteer force within the city under Précy's command. Thus a true counter-revolution would be initiated, and Britain would, because of the assistance given to the resurgence of royalism, gain a preponderance in French affairs.[4]

Although Grenville was more cautious than his envoy in weighing the chances for success, he came increasingly to share Wickham's views. At first, Grenville had maintained that the Franco-Prussian peace (concluded on 5 April 1795) would deter Austria from undertaking fresh offensive operations. Assistance to Lyons was therefore out of the question.[5] Nevertheless, because there appeared to be no immediate expectation of Austrian assistance for Condé, only a small sum of £20,000 should be advanced to him, as his force would bear the brunt of the fighting.

[1] Wickham to Grenville, 26 April 1795, F.O. 74/6.

[2] Wickham to Grenville, 10 May 1795, ibid.

[3] The representative of the Committee of Public Safety at Lyons, Bonnet, informed his superiors that cries of 'Long live Précy!' were to be heard everywhere in Lyons. Cited by Mathiez, *La Réaction thermidorienne*, p. 227. The *Moniteur* printed a letter dated 3 May from Lyons: 'These days, every republican is looked upon as a Terrorist, and their lives are in danger. Republicans have been massacred. Précy's general staff has been reconstituted. . . . The *émigrés* are returning *en masse* to the city.' Cited in Blanc, *Histoire de la Révolution française*, ii. 618.

[4] Wickham to Grenville, 12 May 1795, *Correspondence of William Wickham*, i. 42–9; Wickham to Grenville, 15 May 1795, F.O. 74/7.

[5] Grenville to Wickham, 5, 12 May 1795, *Correspondence of William Wickham*, i. 34–9, 40–2.

Despatches from Eden in Vienna completely dissipated the foreign secretary's prudence. It now became clear that the Austrian chancellery was intent on moving into Franche-Comté with Condé in the advance guard free to act as circumstances warranted. On the strength of these assurances, Pitt and Grenville sent colonel Charles Craufurd to Condé's headquarters with authorization to make available up to £140,000 for the prince's needs. Craufurd was also empowered to transfer as much as £30,000 to Wickham for his requirements at Lyons.[1]

During most of this preparatory period, the irregularity of communication with London forced Wickham to assume major responsibilities. In keeping with his project of using the clergy to stir up dissatisfaction, he asked Monciel to discuss the matter with La Champagne. Monciel reported that the clergy would commit themselves only with the approval of their bishops and grand vicars; the bishop of Lausanne, acting as interim bishop for the Besançon diocese, and the abbé de Chaffoy, one of his grand vicars, were likely to co-operate.[2] This was good news. Wickham then proceeded to extend his intelligence operations to Besançon and the frontier region from Lac de Joux in the south of Switzerland to La Chaux de Fonds further north.[3] However active Wickham was, the unsympathetic reactions of Trevor and Précy to his proposals momentarily shook his confidence. Précy refused to budge from Turin: the time for action had not yet arrived, and until it did, Lyons could better occupy itself in storing provisions, gathering arms and stirring up opinion.[4] Trevor was even less assuring. He reminded Wickham that an offensive commanded by De Vins in Savoy supported by British naval forces off the French coast could not be undertaken till the end of July. De Vins preferred, moreover, to make the Savoy manœuvre a defensive diversion, with naval action reducing Toulon in preparation for an invasion of Provence. A serious difference of opinion between the two envoys centred on the presumed advantages of Wickham's counter-revolutionary strategy. Would an armed insurrection confined to one area turn the tide? Trevor was doubtful. Foreign intervention could promote a true counter-revolution only when

[1] Grenville to Wickham 22 May 1795, *Correspondence of William Wickham*, i. 49–51.
[2] Monciel to Wickham, 17 May 1795, F.O. 74/7.
[3] Wickham to Grenville, 24 May 1795, ibid.
[4] Précy to Wickham, 26 May 1795, *Correspondence of William Wickham*, i. 59–61.

France, as a whole, turned against the Republic. The natural rallying point was unquestionably the monarchy but the aversion towards the comte de Provence was deeply-rooted even among royalists.[1] The obvious means to convert French opinion would be a declaration the same as, or similar to, that proclaimed in Toulon in 1793 to which all the allies had subscribed.[2]

Trevor's observations served to sharpen the outlines of Wickham's plans. The very vagueness of Wickham's original instructions, at a time when inactivity and procrastination were abhorrent to him, gave him an opportunity to elaborate his thoughts. The prospect of converting Lyons into the counter-revolutionary capital of France[3] was not to be separated from the larger scheme of overthrowing the government at Paris.[4] He enumerated the obstacles to the alternative plan for an invasion of Provence. Such an invasion would necessarily be confined to the immediate coastal area, for so long as the French controlled the Rhône and Saône the landing army could not advance to the north without risking the loss of its source of supplies. Moreover, the required strength of such an invading army would necessitate the diversion of forces from the Sardinian frontier and leave it exposed to enemy attack. Far better to combine a naval blockade of France's Mediterranean ports, sealing them off from grain supplies, with an overland invasion from Savoy directed towards Lyons. Once it was in the grasp of the Allies, France would be divided in two and the north would be deprived of supplies. Another argument, favouring Lyons as the crucial target, was that the entire Franche-Comté operation hinged on it. With the south-east in allied hands, an army entering Franche-Comté from the east would suffer little or no exposure to republican armies from Savoy, Bresse, Bugey, and Bex, particularly if a

---

[1] Trevor to Wickham, 26 May 1795, ibid., 56–9.

[2] Trevor to Wickham, 6 June 1795, F.O. 74/9. The Toulon Declaration stated, as we have seen, the British government's desire for a limited monarchy, a much less royalist preference than that professed by Britain's allies.

[3] In the following extract from a report by Gonchon, one of the commissioners sent by the Committee of General Security to Lyons, may be seen what can be taken as an expression of opinion current in the city at the time. It is also interesting as corroborating Wickham's views on the situation at Lyons. Gonchon reported the following conversation he had with a local citizen: 'It won't be long before we proclaim young Capet king of France. Lyons will then become the capital of the kingdom.' Cited by Blanc, op. cit., ii. 618.

[4] Wickham to Trevor, 2 June 1795, *Correspondence of William Wickham*, i. 73–4.

force were posted along the frontiers of Dauphiny and Savoy. But an uprising in Franche-Comté would never get off the ground unless Lyons took the first step, and Lyons would not commit itself unless it could expect support from an invasion through Savoy. It was therefore vital to persuade Vienna and Turin to hasten their preparations.[1]

Wickham felt committed by his instructions to support the combined invading forces by aiding the royalists in the Midi area. Premature royalist action in any one area was naturally to be avoided.[2] To prevent it, agents were stationed in key positions along or near the frontier of Franche-Comté and relay stations were established connecting it and Lyons. Once this system of communications was under way, Wickham sought to win over the commander of the National Guard at Lyons, Sériziat, whose connections with the commander-in-chief of the army of the Alps, general Kellermann, would be extremely useful.[3] Communications between Condé, Sériziat and the royalists in the Jura department were also essential. Condé, indecisive on this point and unwilling to defile pure royalist principles by co-operating with constitutionalists, offered instead to extend the hand of friendship after Sériziat and the Jura leaders swore to fight as partisans of Louis.[4]

During the first week of July, Wickham was able to throw off the anxieties he must have felt because of the vagueness of his original instructions, although Grenville's declaration that entire discretion in the planning and efficacy of the Lyons affair was to devolve upon Wickham[5] doubtless added a fresh source of apprehensions. In a private despatch, he informed Wickham of a projected invasion of Brittany which, if successful, would be fol-

---

[1] Wickham to Grenville, 15 June 1795, *Correspondence of William Wickham*, i. 89–98.

[2] Wickham to Trevor, 25 June 1795, ibid., 108–13.

[3] Two other high-ranking officers in the National Guard had already been gained. Wickham to Craufurd, 24 June 1795, ibid., 100–2. Wickham made no mention of the extent of the connections between the government's commissioners at Lyons and the royalists. Boisset, one of the former, distributed, in the wake of the Paris uprising in Prairial, some ten thousand rifles to the National Guard at Lyons, which was entirely made up of members of the 'Company of Jesus'. They were disarmed, at the command of the government, only a month later. There is no reason, however, to doubt that the National Guard at Lyons remained an anti-revolutionary force. See Mathiez, *La Réaction thermidorienne*, pp. 225, 228.

[4] Craufurd to Wickham, 26 June 1795, *Correspondence of William Wickham*, i. 103–7; Craufurd to Grenville, 6 July 1795, F.O. 29/5.

[5] Grenville to Wickham, 6 June 1795, ibid., 74–5.

lowed by the landing of the comte d'Artois in the area. Victory
in the west would stand a greater chance of success if a diversion
in the south-east could be effected.[1] Unfortunately, Vienna was
again having second thoughts about undertaking a Rhine offensive and permitting De Vins to advance through Savoy. It was
for Wickham to decide, Grenville concluded, whether an allied
offensive in the future would be better than an immediate insurrection in Lyons.[2] Grenville, meanwhile, alerted Trevor to co-
operate to the utmost with Wickham in promoting the formation
of an internal royalist force.[3]

The urgency of Grenville's observations confirmed Wickham
in his determination to speed up the plans he had already set in
motion. He had already advanced the small sum of £300 to the
marquis de Bourmont towards the end of June for the purpose of
linking the activities of the Vendée with those at Lyons.[4] Bourmont, a month later, put Wickham in touch with Chavanne, a
cavalry officer who had served under d'Autichamp in the west;
Wickham entrusted him with the mission of establishing communications between the Lyons royalists and Charette who was
pleading for an instant diversion in the Midi.[5] He then requested
Eden to exert pressure on the Austrian court to throw their
armies across the Rhine. The Austrians were the stumbling block.
While they promised to attempt a diversion in Upper Alsace at
once, they were disinclined to place much trust in Condé who,
they said, lacked the confidence of his compatriots in the interior.[6]
Wickham protested that the counter-revolutionary activity in
Lyons was being fanned by the young men, who were fearful that
an undisguised foreign invasion would unleash panic and destroy
all hope of rallying royalist opinion.[7] There was, Wickham argued,
no choice between two tested solutions. There was only a choice
of the lesser of two evils: the lesser evil was to risk the entrance
of Condé's army, no matter how small.[8] How else disabuse
Frenchmen of their fears that Austria's major goal in the war was

[1] Grenville to Wickham, 8 June 1795, ibid., 82–4.
[2] Grenville to Wickham, 8 June 1795, separate from above, ibid., 75–82.
[3] Grenville to Trevor, [?] June 1795, F.O. 67/17.
[4] Wickham to Grenville, 14 May 1796, F.O. 74/17.
[5] Bourmont to Wickham, 14 July 1795; Wickham to Grenville, 20 July 1795,
F.O. 74/10.
[6] Eden to Wickham, 30 July 1795, *Correspondence of William Wickham*, i. 127–9.
[7] See Fuoc, op. cit., p. 59.
[8] Wickham to Eden, 6 August 1795, *Correspondence of William Wickham*, i. 135–9.

the cession of Alsace? At Mulheim, Condé's headquarters, Wickham and his colleague Craufurd, persuaded Bellegarde, the Austrian general, of the imperative need to allow Condé to use Louis' name immediately upon entering French territory and to desist from taking any French town in the emperor's name. The interior was prepared and the plan would surely succeed if these conditions were met. The grand design had now fully blossomed in Wickham's mind: armed insurrection within France set off by the appearance of Condé on French soil; and a rapid advance by Charette in the Vendée against Hoche, the republican commander. France would thus be cut in two by the synchronization of the three movements.[1]

Of all the uncertainties that plagued Wickham, Austria's apparent indecision, both in regard to the Rhine and to the southern operations in which De Vins was the key figure, gradually undermined his belief in the possibility of ending the war in 1795. Bellegarde, he learned with dismay, had no real authority; it was general Wurmser who held the destiny of France and of the Allies in his hands.[2] Though Wickham tried to regain his self-confidence in the face of a desperate situation by stressing to Trevor the reciprocal nature of the Savoy and Rhine campaigns,[3] he could not conceal from Grenville his suspicions of the ministers at Vienna, whom he accused of deliberate inactivity.[4] The opportunity of fulfilling Grenville's request[5] to create a diversion in the south-east was becoming remote. For the first time, too, Wickham began to question the possibility of making any impression upon the myopia of Louis and his ministers, whose ill-considered sentiments in the Verona Declaration were proof of their refusal to recognize how slender were the chances of success.[6] Nothing but fear had been inspired by the Declaration, so much so that Franche-Comté was as likely to submit to the Convention's appointment of new local administrators in the Jura as welcome Condé.[7] The stalemate on the Rhine, which was

[1] Wickham to Eden, 8 August 1795, *Correspondence of William Wickham*, i. 141–51.
[2] Ibid.
[3] Wickham to Trevor, 2 August 1795, ibid., 129–35.
[4] Wickham to Grenville, 12 August 1795, ibid., 152–4.
[5] Grenville to Wickham, 24 July 1795, F.O. 74/10.
[6] Wickham to Grenville, 19 August 1795, F.O. 74/11. For a fuller discussion of the Verona Declaration, see pp. 82, 95–7.
[7] Wickham to Grenville, 26 August 1795, *Correspondence of William Wickham*, i. 161–5.

allowing the French to detach large reinforcements from the lower Rhine to Savoy and Dauphiny—about 15,000 troops had passed through Lons-le-Saunier—added to Wickham's general gloom.[1]

Faced with Austria's stubborn refusal to make use of Condé's army,[2] Wickham reluctantly concluded that any expectation of a simultaneous internal and external onslaught against the French armies had ended.[3] Yet as the preparations in Lyons and the surrounding countryside were proceeding without let-up, he felt that he could not peremptorily call a halt. He therefore granted an additional sum of £300 to the former mayor of Lyons, Imbert-Colomès[4] who had taken a leading part in the royalist uprising in 1793, for use in that city and another £7,000 to his agents, mainly priests, in Bourg-en-Bresse, Mâcon, and Montbrison.[5] The return of Imbert-Colomès to active duty was a fortunate circumstance, as he could be of great assistance to Précy. Although no longer a young man, Imbert-Colomès possessed great energy, invaluable political experience, and as open a mind as could be expected from one who had suffered great losses. He was certainly not a blind traditionalist.[6] In a sense Austria's weakness on the Rhine may have provided Wickham with some consolation; Imbert-Colomès cautioned him that an immediate Austrian offensive would, instead of encouraging the electors to reject the Convention's candidates in the forthcoming elections, throw them panic-stricken into the arms of the Republicans.[7] This observation from Imbert-Colomès provided the only note of optimism in a rapidly deteriorating situation.[8]

During much of September and the early part of October, Wickham began to expect some positive results from the growing sense of dissatisfaction with the Convention's decision to limit

[1] Wickham to Grenville, 26 August 1795, *Correspondence of William Wickham*, i. 161–5.

[2] Eden to Wickham, 22 August 1795, ibid., 158–61.

[3] Trevor to Grenville, 14 September 1795, F.O. 67/18.

[4] See Poidebard's biography, op. cit., for information on Imbert-Colomès' early career.

[5] Wickham to Grenville, 6 September 1795, F.O. 74/11.

[6] Madame Roland dismissed him as a tradesman. See Vingtrinier, op. cit., i. 97–8. But Mallet du Pan admired him as a man of principle, although not overly-endowed with good judgement, Sayous, op. cit., ii. 299.

[7] Imbert-Colomès to Wickham, 1 September 1795, F.O. 74/11.

[8] Wickham to Grenville, 26 August 1795, *Correspondence of William Wickham*, i. 161–5; Trevor to Grenville, 29 August 1795, F.O. 67/18.

the free election of members to the new national assembly or *Corps législatif*. Agitation within the Parisian sections against the decrees of 5 and 13 Fructidor, which were designed to prolong the legislative careers of two-thirds of the Conventionals, was gaining strength. Confident that his agents' preparations in Lyons were sufficiently far advanced to support the sections of Paris when they declared themselves, he sent Bayard to the capital from Lyons on 9 September to perfect communications between the two cities.[1] He even ventured the prediction—this the day before the fatal encounter between the insurgent Parisian sections and the army—that a timely conciliatory statement from Louis would induce the leaders of the sections to welcome Charette, and in this way topple the Republic. To hasten this eventuality, Précy must be persuaded to head the insurrections forming in the south. As Wickham saw it, France was in the final throes of disintegration impelled by forces converging on Paris.[2]

The collapse of the Republic appeared to be at hand. While its armies threw back the Austrians, the latter were not routed. On 6 September Jourdan's forces succeeded in forcing Clerfayt to retreat to Mainz. A fortnight later, Pichegru, commanding the now unified army of the Rhine and Moselle, captured Mannheim. However, Pichegru failed to invest Heidelberg and lost the opportunity of dividing the two Austrian armies under Clerfayt and Wurmser. At the beginning of October, the Austrian generals gained the offensive. The appearance of renewed Austrian energy seemed a favourable opportunity for utilizing the opposition that was building up in Lyons and its surrounding area. Consequently when the agent Tessonnet appeared at Condé's headquarters to tell of Imbert's decision to call off the Lyons plan, Wickham, with support from Condé and the comte d'Avaray, Louis XVIII's most trusted adviser, gave instructions to launch the projected movement when the French armies were defeated in Germany.[3] Such a decision seemed to gain additional strength from the nature of the reports from the chevalier de Guer. His description of royalist fever as far south as Marseilles and as far west as the

---

[1] Wickham to Grenville, 16 September 1795, F.O. 74/11; Bayard to Wickham, 9 October 1795, F.O. 74/12. Wickham correctly anticipated Grenville's instructions, Grenville to Wickham, 8 September 1795, *Correspondence of William Wickham*, i. 155–8.

[2] Wickham to Macartney, 4 October 1795, ibid., 176.

[3] Wickham to Grenville, 11 October 1795, F.O. 74/12.

department of Haute-Vienne, encompassing fifteen departments in all, was striking even if half the claims were accurate.[1]

While Précy did not agree that this was the right moment for a successful uprising, he submitted to Wickham's appeals to be ready to join and head the insurgents.[2] The news from Lyons seemed so promising that Wickham wrote hurriedly to London advising Grenville that he would require an additional sum of some £40,000.[3] On 10 November he received the dramatic news that Wurmser was intending to give Condé's force a share in the Rhine offensive.[4] The longed-for moment had arrived, and there was barely enough time to set the Lyons and Franche-Comté machines in motion! Wickham immediately transmitted funds to Imbert-Colomès in Lyons, wrote to Précy to hold himself in readiness, and sent off instructions to his agents in Franche-Comté. Funds were obviously required. To the agents in Franche-Comté Wickham made £6,000 available; to Imbert-Colomès and Précy he forwarded over £25,000.[5] These were the actual sums sent; they fell short of the amounts Wickham had originally intended to expend, for his first estimate had come to £50,000 for Lyons and Besançon, not including a reserve of £10,000 for emergency purposes.[6] A portion of the funds sent to Imbert-Colomès was destined as payments to Colinet, adjutant-general of the army before Lyons and general Lapoype,[7] commanding general at Lyons, both of whom had given unmistakable proof of their support.

But the defection of still another general was Wickham's greatest hope. Following the spectacular conquest of Holland, the name of the thirty-four-year old Pichegru, was the most

---

[1] De Guer to Wickham, 13 October 1795, ibid.

[2] Trevor to Grenville, 28 October 1795, F.O. 67/19.

[3] Wickham to Grenville, 6 November 1795, F.O. 74/12.

[4] Condé to Wickham, 6 November 1795, *Correspondence of William Wickham,* i. 186-9.

[5] Wickham to Grenville, 14 May 1796, F.O. 74/17.

[6] Wickham to Grenville, 10 November 1795, F.O. 74/12.

[7] Lapoype, a native of Lyons, was of noble parentage, and an old army man. He rose to become brigadier general in 1793. He was Carteaux's temporary successor as commander at Toulon that year. The Convention dismissed him for incompetence, but he seems to have succeeded in obtaining a command in Lyons in 1795. See Dr. Robinet, A. Robert and J. le Chaplain, *Dictionnaire historique et biographique de la Révolution et de l'Empire 1789-1815* (2 vols., Paris, n.d.). Kellermann had also been approached but without success. See Wickham to Grenville, 18 November 1795, *Correspondence of William Wickham,* i. 207-9.

widely circulated in France. Rumours of possible co-operation between Pichegru and the royalists had been reported by Mallet du Pan as early as May.[1] Apparently he had grown more and more disgruntled by the government's disregard—he considered it callous—of his army's elementary needs. On a more personal plane, he seems to have resented the Spartan regime into which he had been forced, particularly since the pecuniary demands of Madame Lajolais, his newly-acquired mistress, were never ending.[2] Condé, on the other side of the Rhine, was well aware of the condition of Pichegru's army and was impressed by the general's suppression of the Paris uprising of the *sans-culottes* on 1 April;[3] his reputation as the saviour of society from the undisciplined mob preceded him upon his return to his command on the Rhine. The young general had qualities which could be turned to good advantage. Condé had hopes of severing his ties with the Austrians by convincing Pichegru that a purely French force could successfully march against the Convention and precipitate its fall. Beginning in May therefore Condé made advances to Pichegru, whose responses although vague, were neither overly-evasive nor excessively hostile. In July Wickham took up Condé's suggestion to deliver Pichegru into the royalist camp.[4] But by September he refused to grant further funds to subvert Pichegru unless Condé divulged the names of the agents in communication with the general. Condé complied, and his agents, Fauche-Borel, a bookseller from Neuchâtel, and Fenouillot, received from Wickham almost £9,000 to be used in bribing Pichegru to surrender Huningen and Strasbourg at the propitious moment.[5] In October, Pichegru sent strong assurances of

---

[1] A. Michel (ed.), *Correspondance inédite de Mallet du Pan avec la cour de Vienne (1794–1798)* (2 vols., Paris, 1884), i. 205, 21 May 1795.

[2] Caudrillier, *La Trahison de Pichegru*, pp. 21–2.

[3] On Pichegru's conduct while commander of the force in Paris ordered to break up the insurrection, see K. D. Tönnesson, *La Défaite des sans-culottes* (Paris and Oslo, 1959), pp. 207, 213–17, 220–1.

[4] Wickham to Grenville, 25 May 1795, F.O. 74/7; Craufurd to Grenville, 6 July 1795, F.O. 29/5; Wickham to Grenville, 8 March 1797, F.O. 74/20. Cf. Phipps, op. cit. ii. 262. Had Phipps possessed more evidence, he would not have dismissed the suggestion that Pichegru was approached as early as May, instead of August as he thought.

[5] Condé to Wickham, 17 September 1795, F.O. 74/12; Wickham to Grenville, 14 May 1796, F.O. 74/17. The precise sum was £8,867. 3s. 6d. The evidence of Pichegru's receipt of money from Wickham is incontrovertible and would have stilled Phipps' doubts. See Phipps, op. cit., ii. 266.

his good intentions.[1] And on 18 and 23 November, Wickham made further advances totalling almost £2,000 to the apparently compliant Pichegru,[2] who left only 4,000 troops in Franche-Comté.[3] Clearly Wickham expected unconditional collaboration.

While these preparations were under way, the most crucial problem remained unresolved. 'The fate of the war hangs on Austria's decision,' Wickham wrote Eden,[4] urging that Thugut be impressed with the need to support Condé's efforts to create a respectable fighting force. The truth was that Condé's army stood at a mere 1,000 men, consisting almost entirely of light troops and cavalry who would be powerless against the enemy's infantry. The bubble of Wickham's waning optimism slowly descended to earth. The French police had not been idle. Into their hands fell papers implicating the agents in Lyons, including Imbert-Colomès who was barely able to make his exit.[5] This débâcle convinced Précy, who conferred with Wickham on 25 November, that all should be abandoned. Précy had consistently opposed Wickham's plan as being too risky;[6] Wickham to the last felt that it was feasible.[7] But Wurmser's sudden decision to remove Condé from Mulheim ended the project.[8]

Not till the next year did Wickham learn of the utter confusion in Lyons following upon the catastrophe of Vendémiaire. The proliferation of agents, their mutual suspicions, the lack of clear directions, and the rapidly changing situation also contributed to the imprecision and chaos. Wickham had for months resented the suspicious and scrutinizing eyes of Condé who refused to accept as agents men who were critical of his pure monarchical princi-ples.[9] But he had sufficient confidence in his own powers to believe

---

[1] Wickham to Grenville, 20 October 1795, *Correspondence of William Wickham*, i. 184–6.

[2] Wickham to Grenville, 14 May 1796, F.O. 74/17.

[3] Wickham to Grenville, 18 November 1795, *Correspondence of William Wickham*, i. 207–9.

[4] Wickham to Eden, 17 November 1795, ibid., 197–207.

[5] Wickham to Grenville, 25 November 1795, ibid., 216–17.

[6] Drake to Trevor, 20 November 1795, F.O. 28/13.

[7] Wickham to Grenville, 27 November 1795, F.O. 74/13.

[8] Condé to Wickham, 28 November 1795, *Correspondence of William Wickham*, i. 217–18. As Macartney, Grenville's special envoy to Louis XVIII, put it: 'Wick-ham's plans . . . are retarded if not entirely disappointed.' Macartney to Grenville, 10 December 1795, F.O. 27/45.

[9] Wickham to Grenville, 10 July 1795, *Correspondence of William Wickham*, i. 115–117.

he would not meet effective resistance from him.[1] Differences between Wickham and Condé might have been kept under the surface, but among the agents they were glaringly apparent. Tessonnet could not get on with Dominique Allier, who, he suspected, was a double-spy, an opinion shared by Wickham but not by Condé.[2] Tessonnet had also taken to brawling with Besignan and Lamothe, who were active in the Forez, and had disputed with de Guer the honour of going to Paris for the purpose of concerting measures with the sections.[3] De Guer, rather than Tessonnet, had Condé's confidence, while in Wickham's case the reverse was true. De Guer's, however, was the dominant personality. The result was a squandering of the funds entrusted to them. Wickham might have added that the discovery by the Paris police of Lemaître's correspondence,[4] incriminating a number of the Midi agents, and French surveillance[5] of the Midi preparations were sufficient cause for failure.

Despite the efficiency of the French intelligence, there can be no doubt that Wickham's net had been thrown wide; perhaps too wide. Barthélemy summed up the nature and extent of the Republic's internal and external foes by pointing his finger at Wickham who was 'the centre of all the links and correspondence'[6] with the interior. From his headquarters had been disseminated the 'poisonous writings circulating in the frontier departments'. Through him, and with passports made available by him, the enemy's agents had found 'the means to penetrate to the Vendée, to Lyons, and into the departments of Meurthe and Rhine'. All the friends of the Revolution were astonished at the ease with which the enemy was preparing the means 'to set aflame in France all the horrors of civil war'. For the time being the civil war was far from being the imminent reality Barthélemy feared. Nevertheless, a number of the seeds Wickham had sown took root and, in the year to come, some of them would flower.

[1] Wickham to Grenville, 14 November 1795, *Correspondence of William Wickham*, i. 196–7.

[2] Tessonnet to Condé, 12 September 1795; Condé to Wickham, 23 September 1795, F.O. 74/12.

[3] De Guer to Wickham, 8 October 1795, ibid.; Bayard's 'Notes sur les suites du 13 vendémiaire et particulièrement sur Lemaître', F.O. 74/14.

[4] See below, passim, for an account of Lemaître and the Paris agency.

[5] Bacher's reports, 17 September, 22 October 1795, A.N., AFIII51A, dossier 186.

[6] Barthélemy's report of 17 December 1795, A.N., AFIII81, dossier 336.

III

Wickham's first year in Switzerland was marked by failure of yet another of his plans. The royalists were ever on guard against the probability of Wickham intending to promote a British-oriented counter-revolution. D'Artéz, at the centre of the intrigue, induced Wickham with surprising ease that he possessed a superior source of intelligence in Paris.[1] Without Wickham being aware of it, d'Artéz was working in close collaboration with Lemaître, the most eccentric member of the Paris agency,[2] whose bulletins were to shape the minister's assessment of the crisis in Paris.

The latest crisis in the French capital had developed as a result of the opposition to the Fructidor decrees—the Convention's desperate attempt to dominate the next Legislature by assuring two-thirds of its seats for the Conventionals. Together with the Constitution of 1795, the decrees required electoral ratification. Intelligence reaching Wickham indicated that the primary assemblies in the sections were dominated by the constitutionalists who felt confident in their ability to have the decrees rejected if the pure royalists were rigidly excluded.[3] Their guidance of the assemblies appealed to Wickham; the revival of disputes among the royalist factions, each with its own candidate for the throne, was to be avoided. Though experience had taught him not to discount rivalries within the royalist camp, he believed they would recede into the background if events took their own course.[4] And since the initiative, so far as he knew, had already been taken by the constitutionalists who preferred to focus opinion on the immediate need to reject the decrees, he gave them his full support.[5]

Wickham therefore awaited the opening of the primary assemblies with some trepidation for, like Grenville, he hoped that the failure of the decrees would prepare the way for a new government, moderate and pacific in temper.[6] The sections seemed to be

[1] D'Artéz to Wickham, 11 August 1795, F.O. 74/10.

[2] See below, ch. v.

[3] Wickham to Grenville, 22 August 1795, *Correspondence of William Wickham*, i. 161. Cf. F.O. 74/11, in which this despatch is dated 26 August.

[4] This opinion was based on information he was receiving from an agent in Lyons, 2, 4 September 1795, F.O. 74/11.

[5] Wickham to Grenville, 22 August 1795, *Correspondence of William Wickham*, i. 161.

[6] Grenville to Wickham, 8 September 1795, ibid., 158.

carrying off the preliminaries so well and the disposition of Lyons and the southern departments seemed so favourable that his optimism was clouded only by the Committee of Public Safety's hold over the army.[1] His expectations of the reception which Paris would accord the decrees and his fears of the army's influence were warranted: the decrees were carried by the votes of the armed forces but were overwhelmingly rejected in Paris. Undismayed, he now awaited news about the composition of the electoral assemblies which were to elect candidates to the *Corps législatif*.

His appraisal of the situation was influenced, in the first instance, by Mallet du Pan's incisive analysis. Mallet allowed Wickham access to his correspondence with a vice-president of one of the Paris sections.[2] From these reports it was clear that the number of pure royalists involved was negligible. Indeed, the sections had named as electors journalists, pamphleteers and former municipal officers known only for their anti-Republicanism and tacit commitment to some form of constitutional monarchy.[3] Mallet's information was, however, contradicted by Lemaître's letters to d'Artéz. These were also made available to Wickham. Recalling his first unpleasant encounter with Mallet, Wickham was unable to feel confident in his motives. He was thus hoodwinked into believing that the pure royalists were a more significant factor than they actually were.

At this point Wickham was afforded the opportunity to establish contact with the other members of the Paris agency, the abbé Brottier and Duverne de Presle. This arose out of Charette's appeals to the British government for funds. Charette's emissary to London, the chevalier d'Andigné, had seen Windham at the War Office just when the fires of the Parisian crisis were being kindled. Complying with Charette's request, Windham agreed to hold Brottier and Duverne responsible for the transmission of funds to him. At the same time, Windham asked Wickham to direct and finance the agency's efforts to procure intelligence.[4] Six weeks later, Grenville also took steps upon the advice of

[1] Wickham to Grenville, 16 September 1795, F.O. 74/11.
[2] Mallet du Pan to Wickham, 25 September 1795, *Correspondence of William Wickham*, i. 170.
[3] Mallet du Pan's letter from Paris, 25 September 1795, F.O. 74/12.
[4] Windham to Wickham 7 August 1795, *Correspondence of William Wickham*, i. 140.

Dutheil,[1] the princes' representative in London, to bring about a liaison between Wickham and the agents. He accordingly informed Wickham that Duverne would be coming to obtain funds from him to promote the royalist campaign in Paris.[2] Early in October, Duverne succeeded in crossing the border into Switzerland. He gave Wickham a partially distorted impression of events in Paris, causing him to believe more firmly that the royalists' rôle in the movement of the sections was not minimal; he therefore instructed Duverne to devote part of the funds he gave him to form a working association with the constitutionalists.[3] Indeed, he was so impressed by Duverne's reports that he advised the constitutionalists to collaborate with the agency.

There was yet another reason for such a manœuvre. Wickham was not certain whether there was any distinction between the leaders of the sections and the politicians clustering around Madame de Staël, general de Montesquiou, Talleyrand, and others whom he suspected of harbouring anti-British sentiments. Because he did not underestimate their gift for political intrigue, and because the outcome of the crisis now appeared doubtful, he feared that unless precautions were taken, they might use their influence to strengthen the Convention's hand. If that were to occur, the ascendancy of a party professing anti-British as well as anti-royalist views would endanger British interests. The only solution was to link the constitutionalists and royalists in a coalition powerful enough to resist this faction.[4]

Duverne's assurances that the agency would co-operate with the constitutionalists were, it transpired, empty promises. Even after the dispersal of the sections on 14 Vendémiaire, Wickham was certain that the two groups had begun to concert their plans

---

[1] Dutheil to Grenville, 19 September 1795, F.O. 27/44. See M. H. Weil (*Un Agent inconnu de la coalition, le général de Stamford* (Paris, 1923), pp. 721-2) for a note on Dutheil, who, before the Revolution, was secretary of the *Intendance* of Paris and later, after its suspension, worked under Bailly, the mayor of Paris. He emigrated twice, in 1790, and in 1792, on the latter occasion joining Artois at Coblentz and, following the partial demobilization of the *émigré* army, was charged with the liquidation of its debts. From Germany he transferred his activities to London.

[2] Grenville to Wickham, 21 September 1795, F.O. 74/11.

[3] Wickham to Grenville, 12 October 1795, F.O. 74/12. Wickham gave the agents a first instalment of £6,000, depositing an additional sum of £17,000 with Messrs. Marcel Carrard & Co., bankers at Lausanne. See also Brottier to Wickham, 15 October 1795, F.O. 74/13.

[4] Wickham to Grenville, 12 October 1795, F.O. 74/12.

and would soon assume the offensive.[1] There was one inconsistency in his reading of the events taking place in Paris. News from the Paris agency after the insurrection deepened his belief that the alleged coalition of constitutionalists and royalists still possessed the resources to renew the struggle. This optimism did not survive for long. Towards the end of December, Wickham was shocked into the unpleasant discovery that he had been both an unwitting instrument of a royalist plan to discredit the constitutionalists and the victim of tampered correspondence. It was not until the published Lemaître letters reached him that he became aware of the deceptions.[2] The letters revealed the connections between Brottier and Lemaître and between Lemaître and d'Artéz, and disclosed the suspicions they entertained of British policy. More significant than these discoveries were the unequivocal statements pointing to the fact that the royalists had had no influence whatever in the sections.[3] Wickham saw at last that the agents had contrived fictitious accounts for the purpose of persuading him to withhold assistance from the constitutionalists.

Wickham's first year of counter-revolutionary efforts had ended. His had been a grand design, comprehending nearly all of France; the scale of operations had been tremendous and the risks great. It had been his firm conviction and also Grenville's that simultaneous movements in the Vendée, the Midi and Paris would provide the catalyst for a mass uprising against the Republic. But too many obstacles had stood in the way of even partial success. Post-Thermidorian France demonstrated many internal weaknesses, but Wickham and his superiors had seriously overestimated them. The disaster of the landing at Quiberon[4] proved that the resources of the royalists in the west, both physical and moral, were at ebb-point. The decisive intervention of the army in Vendémiaire was another signpost. It was a precedent which would not be lost on those who would be forced to defend the Revolutionary regime against future threats. The Republic's resilience did not extinguish Wickham's hopes. In the next two years, because of the Directory's continuing strains, Wickham's failures were almost converted into success.

[1] Wickham to Grenville, 13 October 1795, F.O. 74/12; Wickham to Windham, 12 October 1795, Add. MSS., 37875.

[2] Wickham to Grenville, 22 December 1795, F.O. 74/13.

[3] *Recueil de la correspondance saisie chez Lemaître*, passim.

[4] For the most recent analysis of the disaster, see Hutt, loc. cit.

5

THE PARIS AGENCY, THE COMTE D'ANTRAIGUES AND FRANCIS DRAKE

THE small coterie of royalist agents, known to historians as the Paris agency, *les Amis de Paris*, and the '*Manufacture*', played a pivotal and often obstructive rôle during the most active period of the counter-revolution. The oldest royalist organization of its kind in France, the Paris agency was not, during its early existence, directly linked either to the rebels in the Vendée or to the *émigrés* who crowded the ante-chambers of nearly every European court, but to the Spanish government, whose ambassador in Paris, Fernan Nũnes, formed it in 1791 with the approval of Louis XVI.[1] Only three men were in its service in those early days. The first was the chevalier Despomelles, a lieutenant-colonel under the old regime who had been interested in army reform. He was an acquaintance of the comte d'Antraigues and had been one of the editors of the royalist *Journal général de France* published by the abbé de Fontenay.[2] Despomelles' colleagues were Pierre Jacques Lemaître, an *avocat* and a former *sécrétaire-général du conseil des finances*,[3] and François Nicolas Sourdat, a former magistrate and lieutenant of police from Troyes.[4] From them Nũnes acquired military and political intelligence which he sent to Madrid, though he frequently sent copies to Las Casas, the Spanish ambassador in Venice.

Although the later activities of the agents are well-documented,

---

[1] An outline of the agency's origins is given by the comte d'Antraigues in two memorials which he drew up in 1809. See his 'Histoire de l'agence secrète de Paris et de la Vendée', A.A.E., France 628 and his, 'Mémoire à consulter', A.A.E., France 641. Cf. A. Mousset, *Le Comte de Fernan Nũnes* (Paris, 1923), in which there is not a single reference to the Spanish ambassador's relations with the agency.

[2] Ibid. See also L. Pingaud, *Correspondance intime du comte de Vaudreuil et du comte d'Artois pendant l'émigration, 1789–1815* (2 vols., Paris, 1889), i. 402. Cf. Vingtrinier, op. cit., i. 289n.

[3] Conseil militaire séant aux ci-devant Filles St. Thomas, Section Lepeletier, 8 November 1795, A.N. BB³4.

[4] See Bayard's 'Notes sur les suites du 13 vendémiaire . . .', F.O. 74/14.

there is no continuous record of their early history. We do know[1] that while Lemaître passed as an exemplary employee in the *conseil des finances*, he was imprisoned in 1785 for printing and selling pamphlets critical of Calonne. Lemaître was one of that numerous tribe of gazetteers or *nouvellistes* who, during the later part of the eighteenth century, swarmed about the cafés and promenades of Paris, selling gossipy news-sheets about the aristocracy and the court.[2] In this way many foreign governments, ever on the prowl for intelligence, sought and obtained news of what was happening in Paris. As a gazetteer, Lemaître was gaining experience for his more clandestine interests under the revolutionary regime. His activities branched out until he was securing first-hand information from government offices. Lemaître's first brush with the revolutionary police dates from August 1792, when he was arrested in the great round-up of suspects following the fall of the monarchy. Thanks to the intervention of Tallien, who was then *greffier* of the Paris Commune, Lemaître was released, only to suffer arrest and imprisonment again a year later on charges of professing royalist views and of consorting with refractory priests. He remained in prison throughout the Terror, but was released after Thermidor.

The other members in the agency distrusted Lemaître. During his imprisonment, they lived in daily fear that he would denounce them to the police. Bayard, however, thought him courageous and enterprising, imaginative and intelligent, a perfect spy if he could get over his impulsiveness.[3] While Brottier acknowledged some of these same qualities, he found it impossible to get on with him:

Lemaître had a brilliant imagination, the true artist's ability to portray men and events, and a bitter sarcasm. Possessing the two former qualities, he knew how to captivate both the stupid and the intriguers, as well as men of experience. . . . He was able, because of his sarcasm, to dominate anyone who wasn't strong enough to resist the envenomed

---

[1] Unless other sources are cited, the details concerning the earlier history of the agents are derived from P. Bessand-Massenet, *La Vie de conspirateur* (Paris, 1956), pp. 21–34. While valuable for its revealing passages concerning the early private lives of the agents, this book cannot conceal the author's predilection for the sensational. It is Lenôtre in new dress.

[2] For a discussion of the *nouvellistes*, see F. Funck-Brentano, *The Old Regime in France* (Trans., London, 1929), pp. 321–42.

[3] Bayard's 'Notes sur les suites du 13 vendémiaire . . .'; plan submitted by Bayard to Wickham for an internal central agency corresponding with Wickham, F.O. 74/14.

darts of a wicked tongue or the malignancy of a sardonic smile. . . . We never wanted to communicate with him.[1]

As we shall see, Lemaître was very much the lone wolf; the agents' suspicions of him were matched by his contempt for them. His only close friend and associate was Sourdat who had been under police surveillance as a suspected counter-revolutionary in Troyes. He came to Paris in 1793 and, after some months in prison during the Terror, became a member of the agency. He was, according to Bayard, calm, cold, reserved, a bit too credulous, however, as he believed all too readily in the reports delivered to him.[2]

Perhaps none of the other agents offered a sharper contrast to Lemaître then Despomelles, the oldest member of the agency, whose contacts with the Spanish government dated from the very earliest stages of the Revolution. Pusillanimous and inactive are the terms that Bayard used to describe him.[3] Again, for want of a more impartial evaluation—Despomelles succeeded in leaving almost no trace of himself in the police records—we must turn to this rather inadequate sketch by Brottier: 'It is truly absurd to suggest that this man who is of help to us only very rarely is still part of the agency; he constantly remains at a distance of more than four leagues from the centre of observation. . . .'[4]

With Lemaître in prison during the height of the Terror and Despomelles increasingly reluctant to risk his life, the burden of work fell upon the abbé André Charles Brottier, who was joined later by Duverne de Presle. After Thermidor, the newcomers appear to have assumed control of the agency. By then Despomelles had voluntarily relinquished most of his power; and Lemaître, upon being released from prison, preferred to work alone.[5]

Born into a devout and fanatically royalist family in the Nièvre district, Brottier entered the minor orders after a period of youthful dissipation. Nephew of the Greek scholar Gabriel Brottier, the

---

[1] Brottier's 'Mémoire sur l'agence de Paris et sur la position des agents du roi', 17 December 1795, Puisaye Papers, Brit. Mus. (Add. MSS.), 8055.

[2] Bayard's 'Notes sur les suites du 13 vendémiaire . . .', F.O. 74/14.

[3] Plan submitted . . . to Wickham . . ., ibid.

[4] Brottier's 'Mémoire sur l'agence de Paris . . .', Add. MSS., 8055.

[5] The exact date of Brottier's first association with the agency is not known, but most of the letters which d'Antraigues received from the agency in 1794 are in his handwriting. See Add. MSS., 8055–6. Duverne probably became a full member towards the end of 1794. See d'Andigné to d'Antraigues, 4 May 1795, A.A.E., France 629.

abbé became a well-known mathematician, numismatist, and a Hellenist scholar who authored treatises on Pliny, Epictetus and Plutarch. He lectured in mathematics at the *École militaire*, was asked to undertake the education of the abbé Maury's nephews, and wrote for the *Journal de la France* and *l'Année littéraire*. His activities as an agent did not go unnoticed by the police whose records tell us that he was transmitting intelligence abroad. What the police did not know was that Brottier had worked with Lemaître for some time before the Revolution. They took no action against Brottier, possibly because he avoided their scrutiny in Belleville where he gave every appearance of living in retirement among his books; he had even gone so far as to discard his *soutane* and join the local National Guard. All who knew him disliked him. The comte de Puisaye believed that Brottier was responsible for the attacks on his relations with the British ministry. He accused Brottier of being an apostate priest, who had been thrown out of the household of the marquis de Labourdonnaye for his immoral and debauched conduct.[1] The Director Barthélemy, who shared with Brottier the pains of deportation after Fructidor, claimed that his 'evil and melancholic character' and his friendliness with the terrorist Billaud-Varenne, had alienated him from the royalists in Sinnamari.[2] Another agent, Berthelot de la Villeurnoy, found him an exceedingly difficult companion.[3] Contempt for his fanaticism is voiced by Mallet du Pan, who declared that Brottier was one of those men who awaited and predicted a counter-revolution with every new phase of the moon.[4]

Even more accomplished in the art of conspiracy was Duverne de Presle, a naval officer before the Revolution, and the youngest member of the agency. Emigrating in 1792, he returned to France on the eve of the Terror. Passing as an almanac salesman, he travelled throughout France, under a variety of aliases, carrying information from one band of royalists to another. In Paris, he went under the name of Theodore Dunan, Swiss citizen, wholesale grocer.[5]

[1] *Mémoires du comte Joseph de Puisaye* (6 vols., London, 1803–8), vi. 354.

[2] *Mémoires de Barthélemy 1768–1819* (Paris, 1914), p. 347.

[3] H. Bonhomme (ed.), *Coup d'état du 18 fructidor an V d'après le journal inédit de la Villeurnoy* (Paris, 1873), p. 213.

[4] *Correspondance inédite de Mallet du Pan*, ii. 227, 15 February 1797.

[5] Interrogation of Dunan, 13 pluviôse an V, A.N., F⁷6371.

After the execution of Louis XVI, the services of the agency were sought by the king's brother, the comte de Provence, from his refuge in Verona. This was accomplished by a minor French *émigré* noble, Louis Emmanuel Henri Alexandre de Launai, the comte d'Antraigues,[1] who had obtained a key position in the Spanish embassy at Venice in 1793. Forty years separated him from his birthplace in Montpellier. His mother was the daughter of the *intendant* of Languedoc, the comte de Saint-Priest; his father's family was of more humble origins, originally Swiss and Protestant. They planned a military career for him but he put the army behind him as soon as he could, and spent a year travelling in central Europe and the near East. Upon his return, he spent the decade until 1789 in the village of Antraigues, living in the traditional style of a well-to-do country noble. His annual income of about 40,000 livres was derived almost entirely from feudal rights. During this period, he began to evince an interest in politics and read both Montesquieu and Rousseau.

In 1788, by publishing his brochure, *Mémoire sur les États-généraux*,[2] he became one of the leading exponents of the aristocratic attack against royal absolutism. After a short term in the Constituent Assembly, he left France in 1790 for Switzerland where he put his facile pen at the service of the princes on whose behalf he wrote several counter-revolutionary pamphlets. They were violent in tone and total in their rejection of compromise. For some time he travelled in the south of Switzerland and northern Italy, under the improbable name of Marco Polo Philiberti, and helped to direct the short-lived royalist conspiracies in southern France. In 1792 he attracted the attention of Las Casas, Spanish ambassador at Venice, who made him a member of his staff and entrusted him with the Paris correspondence. Venice was, since Spain's declaration of hostilities, receiving the Paris reports. The Spanish court permitted d'Antraigues to send copies to the comte de Provence but reserved the right to delete all intelligence relating to Spanish affairs. In this way the agents of Madrid also became the agents of the princes. D'Antraigues' official link with the Spanish legation served to conceal his less official activities as royalist propagandist *par excellence*. For, in addition to the intelligence he conveyed to the comte de Provence and the tracts

[1] See Pingaud's biography, op. cit.
[2] See Beik, op. cit., pp. 11–13 for a discussion of d'Antraigues' *Mémoire*.

he wrote denigrating the Revolution and exalting the old order, he devoted much attention to the composition of bulletins of information destined for London. Boldly, often recklessly, he used every literary device, exploited every plausible bit of information supplied him by the agents in Paris, and even invented news to plead the cause of counter-revolution before the imperturbable officials of the British Foreign Office.[1] Extreme in his views and conduct, his advocacy of the rights of the French monarchy was very likely compensation for his unorthodox young manhood during which he had travelled in and extolled the pleasures of life in Turkey, befriended the *philosophes*, knew Rousseau well enough to have received one of his manuscripts, and, to the dismay of his mother, took for his mistress the most famous singer of the day, Madame Saint-Huberty, whom he later married.

II

Consideration of d'Antraigues' activities as a purveyor of political intelligence provides the key to the significance of more than one hundred lengthy bulletins which he wrote for the purpose of influencing Britain's war policy. Since, with few exceptions, the letters that the comte received from the agents in Paris were written in invisible ink,[2] we can only assume that they provided

[1] For an analysis of d'Antraigues' relations with the British government, see my article, 'Francis Drake and the comte d'Antraigues: A Study of the Dropmore Bulletins, 1793–1796', *Bulletin of the Institute of Historical Research*, xxix (1956), 123–44, from which most of the material dealing with d'Antraigues in this chapter is taken. My article is based on an examination, first, of the twenty-eight bulletins originally published by the Historical Manuscripts Commission in the second volume of the *Dropmore Papers*, second, the bulletins included in the Drake Papers deposited in the British Museum, third, those in the foreign office correspondence with Genoa, and finally those which were deposited in other Foreign Office records. In 1958, A. Rufer, archivist in Vienna, published a number of bulletins authored by d'Antraigues, 'En Complement des Dropmore Papers', *Annales historiques de la Révolution française*, xxx (July–September 1958), 14–43. Only two, those of 25 February 1795 and 16/22 January 1796, are not to be found in the British records, apart from those dealing with the period after 1796, when d'Antraigues brought this British series of bulletins to an end. Those treating the period from 1793 to 1796, with the exception of the two cited above, are in the British archives, and four of the bulletins reproduced by Rufer are truncated versions of the bulletins in British repositories. D'Antraigues' personal correspondence with Drake continued after 1796 and may be seen in the Drake Papers in the British Museum.

[2] These blank sheets of paper are preserved in the Quai d'Qrsay, A.A.E., France 628–9, and in the British Museum, Add. MSS., 8055–6. The agents tried to conceal their identity in the correspondence by using assumed names and code. For example,

d'Antraigues with the basis for the bulletins which he drew up and transmitted to London through the intermediary of the British minister at Genoa, the twenty-nine-year-old Francis Drake. For nearly three years, from August 1793 to February 1796, with one major gap between mid-November 1794 and mid-January 1795, Drake forwarded the d'Antraigues' bulletins to the Foreign Office. Although the first bulletin dates from August 1793, it was not until the end of October that Drake and d'Antraigues met for the first time. Their secret place of rendezvous was the small town of Novi near Genoa. There they arranged payment for the correspondence, and the frequency with which the bulletins would reach Drake.[1]

To ask what importance can be ascribed to the d'Antraigues' bulletins as a source of information about the momentous decisions of the small number of men who were responsible for the triumph of revolution in France and its advance in Europe is immediately to be confronted with the need to examine d'Antraigues' motives. This is a far more useful inquiry than that carried out by the first group of historians who studied the original twenty-eight bulletins when they were first published. Clapham, Aulard and Glagau dismissed the bulletins as being unworthy of the historian's attention, without considering the significance of the mind responsible for them and the insight they could furnish into royalist fears and hopes.[2] The authorship of the bulletins was guessed, but not proved, by FitzPatrick and Mathiez, and did not attract too much notice from d'Antraigues' biographer.[3] In our own time, some historians have adopted an

---

Lemaître went by the name of Le Traime; Despomelles, by that of Thibault; Brottier by that of Corbeau or the number 99; Sourdat by that of BB; Duverne by that of Dunan.

[1] D'Antraigues to Drake, 5 November 1793, Add. MSS., 46831. D'Antraigues wrote: 'I need hardly say anything, Monsieur, of my pleasure in having seen you.'

[2] J. H. Clapham, 'A Royalist Spy during the Reign of Terror', *English Historical Review*, xii (1897), 67–84; F. A. Aulard, 'Les Bulletins d'un espion royaliste dans les papiers de Lord Grenville', *La Révolution française*, xxxii (1897), 121–8; H. Glagau, 'Achtundzwanzig Bulletins über den Wohlfahrtsausschuss', *Historische Zeitschrift*, lxxviii (1897), 217–37.

[3] W. FitzPatrick in his introduction to the third volume of the *Dropmore Papers*, xxix; Mathiez in chapters vii and ix of *La Conspiration de l'étranger*; Pingaud, op. cit.; G. Bord (*Etudes sur la question Louis XVII. Autour du Temple* (Paris, 1912)) attributed the authorship of the bulletins to Baldwin, whom Drake had pointed out as a French agent! It should also be added that J. Hall, in his book on Pichegru, op. cit., commented on the bulletins without solving the mystery.

even less critical approach.[1] A recent biography of Saint-Just is based rather uncritically on the bulletins' revelations of the key figures of the Committee of Public Safety, a rather dangerous procedure.[2] The same attitude is revealed in an investigation by M. de Grandsaignes.[3] He admits that the bulletins' reports of the inner deliberations of the Committee of Public Safety will probably never be authenticated. Nevertheless, he insists that d'Antraigues had no reason to fabricate his information because he had a European-wide reputation of trust to safeguard. Unless some miracle restores the handwriting in the letters received by d'Antraigues from Paris, it will not be possible to test to what extent the bulletins differ from their alleged models. It seems far more profitable to look at the bulletins as a reflection of d'Antraigues' political personality. This approach is further justified by the availability of his correspondence with Drake, for it elucidates many of the matters discussed in the bulletins.

It is not difficult to detect the nature of d'Antraigues' intentions. The bulletins often exceeded the limits of credibility by creating the impression that the Committee of Public Safety would be overwhelmed by Britain's recognition of the Bourbons and the infusion of strength to the Vendée. D'Antraigues' private letters reinforced the same thesis. Thus the bulletin of 25/30 November 1793 represents the Committee as relieved to learn from Talleyrand that Grenville held the royalists in great disfavour and would never consent to intervention in the Vendée.[4] Another bulletin

---

[1] Published after his death, Guglielmo Ferrero's *Les Deux Révolutions françaises* (Neuchâtel and Paris, 1951) is an unconvincing analysis of the Dropmore Bulletins. Ferrero's uncritical acceptance of the bulletins' unsubstantiated statements is unworthy to stand alongside this historian's more judicious studies.

[2] A. Ollivier, *Saint-Just et la force des choses* (Paris, 1954).

[3] See his article 'Enquête sur les bulletins de Dropmore', *Annales historiques de la Révolution française*, xxix (1957), 214–37. M. de Grandsaignes' article followed mine, op. cit., by less than a year and consequently could not deal with it. His treatment of the subject is directly opposed to mine and in obvious conflict with its conclusions. For additional discussion of the Grandsaignes position, see J. Godechot, 'À Propos de Vannelet: Deprez et Daru', ibid., xxx (Oct.–Dec., 1958), 1–12; M. Reinhard, 'Dropmore papers et méthode historique', ibid., 13–16; and M. de Grandsaignes' reply, ibid., 16–20. Godechot reviews his attitude in an article, 'Essai d'identification de quelques correspondants du comte d'Antraigues', *Bulletin de la société d'histoire moderne*, 11th series, n. 10 (1959), 5–9. Godechot develops his arguments more fully in his *La Contre-Révolution*.

[4] Bulletin of 25/30 November 1793, *Dropmore Papers*, ii. 473. This bulletin was written on the eve of the departure of Lord Moira's expedition to the Vendée and Brittany. See above, pp. 36–7.

pictures the Committee brushing aside the dangers of invasion from the east to concentrate on the greatest danger of all—the increasing and unrelenting pressure of the rebels in the Vendée.[1] By February 1794, when the British were transferring the bulk of their resources to Flanders, d'Antraigues was arguing that the improved military situation in the Vendée made a union of British and rebel forces opportune. But he warned that the union could be effective only if Britain gave immediate recognition to the Bourbons.[2] In the same spirit, he had earlier suggested to Drake that the loss of Toulon to the French would not have occurred had not Hood frustrated the hopes of the royalists who had demonstrated in favour of the comte de Provence.[3]

The longer the British withheld aid from the Vendée and refused to commit themselves to unqualified support of the Bourbons, the more virulent became the criticism of what were labelled Britain's Machiavellian designs. Indeed, the arguments employed rather doubtful evidence. For example, the authority of Saint-Just was adduced to prove that the Republic need not fear any attack from Britain in the Vendée because the prevention of a Bourbon Restoration was more important to British designs than the defeat of the Jacobins.[4] After the defeat of the allies at Fleurus, d'Antraigues insisted that a properly-timed diversion in the Vendée could have prevented a French victory on the Flemish front.[5] It was essential that once Britain had helped to launch a civil war in the Vendée, she act as an auxiliary in order to preserve the national character of the struggle—'the nation forgives the misfortunes that she inflicts upon herself; this is not the case when the foreigner is responsible for the misfortunes'.[6] In defence of Britain's policy, Drake contended that aid to the Vendée

[1] Bulletin of 28 December 1793; bulletin of 1/7 February 1794, ibid., 487, 518.

[2] Bulletin of 16/29 February 1794, ibid., 529–32. See also, bulletin of 4/12 April 1794, ibid., 560–3.

[3] D'Antraigues to Drake, 18 January 1794, Add. MSS., 46832.

[4] Bulletin of 4/9 May 1794, *Dropmore Papers*, ii. 567–70. See also, bulletin of 17/24 May 1794, ibid., 574–7. According to the latter bulletin, Saint-Just accused Robespierre of creating royalist phantoms for the purpose of arrogating power to himself, claiming that there was evidence to prove that Britain had abandoned the royalists.

[5] D'Antraigues to Drake, 7 August 1794, Add. MSS., 46833. Cf. F.O. 28/9 in which a copy of this letter bears the date 24 July 1794.

[6] See Trevor's opinion of d'Antraigues, whom he described as 'very clever and agreeable; but en fait de raisonnements sur la Révolution—c'est une tête exaltée', Trevor to Drake, 26 November 1794, Add. MSS., 46825. Cf. Mallet du Pan's estimate of him as the 'authentic aristocratic terrorist', Mallet du Pan to Trevor,

would be possible only if the royalists retreated from their narrow ideological base and broadened their outlook to include men from all parties opposed to the Convention.[1] In any case the British could muster only a small invading force which could not possibly achieve success unless internal preparations preceded a landing.[2] When in the winter and spring of 1794, the bulletins reported feverish preparations for a large-scale offensive in the Vendée, he warned d'Antraigues that Britain could not be held responsible if the impending action failed.[3]

The main issues in d'Antraigues' wish-and-fear world arose from his suspicion of Britain's attitude towards the royalists. According to Drake the prime consideration was the restoration of order in France. 'When this is effected,' he wrote, 'the rest will follow.'[4] In d'Antraigues' eyes, Britain's refusal to recognize the royalists only meant one thing: that the destinies of Britain's French policy had been entrusted to his most hated political opponents, the constitutional monarchists. His bulletins and letters clearly point to the belief of the pure royalists in the conspiracy view of history. D'Antraigues maintained that the constitutionalists were enjoying Grenville's exclusive confidence,[5] and charged that true royalist principles had been sacrificed at Toulon because of the connivance of the constitutionalists with the British.[6] His comments on letters alleged to have been written by Mallet du Pan, and reported in the bulletins as having been found among Hérault de Séchelles' papers, amply demonstrate the magnitude of his obsession.[7] He accused Pitt of wishing to sacrifice the clerical and *émigré* interests in France in order to pave the way for a negotiated peace with the constitutionalists who were still in France;[8] and, in commenting upon his reports from the Vendée, he insisted that the rebels would never treat with any

---

8 September 1795, F.O. 67/18. Montlosier's *Souvenirs*, op. cit., p. 297, quotes d'Antraigues as saying 'Montlosier finds me implacable; I will be the Marat of the counter-revolution; I will cause 100,000 heads to fall and his will be the first.'

[1] Drake to d'Antraigues, 31 January 1794, A.A.E., France 632.
[2] Drake to d'Antraigues, 7 March 1794, ibid.
[3] Drake to d'Antraigues, 14 March 1794, ibid.
[4] Drake to d'Antraigues, 30 May 1794, ibid.
[5] Bulletin of 25/30 November 1793, *Dropmore Papers*, ii. 473.
[6] D'Antraigues to Drake, 18 January 1794, Add. MSS., 46832.
[7] D'Antraigues to Drake, 19 April 1794, ibid.
[8] Bulletin of 15/21 March 1794, *Dropmore Papers*, ii. 548.

government dominated by constitutionalists.[1] The belief that Britain and her allies were more intent on gathering spoils than in restoring France's pre-revolutionary status is also evident. D'Antraigues claimed that the Jacobins were attracting the support of royalists and other opponents of the Revolution by their skilful exploitation of French fears of allied aims: 'We will not tolerate the partition of France on the Polish model. She will be a Republic or a Kingdom; but she will not be divided . . .'[2]

The bulletins made a great deal of the divisions in the French government. While the course of the Revolution was punctuated by personal and ideological rivalries, d'Antraigues' version of them was hardly accurate. His prime motive was to convince the British that there did not exist any stable or reliable faction or body in revolutionary France with which Britain could treat for peace. The Committee of General Security was made to appear even more determined than the Committee of Public Safety to carry on factional intrigues.[3] Discord between Robespierre and Saint-Just, based on the latter's fear that Robespierre was contemplating peace negotiations, was said to have succeeded the earlier antagonism between Robespierre and Hébert.[4] The alleged enmity between Robespierre and Saint-Just continued until the eve of Thermidor when they buried their differences to prevent the dismantling of the terrorist state.[5] After Thermidor the divisions between the Thermidorians and the Robespierrists were emphasized.[6] If d'Antraigues intended to stress the instability of the French government, the bulletins, read in isolation from other sources of information, would certainly have given such an impression. Indeed, he rather overshot the mark at this

[1] Bulletin of 4/12 April 1794, ibid., 563.

[2] D'Antraigues to Drake in a note accompanying the bulletin of 24/28 June 1794, F.O. 28/8.

[3] Bulletin of 13 November 1793, ibid., 466.

[4] Bulletin of 25/28 March 1794, ibid., 553.

[5] The record of this antagonism may be seen in the bulletins from the end of June until the middle of July 1794, Add. MSS., 46828 and F.O. 28/9. On the divisions in both committees, see Mathiez's two articles, 'Les Divisions dans les comités à la veille de thermidor', *Revue historique*, cxviii (1915), 70–87 and 'Les Séances du 4 et 5 thermidor aux deux comités du salut public et de sûreté générale', *Annales historiques de la Révolution française*, iv (1927), 193–222. A few observations, by R. Cobb ('Le Témoignage de Ruhl sur les divisions au sein des comités à la veille du 9 thermidor', ibid., xxvii (1955), 110–14), are also useful.

[6] Add. MSS., 46828. The bulletin of 17/23 August 1794 set the tone for those that followed. Tallien was given the rôle of chief moderator of the Revolution.

point. Drake was puzzled by the apparently senseless oscillations of power between the moderates and the surviving terrorists.[1] He disclosed his doubts to Grenville, by criticizing the tone of the bulletins as being similar to the views current at Verona and expressed 'by the royalist *émigrés* in every part of Italy who are at this moment extremely active in propagating their opinions as to the impossibility of any accommodation between the allied powers and the present ruling party in France . . .'[2] To d'Antraigues, Drake suggested that peace might after all be the best solution for all concerned: since the army had become the backbone of revolutionary France, the Republic would disintegrate under the problems of demobilization.[3] Drake's analysis of the military and diplomatic situation in Europe paralleled that of Grenville and Pitt who, as we have seen, decided at this time to send Wickham to Switzerland to explore the channels of communication with the group connected with Tallien.[4]

The first period of the correspondence was drawing to a close. In mid-September 1794 Drake informed d'Antraigues that he had been granted a leave of absence to return to London; he hoped that d'Antraigues would continue to send his bulletins, intimating that they would perhaps receive closer attention in London than they had in the past.[5] Before he left he met d'Antraigues and completed arrangements for the despatch of future bulletins to London during his absence from Italy. They also agreed on a code to permit the transmission of more confidential information.[6] It should be noted that Drake still preserved the secrecy of the authorship of the bulletins. His unwillingness to provide any more information about d'Antraigues was presumably at the latter's request, and the reason is not difficult to guess. Although the Spanish court permitted d'Antraigues to send some, but not all, of the intelligence gathered by its agents in Paris to the comte de Provence, there is no reason to suppose that Madrid had any knowledge that copies were also going to Whitehall. Spain, fearful of Britain's potential domination of the Mediterranean, would hardly have approved of the idea of facilitating her sources of

---

[1] Drake to d'Antraigues, 11 October 1794, A.A.E., France 632.
[2] Drake to Grenville, 1, 8 November 1794, F.O. 28/10.
[3] Drake to d'Antraigues, 8 November 1794, A.A.E., France 632.
[4] See above, pp. 38–9.
[5] Drake to d'Antraigues, 17 September 1794, A.A.E., France 632.
[6] D'Antraigues to Drake, 25 October, 6 December 1794, Add. MSS., 46833.

information, and the revelation of the secret would thus probably have resulted in the elimination of d'Antraigues from the Spanish payroll as well as the cessation of the Paris correspondence.

The bulletins were resumed early in 1795 when the Convention was earnestly trying to end the civil war in the west. The Vendée, exhausted and full of despair, was more disposed to listen to its overtures. As d'Antraigues surveyed the scene in the Vendée, he was alarmed by the conferences some of its leaders were having with representatives of the Convention.[1] Again he urged that Britain clarify her position towards the rebel armies by asserting that the royalists were and would continue to be the sole bene-ficiaries of her aid.[2] Hesitation would only increase the suspicions of the Vendée and throw it into the arms of the Republic.[3] At the same time, d'Antraigues took care to show that the Vendée was still a viable theatre of war. News had been received that Charette was keeping an army of 90,000 Republicans occupied; guerilla warfare, disease and lack of food were also helping to drain the strength of the 'patriots'.[4] Pacification of the Vendée would materialize only if Britain failed to meet her obligations: 'The Vendée is lost and without resources if she is not given assistance.'[5] But by May, a truce in the Vendée was negotiated. Even Charette and Stofflet, the sturdiest defenders of throne and altar, had agreed to halt hostilities, and d'Antraigues' importu-nities gave way to sarcasm in his denunciation of British equi-vocation as being responsible for the disaster.[6]

Meanwhile, d'Antraigues was feverishly working to establish a closer connection between the rebel leaders and Verona. Despite the pacification, the Vendée appeared to be the only true strong-hold of the monarchy in France. It was time to inject new hope into the Vendée by corresponding directly with its chiefs. Because of his liaison with the agents in Paris, d'Antraigues was asked to arrange this. Earlier efforts in 1794 had produced negative results[7]

[1] D'Antraigues to Drake, 17 February 1795, Add. MSS., 46834.
[2] Ibid.
[3] D'Antraigues to Drake, 25 February 1795, ibid.
[4] Bulletin of 16/22 January 1795, F.O. 28/11.
[5] Bulletin of 9 February 1795, ibid.
[6] D'Antraigues to Drake, 9 May 1795, ibid.
[7] Brottier to d'Antraigues, 21 April 1795, A.A.E., France 629. D'Antraigues and the comte de Provence were not only trying to assure Charette and the other Vendean leaders of their support but also instructed him to undertake a secret and direct correspondence with Spain for the purpose of obtaining Spanish aid. Cf.

and it was only in May 1795 that contact was established with Charette and his followers.[1] Although Charette had made his peace with the Republic, he gave his allegiance to the comte de Provence[2] and protested his loyalty to the royalist cause.[3] In the early summer of 1795 d'Antraigues' mood changed, as a result of d'Andigné's successful mission—he was the rebel leaders' emissary—to solicit funds from the British government.[4] The comte could take comfort from d'Andigné's enthusiastic report of his treatment in London: 'With the pecuniary assistance accorded us by the British government, we will be able to act effectively for the first time!'[5]

The clouds seemed to be lifting, but the status of the comte de Provence was still pressing. The death of Louis XVII in June made a declaration from his successor imperative. The Verona Declaration, as Provence's manifesto came to be known, did more harm than good. Vengeance was its keynote, repudiation of the Revolution its promise, and the sovereignty of the king, surrounded by wise and benevolent ministers, its only 'concession' to constitutional monarchy.[6] Plans were made to see to its distribution in France. Charette seemed the obvious choice for the unfurling of the manifesto, but his feigned acceptance of the truce with the Republic ruled him out.[7] It was therefore decided that the agents in Paris be held responsible for the immediate distribution of the Declaration.[8]

The summer and autumn of 1795 were a time of great hope for the royalists, but also a time of great anxiety. So much seemed at

---

d'Antraigues' memorandum written after Spain made peace in July, in which it is evident that he still placed more confidence in Spain than in Britain: '. . . It is time we realized that all illusions about any assistance that we can expect from the powers have vanished; the cause of the king is the cause of none of them except Spain.' A.A.E., France 634.

[1] D'Andigné to d'Antraigues, 4 May 1795, A.A.E., France 629.

[2] Charette to d'Antraigues, [?] July 1795, ibid.

[3] Flachslanden to d'Antraigues, 8 July 1795, Add. MSS., 8055.

[4] D'Andigné to d'Antraigues, 7 July 1795, Add. MSS., 8056; d'Andigné to Windham, 4, 13 July 1795, Add. MSS., 37859.

[5] D'Andigné to d'Antraigues, [?] August 1795, A.A.E., France 629. Cf. D'Andigné's *Mémoires* (2 vols., Paris, 1900), which omits any mention of his relations with d'Antraigues or the Paris agency.

[6] A copy of the Verona Declaration with a few corrections in d'Antraigues' handwriting may be seen in A.A.E., France 588.

[7] Flachslanden to d'Antraigues, 8 July 1795, Add. MSS., 8055.

[8] D'Avaray to d'Antraigues, 8 July 1795, Add. MSS., 8056.

stake: the combined Anglo-royalist landing in the west; the projected invasion of France in the east; and the increasing chances of a reversal of power in Paris. To take full advantage of the manifold opportunities open to the adherents of the old order, the ministers of the *émigré* king told d'Antraigues to utilize the efforts of the Paris agency in blocking the plans of all but the pure royalists. Convinced that the allies would not hesitate to impose a crippling peace upon France and that a number of political factions were conspiring to gain power, the ministers at Verona insisted that it was mandatory for the agents to combat the intrigues of the enemies of the comte de Provence, and, above all, to bring the so-called English faction, presumably the constitutionalists, to accept the views of the pure royalists.[1]

III

With these directives, the members of the Paris agency took up positions along two fronts. As we have seen in the preceding chapter, a channel of communication, via d'Artéz, was established in August between Lemaître and Wickham, and another link between the agency and the British minister was forged by d'Andigné and Dutheil. In this way, the royalist agency in the capital controlled the bulk of intelligence reaching Wickham and hoped to influence any decisions the British government might take when the moment of crisis arrived. Indeed, both Wickham in Switzerland and the ministry at Whitehall received the same version of French events, for the information contained in d'Antraigues' bulletins was, in its treatment of the preliminaries and consequences of Vendémiaire, almost identical with that sent to Wickham by the Paris agency itself. The significance of the intrigue is not only that Wickham was deceived with regard to the connections between the various members of the agency and with d'Antraigues, but also that Drake and Grenville were unaware of the ties between the agency and d'Antraigues. Moreover, Wickham had no knowledge of the d'Antraigues-Drake correspondence nor of the bulletins being sent to Grenville. Essentially, therefore, British interpretation of what was happening in Paris during this period, was monopolized by the pure royalists. Most of the information we possess about the agency's attitude to the

[1] Instructions to d'Antraigues, [?] 1795, Add. MSS., 8055.

agitation in the sections is to be found in these bulletins. The comments in this series seem to be those of the agents, while the bulletins of the previous year contain no personal allusions and give the impression of having been edited. Those dealing with the period up to and including the insurrection itself have a sense of immediacy, of being the views of persons *en scène* and may for that reason be considered more authentic than those of the earlier period.

The organizers of resistance in the Paris sections culminating in the Vendémiaire insurrection were hardly inspired by principles of pure royalism; they were chiefly determined to prevent the prolongation of the Convention's powers, and if they could manipulate the new Constitution to their own ends, all the better. If the 'two-thirds decrees' were rejected, they felt confident in their ability to elect their own candidates to the new assembly. Only then, by the gradual processes of constitutional government, could the ground be prepared for the transformation of the Republic into a moderate constitutional monarchy. The main core of opposition to the Convention's decrees was furnished by the richer sections of the city, firmly supported by the National Guard.[1] While all the Parisian sections had gradually purged their committees and general assemblies of Jacobins, the sections in the western sector of the city, where the *nouveaux riches* who had benefited by the government's economic policies lived, were the most determined political agitators against the Convention. Paradoxically, these same sections were the homes of *rentiers* and small proprietors who were suffering from the effects of inflation and rising prices—sufficient cause for the hatred shown by them to the Convention.[2] The Convention further intimidated the sections by its decision to bring troops into the city and by its decree of 2 September, allowing former terrorists to vote in the primary assemblies.

The agents in Paris anticipated the nature of the opposition to the Convention which became increasingly vocal during August and September. On the whole they concluded accurately that the constitutionalists were providing the main impulse to the

[1] For the only full-length study of this *journée*, see H. Zivy, *Le Treize vendémiaire an IV* (Paris, 1898).

[2] See G. Rudé, *The Crowd in the French Revolution* (Oxford, 1959) p. 163 for an interesting discussion of the effects of the government's economic policy on the various strata of the Parisian population.

movement. As early as July they observed and criticized the activities of their rivals. A fear that some members of the Convention were ready to reach an agreement with the constitutionalists was doubtless responsible for the agents' assertion that Sieyès was suggesting the recall of Mounier, the foremost advocate of a limited monarchy.[1] They were also irritated by Mounier's *Adolphe*—it bears no resemblance to Constant's classic novel—because of its criticism of the 'ancient constitution' and its support of a bicameral legislature.[2] The widespread confidence in the leaders of the primary assemblies expressed by some of the constitutionalists was no less disconcerting.[3] What upset the agents even more were the efforts of Madame de Staël to persuade the Committee of Public Safety to permit the return of such prominent *émigré*-constitutionalists as the Lameths; her salon was the headquarters of those political amateurs who were hatching plots to found a new dynasty on the basis of a revision of the 1791 Constitution.[4] To be sure, signs of growing resistance to the decrees were to be welcomed, but the moves of the *feuillants* outside, and the moderates in, the Convention to nurture propaganda in favour of a constitutional monarchy were to be deplored.[5] Equally nightmarish was the press's sellout to the constitutionalists: what was inexplicable was the sudden loss of judgement of such far-sighted journalists as Lacretelle and La Harpe.[6]

The information which d'Artéz received from Lemaître and passed on to Wickham concurs with that in the bulletins. According to Lemaître, there was mounting evidence that the movement in Paris was the work of a strange amalgam of parties including prominent non-*émigré* constitutionalists mysteriously connected with their *émigré* supporters, of whom Mallet du Pan and Malouet were the chief figures; moderates who clustered around Madame de Staël;[7] certain members of the Convention,

---

[1] Bulletin of 8/13 July 1795, Add. MSS., 46828.   [2] Ibid.

[3] Bulletin of 27 July–4 August 1795, ibid.

[4] Bulletin of 18/24 August 1795, ibid. and F.O. 28/12. That the removal from the list of *émigrés* of her constitutionalist friends was one of the reasons for Madame de Staël's return to Paris is confirmed by J. C. Herold in his recent biography, *Mistress to an Age* (London, 1959), p. 155.

[5] Bulletin of 24/31 August 1795, Add. MSS., 46828.

[6] Bulletin of 7/14 September 1795, F.O. 27/44.

[7] According to Wickham who dined with Madame de Staël upon her return to Switzerland, that famous lady acknowledged her support of the sections in the early stages of the agitation, withdrawing it, however, when she found that royalist

most notably Boissy d'Anglas; and even Barthélemy, the minister in Switzerland.[1] Lemaître warned that the 1791 Constitution would triumph unless the British abandoned their equivocal policy by a public declaration of support for the Bourbons;[2] sentiment could be swung in their favour if the British permitted Artois to land in France.[3]

It is evident that the agents thoroughly disapproved of the movement in Paris. It is also abundantly clear that they took no part in it, wavering between an optimistic appraisal of the strength of the sections and a despair of the absence of any genuine royalist motivation among its leaders. They counted on one of two things to result from the inevitable clash between the Convention and the sections: the sections would either gain the upper hand, in which case they might be guided to embrace the royalist cause more firmly; or the Convention would crush the sections, in which event the constitutionalists would disappear as a political force. The army's final destruction of the sectional uprising on the morning of 14 Vendémiaire (6 October) laid bare their bitter animus towards the electors whom they contemptuously branded as 'scribblers, petty poets and insignificant philosophers', who 'were proposing co-operation with the constitutionalists'. As an afterthought they added that they had hoped 'to thwart their devilish moderatism'.[4] Unable to accomplish this, they attributed the failure of the movement to the weakness, stupidity and fright of the constitutionalists. They admitted the impotence of the pure royalists in the struggle; their hope lay in a civil war which might contain the seeds of a legitimate restoration.[5] Indeed, they were overjoyed at the discomfiture of the constitutionalists, whom they described as having been utterly discredited and as having suffered irreparable losses.[6] That the

---

propaganda was making too much headway. Wickham to Grenville, 4 January 1796, F.O. 74/14. Madame de Staël foresaw that the Jacobins would side with the Convention against the sections. This is pointed out by Herold, op. cit., p. 158.

[1] Lemaître to d'Artéz, 12 September 1795, F.O. 74/12.

[2] Ibid.

[3] Lemaître to d'Artéz, 25 September 1795, ibid. This was wishful thinking. The Quiberon expedition had been a tragic failure, and Artois at the head of 4,000 men was unable to effect a landing on the Breton coast, so firmly was it defended by Hoche.

[4] Bulletin of 28 September–2 October 1795, Add. MSS., 46828 and F.O. 28/13.

[5] Bulletin of 5 October 1795, F.O. 28/13.

[6] Letter from Paris, 13 October 1795, F.O. 74/13.

constitutionalists had received considerable support they did not deny, ascribing it to skilful manipulation of the hopes and fears of 'the purchasers of national property and of those who had profited from the Revolution'.[1] They spared no words in justifying their own conduct and in heaping contumely on the constitutionalists; they even imputed to the latter aims similar to those of the Convention.

However, while the agents' rôle in the struggle was negligible, one of their number, Lemaître, was condemned to death by the military court of the Lepeletier section.[2] Here we encounter one of the mysteries of the organization of the Paris agency. It seems that there was a complete rupture between Brottier and Lemaître on the question of tactics. Lemaître made his own plans, from which Brottier dissociated himself.[3] It may be that the root of the trouble lay elsewhere; in Venice, where d'Antraigues, for reasons that remain unfathomable, confided in Lemaître without Brottier's knowledge.[4] Bayard, Wickham's agent, guessed that d'Antraigues tried to placate the agents by secretly giving each the impression that full authority was his.[5] Lemaître, in the full belief that he was the only accredited agent, proceeded with the aid of Sourdat, his faithful lieutenant, to formulate a fantastic plan. He wrote of his intimacy with two members of the Convention, Saladin and Rovère, from whom he received assurances that there were at least one hundred deputies willing to overthrow the Convention in preparation for the restoration of the Bourbons.[6] Encouraged by d'Artéz,[7] Lemaître became so confident that he asked d'Antraigues to promise royal pardon to the deputies. D'Antraigues complied, but cautioned Lemaître to beware of traps.[8]

---

[1] Letter from Paris, 13 October 1795, F.O. 74/13.

[2] According to Wickham, Colleville, a poor *émigré* from Caen, who was a double agent, betrayed Lemaître, Wickham to Grenville, 23 July 1796, F.O. 74/18. For additional information concerning Colleville, see Forneron, op. cit., ii. 86-7.

[3] Brottier's 'Mémoire sur l'agence de Paris . . . ; Add. MSS., 8055.

[4] Bayard's 'Notes sur les suite du 13 vendémiaire . . .', F.O. 74/14.

[5] Ibid.

[6] Ibid. See also Brottier's 'Mémoire sur l'agence de Paris . . .', Add. MSS., 8055 and Lemaître to d'Artéz, 25 September 1795, F.O. 74/12.

[7] Lemaître to d'Artéz, 30 September 1795, ibid. Lemaître wrote: 'I have thought it useful and *as part of your plan* to dine once a week or more often if necessary with three or four leaders who are in touch with the others. This is the way to hold the thread and turn the spindle.' (My italics.)

[8] D'Antraigues to Lemaître, 10 October 1795, *Recueil de la correspondance saisie chez Lemaître.*

Is it possible to ascertain whether Lemaître had really established connections with the deputies? At least four versions of what happened are available. The first is Brottier's, which is supported by Bayard: Lemaître did have dealings with a number of deputies who backed out at the last minute.[1] The bulletins offer an alternative explanation: some deputies, notably Tallien and Sieyès, seeking to justify the action of the Convention against the sections, charged Lemaître with having formed ties with the constitutionalists and of having conspired with the royalists in exile and with Wickham. This account goes on to suggest that Tallien did not charge Lemaître with complicity with the deputies for fear that he himself might have been implicated.[2] The third is that Lemaître constructed his plan on the basis of Sourdat's over-optimistic reports but that he never executed it.[3] The last is that he really did enter into a relationship with some deputies whose vague leanings towards royalism convinced him of their support. There is no proof beyond Brottier's assertions and Lemaître's alleged statements at his trial that the latter planned to or had indeed won over any deputies. However, there were many deputies, including Saladin, who were sympathetic to the constitutionalists, and both he and Rovère were arrested for conspiring to overthrow the government. The Convention's charge that Lemaître had a special connection with the constitutionalists was a fabrication, but the accusation that he had been conspiring with royalist émigrés was true. He was, however, not in league with Wickham, who did not discover until later his relationship with d'Artéz. The few grains of fact that we have been able to extract from the contradictory evidence does at least confirm Brottier's statement that he had broken with Lemaître. Brottier was arrested along with Lemaître but British money probably saved his life.[4]

---

[1] Brottier's 'Mémoire sur l'agence de Paris . . .', Add. MSS., 8055; Bayard's 'Notes sur les suites du 13 vendémiaire . . .', F.O. 74/14.

[2] Bulletin of 19 October 1795, F.O. 27/44; bulletin of 30 October–9 November 1795, F.O. 28/10.

[3] Bayard's 'Notes sur les suites du 13 vendémiaire . . .', F.O. 74/14.

[4] Duverne to Wickham, 23 November 1795, F.O. 74/13. See also Wickham's note to d'Avaray, 15 November 1795, A.A.E., France 588.

IV

One other matter requires clarification. D'Antraigues and the agents were certain that the British government was working with the constitutionalists and that the British secret service, by promoting their interests, was retarding the counter-revolution. He made curious allusions to the marquis of Lansdowne, 'that petty English Mirabeau';[1] and the agents scornfully referred to his supposed correspondence with the abbés de la Roche, Morellet,[2] Cabanis and Sieyès, all of whom were purportedly acting in the name of a fairly large party 'which wants the English constitution'.[3] The absurdity of this was matched by their statement that Treuil whom they singled out as one of the master agents in the British secret service was in touch with Madame de Staël![4] Brottier and Lemaître reported that a club made up of constitutionalists near Altona, a suburb of Hamburg, was corresponding with friends in Paris through the duc de Chartres (the future Louis Philippe), and that Treuil was also involved in this intrigue.[5] The Spanish ambassador in Paris, Campos, whose informant was undoubtedly d'Antraigues, wrote to Madrid in September 1795 that the constitutionalists were in touch not only with Treuil, but also with two other agents, Lambert and Solier.[6]

It was perhaps inevitable that d'Antraigues and the agents would discover the identity of some of the agents in the British secret service. There appears to be some truth in the suggestion that Treuil *was* a British agent.[7] An abbé Lambert *was* co-operating with Dutheil in forwarding letters from Paris.[8] And of course

[1] D'Antraigues to Drake, 27 February 1795, Add. MSS., 46834.
[2] Bulletin of 1/9 February 1795, F.O. 28/11.
[3] Paris agency to d'Antraigues, 11 May 1795, Add. MSS., 8056.
[4] Bulletin of 10/13 August 1795, Add. MSS., 46828.
[5] D'Antraigues to d'Avaray, 17 August 1795, A.A.E., France 588.
[6] Campos to d'Alcudia, 30 September 1795, Madrid, Estado de l'Archivohistorico 4787.
[7] Treuil's name appears in the records of the Home Office as early as March 1796, Home Office to Newport, 16 March 1796, H.O. 5/1. Reinhard, the French minister at Hamburg, cited him as a dangerous British agent, Reinhard to Delacroix, 8 December 1796, 30 April 1797, A.N., AFIII59, dossier 231.
[8] Report drawn up by count Butler, 27 October 1795, F.O. 27/44. Reubell sent the minister of police some details on the abbé Lambert who, he wrote, had taken part in the Vendémiaire insurrection, Reubell to Cochon, 6 February 1797, A.N., F⁷6371.

Madame de Staël and her friends were discussing politics and the merits of the Constitution of the year III. But there is no proof that this small handful of agents was actively conspiring with constitutionalists or with the conservative republicans of whom Madame de Staël was the centre. What is true was that Wickham was making strenuous efforts to reconcile the constitutionalists and the royalists. In the strange mind of d'Antraigues, however, this amounted to treason, and he had no difficulty in assuming the existence of underground links between British agents and his most hated adversaries. He therefore sought to destroy the credit of the latter by attacking the former.

It was with this intention that he sent Drake a copy of a letter from Gamon, proposing that the British government put its French secret service activities under his direction. Gamon was a young man of twenty-eight who came from Antraigues, the count's natal village, where his father had managed d'Antraigues' estates before the Revolution. Upon completion of his law studies at Toulouse, young Gamon became an *avocat* to the *Parlement* of that city. In 1791, the Ardèche department elected him to the Legislative Assembly to take the seat of its resigned deputy and he continued to represent the department in the Convention.[1] He left France in protest against the purge of the Convention in May–June 1793, settled in Switzerland, married a Swiss woman and lived under the assumed name of Fillion.[2] After Thermidor, he emerged from exile and was permitted to resume his seat in the Convention. As some of the bulletins reveal, he was acting as one of the Paris agency's sources of information.[3]

Gamon's letter gives an impression of having been concocted in collaboration with d'Antraigues. In it he criticized the careless and imprudent methods of agents like Treuil, and asked to be given authority as Britain's chief agent in France. He needed five hundred *louis d'or* to begin his operations. If things went badly, he wanted a guarantee from the British of a refuge and pensions

[1] Pingaud, op. cit., p. 116; A. Kuscinski, *Dictionnaire des Conventionnels* (Paris, 1920); *Biographie nouvelle des contemporaines* (Paris, 1822).

[2] My thanks are due to Madame Cecille Delhorbe of Lausanne for discovering Gamon's assumed name.

[3] The person known as 'xx' in the bulletins was undoubtedly Gamon. See bulletin of 16/22 June 1795, Add. MSS., 46828. According to d'Antraigues, Gamon overcame all obstacles in facilitating the circulation of the Verona Declaration in Paris, d'Antraigues to d'Avaray, 17 August 1795, A.A.E., France 628.

90

for the four agents whom he planned to station at Lyons, Rennes, Ostend and Dolle. For himself he asked not only the same assurance but also permission to bring to Britain 400,000 francs in merchandise and in specie.[1] Gamon's letter was the opening shot in d'Antraigues' new campaign to induce the Foreign Office to modify British policy. D'Antraigues' next move was to attempt to bring Wickham into disrepute, for which purpose he deluged Drake with copies of letters from Gamon. At first they stressed the risks of employing incompetent agents.[2] Lemaître's arrest was indirectly imputed to Wickham, on the grounds that d'Artéz had been grossly negligent; he had, in his correspondence with Lemaître, overlooked the elementary precaution of concealing his name and address.[3] Another agent in Wickham's employ, de Guer, was ridiculed as singularly stupid,[4] a conclusion reached by Wickham himself. All the while d'Antraigues persistently appealed for a speedy reply to Gamon's offer.

Although the sequel to this episode belongs to a later period, it is appropriate to relate part of it now. Early in 1796 d'Antraigues, still without a reply from Drake, announced that the final date for the acceptance of Gamon's offer was 20 February.[5] Drake, at first, had been wary of d'Antraigues' newest venture. Nevertheless he referred the matter to Grenville,[6] and took steps to warn Wickham that de Guer was untrustworthy.[7] Moreover, he came to share d'Antraigues' view of Wickham as reckless and impulsive.[8] He was, of course, unable to assume the responsibility for accepting Gamon's proposal without obtaining authority from London, and was therefore sincere in his protests to d'Antraigues that the

---

[1] Add. MSS., 46828. The letter took the form of a bulletin dated 10/13 August 1795. Godechot ('Essai d'identification de quelques correspondants du comte d'Antraigues', p. 7) gives the impression that Gamon made his offer in June 1796, whereas his first offer dates from the previous summer.

[2] D'Antraigues to Drake, 17 October 1795, Add. MSS., 46834.

[3] D'Antraigues to Drake, 7 November 1795, ibid.

[4] Ibid.

[5] D'Antraigues to Drake, 5 February 1796, Add. MSS., 46835.

[6] Drake to Grenville, 5 September 1795, F.O. 28/12.

[7] Trevor to Drake, 18 November 1795, Add. MSS., 46825: 'Without committing anybody, I shall put him [Wickham] on his guard with respect to de Guer, having other grounds and reasons for doing so.'

[8] Trevor to Drake, 30 September 1795, 'With respect to the sanguine expectations of the result of the present crisis at Paris—I cannot indulge them any more *than you...*' ibid. (My italics.) The abbé Villefort, one of d'Antraigues' informants, told him that Drake had confided in him of his disapproval of Wickham's tactics, Villefort to d'Antraigues, 20 April 1796, Add. MSS., 8056.

matter was out of his hands.[1] His requests to the Foreign Office went unanswered, and Gamon withdrew his offers in February 1796. The bulletins ceased the same month, ending a series that had begun in August 1793. There are three probable reasons for the end of the bulletins. First, while the agents at Paris continued what was becoming a less frequent correspondence with d'Antraigues, they were, in the winter of 1795-6, turning their attention to more pressing matters. They protested to Verona that their functions were too circumscribed, and they demanded 'a function other than that of simple correspondents'.[2] In the second place, Gamon, who had been as early as June 1795 their principal informant, gave up that duty in mid-November, because the references to his name in the Lemaître correspondence made it too dangerous for him to continue.[3] Finally, d'Antraigues was too occupied in trying to persuade Drake to accept Gamon's offer to devote much attention to the bulletins. We shall examine the implications of d'Antraigues' continuing efforts at a later time.

V

During the crisis in Paris, d'Andigné succeeded in obtaining the funds he had requested from the British.[4] While in London he confided in Dutheil, whose management of Artois' affairs gave him an entrée to the Foreign Office. Dutheil was anxious to assume control over the Paris agency. For a time, during 1795, his only link with the agency was Lemaître, but he suspected that the latter's grudging association with the other members was depriving him of important information.[5] As he was sure that he would be unable to sever Brottier's close attachment to d'Antraigues, he cleverly schemed to tempt Duverne with the prospect of replacing his colleague as chief of the agency.[6] D'Andigné fell in with the plan. He informed the agents that Windham had decided that the greater part of the funds destined for Charette

---

[1] Drake to d'Antraigues, 27 January, 2 March 1796, A.A.E., France 632.

[2] Brottier's 'Mémoire sur l'agence de Paris . . .', Add. MSS., 8055.

[3] Bulletin of 11/17 November 1795, F.O. 28/13.

[4] See above, pp. 66, 82.

[5] Dutheil to Lemaître, 24 July 1795, *Recueil de la correspondance saisie chez Lemaître*. See also Dutheil to Valdené, 12 January 1796; Wickham to Grenville, 18 February 1796, F.O. 74/15.

[6] Brottier's 'Mémoire sur l'agence de Paris . . .', Add. MSS., 8055; Bayard's 'Notes sur les suites du 13 vendémiaire . . .', F.O. 74/14.

should be obtained from Wickham. At the same time d'Andigné recommended that Duverne should visit Wickham and arrange for the transfer of the money from Switzerland to Paris.[1] Once Duverne was in Switzerland, Dutheil's agent, the abbé Villefort, would be there to tell him of the plan to make him head of the agency. Dutheil's plan failed, for Duverne's suspicions both of him and Villefort made him stick by Brottier.

They now set about rather hesitantly and belatedly to fulfil the tasks for which they had been granted funds. To be sure, Brottier had already distributed a portion of the funds to Charette, and the other rebel leaders, including Leveneur, Rochecotte and Bourmont, and he was optimistic that the fighting spirit of the west would be revived.[2] But Brottier made this estimate before the disarrangement of the agency's affairs, and before he received the disturbing news of Dutheil's intentions. Therefore his acquittal was, in a sense, not only a return to freedom, but also to the direction of the agency from which, but for Duverne's loyalty, he had almost been removed. Both he and Duverne were now on their guard against a possible renewal of police action, and against the interference of Dutheil and d'Andigné.

In assessing the causes of the stalemate in the west, these important psychological factors must be considered in addition to Hoche's superior forces, and the antagonism between Charette and Stofflet.[3] In the first place, Brottier's arrest discouraged the western rebels from corresponding with him so that he rarely had a clear picture of events. Secondly, the antagonism between Brottier and d'Andigné served to aggravate the existing confusion. On his return to France in the middle of October,[4] d'Andigné, armed with instructions from Dutheil and Windham, attempted to rally the rebels around Puisaye. Brottier, on the other hand, taking his cue from Verona, distrusted Puisaye, because of his undisguised reliance on the British government; his main aim was to increase Charette's power. He accused

[1] D'Andigné to Brottier, 9, 18 August 1795, Add. MSS., 8056. In his letter of the 18th, d'Andigné specifically asked Brottier to send Duverne as the emissary to Wickham. In his previous letter of the 9th, he made no such specific proposal.
[2] Paris agency to Wickham, 13, 15 October 1795; Duverne to Wickham, 23 October 1795, F.O. 74/13.
[3] The antagonism between the two leaders was admitted by Duverne in a letter to Wickham, 23 November 1795, ibid.
[4] Bouillon to Windham, 14 October 1795, F.O. 95/605.

d'Andigné of intercepting the letters he was sending to Charette for the purpose of delivering them to Puisaye; d'Andigné protested that his sole mission was to reconcile all the rebels.

Having no news from Leveneur and Charette, learning of Stofflet's inactivity, and receiving conflicting reports concerning the activities of Bourmont and Rochecotte, Brottier and Duverne decided in mid-November to send Bayard on a tour of inspection of the troubled area. What he saw and reported was discouraging. Stofflet's popularity with the rebels was arousing Charette's jealousy and was preventing co-operation between them;[1] Leveneur and Rochecotte were marking time and the other leaders were equally inactive.[2]

Towards the end of the year, Brottier prepared a memorandum suppressing the details of his own responsibility and tracing the deadlock in the west to lack of consultation between Louis and Artois. He rejected Dutheil's suggestion to correspond directly with him, flatly stating that he would co-operate, if necessary, only with Artois. He asked for authority to be granted the agency to define the extent and limits of the commands of each of the western leaders; to permit Charette to bestow promotions among his officers; to appoint Mallet, the Swiss officer whom Wickham had sent to assist Leveneur, as the latter's second-in-command; to acknowledge the work of Sapinaud, Scépeaux, Rochecotte and the abbé Bernier; and to promise Cormatin, who had been Hoche's prisoner since May, special powers as soon as he gained his freedom. Characteristically, there was no mention of Puisaye except in the familiar derogatory manner.[3]

Thus, as for Wickham, the year 1795 ended dismally for the agents. The execution of Lemaître and Brottier's own narrow escape had weakened and dispirited them. They soon rallied, however, with proposals for the reorganization of their activities. Both the agents and Wickham, in reassessing their respective positions, came to similar conclusions, thus paving the way for the next round of counter-revolutionary efforts.

[1] Wickham to Grenville, 7 January 1796, F.O. 74/14.
[2] Duverne to Wickham, 23 November, 8 December 1795, F.O. 74/13.
[3] Brottier's 'Mémoire sur l'agence de Paris . . .', Add. MSS., 8055.

6

THE PARIS AGENCY CUTS
THE CORD

THE decision to give the Paris agency extensive powers lay with
Verona, but confusion, intrigue and jealousy rather than harmony
and statesmanship were the order of the day. A profound malaise
lay at the root of the thinking of all the royalist ministers. As a
compensatory device they concealed their true feelings and beliefs
under an assumed optimism, which, as time was to prove, would
blind them to the real nature of events. Essentially they were relics
of a vanished age, unable and unwilling to take measures to meet
the realities of a new one. They clung desperately to their precious
bits of empty authority, fearful of assuming the responsibilities of
collective action.

Lord Macartney's mission[1] to the comte de Provence, who had
taken the title of Louis XVIII after the death of his nephew,
proved futile; Grenville's special envoy arrived too late to prevent
the release of the Verona Declaration, which likened the Revolution to the hydra-head of anarchy. It spoke of restoring the ancient
constitution, 'for fourteen centuries the glory of France', with
provision for the re-establishment of the three orders, the *Parlements* and religion. The Declaration's threats against the regicide
members of the Convention further alienated responsible moderate
opinion. As Grenville pointed out, allowance had to be made even
for the regicides who had acted out of fear; they could expiate
their crimes by performing great services for the monarchy.[2] Like
Wickham[3] and Trevor,[4] Grenville found the Declaration un-
acceptable: the narrowness of the amnesty was driving the French
into the arms of the Republic. In any case an interim military

---

[1] Grenville to Macartney, 10 July 1795, F.O. 27/45. Cf. Grenville's note to Harcourt asking him to use his influence with the comte de Provence to be moderate
in his public statements, Grenville to Harcourt, 22 June 1795, A.A.E., France 588.
[2] Grenville to Harcourt, 27 August 1795, A.A.E., France 624.
[3] Wickham to Grenville, 19 August 1795, F.O. 74/11.
[4] Trevor to Grenville, 19 August 1795, F.O. 67/18.

regime would very likely be imposed upon France before the monarchy could be restored.[1]

In private conversations with Louis, Macartney found him intelligent, informed, communicative, and sensible when he was momentarily able to overcome the prejudices of his education and of his advisers. While his ministers' political ideas were inconsistent, Macartney concluded generously that Louis' own ideas were 'much less tinctured with prejudices than theirs .... He appeared to me to reason justly and with great moderation.' Louis regarded Necker's publication of the *Compte Rendu* as the first step towards the Revolution; an error of equal, perhaps, greater magnitude was the crown's submission to the demand that the Estates meet as one body. Louis XVIII would not be guilty of this error![2] The social creed of the privileged orders could not have been better expressed. Moving on to more recent events, Macartney found that the Convention's victory over the Parisian sections in Vendémiaire did not disturb the equanimity of Louis' court; indeed it was satisfied that the defeat was a blessing in disguise in view of the insurgents' avowed dislike for the 'old government'.[3]

That the Verona Declaration had stimulated universal hostility and suspicion was the burden of a memorandum submitted to Louis and his ministers. Unsigned and undated, but obviously written after the elections to the new assembly, the writer attempted an assessment of the Declaration's effects, showing how its allusions to vengeance and the restoration of feudal dues had divided the primary assemblies, strengthened the Convention, and harmed the progress of the counter-revolution. Negotiation with the bourgeois masters of revolutionary France was a far wiser course than reliance on outside force. Even now, the baneful consequences of the Declaration could be mitigated by acknowledging

[1] Grenville to Macartney, 8 September 1795, F.O. 27/45. Drake summed up official British opinion best in some observations meant for Grenville: '. . . The greater part of those persons who are more enthusiastically attached to the court of Verona are desirous of re-establishing the ancient system in France, purely and simply, and without any of those modifications which the present times and circumstances might perhaps render necessary.' Drake to Grenville, 15 August 1795, F.O. 28/12. Monciel observed at the same time that the best proof of the Declaration's bad effect was the Convention's order to have more copies printed at Paris! Monciel to Wickham, report on observations during August and September 1795, F.O. 74/12.

[2] Macartney to Grenville, 27 September 1795, F.O. 27/45.

[3] Macartney to Grenville, 15 November 1795, ibid.

the constructive aspects of the Revolution.[1] This realistic appraisal of the royalists' position apparently made some impression on Louis and his ministers, who instructed their agents in France to 'explain and interpret the certain parts of the Manifesto in such a manner as to remove many of the objections that were made to it'.[2]

Harmony between Louis' ministers and d'Antraigues was equally lacking. D'Antraigues was determined to retain his control over the Paris agents, and he took the opportunity of Bayard's visit to Venice to alter their report by styling himself as their sole intermediary with the king.[3] From d'Antraigues' acidulous criticism of Louis' advisers, Bayard gathered that with the exception of Flachslanden, none was worthy to hold high position: d'Avaray, Louis' favourite, was unbearably arrogant; la Vauguyon appropriated and sought credit for the plans of others while taking care to ingratiate himself with everyone; Jaucourt was a contemptible automaton.[4] Bayard's impressions of the court at Verona were doubtless coloured by d'Antraigues,[5] who nevertheless was no mean judge of character: Bayard's conversations with Louis and his entourage were disappointing. They simply refused to assess the gravity of the situation. The recommendations Bayard brought from Brottier and his own analysis of royalist weakness displeased them; they had the preconceived notion that France was daily growing more royalist. Instead of adopting the agency's proposals, plans for isolated insurrections still appealed to them; and they could not rid themselves of the illusion that the forces of the Republic would melt away the moment the king appeared on French soil.[6] Thus Bayard returned to Venice empty-handed. D'Antraigues was furious, for he rightly suspected that the ministers' jealousy of his undeniable hold over the agency was behind their refusal to sanction its plans. Without wasting words, he informed Flachslanden that the dictates of security ruled out a scheme whereby the agents would be answerable directly to the

[1] 'Note sur l'état actuel de la France, 1795', A.A.E., France 588.
[2] Macartney to Grenville, 19 November 1795, F.O. 27/45.
[3] The alterations can be seen in the agency's 'Mémoire sur l'agence de Paris . . .', 17 December 1795, Add. MSS., 8055.
[4] Bayard to Wickham 16 February 1796, F.O. 74/15.
[5] 'Notice sur Vérone, le Roi, ses entours, leurs moyens et leurs projets', in Wickham's despatch to Grenville, 8 April 1796, F.O. 74/17.
[6] Bayard to Wickham, 16 February 1796, F.O. 74/15.

king. Then, in threatening language, he declared that it was some-
times necessary to serve the institution of the monarchy rather than
the person of the king.[1]

His suspicions were well-founded, because the ministers, especially la Vauguyon and d'Avaray, wanted to grant the powers
demanded by the agency without increasing d'Antraigues' authority over it. It was necessary to accomplish this without
arousing his suspicions. Indeed, it was essential to force Brottier,
even against his will, to consult directly with them in Verona and
with Dutheil in London. To ensure that he would do so, they
gave him all the powers he had demanded, and even permitted
him to correspond with d'Antraigues. But their instructions were
so designed that Brottier was bound decisively to be governed by
their will. It is worth looking at them in some detail.[2] Since
Britain, alone among the great powers, was prepared to offer
assistance to the royalist cause, Louis' ministers informed the
Paris agency that the comte de Moustier would assume, under
British direction, supervision of the aid destined for the insurgent
west; Précy and Imbert-Colomès would continue to concert
measures with Wickham; and Villecrose, the chief royalist agent
in Provence, would co-operate with Drake. The ministers directed
Brottier and Duverne to extend their scrutiny over all royalist
operations in France, for which purpose the country would be
divided by the Loire. Efforts to attract not only royalists but all
properly penitent opponents of the Republic and the establishment of paramilitary organizations in all the departments also fell
within their terms of reference. As Paris was the hub of the
nation, the agents were to continue their work of propaganda
there; to appraise the strength of the various factions—the
Orléanists, the constitutionalists, etc.—utilizing them whenever
possible to advance true royalism; and to seek friends in the
Directory, the ministries, among the clerks, the National Guard,
and the newly elected members of the *Corps législatif*. Should the
prospect of a new 'explosion' on the model of Vendémiaire
materialize, the agents were instructed to gain the support of the
insurgents so as to ensure the proclamation of the monarchy once
the Republic disintegrated.

The instructions did not reach the agency until some time in

---

[1] D'Antraigues to Flachslanden, 11 February 1796, A.A.E., France 589.
[2] Instructions to the Paris agency, circa March or April 1796, Add. MSS., 8055.

March or April. In the interval, Brottier and Duverne agreed to correspond with Dutheil, through whose offices they hoped to obtain additional British funds. For this purpose, they asked François[1] to make his way to London. When their instructions from Verona finally came, they decided to divide their functions. Brottier agreed to remain in Paris to direct the major part of the operations; and Duverne consented to settle in Switzerland for the purpose of expediting the correspondence between Verona, Paris and other parts of France.[2] It was their intention to take advantage of any evidence of growing royalist agitation, to direct it, and to act in the name of Louis XVIII if the deputies were willing to work towards his restoration.[3] La Vauguyon approved, and they made some headway even before Duverne departed for Switzerland. They gained the collaboration of Jean François Vauvilliers, a former professor of Greek at the Collège de France. He had just given up a post in the ministry of the interior as Bénézech's chief agent *pour les subsistances*, but apparently utilized his old contacts to secure intelligence from the public offices.[4] They sought the services of the editor of the royalist journal, the *Accusateur public*, Richer-Sérisy, who had been in the forefront of the agitation during Vendémiaire.[5] They also mentioned Jean François Marmontel, the distinguished *littérateur*, as one of the writers who would probably put his prestige and literary talents at the service of the royalists.[6] They spoke in similar terms of the editor of *Véridique*, Jacques Corentin Royou, the brother of the abbé Royou with whom he had edited the *Ami du roi*; and of Montjoie, who had also contributed to the abbé's journal.[7] Finally, they even made friendly references to La Harpe and Morellet, both of whom had earned their scorn during Vendémiaire. This indeed was a novel departure!

[1] Paris agency to Dutheil, 9 February 1796, F.O. 27/47. On the background of Jean Marie François, an *émigré avocat* from Mâcon, see P. Montarlot, 'Un Agent de la police secrète 1800–1817, Jean Marie François', *Revue des questions historiques*, xciv (1913), 94–119. He composed the daily police bulletins for Fouché during the Napoleonic regime.

[2] Brottier to d'Antraigues, 16 April 1796, Add. MSS., 8057.

[3] Duverne to d'Antraigues, 6 May 1796, ibid.

[4] Duverne to d'Antraigues, 21 April 1796, ibid. Vauvilliers, implicated in the Brottier conspiracy of 1797, won his acquittal. See his interrogation by the police on 2 February 1797, A.N., F⁷6371. He was deprived of his seat in the *Conseil des Cinq-Cents* after Fructidor, took refuge in Switzerland, and died in Russia in 1801.

[5] Brottier to d'Antraigues, 22 April 1796, Add. MSS., 8057.

[6] Ibid.　　[7] Ibid.

An even more astonishing reversal of policy followed. It had its origins in at least two events. The first was Brottier's and Duverne's decision to make overtures to members of the *Conseils*. Probably they did so with the same reservations with which Louis and his ministers were to sanction such an approach; any deputy who would be willing to assist in the achievement of royalist aims could expect a reward at the appropriate time. One of the greatest obstacles to the search for new adherents to the cause was the obscurantism of the Verona Declaration. It was this barrier that was causing hesitation among deputies who might otherwise consider lending their support to the royalist cause. The second reason for the new direction taken by the agents was the distressing news from the Vendée, Brittany and Normandy. Both Charette and Stofflet had abortively taken up arms again early in 1796, and then joined with the other insurgent leaders in an appeal to the British and Artois for help. Britain promised at least £30,000 monthly for Puisaye, Charette, Stofflet and Scépeaux. Heartened, and believing that the next engagement with Hoche would be the final one, they prepared for battle. But before the campaign could begin, Stofflet was taken prisoner and was executed on 25 February. Charette shared his fate on 29 March and Scépeaux's submission to Hoche soon followed. Only Frotté and Rochecotte were left in Normandy while Puisaye remained inactive. Henceforth the Vendée could no longer be regarded as the centre of royalist strength.

These two factors were instrumental in shaping a new approach to the problems of the counter-revolution. Without first seeking authorization from Louis and his ministers, Brottier and Duverne proceeded to negotiate with certain members of the *Conseils*, chiefly Lemerer, deputy to the *Conseil des Cinq-Cents* from the department of Ille-et-Vilaine, and Mersan, deputy to the same body from the Loiret department, whose intentions were made known to, and evidently had the support of, general Moreau.[1] Gamon, whose connections with the agency and with d'Antraigues we have already examined, and Madier, his fellow-deputy from the Ardèche department were also members of the group of

---

[1] Wickham to Grenville, 10, 16 July 1796, F.O. 74/18. In 1797, Duverne revealed to the police that Lemerer and Mersan were the two leading deputies with whom the agency was in direct consultation. See *Deuxième déclaration de Dunant, annexée au registre secret du Directoire Exécutif, 17 ventôse an V* (7 March 1797), Brit. Mus. Pamphlet, R. 168.

deputies with whom the agents were working.[1] These politicians agreed that the monarchy could be restored only by pursuing a policy of moderate opposition to the Directory through the Legislature. Since they were determined to proceed with or without Louis' consent, the agents endeavoured to gain his support.

Gamon himself elaborated his belief in such a policy in letters to Drake which reached him through d'Antraigues. The preconceptions and wishful thinking of the great majority of royalists were not shared by Gamon. Three out of four Frenchmen, he declared, were opposed to the restoration of the unreformed monarchy. It would be sheer waste to establish any contacts with that segment of the population favouring the king, because it was isolated and utterly lacking in resources for action.[2] It would also be futile to persist in the conquest of France, for the armies of the Republic were inspired by appeals to preserve the inviolability of French territory and by the equally firm conviction that they were waging a defensive war. How could the war be ended? By destroying the Directory—the house of cards would collapse ignominiously under the impact of legislative criticism of its disastrous financial policy.[3] The way would then be opened to the seizure of power by the royalist deputies and the return of Louis XVIII.[4]

A similar analysis was the burden of the agency's recommendations to Louis.[5] While awaiting a reply from him, they acquired the services of Berthelot de la Villeurnoy, a former *maître des requêtes* from Toulouse, a veteran of Coblentz, and a survivor of the terror in Paris.[6] When they estimated their needs, they asked for a preliminary sum of £7,000 to finance the plans of their deputy friends and to win potential recruits from the army when the time for open opposition to the government arrived; and they demanded a much larger sum from the British government for the

---

[1] Proof of the collaboration between Gamon and Madier and their membership in this group is to be seen in a letter from d'Antraigues to la Vauguyon, 2 February 1797, A.A.E., France 610.

[2] Gamon to Drake, [?] 1796, in Drake's despatch to Grenville, 17 June 1796, F.O. 28/15.

[3] Gamon to Drake, 3 July 1796, ibid.

[4] Gamon to Drake, 23 August 1796, ibid.

[5] La Vauguyon to Brottier, 11 July 1796, F.O. 74/18.

[6] See A.N., F⁷6371 for his interrogation by the police, 12 pluviôse an V (31 January 1797). According to Dutheil, La Villeurnoy was known to Grenville, Dutheil to Grenville, 18 August, 1796, F.O. 27/48.

purpose of co-ordinating their activities with those of Rochecotte, Frotté, Puisaye and Leveneur.[1] They intended to rely heavily on Rochecotte who, it seemed, had won the confidence of Hoche's second-in-command, Beauregard.[2] What they were really planning was the infiltration of the armed forces in Paris with royalists in preparation for an assault on the government: they clearly expected that the deputies would sustain the momentum of their attack on the Directory, which would paralyse its administrative organs and discredit it in the eyes of the people and the army. That these plans were known to Lemerer, Mersan and their friends is extremely doubtful; if they were it seems improbable that they would have approved. Most of them had not yet realized, and indeed, few were to become aware of, the violence implicit in their opposition to the Directory. The agency, less given to moralizing, had incorporated into its plan what it had always believed was the most effective means of overthrowing the Directory. For the agency, the rôle of the army on two critical occasions, in Prairial and Vendémiaire, was clear and decisive. With the army at its disposal, the Directory could resist any attack; without the army it would succumb.

The reply from Louis and la Vauguyon reached the agency in July. They approved of la Villeurnoy's membership in the agency and praised the plan of co-ordinating the activities of the western insurgents.[3] But they refused to authorize the request to work with the deputies. Duverne, who was then in Switzerland, begged Louis to reconsider, but was coldly reprimanded. It was only because of Wickham's intervention that la Vauguyon did not reject the project outright. As a concession, la Vauguyon suggested that a representative of the deputies might visit Blankenburg, the king's new residence, and negotiate a basis for co-operation.[4]

[1] Brottier to Wickham, extracts of despatches from 15 to 22 May 1796, F.O. 74/17; Brottier to Dutheil, 22, 27 June 1796; François to Dutheil, 27 June 1796, F.O. 27/48.

[2] Brottier to Dutheil, 27 June 1796, F.O. 27/48; Wickham to Grenville, 28 October 1796, F.O. 74/19. The agents informed Wickham that Beauregard had given them intelligence concerning the projected invasion of Ireland.

[3] La Vauguyon to Brottier, 11 July 1796; Louis XVIII to Brottier, 11 July 1796, F.O. 74/18.

[4] Wickham to Grenville, 18 July 1796, *Correspondence of William Wickham*, i. 420–426. During his interrogation by the police, Duverne gave substantially the same version, *Déclarations de Duverne de Presle ou Dunan, annexées au régistre secret du Directoire Exécutif, le 11 ventôse an V* (1 March 1797), Brit. Mus. Pamphlet, R. 168.

II

The reply from Blankenburg hardly fulfilled Brottier's expectations, but it did not deter him from acting. He began to examine the administrative problems of establishing an efficient clandestine organization. In consultation with Despomelles, whom he persuaded to resume a more active rôle in the agency, the decision was made to concentrate operations within a 150 mile arc surrounding Paris. Most of this area was west and south of Paris; it extended as far north as Rouen and Beauvais and to Auxerre in the south-east. Within this arc, a system of communications was to be set up linking eight principal regions to Paris, each of which was to be centred in an important provincial town: Rouen; Beauvais and Senlis (which were treated as one centre); Auxerre; Melun; Orléans; Tours; Le Mans; and Evreux. Each of these units was to be commanded by a *président*, who would be responsible for establishing a communication system with Paris. For example, Rochecotte would take charge of the Le Mans area, which would be linked in two ways to Paris: the first extended from Le Mans to Paris by way of Ferté-Vidame, Senouches, Chateauneuf, Maintenon, Epernon, and Versailles; the second by way of la Ferté-Bernard, Nogent le Retrou, Chateauneuf, Maintenon, Epernon, and Versailles. The *présidents* would be in touch not only with Paris but with one another. Of the £10,000 the agents hoped to have at their disposal, at least £1,000 would be distributed to each of the *présidents* who would use the funds (1) to set up their relay systems and (2) to purchase arms. With the remaining £2,000, the agents intended to influence public opinion through the press, to encourage desertion in the army, to maintain their relations with the deputies, and to defray the costs of their own living expenses.[1]

The purpose of this transmission belt was not, in the first instance, directed towards stimulating a series of simultaneous uprisings against the central and departmental administrations. The agents insisted that violence would produce more harm than good. They were confident that the Directory's financial difficulties contained the seeds of its inevitable destruction, especially if the deputies carried out their plan to oppose the Directory's fiscal programme. Emphasis should rather be put on the forthcoming

---

[1] Paris agency to Dutheil, 6 August 1796, no. 1, F.O. 27/48.

electoral campaign; if successful, it would return a majority of royalists and '*honnêtes gens*'—the men of wealth—to the *Conseils*. The armed forces in the area around Paris would then, if still necessary, be employed to destroy the vestiges of Directorial power.

What the agency had in mind was a secret organization masking its clandestine activities under the cover of an open one. It hoped that in time it would be extended to the entire country. At the summit in each department there would be a commandant, known openly as the *président des amis de l'ordre*. He alone would be in a position to correspond with Paris and know the true aims of the organization. Next in command there would be a *sous-chef* or *vice-président* who would be aware of the *président's* functions but would not have access to his correspondence with Paris. Each department would be divided into units headed by *secrétaires des amis de l'ordre*; but they too would remain unaware of the society's connections with Paris. Ostensibly each departmental society would function independently, its chief concern being to disarm the Jacobins and to gain control of the local organs of government. This would serve as a preliminary step to the society's domination of the primary and electoral assemblies. All references to the monarchy were to be avoided. As much as possible, the local authorities were to be lulled into the belief that the movement was normal, peaceful, spontaneous, and legitimate. The agents envisaged the organization's encouragement of the electors to support the 'right' candidates and to meet as a body when the occasion demanded.[1] Such was the outline of the plan for the famous *Institut philanthropique*.

Before the *Institut* could be established, funds were needed. The sum of £20,000 which Wickham had put at the disposal of the agency in the autumn of 1795 was already exhausted. In May François brought the agents £4,400 from Windham and Grenville for the rebels in Normandy, but the drafts had been drawn inaccurately and could not be used.[2] At the end of June, Wickham

---

[1] Paris agency to Dutheil, 6 August 1796, no. 1, F.O. 27/48.

[2] François to Dutheil, 1 June 1796; Harcourt to Grenville, 16 June 1796; Tryon to Grenville, 7 September 1796, F.O. 27/48. Tryon was employed by Windham to transmit funds to Frotté and Puisaye. He also occasionally carried despatches to and from the agency. See Windham to Pitt, 10 July 1796, Add. MSS., 37844 and Tryon to Grenville, 12 September 1796, F.O. 27/48. Earlier in the year Tryon was sent on a mission to Scépeaux, Tryon to Windham, 27 June 1796, W.O. 1/663. Cf. V. Pierre, *18 Fructidor. Documents pour la pluparte inédits* (Paris, 1893), pp. 195–6.

allowed them the use of £3,000, which he had originally earmarked for Rochecotte's use.[1] In July Duverne and la Vauguyon urged Wickham to increase this amount, but he was unwilling to do so without authorization from Whitehall.[2] Dutheil and Harcourt then pressed Grenville and Windham to supply the agents with at least £7,000.[3] Finally, on 11 September, Grenville, having first presented their arguments before the Cabinet, assured Dutheil that the agents could have the funds on the understanding that the amounts already sent would be subtracted from the total sum. By this time, Wickham was also ready to accede to their requests.[4]

The agents were now reasonably certain of financial resources. Louis and his ministers were enthusiastic, and directed them at the beginning of October to use the funds to promote royalist candidates during the spring elections. They were also anxious to receive the representative of the deputies with whom Brottier and Duverne said they were co-operating.[5] Perhaps the royal exiles were at last willing to support a counter-revolution based on constitutional methods. In part the determining factor in their awakening was their fear that the Spanish ambassador at Paris, del Campo, had been duped by Tallien, who was rumoured to be urging the restoration of the monarchy with a Spanish claimant at its head. There had been many rumours, ever since Spain's treaty of peace with France in 1795, that one of its secret clauses stipulated the restoration of the monarchy headed by a Spanish Bourbon. Speculation flared anew at the conclusion of the Franco-Spanish alliance in August 1796. Even Wickham reported 'on the best of authorities' that Tallien and Cabarrus, his father-in-law, had inserted a provision into the treaty for bringing a Spaniard to the French throne.[6] Drake reported the same news in a ciphered

---

[1] Wickham to Grenville, 30 June 1796, F.O. 74/17. Actually Wickham arranged for the sum of £4,000 to reach them, but he reserved £1,000 to be used in facilitating the escape of Sir Sydney Smith who was imprisoned in the Temple.

[2] La Vauguyon to Wickham, 10 July 1796, A.A.E., France 609; Duverne to Dutheil, 20 July 1796; Brottier to Dutheil, 6 August 1796, F.O. 27/48; Wickham to Grenville, 4 July 1796, Dropmore Papers, iii. 216.

[3] Harcourt to Grenville, 23 August 1796, F.O. 27/48; Dutheil to Windham, 11 September 1796, Add. MSS., 37862.

[4] Ibid. Windham to Grenville, 9 September 1796; Grenville to Windham, 11 September 1796, Dropmore Papers, iii. 244, 249; Wickham to Grenville, 2 September 1796, F.O. 74/18.

[5] Note to Paris agency and Harcourt, 2 October 1796, A.A.E., France 609 and 625.

[6] Ibid. Wickham to Grenville, 7 September 1796, F.O. 74/18. Cf. Trevor's remarks to Lord Bute, ambassador at Madrid, 2 March 1796, Add. MSS., 36811.

message to Grenville.[1] The story evidently caused Louis some anxiety, for he instructed the agents to warn del Campo of Tallien's treachery and to win for the royal cause those deputies who seemed to be favouring a Spanish claimant.

There seems to be no doubt that Louis and la Vauguyon were now prepared to negotiate with the representative of the deputies. D'Antraigues dissented. To be sure, he could not rule out a *rapprochement* with the constitutionalists but only on condition that they accept Louis' earlier promises of an amnesty. Co-operation with them was permissible if they agreed to accommodate their politics to the pattern of the *ancien régime*. It is not possible to discover the basis for negotiation with the deputies, but d'Antraigues' alarm suggests that Louis and la Vauguyon were considering greater concessions than in the past.[2] D'Antraigues' attitude was clearly that of a bitterly disappointed man. His uneasiness arose not so much because his cherished principles were being mutilated, but rather because his personal position was being threatened by events. Frantically he resumed his efforts to seek British approval for Gamon's plan; again he used Drake as his intermediary;[3] and again he failed. Why? The entire system of operations in the Midi radiated from Wickham's Swiss headquarters, and the British were committed to Wickham's plans; they had sanctioned and encouraged them. Since the success of Wickham's proposals rested on a royalist electoral victory in 1797, there was no unique advantage in abandoning them in favour of Gamon's which were not essentially different; moreover, why lend support to an arch-royalist like d'Antraigues whose trustworthiness and motives could only arouse suspicion.

D'Antraigues was obviously in rivalry with Wickham. Gradually he was being pressured to relinquish his control of the agency in Paris. He could not tolerate the thought of accepting a position in which he would be subordinate to Wickham.[4] To preclude this possibility, he had asked Grenville in June for a greater share of responsibility, but he was told to look to Wickham and Drake for orders.[5] D'Antraigues' request, it should be noted, was made at

---

[1] Drake to Grenville, 19 August 1796, F.O. 28/15.

[2] D'Antraigues to la Vauguyon, 13 October 1796, A.A.E., France 634.

[3] Drake to Grenville, 16 September 1796, F.O. 28/15.

[4] Macartney to Drake, 2 February 1796, Add. MSS., 46829. Macartney expressed the hope that Wickham's 'circumspection' would neutralize d'Antraigues' 'impetuosity'.

[5] Macartney to d'Antraigues, 20 June 1796, Add. MSS., 46835.

the same time as his renewal of Gamon's offer to Drake; obviously he was exploring every expedient to restore his influence. Upon the rejection of this last appeal, Drake asked Grenville whether d'Antraigues would be permitted to seek refuge in England with the remains of his fortune, amounting to some £12,000.[1] There was apparently no response. When it became evident that Grenville's confidence in Wickham could not be shaken, d'Antraigues reverted to his earlier, more characteristic hostility towards any scheme that smacked of reconciliation with, and recognition of, the growing powers of the constitutionalists. However, he did approach Drake for aid to finance the royalist campaign in the southern departments in the forthcoming elections,[2] only to be told that the British ministry had given Wickham full authority to achieve the same ends.[3]

While d'Antraigues was exploring solutions for his dilemma, Louis and his ministers awaited the representative from the deputies. The meeting never took place.[4] In Paris, the agents were forced to mark time, because of delay at Whitehall in transmitting funds,[5] but at last on 6 October the money was made available.[6] In the interval, the agents concluded that the normal channels through which all government decisions in London had to travel was another example of British procrastination. Moreover they required additional funds. They so informed Dutheil, who learned in this way that Duverne would himself visit London to press the case.[7]

There was still another reason for Duverne's voyage to London. The British ministry was about to undertake peace negotiations

[1] D'Antraigues to Drake, 5 September 1796; Drake to Grenville, 6 September 1796, F.O. 28/15. I have been unable to find any record of Grenville's reply to this request.

[2] D'Antraigues to Drake, 26 December 1796, Add. MSS., 46835.

[3] D'Antraigues to Drake, 25 January 1797, Add. MSS., 46836.

[4] La Vauguyon to d'Antraigues, 19, 27 October 1796, A.A.E., France 609. Duverne was to state at his interrogation by the police that a representative acting for 184 deputies *may* have visited Louis in December 1796 or early in January of the following year. There is no other record of the alleged meeting. *Déclarations de Duverne de Presle ou Dunan, annexées au régistre secret du Directoire Exécutif, le 11 ventôse an V* (1 March 1797).

[5] Dutheil to Grenville, 14 September 1796, F.O. 27/48; Windham to Grenville, 25 September 1796, Add. MSS., 37846.

[6] Dutheil to Canning, emploi des £7,000 remises par M. Canning le 6 octobre 1796, F.O. 27/48; Grenville to Wickham, 14 October 1796, F.O. 74/19.

[7] Dutheil to Grenville, 6 October 1796, F.O. 27/48. The agents informed Dutheil of their decision in a letter dated 30 September 1796.

with the Directory; it had been trying to do so since early in the year. At last, in September, the Directory appeared willing to negotiate, and on 16 October, Lord Malmesbury, Britain's veteran ambassador, who had in 1787 engineered the triumph of the Orange party in the United Provinces, left for the French capital. Malmesbury's mission naturally alarmed the royalists. Dutheil instructed the agents to assist the British negotiator in acquiring intelligence, but not to subordinate the interests of Louis to Britain's needs.[1] Dutheil's cautionary note to the agents earned the displeasure of the comte d'Artois, who, upon hearing of it, directed the agents to lend Malmesbury every assistance.[2] Artois' instructions contradicted Dutheil's only on the surface, for both were convinced that Malmesbury's mission would prove abortive. In a conference with Malmesbury at the Foreign Office on the eve of his departure, Dutheil surmised that neither Grenville nor Malmesbury believed in a successful conclusion to the negotiations.[3] The agents were suspicious, however, and were not content to await the unpredictable issue of the negotiations. Duverne and François must be sent posthaste to London to convince the ministry that the Directory was not really serious in seeking an end to hostilities.

III

Towards the end of October Duverne and François were in England.[4] Duverne went directly to Edinburgh to inform Artois that Louis desired the duc de Bourbon, Condé's son, to return to France to hold himself in readiness to act as the representative of the princes should the country move towards a restoration.[5] When Duverne returned to London in mid-November new instructions from d'Avaray were awaiting him. To prevent the possibility of a party forming on behalf of the Condés, the royalist standard bearer would be Artois' younger son, the duc de Berry. However, everything was to proceed as before, for secrecy was essential to the success of the venture. Hence young Condé's voyage to the

[1] Dutheil to Brottier, 15, 16 October 1796, A.A.E., France 589.
[2] Artois to Dutheil, 18 October 1796; Artois to Brottier, 18 October 1796, ibid.
[3] Dutheil to Harcourt, 14 October 1796, A.A.E., France 625.
[4] King to Collector of Customs at Brighton, 31 October 1796, H.O. 5/2.
[5] Dutheil to Canning, 7 December 1796, F.O. 27/48.

continent was to be publicized in order to divert attention from Berry's movements.[1]

While Duverne kept this information secret from everyone, including Dutheil, together they awaited the end of the peace negotiations. But they were not inactive. With reports furnished by Brottier telling of French preparations for an invasion of Ireland and England, they did their best to create the impression that the Directory was prolonging the negotiations in order to divert Britain's attention from its aggressive designs.[2] At the same time, they sent Grenville intelligence of increasing opposition to the government in the departments neighbouring Paris.[3] The exertions of the royalists were superfluous, for by mid-December it was clear that Malmesbury's peace mission had failed. Even before Malmesbury's departure for Paris, Grenville had expressed his doubts about the wisdom of the mission, going so far as to urge Wickham 'to profit from the discontent which the continuance of the present calamities, aggravated by disappointment from the failure of the negotiations for peace, may reasonably be expected to excite'.[4] With the failure of the negotiations, he felt that every possible source of resistance to the Directory should be explored. He had no illusions about the reliability of the agents, but he was ready to support their request for more funds.[5] As he was to confide to Windham later, Paris rather than the provinces was the key to the future of the monarchy.[6]

The agents in Paris required additional funds for three general purposes. British needs would be served by establishing more reliable sources of intelligence in Paris; the *Institut philanthropique*, already making preparations for the forthcoming elections, could not operate unless it was adequately supported; and the financing of a military machine in Paris and its environs was essential.

---

[1] Wickham to Grenville, 8 March 1797, F.O. 74/20.

[2] Intelligence provided by Duverne, 18 November 1796, F.O. 27/48.

[3] 'Notes sur la police intérieure' in Dutheil's note to Grenville, 17 December 1796, ibid.

[4] Grenville to Wickham, 14 October 1796, F.O. 74/19. Grenville, unlike Pitt, had opposed the negotiations. An excellent account of Malmesbury's mission is to be found in R. Guyot, *Le Directoire et la paix de l'Europe 1795-1799* (Paris, 1911), pp. 261-305. In analysing the breakdown of the negotiations, Guyot apportions the blame equally between Grenville and the Directory.

[5] Grenville to Wickham, 27 January 1797, *Correspondence of William Wickham*, ii. 6-8.

[6] Grenville to Windham, 5 February 1797, Add. MSS., 37846.

Grenville had Duverne's assurance that the military force would be held in reserve until after the elections unless there was proof that the Directory planned to delay or suspend them. Upon this condition the Cabinet authorized Grenville to promise the agency £60,000 for the first quarter of 1797; a further sum of £45,000 would be forthcoming if an underground military force were formed.[1]

With this offer, Duverne left for Paris on 13 January.[2] Only one more item on the royalist agenda remained to be tackled. The agents planned to co-ordinate their activities with Frotté as well as with Rochecotte. Frotté, who had been in London since September vainly trying to interest Pitt in renewing the war in the west,[3] learned that the funds accorded the agency did not include a penny for his needs. Dutheil now set to work to procure funds for him.[4] During the remainder of January, he bombarded the Foreign Office with requests on behalf of Frotté's preparatory plans in Normandy,[5] buttressing his arguments with letters from the agents in Paris urging speed. On 26 January, Dutheil informed Grenville that the agents had summoned the prince de la Trémouille to command the clandestine military force they were organizing in the Paris region, which neighboured on Frotté's; consequently his presence was essential.[6] Finally, on the 30th, Dutheil learned that Frotté was to be offered £500, a minute fraction of the £10,000 for which he had applied.[7] In the next few weeks, his problems were eclipsed by startling and perplexing news from Paris. On 31 January the Directory arrested most of the members of the agency.

The news of the arrest caught London and Blankenburg completely off guard. The circumstances surrounding the arrest are well known. During Duverne's absence in London, Brottier and la Villeurnoy took into their confidence two military commanders who, they rashly believed, were eager to collaborate with the

---

[1] Cabinet minute of 2 January 1797; minute of Lord Grenville, 30 March 1797, *Dropmore Papers*, iii, 291, 305.

[2] Dutheil to Grenville, 13 January 1797, A.A.E., France 626.

[3] Frotté to Pitt, 5, 28 September, 11, 24 October 1796, PRO 30/8/137.

[4] Dutheil to Grenville, 13 January 1797, A.A.E., France 626.

[5] Dutheil to Grenville, 11 January 1797; Dutheil to Hammond, 21 January 1797, F.O. 27/51.

[6] Dutheil to Grenville, 26 January 1797, ibid.

[7] Dutheil to Hammond, 30 January 1797, ibid.

royalists. One was colonel Malo, commander of the 21st regiment of Dragoons; the other was adjutant-general Ramel, commander of the Grenadiers of the *Conseils*. The first, because of his suppression of the Jacobin attempt to incite troops in the Grenelle camp, seemed good game. The second, because of his command of the Legislative Guard, was deemed a key figure. When the agents approached them, they struck a royalist pose; Malo even spoke enthusiastically about moving against the Directory immediately. Actually he and Ramel were betraying the agents: they kept the Directory informed of every detail; and Cochon the minister of police instructed them to lure the agents into a trap.[1] Brottier and la Villeurnoy met with Malo a few times, and, together with Duverne, agreed to meet the colonel in his quarters at the *Ecole militaire* on the evening of the last of January. The encounter was fatal, for when the agents left Malo's apartment they were arrested by the police. Fourteen other persons were apprehended almost as quickly.

The information given the Directory by Malo and Ramel corroborated revelations from another source, for the agents had in fact been betrayed by la Vauguyon's son, the prince de Carency, a voluptuary, an adventurer and a swindler. The young fraud was also an accomplished impersonator; he had posed as a messenger in the British service, intercepted letters addressed to Condé and Craufurd, and extorted money from Wickham's Swiss banker.[2] The French naturally had their eyes on him.[3] Towards the end of 1796 Brottier had welcomed him to Paris.[4] At the very moment that Brottier was preparing to entrust him with an important mission,[5] Carency was disclosing the agency's secrets to Barras.[6] He divulged more of them to the *Journal général* and the *Journal des hommes libres*.[7] The Directory, therefore, had sufficient evidence to order the arrest of the agents, but waited for Malo to collect more information; and he was doing this so effortlessly. What is

---

[1] G. Duruy (ed.), *Memoirs of Barras* (4 vols., London, 1896), ii. 335.

[2] Wickham to Grenville, 15 December 1796, F.O. 74/19.

[3] Reinhard to Delacroix, 20 May, 21 June 1796, A.N., AFIII59, dossier 230, plaquette unique.

[4] Wickham to Grenville, 11 December 1796, F.O. 74/19.

[5] Wickham to Grenville, 18 December 1796, ibid.

[6] Barras, *Memoirs*, ii. 383. Barras speaks obliquely of the information Carency brought him, but dismissed it at first as being too trifling to deal with.

[7] Wickham to Grenville, 4 January 1797, *Dropmore Papers*, iii. 292; Précy to d'Avaray, 6 January 1797, A.A.E., France 590.

surprising is that Carency had been able to dissipate Brottier's customary suspicions. Duverne was a superior judge. He had seen through Carency, but the damage was done during his absence in London, and Wickham's feverish notes to Grenville to warn the agents of Carency's double-dealing were of little use in the circumstances.[1]

IV

The official version of the so-called Brottier conspiracy—Brottier must surely have derived immense satisfaction from the Directory's recognition of his pre-eminence in the agency—was created during the trial of the accused by a military court. It was revealed that a conspiracy had been organized to storm the principal government offices and military establishments, overthrow the Directory, disperse the Legislature, and arrest all the prominent Jacobins. Malo testified that the agents had been planning to provoke an uprising in the working-class faubourg of Saint-Antoine in order to rouse the wealthier sections and thus create an atmosphere favourable to royalism. The documents seized by the police further disclosed that the agents had even compiled a list of ministers for a royalist cabinet. It included, as possible nominees for the post of police minister, Cochon who was in that post under the Directory and was responsible for the rounding up of the agents, as well as the names of Portalis and Siméon, members of the *Conseils*. The same list designated Barbé-Marbois as minister of the Indies (presumably because of his pre-revolutionary experience as *intendant* in Santo Domingo); Hennin, a diplomat in the service of the *ancien régime*, was named as minister of foreign affairs; and Fleurieu was to be appointed to the position he had held at the ministry of the navy before 1789. The government also used Ramel's evidence to reinforce its case. He testified that the royalists had shrewdly planned to announce a general amnesty for the purpose of gaining wide support. Since the *Parlements* would be revived under the restoration, they would be expected to annul such a sweeping act, and the arrest of the constitutionalists would proceed without mercy. Of interest also is another of Ramel's statements accusing Tallien of being a party to the plot. This is so highly improbable that it suggests the Directory was grasping at

[1] Wickham to Grenville, 18 December 1796, F.O. 74/19.

the opportunity to discredit him for his opposition to its suppression of the Babeuvists.

The military court's right of jurisdiction was challenged at once by the defence on the premise that charges of conspiracy could be heard only in the civil courts. These objections were overruled, but the defendants appealed to the Court of Cassation which signified its willingness to hear the evidence on 22 March. The royalists in the *Conseils* were naturally eager to have the case quashed, for successful proceedings against the accused would, they feared, not only harm their cause but very probably their persons. They consequently contested, as had the defence, the right of the military court to hear the case, and were vindicated by the Court of Cassation's finding that the military tribunal was indeed exceeding its jurisdiction. At this point, the Directory set aside this judgement by forbidding the minister of justice to transfer the trial to the highest court of the land. After more than a month's hearings, the military court countered the Directory's flagrant defiance of judicial procedure and independence by acquitting fourteen of the defendants. However, the evidence against Duverne and Brottier appeared too overwhelming to be dismissed: they were sentenced to ten years' imprisonment. La Villeurnoy got off more lightly with a one-year sentence.

But the affair did not end there. The Directory was determined to renew the case in the ordinary courts, but the months passed without the reopening of the trial. An easier way was found to dispose of the accused; they were deported in the aftermath of the *coup d'état* of Fructidor. Only then did the government publish Duverne's confession: he had given his colleagues away on 28 February to save his own neck. The Directors were thus aware of the additional ramifications of the conspiracy: the workings of the *Institut philanthropique*; Britain's supply of funds; the assistance rendered by Wickham; and the liaisons the agency had formed with members of the *Conseils*. Instead of acting upon this information in February, the Directory preferred to wait for a more opportune time. In the interval its inaction, as we shall see, permitted the royalists to make gains in the elections and to further their plans during the summer.

Certain details in the published account of the conspiracy and trial are undeniably authentic. But a comparison between it and other sources reveals some discrepancies. The government's case against the agents was constructed on the assumption that they were planning to use military force against the regime at the time or within a few days of their arrest. What is surprising is that, with one exception, historians have accepted this interpretation without seeking any other evidence to support it,[1] other than the incomplete minutes of the trial and Duverne's confession, which, moreover, Barras tells us, was cut short by his unwillingness to divulge more.[2] It is therefore necessary to examine the additional available evidence to ascertain the nature of the agents' plans immediately before their arrest.

Of specific pertinence are the letters sent to Dutheil by his agent, the comte de Butler.[3] Towards the end of 1796, he had been commissioned to ensure regular communications between London and the Paris agency and to survey French naval preparations along the Channel. He was thus in an excellent position to comment on events in Paris in the weeks before the arrest. On 14 January Butler reported to Dutheil rumours circulating in Paris of a Jacobin movement[4] against the government. To forestall it, the Directory was taking precautions to ensure that the March elections would take place under normal conditions.[5] Two days later he wrote that bands of deserters on the frontiers of Alsace were molesting the republican troops and were impatiently awaiting a leader to reconquer France for the monarchy.[6] In yet

---

[1] Daudet (*Histoire de l'émigration*, ii. 61) admits that the minutes of the trial baffled him; Caudrillier (*La Trahison de Pichegru*, pp. 321–2) and Hall (op. cit., pp. 182–4) are surprisingly lacking in curiosity. Only Lefebvre has, in a review of a study on Rochecotte, suggested that Duverne's testimony was either edited or incomplete. See his review of C. Girault, *Rochecotte et la chouannerie Mancelle* (Laval, Goupil, 1949) in *Annales historiques de la Révolution française*, xxv (1953), 273.

[2] Barras, *Memoirs*, ii. 453.

[3] Of Irish origin, Butler had been a captain in a regiment of royal dragoons before the Revolution and had fought in the *émigré* corps during the 1792 campaign as colonel of a cavalry regiment. In 1793 the British employed him to inspect French naval forces in the Channel ports. Two years later he accompanied the baron de Nantiat on a British-inspired mission to Charette with instructions to assess royalist strength in the Vendée and public opinion in the area neighbouring the royalist stronghold. Throughout the early months of 1796 he made repeated but unsuccessful efforts to suborn, in connivance with their commanders, the troops in the Pas-de-Calais area, who would thus be transformed into a counter-revolutionary cadre. See Butler's report, 5 June 1793, F.O. 95/2; *Dropmore Papers*, iii. 105–24; F.O. 27/48; F.O. 27/51.

[4] Cf. Barras, *Memoirs*, ii. 330. Barras relates how Carnot was deeply shaken by the reports of Jacobin activity at the beginning of January 1797.

[5] Butler to Dutheil, 14 January 1797, F.O. 27/51.

[6] Butler to Dutheil, 16 January 1797, ibid.

another letter he wrote enthusiastically of the wholesale opposition in the departments bordering Paris to the requisition of troops, of the open return of *émigrés*, and the unconcealed church attendance.[1]

The agency's reports for the same period bear out Butler's. On the 20th the agents informed Dutheil of their fears that the Directory was preparing to take steps to manipulate the elections.[2] A few days later, on the 24th, they reported that *agents-provocateurs* were stirring up the working-class faubourg Saint-Antoine, but they were confident that the agitation could be countered by the soldiers in Paris who were sympathetic to the *amis de l'ordre*.[3] On the 26th, they wrote that the instigators of a Jacobin plot at Senlis had been arrested.[4] On the 29th, Duverne informed Dutheil that the agents were awaiting the arrival of la Trémouille and that the forthcoming convocation of the primary assemblies was stimulating a great deal of interest.[5] Two days later the agents were arrested.

This seems to endorse the Directory's claim that the agents were making preparations for a *coup d'état* in the immediate future, that is, before the elections were to take place. British aid to the agents, it should be recalled, had been approved on condition that force was to be avoided until after the elections unless there was overwhelming evidence that the Directory was planning to suspend them. The alarmist tone of the agents' reports, particularly their observations of Jacobin activity, coupled with their expressions of confidence in the increasing opposition to the Directory, certainly create the impression that they were contemplating immediate military action against the Directory. This seems borne out by the fact that la Trémouille was on his way to Paris to direct the armed forces they had been organizing. At the same time, however, they were awaiting Frotté's return to France. Would they have undertaken military action without waiting for the return of Frotté whose presence in Normandy was an essential part of their plan?

---

[1] Butler to Dutheil, 18 January 1797, ibid.
[2] Paris agency to Dutheil, 20 January 1797, ibid.
[3] Paris agency to Dutheil, 24 January 1797, F.O. 27/51. The agency's reports on Jacobin activity are amply substantiated by those of the police during the same period. See F. A. Aulard, *Paris pendant la réaction thermidorienne et sous le Directoire* (5 vols., Paris, 1898–1902), iii. 677, 696, 699, 700, 718 (5, 16, 17, 18, 26 January 1797).
[4] Paris agency to Dutheil, 26 January 1797, F.O. 27/51.
[5] Duverne to Dutheil, 29 January 1797, A.A.E., France 590.

In addition, Duverne's references in his letter of the 29th to the great interest shown in the election campaign is consistent with the carefully nurtured plans of the agency.

When the news of the agents' arrest reached d'Antraigues, he expressed astonishment.[1] Although he admitted that his only direct news from Brottier since April 1796 was inconsequential, he had known from Gamon and Montjoie that the agents had firmly insisted that the election campaign should not be marred by violence. To be sure Gamon had expressed his anger to d'Antraigues over the agency's intemperate actions; for Gamon the Directory's case against Brottier and his colleagues was proven. D'Antraigues felt that Gamon and his friends in the *Conseils*, with whom the agency had reached accord on non-violent opposition to the Directory, had fallen into a skilfully prepared trap. The Directory must have deliberately distorted the evidence to drive a wedge between the royalists and the constitutionalists. The possibility that Brottier and Duverne had been carried away by their zeal could not be ruled out, d'Antraigues admitted, for only a temporary aberration could explain their actions. But to accept the Directory's version of events belied what they had so patiently laboured to create, both with respect to the *Institut* and their promises to the deputies in the *Conseils*. The Directory, d'Antraigues noted further, had chosen to divulge its information just at the time of the approaching meetings of the primary assemblies. It had actually possessed, he believed, sufficient information to act the previous November.

No clear answer can be given on the available evidence. It is permissible, however, to advance the view that the agents were not planning an immediate show of force against the Directory. They may have been pursuing their efforts to obtain military support in anticipation of any contingency that might arise after the elections. This was in accord with their commitments to the British. After all, this was why they were in touch with Frotté and Rochecotte. Their appeal to la Trémouille to come to Paris may have been prompted by their desire to acquaint him with the force ultimately to come under his command. Frotté was still in London soliciting funds, and surely any military action would have been postponed until his return to his command. The agency's reports to Dutheil may be seen as the product of men who were, in the

---

[1] D'Antraigues to la Vauguyon, 22 February 1797, A.A.E., France 610.

circumstances, on the lookout for any evidence of increased police scrutiny. The evidence seems to point to the conclusion that the agency's search for armed support was in keeping with its long-term prospects of subverting the Directory by non-violent means but that it was not ruling out the possibility of using force—after the elections, if necessary. Finally, it is essential to distinguish between the ultimate aims of the agency and the feeble means at its disposal; for the agents were capable of such human errors as haste, anxiety, misguided enthusiasm, gullibility, wishful thinking, and inadequate preparation.

7

WICKHAM'S HOPES REVIVED

THE year 1796 was to be for Wickham a time of reflection and re-evaluation. Yet in the first months of the new year, he still found the plan to encourage resistance in Lyons attractive and feasible: Précy pledged himself to return to Lyons if the allied offensive were resumed; and he also promised to organize, with the help of Tessonnet and Imbert-Colomès, the work of a corps of agents in five districts surrounding the city. Low morale and desertion in the French armies and the apparent ease of subverting their generals and administrators was another reason Wickham adduced for his contention that Lyons would maintain itself against the forces of the Directory. The defection of three officers who had been stationed at Lyons—Lapoype,[1] Colinet, Montchoisy[2]—and now, La Cours[3]—seemed to presage success. Of the £50,000 necessary for this latest undertaking Wickham still had £28,000, and he asked Grenville for his support and additional funds.[4]

Crucial to the success of the spring operations were Pichegru's plans, but their precise nature was a mystery to Wickham and Craufurd. For some time after the beginning of the year, the two men tried to analyse the general's motives during the previous autumn and to weigh the worth of his promises in the months ahead. Despite Pichegru's retreat behind the Wissembourg Lines and his consent at the end of December to an Austrian armistice, Wickham and Craufurd were puzzled by his apparent failure to do more than this. Gradually, however, they were able to assess the situation more clearly and gain a fuller appreciation of the dangers

---

[1] Lapoype was dismissed from the service in October 1795, but recalled by the Directory in September 1797. See G. Six, *Dictionnaire biographique des généraux et amiraux français de la Révolution et de l'Empire (1792–1814)* (2 vols., Paris, 1934).

[2] In 1798, general Montchoisy officially protested against the imputation that he had bestowed his protection upon the '*égorgeurs*' at Lyons. See *Réimpression de l'ancien Moniteur* (31 vols., Paris, 1850–54), xxix. 319.

[3] Despite searches, the identity of La Cours could not be ascertained.

[4] Wickham to Grenville, 5 January 1796, *Correspondence of William Wickham*, i. 234–40.

of Pichegru's position. Their earlier doubts concerning Pichegru's failure to surrender Huningen and Strasbourg to Condé during the autumn campaign were dissipated by the general's reasonable disclaimer that suspicion would have been attached to such an action in view of the small and ineffectual force under Condé's command. Surely Pichegru's defeat at Handschuhsheim, when his army of 15,000 failed to overcome 4,000 Austrians who were barring his way to Heidelberg, was sufficient cause for suspicion at Paris. Would not defeat at the hands of the miniscule force under Condé have confirmed the Directory's apprehensions, leading perhaps to his disgrace and dismissal? On this much Wickham and Craufurd were agreed: Pichegru could not have done more than he had.[1]

Nevertheless Craufurd and Wickham had difficulty in trying to unravel the nature of the general's future intentions. Fauche-Borel, one of the agents close to him, assured them that Pichegru had no doubt that the army was the key to the Directory's overthrow. The key would fit, however, only with Austrian military co-operation and British financial assistance; but organization of partial insurrections must cease.[2]

Could these protestations of good faith be accepted? Craufurd, while conceding that 'real fraud and treachery are foreign from his [Pichegru's] nature' and that 'he may be under the necessity of practising much political subtilty (*sic*) and circumspection at present', urged Wickham not to rely on the incidental advantages of Pichegru's assistance but rather to base the next campaign on actual military calculations.[3] Wickham refused to share Craufurd's scepticism. Pichegru's defection would be, he protested, extremely valuable and potentially decisive, unless the Austrians seized the opportunity of turning his receptivity solely to their advantage; in that event the future of France would be entirely in Austria's hands.[4] Moreover, Wickham insisted that Pichegru was honest in his dealings with the agents, even if he was not as capable as it had originally been thought. That 'the work he [Pichegru] has undertaken is above his powers' did not deter Wickham from acceding to a demand for a sum of almost 500,000 louis, the expenditure of

[1] Craufurd to Wickham, 22 January, 12 February 1796, ibid., 244–52, 274–9.
[2] Craufurd to Wickham, 12 February 1796, ibid., 274–9; Wickham to Craufurd, 13 February 1796, ibid., 279–91.
[3] Craufurd to Wickham, 12 February 1796, ibid., 274–9.
[4] Wickham to Craufurd, 13 February 1796, ibid., 279–91.

which had been approved by Grenville.[1] Indeed, the potential Monck should be given every encouragement;[2] his departure for Paris had to be viewed as part of an overall royalist intrigue, which had already seen the replacement in the Lyons command of general Carteaux by Montchoisy. 'Extensive and beneficial results' were to be expected from this favourable combination of events.[3]

Craufurd offered a somewhat less hopeful interpretation of Pichegru's movements. He agreed with Wickham that Pichegru was not deliberately aiming to deceive them, but suggested an alternative and more subtle explanation of the general's motives. According to Fauche-Borel, Pichegru was planning his Paris expedition as a means of canvassing the conditions for a successful deposition of the government. To Craufurd this was absurd. Surely, the Directory would not overlook the elementary necessity of ensuring the loyalty of the army in the neighbourhood of the capital to forestall any anti-government measures. And, why, Craufurd continued, was Pichegru entrusting his army to Desaix, a young and ambitious republican? Was this the best way to maintain and extend his hold over his army? Craufurd argued that, as Pichegru was under suspicion in several quarters, he would probably do all in his power to retain his command, the only tangible asset left to him. This was what was impelling him to go to Paris, and this was why he was not to be trusted. Greater faith in him would have been warranted if he had stayed with his army, created the means for Austria's movement into Alsace, and arranged for concerted action with Condé. If the latter conditions could be met in the future, Craufurd was willing to continue the further expenditure of funds to ensure his defection, but nothing in Pichegru's recent conduct justified it. Moreover, Craufurd was almost certain that the Directory would never allow Pichegru to resume his command.[4]

Of the speculations surrounding Pichegru's goals, whose were more accurate, those of the military expert or the diplomat? Pichegru had asked for a leave of absence in January and was granted this request. Craufurd's belief that Pichegru's motives were to remove suspicion from himself was well-founded, since

---

[1] Wickham to Craufurd, 9 March 1796, *Correspondence of William Wickham*, i. 297–9.
[2] Wickham to Grenville, 17 March 1796, ibid., 311–12.
[3] Wickham to Grenville, 26 March 1796, ibid., 319–20.
[4] Craufurd to Wickham, 17 March 1796, ibid., 304–10.

Pichegru suspected that his rôle in the royalist conspiracy had been disclosed by the papers seized by the police at Besançon in January following an abortive royalist uprising in that town.[1] It is also possible that Pichegru wished to avoid carrying out the Directory's orders to arrange with the Austrians an exchange of prisoners, since some of the French repatriates were destined for Franche-Comté, the very area which he had promised Condé to keep as poorly garrisoned as possible![2] However much he may have feared for his position, Pichegru did not expect dismissal, which was decided by the Directory on 13 March. Craufurd was, in the main, on the mark in his assessment, and his prediction of the dismissal was just as accurate. His analysis was clearly superior to Wickham's.

That Pichegru was rapidly losing his credit with the government had become generally known in informed quarters. The Directory, as early as December, had been in receipt of incriminating information, from its special agent, Bassal,[3] and it was this same Bassal whom Pichegru was said to have accused of revealing his relations with Condé.[4] Of course, Bassal's disclosures were only one source of the Directory's intelligence; Bacher, the Directory's minister at Basel, was another.[5] It is not surprising that Pichegru's negotiations with Condé should have come to the Directory's attention. News of his attitudes and his mysterious activities was no secret. Mallet du Pan knew of them,[6] and Wickham complained of the indiscretions of Condé's agents, particularly Montgaillard who had boasted of his exploits to Mallet.[7] Mallet was indeed puzzled by the Directory's leniency towards Pichegru, and astonished that it would appoint him as ambassador to Sweden.[8] Realizing that the Directory's offer of an appointment to the Swedish embassy was, as Mallet also suggested, a means to rid itself of a threat to its power,[9] Pichegru asked for a prolonged leave to give the offer careful consideration. The Directory

---

[1] Caudrillier, *La Trahison de Pichegru*, p. 221.
[2] Ibid., p. 220.
[3] Ibid., p. 185.
[4] Demougé to Fauche-Borel, 2 May 1796, F.O. 74/17.
[5] Caudrillier, *La Trahison de Pichegru*, p. 230.
[6] *Correspondance de Mallet du Pan*, ii. 7, 28–9, 32, 52.
[7] Wickham to Grenville, 5 May 1796, F.O. 74/17.
[8] *Correspondance de Mallet du Pan*, ii. 52. Doubtless the Directory's fears of a royalist *coup* were at that moment submerged by their alarm over the Babeuf conspiracy.   [9] Ibid.

granted the request without too much trepidation, for by this time Bonaparte's exploits in northern Italy were reassuring evidence of military support in case of need.

II

It was by no means certain that Pichegru's loss of his command would end his usefulness to the royalists. Wickham's analysis that the Directory derived its strength from the army was valid.[1] Reports of dissension within the government and increasing popular dissatisfaction continued to reach him. There was no doubt that this state of affairs could be converted into an asset if the generals devoted to the Directory could clearly see a worthy substitute for it. Either their defection or destruction was essential, and for this reason Wickham insisted that Pichegru was of the utmost importance in any plan to overthrow the Directory. All could be arranged but for the machinations of the Austrians; unfortunately they were not prepared to co-operate.[2] Until the Austrians gave proof of their determination to commence hostilities on the Rhine, Wickham felt justified in spending only small amounts to keep alive the royalist spy-net in the Midi. Royalist agents, he informed Grenville, were making headway in the Jura, and had therefore to be supported; Précy and Imbert-Colomès would be given an additional 12,000 louis for the purchase of arms and ammunition; and 6,000 louis would be used to acquire 6,000 rifles, to be transferred to the royalists on the eve of the insurrection.

Wickham's revised plans were fully endorsed by Grenville. In language uncharacteristic of this cold and aloof man, Grenville told his envoy that he was 'filling the most laborious and one of the most difficult situations in the King's foreign service'.[3] Success could now only come from France's perilous internal situation, not 'from what is called a counter-revolution, or the decided prevalence of a royalist party', but from successive or simultaneous explosions of violence. Grenville's enthusiastic outburst was prompted by news of a revolt in the department of the Cher,

[1] Wickham to Grenville, 7 April 1796, F.O. 74/17.

[2] That the Austrians had no intention of giving Condé a free hand can be seen in Morton Eden's remarks to Wickham, *Correspondence of William Wickham*, i. 321–4, 2 April 1796.

[3] Grenville to Wickham, 15 April 1796, ibid., 342–3.

reported in the Paris newspapers, and he instructed Wickham to 'employ with a liberal hand the means and powers given you'. Wickham lost no time in directing Duverne to furnish £3,000 to the insurgents in the Cher; he had another £4,000 for them if they could manage to get it from Switzerland.[1] At the same time he was prepared to give financial assistance to the rebels in the south of France at the foot of the Cévennes, where a 'formidable insurrection' had also erupted.

It was at Fribourg-en-Brisgau, on 30 April, that Wickham received, by special messenger from Berne, Grenville's encouraging instructions. He had reached Fribourg on the 27th, having arranged to meet Craufurd there. The next day they travelled the few miles to Condé's headquarters at Riegel, and were unexpectedly presented to Louis XVIII and his ministers, who had secretly made their exit from Verona, where their stay had been cut short by the Venetian government's orders of expulsion. Wickham and Craufurd then returned to Fribourg to await the reports of Condé's agents who had previously been instructed to renew negotiations with Pichegru at Strasbourg. Finally, on 4 May, Wickham and Craufurd took the road to Riegel again, and conferred with Louis, his chief ministers and Condé to assess the intelligence brought by the agents from Pichegru. The months of uncertainty and speculation were about to end.

Pichegru's views had a sobering effect on Wickham. The general did not conceal that he had committed a serious error: he had failed, he admitted, to gain the confidence of his army and now saw no prospect of using it to further a counter-revolution. Pichegru had, Wickham now surmised, an utterly naïve view of the French political situation. Before going to Paris Pichegru had been isolated from politics and had given little thought to the causes of the Revolution. His sojourn in Paris had disabused him of the belief that the country was divided into two great blocs, the supporters and the opponents of the Revolution. He had discovered instead that only a very small minority of some eight or ten deputies from the southern departments were devoted to the *ancien régime*; the greatest number of the Directory's opponents favoured a constitutional monarchy.[2] The Directory's most potentially successful enemies were, in short, the constitutionalists.

---

[1] Wickham to Grenville, 30 April 1796, F.O. 74/17.
[2] Wickham to Grenville, 4 May 1796, *Correspondence of William Wickham*, i. 356–8.

Pichegru had at last learned what Wickham had always known: the opponents of the Revolution were not necessarily committed to a Bourbon restoration. Although he had never overlooked this unalterable fact, Wickham had, as we have seen, been counting heavily on military action to dislodge the revolutionaries from their seats of power and thus resolve the disturbing political problem. Pichegru's political coming-of-age partially restored Wickham's political sense.

Had the time then come for a major shift in strategy? Ought Pichegru and other key persons to be encouraged to support the proponents of a constitutional monarchy? These were the queries Wickham addressed to Grenville the day after the meeting at Condé's camp.[1] As if to give weight to a positive reply from Grenville, Wickham enclosed a copy of Demougé's letter to Fauche-Borel, reporting part of his conversation with Pichegru. Not only had Pichegru referred to the certainty of civil war which a pure restoration would cause, but he had stressed that there were a number of powerful supporters of an Orléanist monarchy, including the Director Carnot.[2] The evidence of these serious breaches in the defences of the pure royalists was not the only factor that Wickham considered in trying to determine his next course. The major portion of the funds he had advanced to the insurrection in the Cher had been squandered by speculators in Paris; the money would probably, he regretted, have been of little help in any case, since the authorities had ruthlessly suppressed the rebels, while the great hopes held out for the Cévennes had not lived up to expectations. The military situation was, moreover, virtually hopeless. Neither the Italian front, which had been decisively changed by Bonaparte's advances, nor the campaign on the Rhine, which had not yet begun, showed promise.[3]

Not only were the prospects of gaining the army bleak, but the laborious and expensive preparations by Précy, Imbert-Colomès and Tessonnet in the Lyons area and further south were in danger of being delayed or even scuttled. Précy and Imbert-Colomès, heeding Wickham's call, had met with him, Craufurd, and the little Bourbon court at Riegel that evening of 4 May. Précy's estimate of the situation had not changed since early January. With

---

[1] Wickham to Grenville, 5 May 1796, F.O. 74/17.
[2] Demougé to Fauche-Borel, 2 May 1796, ibid.
[3] Wickham to Grenville, 5 May 1796, ibid.

support from Wickham, he had told the group that, until the Austrians resumed offensive operations powerful enough to induce the Directory to divert forces from Lyons, it would be fatal to launch an uprising in the Midi. Since this was still problematical, Précy and Imbert-Colomès agreed to accept £18,000 to purchase arms and ammunitions at Geneva and in Germany; if the Austrians undertook an offensive they estimated their preliminary needs at £150,000.[1] Wickham was hardly optimistic, even though he did not hesitate to commit his government financially to what appeared to be a doomed enterprise. Italy was at the mercy of Bonaparte's lightning-like thrusts, and Austria was giving no evidence of sending reinforcements to aid their general Beaulieu who was bearing the brunt of the French attack. Consequently, Wickham could not but feel that the loss of the initiative to the French in Italy and Austria's refusal to give Condé any aid had already settled the question of supporting a southern insurrection.[2]

Thus had conditions been altered. The French army remained the key to success in the struggle that would decide the fate of revolutionary France, but the fist that held the key had become more tenacious than ever. Without waiting for specific comment from Whitehall and because he had almost unlimited discretionary powers, Wickham shifted his strategy, with Louis' reluctant cooperation, to meet the new circumstances. Louis and his chief advisers, d'Avaray and la Vauguyon, were less than pleased with Pichegru's advice that compliance with the wishes of the constitutionalists in Paris was essential to their hopes. All of Wickham's persuasive powers were necessary to convince Louis and particularly d'Avaray, who had 'the most absolute dominion over his [Louis'] mind', that Pichegru's friends in Paris should be reassured as to royalist moderation, conciliation and readiness to make sacrifices 'for the good of his people'. Even so, Wickham was not at all sure that Louis' ministers had complied with his proposals.[3] Taking the view that unremitting pressure was the only way to dispel their illusions, he mixed flattery and plain talk. He appealed to their vanity by treating them as the wise men surrounding a feeble king, who needed their expert guidance.[4]

[1] Wickham to Grenville, 16 May 1796, *Correspondence of William Wickham*, i. 366-8.
[2] Trevor to Wickham, 7 May 1796, ibid., 358-61.
[3] Wickham to Grenville, 14 May 1796, ibid., 361-5.
[4] Wickham to d'Avaray, 30 May 1796, ibid., 370-2.

III

In its essentials, Wickham's new strategy was not new at all. He had been a consistent advocate of co-operation between the two large groups of royalists, almost from the start of his mission, and that objective had been obscured only during the preliminaries and actual course of the Vendémiaire insurrection. He retained his scepticism of the constitutionalists, in whom he refused to place complete trust. He did not question the validity of their assessment of French political affairs, but he found it difficult to accept the inflated view they had of themselves as practical men of politics. As we shall presently see, Wickham's confidence in them grew as the military situation deteriorated but more particularly because their analysis of the Directory's weak spots coincided with those of Pichegru and the Paris agency.

Early in January there had come into Wickham's hands the copy of a memorandum which had also been sumitted to Verona. He was sure that it was the work of the constitutionalists, chiefly Duport, for its phraseology and sentiments were strikingly similar to those of the reports which had brought him to Switzerland in 1794.[1] Points made in the document[2] leave no doubt that it was authored by the constitutionalists. Ranging over the wide spectrum of internal and international politics, it dealt with the successive abortive attempts to restore the monarchy and outlined the steps required to achieve it. Four years of war had entrenched the revolutionary regime; indeed, with the inevitable withdrawal of Piedmont from the war, only Britain and Austria would remain in the field against the Revolution. The slender hopes of British success on the Brittany coast and the impotence of the Vendée, as well as the difficulties in igniting insurrection throughout France, were a dismal testament of the futility of military action, whether internal or external. How then destroy the Revolution? Contrary to what might have been expected from the premises laid down, the constitutionalists advised the continuance of the war on the ground that conscription, requisitions and taxation would alienate the great mass of peace-loving Frenchmen. The war, however, should be waged without *émigré* participation.

[1] Wickham to Grenville, 5 January 1796, F.O. 74/14.
[2] Memorandum of 21 December 1795, ibid.

This would end the fears the average Frenchman entertained of the king's alleged concessions to the coalition. In short, the counter-revolution's ties with the enemies of France had to be severed; the early accomplishments of the Revolution had to be accepted; and the cultivation of the right-minded deputies in the *Conseils* had to be undertaken. With the fulfilment of these conditions, the power of the royalists in the chambers would become irresistible. Peace negotiations could then be initiated and the restoration of a constitutional monarchy would follow.

Wickham's reaction was cautious but not hostile.[1] He recalled that in June of the previous year the constitutionalists, in the person of Monciel, had made overtures to Condé with the hope of erasing the asperities that had blinded the two groups of royalists. These had been rejected. The repute and influence of the constitutionalists had then risen during the latter half of 1795, due largely to the impetuousness of the drafters of the Verona Declaration. This manifesto had also had the unfortunate consequence of throwing the constitutionalists' support behind the duc de Chartres, the future Orléanist king. Wickham could not ignore information gathered both by partisans and opponents of the Orléanists. A portion of that intelligence had, to be sure, dangerously skirted the wide area of gossip.[2] But in almost every other respect, the association of such names as Madame de Staël, Dumas, Montesquiou, Mathieu de Montmorency with that of Orléans was given such wide currency that it could not be discounted as mere circumstance.[3] At the same time, Wickham did not dismiss reports of Sieyès' behind-the-scenes' support of a marriage between Chartres and Madame Royale, although he seemed to think that there were others who preferred such a marriage with Artois' son, the duc d'Angoulême.[4]

Why then were the constitutionalists urging a conciliatory policy with the royalists, if even one of the most devoted followers of the Bourbons, the abbé Aimé, had scathingly denounced the 'threats and pretensions' of the *émigré* princes.[5] Surely this in itself

[1] Wickham to Grenville, 5 January 1796, ibid.
[2] Unidentified letter from Paris, 30 September 1795, F.O. 74/13.
[3] ibid., and Monciel to Wickham, report of observations during August and September 1795; Lemaître to d'Artéz, 30 September 1795, F.O. 74/12.
[4] Duverne to Wickham, 18 December 1795; Wickham to Grenville, 6 January 1796, F.O. 74/14.
[5] Abbé Aimé to Condé, 13 December 1795, ibid.

was sufficient proof of the disenchantment with the dead king's brothers. To the superficial observer, the colours of the constitutionalists should have been waving in a favourable breeze, but Wickham knew that the contrary was true. The constitutionalists had enormously exaggerated the extent of their power to influence the Directory.[1] In fact, such faltering constitutionalists as Montesquiou and Madame de Staël were said to have sold out to the Directory.[2]

Mallet du Pan's intelligence from Paris confirmed this.[3] Mallet compared the total bankruptcy of every species of royalist in Paris with the impotence of the *feuillants* in 1792. He lamented their inability to form a cohesive party or agree on tactics, their excessive fears and incoherent actions, and the ease with which they lost their bearings under attack. Self-distrust was driving the constitutionalists into an alliance with all groups dedicated to the overthrow of the Directory. This, Wickham was certain, was the chief motive of the men who had approached Louis. Yet he urged that their offers ought not to be rejected.[4] He reasoned that the longer the pure royalists retained their unaccommodating attitude, the more hostile would opinion towards Louis become.[5] Mallet du Pan, who was on intimate terms with the leading constitutionalists, favoured the same course of action.[6] The implication was clear: the royalists now had the opportunity to make the best of their enhanced bargaining power *vis-à-vis* the constitutionalists, namely, to make some concessions in exchange for their demonstration of cordiality. The memorialists' overtures to Verona were rejected, as Wickham had predicted.[7] Then at his request the abbé de Lacombe, who had been active in Lyons the year before, sent Louis and his councillors an account of a conversation he had had with d'André, the well-known constitutionalist who was living in Switzerland at the time.

[1] Wickham to Grenville, 5 January 1796, F.O. 74/14.
[2] Wickham to Grenville, 4 January 1796, ibid. The tone of letters from Mathieu Dumas to Theodore Lameth which Wickham had seen, and his conversations with Montesquiou's correspondents in Switzerland was the basis for this estimate.
[3] Mallet du Pan to Wickham, 5 January 1796, ibid.
[4] Wickham to Grenville, 5 January 1796, ibid.
[5] Wickham to Grenville, 7 January 1796, ibid.
[6] Mallet du Pan to Wickham, 23 January 1796, F.O. 74/15.
[7] Wickham to Macartney, 19 January 1796; Macartney to Wickham, 2 February 1796, *Correspondence of William Wickham*, i. 240-8, 263-9.

This was a turning point in the history of the counter-revolution. Antoine Balthazar Joseph d'André de Bellevue, three times president of the Constituent Assembly, followed an underground career as Wickham's most valuable agent during 1796–7.[1] Born at Aix in 1759,[2] he studied law at the University of Toulouse and at nineteen became *conseiller* to the *Parlement* of his native city. The nobility of Provence elected him as one of their deputies to the Estates-General. As one of the liberal nobles who had approved union with the Third Estate, he stood by Lafayette during the royal session of 23 June in opposing the expulsion of the deputies of the Third. His courage and his liberal views earned him a place on the committee which drafted the 1791 Constitution. Commissioned in September 1789 to liquidate the *conseil des échevins* in Marseilles and to prepare the city's municipal elections, d'André's attempts to restore order to that strife-torn city marked the beginning of his shift to the Right.[3] He gravitated to the group which included Lafayette and Mirabeau who counselled strong measures, including martial law if necessary, to suppress the disorders in the provinces. After Mirabeau's death and the flight to Varennes, he joined the ranks of those who were working for a conservative revision of the Constitution. With the close of the Constituent, he turned to the wholesale grocery trade, and was attacked in the Jacobin papers as a hoarder and monopolist in colonial produce. When his premises were pillaged by a mob in 1792, he managed to emigrate with his family to London. From that date until 1796, very little is known of his activities. A small trace of him can be found in the British War Office records. A single memorandum on conditions in Provence permits us a glimpse of his ideas in 1793. He insisted that the monarchy would never be restored on the basis of the *ancien régime*.[4] In May 1795 we find him in Switzerland, writing to François d'Ivernois, the Genevese financial expert then living in London.[5] This presumably

---

[1] Lebon, op. cit., p. 228, evidently believed that d'André and Berger, which was one of his assumed names, were two different people.

[2] See the references to d'André in O. Teissier, *Biographie des députés de la Provence à l'assemblée nationale de 1789* (Marseilles, 1897), pp. 31–8 and J. Balteau, M. Barroux and M. Prevost, *Dictionnaire de biographie française* (9 vols., Paris, 1933– in progress).

[3] D'André to Louis XVIII, 18 March 1796, F.O. 74/18.

[4] Dated [?] July 1793, W.O. 1/392.

[5] D'Ivernois to Windham, 25 May 1795, Add. MSS., 37859. Unfortunately Windham, to whom d'Ivernois forwarded d'André's letters, did not preserve them.

led the War Office to seek his services, but the records are silent on their nature.[1]

Although the details of his life are shrouded in mystery during this four-year period, the nature of his personality is not so elusive. Etienne Dumont, the celebrated Swiss publicist, translator of Bentham, and observer of the politics and politicians of France during the first years of the Revolution, has left us a remarkably vivid portrait of d'André.[2] Dumont describes a coarse-looking man, diffident in manner and self-effacing. He had none of the pretensions cultivated by most men of importance and influence; he had good sense, quick judgement, clarity of thought and expression, but he lacked the oratorical flourishes of men like Mirabeau.[3] He was at his best in managing men and situations. Dumont tells us that no one in the Constituent Assembly excelled d'André's skill in committee work. His association with the men of his own party, whose weaknesses and strengths he came to know at first hand, left him with no illusions concerning their worth. He complained to Dumont of their indolence, their indecisive deliberations, and their paralysis under attack in the Assembly. He did not spare the court either; Louis had ruined his chances by trying to please everyone and by his endless intrigues.[4]

Dumont's observations are supported by Reubell who was the most competent of the Directors.[5] In a conversation with Bonaparte, Reubell described d'André as a man with a first-class mind.[6] He was, Reubell recalled, the most consummate improviser in the Constituent, knowing how to assess the situation in the Assembly and perfectly aware of how to reach his goals without alienating important supporters. These qualities made him the most dangerous man Reubell had ever known. Reubell's colleague on the Directory, La Revellière-Lépeaux, who cannot be called a friendly witness because of his devotion to the Republic and d'André's hatred of it, was grateful for his assistance at the time of the first Restoration.[7] La Revellière's respect for d'André's generosity is

[1] Receipt for £53 dated 5 September 1795, Huskisson Papers, Brit. Mus. (Add. MSS.) 38769.

[2] Dumont, *Souvenirs sur Mirabeau*, pp. 191–2.

[3] Ibid.

[4] Ibid., pp. 181–2.

[5] Lefebvre, *La Révolution française*, p. 454.

[6] 'Conversation de Reubell avec le premier consul, le 3 ventôse an x (22 fevrier 1802)', *Nouvelle revue rétrospective*, xx (1904), 383–4.

[7] L. M. La Revellière-Lépeaux, *Mémoires* (3 vols., Paris, 1895), i. 82.

consistent both with Dumont's tribute and d'Ivernois' esteem for d'André's acute analysis of men and politics.[1]

This then was the man whom Wickham began, cautiously at first, to take into his confidence. A skilled and knowledgeable politician, an expert manipulator and a clever compromiser, d'André seemed to possess the qualities for which Wickham was searching. He was, moreover, a man who had worked with devotion for the monarchy and could not be accused of the opportunism characteristic of so many constitutionalists.

Louis and his circle could not deny d'André's ability and trustworthiness, but they dismissed the notion that he could be of decisive influence in changing the political climate in Paris.[2] Wickham was inclined to agree, but he was not prepared to jeopardize his usefulness without further investigation. D'André was in touch with a secret committee in Paris,[3] which had assumed the name *Comité Constitutionnel* and was composed of his former colleagues from the Constituent Assembly and deputies belonging to the new third. Because of their fear of police surveillance, they rarely took the lead in debates in the chambers, apart from objecting to legislation threatening the property of *émigrés*. D'André avowed little faith in their vitality or effectiveness. His frank appraisal left little doubt in Wickham's mind of their nullity.[4] Nevertheless there was little to lose and perhaps much to be gained by learning more about their plans and activities, and d'André was the person who could do this. But first Louis' approval was necessary. Wickham persuaded d'André[5] to offer his services to the king in a properly deferential manner;[6] precautions were also taken to suppress the constitutionalists' criticism of Louis.[7] This time the overtures proved more successful, for on 3 April Louis replied in friendly terms.[8] Wickham's infinite patience had at last been rewarded by this slender sign of a *rapprochement* between the two royalist factions.

[1] D'Ivernois to Windham, 25 May 1795, Add. MSS., 37859.
[2] Macartney to Wickham, 2 February 1796, *Correspondence of William Wickham*, i. 268.
[3] Report of a conversation between Lacombe and d'André, 22 February 1796, F.O. 74/15.
[4] Wickham to Grenville, 23 February 1796, ibid.
[5] Wickham to Grenville, 3 July 1796, F.O. 74/18.
[6] D'André to Louis XVIII, 18 March 1796, ibid.
[7] Wickham's marginal notes in Lacombe's report of his conversation with d'André, 22 February 1796, F.O. 74/15.
[8] Louis XVIII to d'André, 3 April 1796, F.O. 74/18.

The scene of the negotiations was then transferred to Paris. D'André sent copies of Louis' reply to Portalis, Durand de Maillane, Siméon, and Dupont de Nemours, asking what measures they and their friends intended to adopt against the Directory. Why did d'André address himself to them? Portalis, who had made a name for himself as a brilliant lawyer and was later to lend his talents to Bonaparte, was at this time a member of the right-wing of the *Conseil des Anciens* and very probably a moderate royalist.[1] Siméon, his brother-in-law, a one-time professor of law at Aix was a member of the *Conseil des Cinq-Cents*; he adhered to Mathieu Dumas' party and was a secret royalist.[2] Dupont de Nemours, who had gained notice as a physiocrat and as a partisan of the *philosophes*, moved from the Constituent Assembly to newspaper ownership, physically defended Louis XVI on 10 August, spent some time in prison, was elected to the *Conseil des Anciens* and published the *Historien*, one of the Directory's most consistent newspaper critics.[3] The Girondin, Durand de Maillane, also a member of the upper chamber, had during the Thermidorian Reaction inspired the law of 22 Germinal which favoured the *émigrés* and had been a super-zealous commissioner in Provence where he purged officials tainted with Jacobinism.[4] These men represented a substantial number of deputies all of whom were opponents of the Directory but whose views on the most efficacious means of overthrowing or replacing it were almost as various as their number. That this was indeed the case can be gauged by the results of the 1795 elections.[5] Of the total number of deputies in both chambers, 88 were known counter-revolutionaries and another 73 were moderate royalists. Thus a right-wing element had been introduced into the chambers. With the moderate republicans, some 139 whose views resembled those of the constitutionalists, they were potentially a pro-monarchist party. Yet they were more in agreement on what they were fighting against than on what they were fighting for.[6]

[1] J. Suratteau, 'Les Élections de l'an IV', *Annales historiques de la Révolution française*, xxiv (1952), 43.

[2] A. Meynier, *Le Dix-huit Fructidor an V* (Paris, 1927), p. 6.

[3] G. Lefebvre (*Le Directoire* (Les cours de Sorbonne) (Paris, 1947), fascicule i, p. 38) believes that Dupont de Nemours' views earn him a place among the moderate constitutionalists.

[4] See his *Histoire de la Convention Nationale* (Paris, 1825), pp. 262, 280, 284.

[5] The 1795 elections have been thoroughly analysed by Suratteau, loc. cit., xxiii (1951), 374–93, xxiv (1952), 32–62.   [6] Ibid., 49.

When d'André's proposals reached his friends in Paris they saw no opportunity to press a policy of overt opposition to the Directory which, because of its military successes in Italy, was at the moment in an impregnable position. They were also impressed by the Directory's anti-Jacobin measures, concluding that it alone stood between moderation and a Jacobin resurgence.[1] The discovery of the Babeuf conspiracy, the danger of which Wickham believed had deliberately been magnified and perhaps even promoted by the Directory,[2] was rallying to its side many men from whom d'André had expected a rather different kind of response. It was not fright alone that was driving them into the arms of the Directory; they had the mistaken notion, Wickham remarked with contempt, of being able to influence some of the Directors and so bring about their fall. He cited as proof the friendly references to the Directory in the *Historien*.[3]

Nevertheless d'André's deputy friends had no intention of permanently relinquishing the initiative to the Directory. They met with fellow deputies and empowered a Committee of Five to reconsider their position. Portalis was the only one of the original group on the Committee. The others were Mathieu Dumas; Dumolard from the *Conseil des Cinq-Cents*; Pastoret who had been in the Legislative Assembly and was now in the lower chamber; and Gilbert-Desmolières, a public servant before the Revolution who had rallied unreservedly to the royalists upon his election to the *Conseil des Cinq-Cents*. At the close of their deliberations, they informed d'André of the policy[4] they intended to pursue in the chambers. Beginning with the principle of the desirability of restoring the legitimate king, they went on to consider how this could be best achieved. They were agreed on the urgent need to press for peace, but insisted that they would not depart from constitutional methods in their representations. Such an approach would virtually ensure the disappearance of the Jacobins as a

[1] Wickham to Grenville, 3 July 1796, F.O. 74/18.

[2] Ibid. Most historians now agree that the Directory had taken great pains to infiltrate the Babeuvists with spies and was therefore aware of their doings and plans. This does not, however, support Wickham's belief that the plot was manufactured by the Directory. There can be no doubt that the Directors, particularly Carnot, were seriously alarmed by the evidence of Jacobin vitality. On this point, see Reinhard, *Le Grand Carnot*, ii. 183–6.

[3] Wickham to Grenville, 3 July 1796, F.O. 74/18.

[4] Copy of propositions made by a Committee of Five, no date, F.O. 74/18 and A.A.E., France 589.

political force, and was essential until the elections of 1797, when a royalist majority could prepare a frontal attack upon the Directory. Meanwhile the *émigrés* must desist from conspiratorial and violent means; otherwise the opportunity of winning adherents in the *Conseils* and even among the Directors would be compromised. They were pressing for a strategy of attrition aimed at preparing opinion for a constitutional return to the monarchy, and they cited their intention to press for legislation favouring the *émigrés* as proof of their good faith.

Wickham supported these proposals and planned to encourage Louis to accept them.[1] As we have seen, Pichegru had reached similar conclusions and urged similar action following his meeting in Paris with members of the constitutionalist group. That the season of internal rebellions was over was also the opinion of the Paris agency. The pressure demanding Louis' approval was thus overwhelming. Yet he refused to abandon his fossilized dogmas, dismissing the agency's plan—he had necessarily to deal with it before considering the Committee's propositions—as if he were already at Versailles.[2] Wickham was in despair. Louis' rejection, not only of his agency's recommendations, but also of similar plans made by Boissy d'Anglas through Précy, was for Wickham the *coup de grace* to the Bourbons. 'Unless', he wrote, 'His Majesty has any influence with Louis and the princes to persuade them to recede from the Declaration of Verona, all is lost for them.'[3] In a private letter to Grenville,[4] Wickham unburdened his hard-pressed soul even more fully. The French people would never return to their senses until the Directory had exhausted its ability to make war. This was unqualified approval for the position taken by the Committee of Five. Even more to the point was his cry of anguish condemning the princes: '. . . One is tempted to believe that God has willed this tremendous revolution, among other purposes, for *their* [his emphasis] particular correction, and that it will not terminate until they and their wretched systems have in great measure disappeared.'[5]

Although he felt that a solution to his difficulties was eluding him, Wickham did not surrender entirely to pessimism. The

[1] Wickham to Grenville, 3 July 1796, F.O. 74/18.
[2] La Vauguyon to Brottier, 11 July 1796, ibid.
[3] Wickham to Grenville, 16 July 1796, ibid.
[4] Wickham to Grenville, 18 July 1796, *Correspondence of William Wickham*, i. 418–420.   [5] Ibid.

apparent futility of the situation forced him to act; he would not permit Louis to commit political suicide. With the help of Duverne, then at Berne, he persuaded la Vauguyon to authorize the Paris agency to conceal Louis' attitude from the deputies and to tell them that he would welcome the opportunity to discuss their plans with one of their representatives.[1] Wickham expected that he would be able to use his influence in the interval 'to make them [Louis and his advisers] act, to a degree, as I should want them'.[2] Besides, although he was certain that the Committee of Five's proposals would meet a similar fate, the very fact that no answer had yet been given bolstered his sinking hopes.

Of Louis' ministers, only la Vauguyon saw the issue clearly and fairly and agreed with Wickham's conciliatory policy towards the constitutionalists. La Vauguyon was impressed by Pichegru's prediction of a successful counter-revolution if Louis accepted some form of constitutional government.[3] Pichegru implored Louis to abandon his pet theories of the *ancien régime* and hinted that there would be time enough for him to become 'absolute master of his Kingdom' once he held the reins of government firmly in his hands.[4] While la Vauguyon appreciated the cogency of Pichegru's remarks, his influence with Louis paled beside d'Avaray's, and Wickham knew only too well how rigid was that minister's respect of, and adulation for, the precedents of a society based on privilege. Nor was the persistence of Orléanist propaganda and the fresh rumours of a party in Paris supporting prince Henry of Prussia of much comfort to the harassed envoy.[5] What Wickham feared most was the possibility that the royalists were even considering some form of co-operation with the Jacobins rather than yield to the constitutionalists. He had a copy of a secret offer said to have been made by Tallien and Barras to Louis, promising their aid on condition that he sever all relations with the British government.[6] His apprehensions were not entirely allayed some two months later when he again referred to the fact that

the Royalists . . . are far more disposed to compromise with the Jacobins than with any other party. All views of humanity, policy, justice

[1] Ibid.
[2] Wickham to Drake, 21 July 1796, ibid., 430–3.
[3] Wickham to Grenville, 21 July 1796, F.O. 74/18.
[4] Wickham to Grenville, 23 July 1796, ibid.   [5] Ibid.
[6] Wickham to Grenville, 3 July 1796: copie du mémoire remis a M. de St. G . . . sur un projet de rétablissement de la royauté en France, no date, ibid.

and interest are nothing when opposed to the desire of humbling and of punishing the first authors of the Revolution. This new plan, for instance, was caught at with eagerness, while the wiser and more reasonable ones were either entirely rejected or received coldly.[1]

Wickham, of course, could not foresee that even la Vauguyon would be fooled by this chimera, but his conviction that Louis would refuse to listen to reason was firmly rooted before this latest delusion. If the royalists were rushing to their rendezvous with a providential fate, Wickham was determined to delay it as long as possible.

Nevertheless he angrily concluded that the lack of trust reposed in the good offices of the British government merited a similar attitude towards Louis and his advisers.[2] From the end of July, he further explored, through the channels opened by d'André, the proposals of the constitutionalists. Support of armed insurrection must now be abandoned in favour of exploiting all the constitutional expedients which presented themselves. Wickham was thus of the same mind as those who saw the existing political situation as a transitional period during which they would throw their support behind the Directory's anti-Jacobin measures and, by so doing, bend it to their will.[3]

What precisely were the features of the policy advocated by d'André? At Wickham's suggestion, he prepared an analysis of the basic weakness of the Directory and the latent strength of its opponents.[4] The important consideration in the not-too-distant-future was the election scheduled for the spring of 1797:

> Only after the elections will it be possible to know what we ought to do. If they go well, the problem will be solved. Even if they do not, there is no need to give up hope. The deeply-rooted corruption of the government, its financial embarrassment, the difficulty of levying taxes in a semi-democratic state, the fickleness of the nation—these are all causes for hope.

The economic and financial bankruptcy of the country was the Directory's most vulnerable point; and the advantage possessed

---

[1] Wickham to Grenville, 7 September 1796, *Correspondence of William Wickham*, i. 449–51.

[2] Wickham to Grenville, 19 July 1796, *Dropmore Papers*, iii. 223.

[3] Wickham to Grenville, 7 September 1796, F.O. 74/18 and *Correspondence of William Wickham*, i. 449–51.

[4] D'André to Wickham, 14 August 1796, F.O. 74/20.

by its critics lay in their ability to marshal public opinion against its financial measures and so dispose the country to vote against its candidates in the next election. It could be weakened in yet another way—by pressing for legislation to recall *émigrés* and priests who could take an active part in the election. With an efficient propaganda campaign and the appointment of reliable men to local administrative posts who could enlist good candidates and ensure that the primary assemblies were well attended by the 'right' people, the election results were bound to be favourable, and the restoration of the monarchy would be assured.

While Wickham did not differ with the essentials of this prognosis, he ridiculed the idea that the opposition to the Directory could outwit it by supporting it. Although he did not deny the advantage of supporting the government's anti-Jacobin measures, he questioned the opposition's ability to maintain its aims in this uneasy coalition.[1] Yet, so long as it managed to prevent its aims from being subordinated to the Directory's will, as for example, by validating the election of the comte de Vaublanc to the *Conseil des Cinq-Cents*,[2] Wickham softened his criticism. He noted that the Directory could not afford to alienate the rightist deputies, whose support was necessary in its anti-Jacobin programme.[3] He did not, however, underestimate the resilience of the dedicated republicans; he expected them to seize the first opportunity to attack their enemies in the *Conseils* and force the Directory to betray them.[4]

In October, as Wickham was to learn some time later,[5] the deputies of the Directorial Committee—so named by him because of its tactical support of the Directory's anti-Jacobin policy— discovered that the government had not carried out its promises: Jacobin administrators in the departments were still at their posts; Merlin de Douai, the minister of justice, had not been dismissed; and worst of all, the government was electioneering in the southern departments. The Directorial Committee was dominated by Mathieu Dumas, whose probity Wickham questioned because

[1] Wickham to Grenville, 3 July 1796, F.O. 74/18.

[2] See Mallet du Pan's references to Vaublanc in *Correspondance de Mallet du Pan*, ii. 133, 304. Vaublanc had been sentenced to death *in absentia* after Vendémiaire.

[3] Wickham to Grenville, 7 September 1796, F.O. 74/18 and *Correspondence of William Wickham*, i. 449–51.

[4] Wickham to Grenville, 21 September 1796, F.O. 74/18.

[5] Wickham to Grenville, 19 December 1796, F.O. 74/19 and *Correspondence of William Wickham*, i. 484–91.

of his intimacy with Carnot. It was made up of virtually the same men responsible for the propositions conveyed to d'André earlier in the year: Gilbert-Desmolières; Portalis; Siméon; Dumolard; but it also included Duplantier and Cadroi whose royalist sympathies were unquestionable. Duplantier had promised Précy and Imbert-Colomès his support in their plans of the previous year,[1] and Cadroi had been an active anti-Jacobin at Toulon in 1795.[2] Holding itself aloof from this group was another committee in touch with the Paris agency and in correspondence with d'André. Comprising Lemerer, Larivière,[3] Thibaudeau,[4] Durand de Maillane and Ribufet, an army contractor, it had dissociated itself from the Directorial Committee on the ground that collaboration with the Directory was bound to fail. Lemerer and Mersan (whose connections were then unknown to Wickham) were in the confidence of the Paris agency, and it was their committee which had deputized Durand de Maillane to maintain contact with d'André in Switzerland. Although the two committees seemed to hold opposite views on the best means of reaching the same objective, there was a close connection between their members, as they were in the habit of meeting at the Clichy club, and it is probable that the composition of the two committees was altered as the deputies changed their ideas on the best methods to oppose the Directory. This doubtless accounts for Wickham's self-confessed confusion in reporting their exact membership.[5]

The news that the assistance given to the Directory by the deputies was coming to an end vindicated Wickham's earlier doubts concerning the expediency of collaboration. He expressed his relief that the disabused deputies were now making attempts to undo their previous errors; for they had requested Duplantier to persuade Theodore Lameth, Duport and other constitutionalists to return to France to stand for election in the spring of 1797. Duplantier, who had gone to Switzerland for this purpose, also approached d'André to induce him to return to Paris and direct

---

[1] Wickham to Grenville, 19 December 1796, F.O. 74/19 and *Correspondence of William Wickham*, i. 484–91.

[2] Robinet et al., *Dictionnaire historique et biographique*.

[3] Larivière, because of his superhuman efforts during the Thermidorian Reaction to purge all Jacobins, was known for his royalist sympathies.

[4] Thibaudeau had a reputation as a moderate.

[5] Wickham to Grenville, 3, 10 July 1796, F.O. 74/18; Wickham to Grenville, 11 December 1796, F.O. 74/19.

the work of all like-minded deputies recruited from the two com-mittees.[1] Duplantier's risks in coming to Switzerland as well as those incurred by Cadroi and Dumolard in their attempts to sound out opinion in the Midi, convinced Wickham that they were now prepared to begin the more active phase of their opposition. He authorized d'André to consent to Duplantier's proposals and promised him financial aid in the forthcoming elections.[2]

As the year was drawing to a close, Wickham could look back upon a time of acute anxiety which was at last being dissipated by an apparently favourable turn of events at Paris. After all, it would be in Paris that the issues confronting the antagonists in the struggle would be decided. His pocket-book was now at the disposal of the constitutionalists and their allies. Pichegru was, as always, something of an enigma, but he was prepared to follow the direction marked out by the deputies. It was possible that a new recruit to the counter-revolution, in the person of Moreau, with whom Pichegru had met on several occasions, would further weaken the Directory, but this contingency was still in ques-tion and Wickham preferred to gamble on political manœuvres to obtain his goals.[3] Just as important in determining Wickham to follow this course was the Paris agency's extraordinary co-operation with the deputies. Moreover, he had acquired a guarded respect for the agency's ability to furnish him with vital military intelligence. The months ahead promised a brighter outcome than that which he had entertained at the beginning of the year.

[1] Wickham to Grenville, 11 December 1796, F.O. 74/19.
[2] Wickham to d'André, 17 November 1796, ibid.
[3] Wickham to Eden, 16 October 1796, *Correspondence of William Wickham*, i. 466–471; Wickham to Grenville, 22 October, 14 December 1796, ibid., 471–3, 491–6.

8

THE ELECTIONS OF 1797

To all the critics and opponents who stood to the Right of the Directory, the electoral campaign in the spring of 1797 was seen as a turning point in the counter-revolution. At stake were one-third of the seats in both *Conseils*. There was more than a remote possibility that the royalist opposition in the Legislature would be transformed into a majority by the return of a full slate of royalist candidates, since there already were some 300 deputies in both houses who were susceptible to monarchist views. Of the latter, less than half—117—had been elected in 1795 for a three-year term; but it was unlikely that their allies among the Conventionals, numbering 183, would all be forced to seek re-election, since the retirement of half the remaining number (465) of Conventionals was to be determined by lot. In the period before the elections, knowledgeable observers estimated that roughly 234 Conventionals would be retiring from the chambers. Even if half of the 183 deputies, who helped make up the royalist faction in the *Conseils*, were to lose their seats, more than 200 of the 300 royalists, constitutionalists and moderate republicans would still remain. And as a certain number of the retiring deputies with royalist views would very probably be re-elected, they, together with the large number of fresh royalist candidates who were expected to win and those whose terms were not yet over, would doubtless comprise the majority in the Legislature.

The Constitution of the year III[1] empowered the primary assemblies to begin their proceedings on 21 March, and stipulated that they were open to all French male citizens who were twenty-one years of age, paid direct land or personal property taxes, and were inscribed in the cantonal registers. Election of deputies to the Legislature was indirect and in two stages; those qualified to participate in the primary assemblies voted for the electors to

[1] All references to the Constitution are taken from J. H. Stewart, *A Documentary Survey of the French Revolution* (New York, 1951), pp. 572–611. For an interpretation of the Constitution, see J. Godechot, *Les Institutions de la France sous la Révolution et l'Empire* (Paris, 1951), pp. 398–405.

the electoral assemblies, although they also had the right to elect justices of the peace, cantonal presidents, and municipal officials. To qualify as an elector, a citizen had to be twenty-five and it was necessary (*a*) in communes of more than 6,000 inhabitants to own real property equal to 200 days' labour, or to lease a dwelling worth an annual income or rental value of 150 days' labour, or to lease a rural dwelling worth 200 days' labour annually; (*b*) in communes with less than 6,000 people, the qualifications were the same with 150 instead of 200, 100 in place of 150, and 100 in place of 200; (*c*) in rural districts to own real property of an annual value of 150 days' labour, or to lease, or to work on shares (*métayage*), real property worth annually 200 days' labour. The electors in turn elected the members of the Legislature and the Court of Cassation, as well as departmental and judicial officials. The Constitution declared that there should be one elector for every 200 citizens, reducing by half the proportion designated in the 1791 Constitution. There were, it is estimated, a total of some 30,000 electors who were actually chosen to elect the national legislators and the administrative and judicial officers in the departments.[1] The drafters of the Constitution, in accord with Boissy d'Anglas who was one of its chief architects, looked forward to a nation controlled by the best elements who, according to their political philosophy, were synonymous with the propertied classes.[2] As the experience of the 1791 Constitution had revealed that only the affluent and most politically minded could afford the luxury of absenting themselves from their daily occupations, it was expected that the same conditions would prevail under the provisions of the new Constitution: the electors normally spent ten days to complete their duties. From this, the royalists drew great comfort; the opportunity of attracting the support of the landed proprietors and those professional

---

[1] Palmer (*The Age of the Democratic Revolution*, pp. 522–6) demonstrates convincingly in his discussion of the 1791 Constitution that in their attempts to estimate the number of electors, historians have confused the number qualified to serve as electors with the number actually chosen. Before the revisions of August 1791, some 3,000,000 qualified as electors, according to the best estimates. The revisions restricted the number of qualified electors, and the number actually chosen was only about 50,000. It is interesting to note that the qualifications for electors in the 1795 Constitution were substantially the same as those in the earlier Constitution, but the number of electors was reduced from one for every 100 active citizens (1791) to one for every 200.

[2] Lefebvre, *La Révolution française*, p. 443.

politicians who were their actual or potential allies was glaringly apparent. There was one major difficulty: how to overcome the resistance of those who had become owners of national property. But this, the royalists believed they could do; they were confident that the constitutional provision forbidding the primary assemblies from naming the same electors every year would give them an opportunity to influence the choice of electors. The future had never looked better, particularly because the Constitution provided for the retirement of one of the Directors in May. The elevation of a royalist to the executive branch of government was therefore possible, if not probable.

Expectation was high for some months before the elections began. The reports of the Directory's police agents contain frequent allusions to the hopes and fears entertained by Parisians, among whom there was a general feeling that the future of French political life would be decided by the elections. The Jacobins and the royalists were of course most vitally interested; the former feared the increasing boldness of the latter and accused the government of tolerating open sedition.[1] The royalists, ever on their guard against what they termed Directorial interference with the laws of the Republic, were suspicious of the Directory's proposals for the retirement of the required number of Conventionals from the *Conseils*.[2]

The Jacobins were despondent and isolated, scowling under their enforced, muted tutelage. Repudiated by the reaction which gathered force after Thermidor, called upon during the insurrection of Vendémiaire to defend the Convention only to suffer a serious setback in the repressions of 1796, they expected the elections to complete their political destruction. They accused the Directory of showing inordinate tenderness towards the *émigrés* and were appalled at the laxity of the conscription laws.[3]

The royalists were by turn optimistic and apprehensive. For them events since Vendémiaire, though far from satisfactory, were more heartening. A silent vow of revenge doubtless inspired their political plans. The police reported that they were monopolizing discussions in the cafés and public places in Paris, 'exhibiting in

---

[1] Rapport du bureau central du 25 décembre 1796, Aulard, *Paris pendant la réaction thermidorienne et sous le Directoire*, iii. 655.

[2] Ibid.

[3] Rapport du bureau central du 6 janvier 1797, ibid., 677.

advance an air of triumph'.[1] They were said to be attacking the
government and openly calling for the 'restoration of the old
order'.[2] They openly declared, however, that the government
might use illegal means to ensure its dominance, even by calling
in the army as it had done during the Vendémiaire crisis.[3] But on
the whole, like the *émigré* Harcourt in London, they regarded this
election year as 'a period which would very probably be decisive
for the future of the counter-revolution'.[4]

The large majority of Parisians regarded the approaching
elections with massive indifference punctuated by distrust. Many
were heard to ask: 'How will it all end? Things cannot become
any worse than they are today; besides, we have too often been
the playthings of factions.'[5] They suspected that the secret
meetings organized by the two dominant factions would result in
'incalculable misfortunes'.[6]

II

Rarely has one party in an election campaign been so completely
prepared as were the royalists and their allies. They concealed
their differences and consented to postpone the question of the
nature of the monarchy until after the elections. Open royalist
sentiment was therefore reduced to a minimum. Even so the
nature of royalist propaganda deceived no one. Its platitudes were
aimed at attracting '*les honnêtes gens*', the proprietors, the relatives
of *émigrés*, the religious-minded, the men whose economic liveli-
hood demanded the end of the war, the secret and the open
royalists, and all the other disaffected groups in French society,
whose desire for stability and order induced in them a receptivity to the royalist programme. Underlying the appeals to these
different interests was constant criticism of the shortcomings
of the Directory and a general condemnation of the Revolution.
The attack on the Directory was total and devastating. One un-
familiar with the issues at stake would be able to discern very
few clues of undisguised royalist propaganda, for though it

---

[1] Rapport du bureau central du 25 décembre 1796, ibid., 655.
[2] Rapport du bureau central du 3 janvier 1797, ibid., 671.
[3] Rapport du bureau central du 9 janvier 1797, ibid., 682.
[4] Harcourt to Bouillon, 22 November 1796, P.C. 1/120A.
[5] Rapport du bureau central du 3 janvier 1797, Aulard, op. cit., iii. 671.
[6] Rapport du bureau central du 9 janvier 1797, ibid., 682.

spoke in Messianic terms of what the defeat of the Directory would mean for France, it was rarely articulate about the hard facts of political life in the event of success.

At hand to launch the campaign of royalist agitation was an almost solid core of royalist and semi-royalist journalists, who borrowed ideas from one another, quoted one another and, apart from the varying degrees of their compositors' skill, edited journals that were remarkably alike in format and content. Their record of resistance to the Revolution, in some cases, dated from 1789 but the majority had launched their newspapers in the post-Thermidorian period. They had been among the leading agitators during the fatal days of Vendémiaire, when they pursued a rather ambiguous policy in support of an undefined form of constitutional monarchy. They were silenced for a short time by the retaliatory measures of the Convention and the Directory but they soon resumed their attacks in the familiar tones of deprecation and vilification. Their journals dominated the Parisian press, swamping the few republican journals such as the government subsidized *Rédacteur* and *Journal des défenseurs de la patrie*. Foremost among the independent journals friendly to the Directory were the *Journal des hommes libres*, the *Sentinelle* and the *Ami des lois*. In sharp contrast to the remnants of the republican press, the royalist and constitutionalist papers were prolific and found their counterparts in the departments. Among those which may be considered as representative of this large number are the *Éclair*, the joint production of the Bertin brothers, and the *Messager du soir* edited by Isidore Langlois, both of which contributed 'a right direction to public opinion'.[1] At least two new papers appeared during the elections: Montjoie's *Journal général de France* was founded by Brottier with funds supplied by Wickham,[2] who also financed Mailhe's *Orateur constitutionnel* or the *Ami de l'ordre et du repos public*.[3] The *Quotidienne*, Michaud's journal, was perhaps the most effective of the lot. Others that added to the royalist cacophony were Fiévée's *Gazette française*; the *Véridique* which counted Poujade-Ladevèze and Royou among its contributors; the *Nouvelles politiques*, the organ of Lacretelle *jeune*

---

[1] Wickham to Grenville, 12 April 1797, F.O. 74/20.

[2] Wickham to Grenville, 18 December 1796, F.O. 74/19.

[3] The journal had 105 subscribers, many of them right-wing deputies. A list of them may be seen in A.N., F⁷4439², cited by Mathiez, *Le Directoire*, p. 285.

and Suard; Gallais' *Censeur des journaux* and Salverte's *Tribune politique*.

Although the elections were not to begin until 21 March, the journals launched their campaign in January, revealing a confidence and a self-assurance which often assumed the impending demise of the Directory. Characteristic of these sentiments was the clarion call of the *Journal général de France*. It described the elections as the 'salvation of all' and appealed to all men of good will to subordinate their personal political opinions for the general good by uniting behind the best qualified candidates.[1] Coinciding with this appeal was a prediction by nearly all the journals of the Right, that the anniversary of Louis XVI's execution would in future be devoted to national mourning.[2] Warnings that public indifference was the Jacobins' greatest hope were repeated *ad nauseam*.[3] Coupled with this admonition was another that the Midi would once again become a scene of slaughter if nothing was done to restrain the 'anarchists' in Toulon and Toulouse[4] or if general Willot was dismissed from his command at Marseilles.[5]

The stage set, the journals, probably by collective agreement, stressed several issues and distorted the Directory's activities as manœuvres to rig the elections. Their most vicious barbs were first aimed at the Directory's trial of the agents; they contemptuously dismissed the Directory's charges by ridiculing its 'naïve' equation of royalism and conspiracy.[6] Gallais was sure that as soon as more details of the alleged plot were made public the Directory's case against the accused would crumble.[7] Michaud's ironic pen gave thanks to 'the salutary action of a tireless police

---

[1] *Journal général de France*, [?] January 1797, cited by M. Peltier, *Paris pendant l'année 1797* (London, 1797), xi. 60–61. A placard, which had wide currency in Paris about this time, *Avis aux honnêtes gens*, made the following points: (1) Though the Jacobins had lost the majority of their supporters, they were still well organized and highly disciplined; (2) since France was sitting atop a Jacobin volcano, the elections were not primarily concerned with political forms but with the final destruction of the terrorists; (3) it was therefore essential to turn out *en masse* to the assemblies and to unite around those candidates known for their 'morality'.

[2] *Censeur des journaux*, 13 January 1797.

[3] Cf. *Tableau de la France*, 22 January 1797.

[4] *Précurseur*, 28 January 1797.

[5] *Gazette française*, 22 January 1797. Since Willot's royalist leanings were well known, his supporters considered his retention at Marseilles essential during the critical period of the elections, which, they felt, he could decisively influence.

[6] For example, see the *Gazette française*, 1 February 1797.

[7] *Censeur des journaux*, 1 February 1797.

force'.[1] Once the documents of the interrogation and the trial of the accused were released, the magnitude of the conspiracy could not be dismissed so lightly. The gravity of the charge was therefore minimized, for it cast its shadow over all the right-wing deputies. Lacretelle *jeune*, echoing Pastoret's views in the *Conseil des Cinq-Cents* on 5 February, insisted that the Directory, by bringing the accused before a military court, was creating a precedent dangerous to all citizens who might be caught in the clutches of an unscrupulous government.[2] The controversy was thus lifted from the mundane plane of conspiracy to the more rarefied air of judicial procedure and individual liberty. This simulated concern for legal niceties was stressed during the months of the trial, while, at the same time, no opportunity was overlooked to press the most savage attacks on Babeuf and his accomplices who were also standing trial.

As if in anticipation of the Directory's decree of 25 February, which struck at the *émigrés'* hopes of returning to vote in the elections, the journals called for the easing of the harsh *émigré* laws.[3] There were approximately 120,000 names on the *émigré* lists, from which 17,000 had been provisionally removed.[4] When the *Conseils* decided to allow the latter to vote in the primary assemblies, the journals praised the measure as a moral victory for the royalists and constitutionalists. As *coincidence* would have it, Lally-Tolendal's new book, *Défense des Emigrés français adressée au peuple français*, was smuggled into Paris from London at the beginning of March and was reviewed ecstatically on front pages of several journals. Nearly all of them seized upon these words in the book as a plea to end the long fratricidal war: 'War between France and her enemies is about to come to an end; will it be perpetuated among Frenchmen?'[5]

Although the elections were still weeks away, many journalists took advantage of the vagueness in the Constitution to claim that the deputies who would be retired by lot on 5 March would be

---

[1] *Quotidienne*, 1 February 1797.

[2] *Nouvelles politiques*, 11 February 1797.

[3] Cf. *Gazette française*, 12 January 1797.

[4] P. J. B. Bouchez and P. C. Roux, *Histoire parlementaire de la Révolution française* (40 vols., Paris 1834–8), xxxvii. 244.

[5] See *Nouvelles politiques*, 8 March 1797. Cf. Louis Mallet's observations to his father, Mallet du Pan, 23 March 1797 in *Mémoires de Malouet*, ii. 504: 'It seems that M. Lally's book has created quite a stir in Paris, and . . . I believe it will hasten the crisis.'

ineligible for re-election.[1] It was better, they insisted, to declare
them all disqualified even if some constitutionalists lost their
seats.[2] This argument proved flimsy, for there was no serious
constitutional challenge to their right to stand again. The supporters of the Directory in the *Conseils* shrewdly included among
the retiring third those who had died and resigned so that only
145 instead of 167 deputies in the *Conseil des Cinq-Cents* were
forced to seek re-election. Similarly, in the *Conseil des Anciens*,
only 71 instead of 83 deputies were retired.[3] Of the retired
Conventionals, 63 were regicides.[4] Among those who also lost
their seats were such right-wing deputies as Fermont, Lanjuinais,
Durand-Maillane, Boissy d'Anglas and Cambacérès. Though the
Conseils were condemned for having retired such faithful public
servants, the *Quotidienne* expressed the gratitude of the nation for
having at last been 'freed from the presence of a few rascals
whose places will be taken by *'honnêtes gens'*.'[5]

On 15 March the Directory asked the *Conseil des Cinq-Cents* to
enact legislation requiring the members of the electoral assemblies
to take an oath of allegiance against royalism and anarchy. This
brought an immediate outcry in the press. On the one hand, it
was condemned as a revival of the Committee of Public Safety's
arbitrary measures, while on the other, electors were advised
that conscience should not stand in the way of taking the pres-
cribed oath, 'so that you may take the proper safeguards for your-
selves and preserve your property from pillage'.[6] The agitation
was premature, for in its final version the oath only required the
electors to swear fidelity to the Republic and to the Constitution
and to defend them against royalist and anarchist attacks.[7] However, there was still a widespread reluctance to swear even this
less offensive oath,[8] and the journals cautioned their readers to
treat the oath with the necessary perspective, suggesting that as
it was demanded by the Republic it could not be binding.

[1] *Gazette française*, [?] January 1797, cited by Peltier, op. cit., xi. 352.
[2] Ibid.
[3] *Réimpression de l'ancien Moniteur*, xxviii. 602–4.
[4] J. Suratteau, 'Les Élections de l'an V aux Conseils du Directoire', *Annales historiques de la Révolution française*, xxx (Oct.–Dec., 1958), 27.
[5] *Quotidienne*, 9, 14 March 1797.
[6] Ibid., 19 March 1797.
[7] Buchez and Roux, op. cit., xxxvii. 245. Cf. L. Sciout, *Le Directoire* (4 vols., Paris, 1895), ii. 315.
[8] Rapport du bureau central du 21 mars 1797, Aulard, op. cit., iv. 15.

The necessity of peace was stressed in the journals. For Fiévée peace was a certainty if the *'amis de l'ordre'* were elected.[1] Montjoie denigrated Bonaparte's military capacities and criticized Dupont de Nemours for urging France to retain Belgium.[2] Lacretelle *jeune* ridiculed speculation that a successful invasion of Ireland would have terminated the war in France's favour. He argued that the extension of the Revolution beyond France's borders had been productive of anarchy. The production of armaments, the continuation of forced loans and conscription could not but end in disaster.[3] In another issue he told his readers that the opening of a new military campaign would turn all Europe against France.[4] The *Éclair* had the courage to demand that the *Rédacteur* refrain from insulting Condé, Berry and other *émigrés*.[5] Michaud assured his readers that bayonets, cannon and other means of terror and oppression could never bring honour and prosperity to France, and urged them to vote for only those candidates who promised to support a policy of peace.[6]

Of course the problems of peace and war were not the only important campaign issues. The sanctity of property was emphasized.[7] Coupled with it was a promise that the defeat of the Directorial candidates would revive the French economy.[8] Religious persecution was vigorously condemned; candidates who made no secret of their religious attachments were praised.[9] Michaud stated that he would even vote for priests if they presented themselves as candidates.[10] The Orléanists were showered with abuse in nearly all the journals; Gallais claimed that there was a diabolical liaison between them and the Babeuvists;[11] Ladevèze parroted this ludicrous accusation;[12] and Michaud attributed to them the fall of the monarchy.[13]

Complete unanimity was not always achieved in the press campaign. The old cleavage between royalist and constitutionalist was perhaps best exemplified in Richer-Sérisy's *Accusateur public* and Dupont de Nemour's *Historien*. Richer-Sérisy's acerbity was

---

[1] *Gazette française*, [?] January 1797, cited by Peltier, op. cit., xi. 352.

[2] *Journal général de France*, 27 January 1797.

[3] *Nouvelles politiques*, 24 January 1797.   [4] Ibid., 17 February 1797.

[5] *Éclair*, cited in *Véridique*, 21 February 1797.   [6] *Quotidienne*, 31 March 1797.

[7] Ibid.   [8] *Nouvelles politiques*, cited by Peltier, op. cit., xi. 801.

[9] *Véridique*, 13 February 1797; *Quotidienne*, 19 February 1797; *Gazette française*, cited by Peltier, op. cit., xi. 352.

[10] *Quotidienne*, 27 March 1797.   [11] *Censeur des journaux*, 24 January 1797.

[12] *Véridique*, 23 February 1797.   [13] *Quotidienne*, 11 March 1797.

unconfined, his perverse gift for contumely bordering on misanthropy, while Dupont's common good sense acted as a valuable corrective. Occasionally the other journals indulged in this intraparty rivalry. The *Véridique* called upon the wrath of heaven to punish the constitutionalists, to whom it ascribed the sorry state of France.[1] On the other side the *Censeur des journaux* lamented the incalculable harm done by extremists like Richer-Sérisy.[2]

In the crucial days after the opening of the primary assemblies the journals insisted on the importance of attending them. Michaud, for example, contrasted the feverish activities of the Jacobins with the apparent indifference of the '*honnêtes gens*'; he exhorted them to brave 'the inclemency of the weather' and to resist 'the intrigues of a dying faction'.[3] As soon as the first election results were made known, the journals began to report the news under the heading of '*Bulletin des assemblées primaires*'. Some of them even published reports from so-called '*correspondants*' in the departments.[4]

When the electoral assemblies began their duties, the question of endorsing certain candidates became more important. Even so, the qualifications necessary for 'good' candidates were outlined before the elections. A pamphlet written by Quatremère de Quincy, *La Véritable liste des candidats*, received close attention in the journals as a guide to electors.[5] Marmontel was suggested as the best candidate in the Eure department; at Versailles, Vauvilliers, Cheron, Hennin and Lacretelle *l'aîné* were said to be worthy of election.[6] Voters were urged to support La Harpe, Lacretelle *jeune*, Richer-Sérisy, Quatremère de Quincy, Chauveau-Lagarde and d'André.[7] The choices seemed to be so favourable that by 8 April Michaud wrote: 'The Constitution created the Directory and will perish when the Directory falls.'[8] Langlois' comments summed up royalist satisfaction:

All writers who prefer the good of their country to the plaudits of a few idiots, who prefer peace and the constitution rather than civil war and Jacobin arrogance, have raised their courageous voices against these nihilists and their intrigues . . .[9]

[1] *Véridique*, 25 February 1797.   [2] *Censeur des journaux*, 1 February 1797.
[3] *Quotidienne*, 25 March 1797.
[4] *Censeur des Journaux*; *Véridique*; *Quotidienne*, passim.
[5] *Quotidienne*, 5 March 1797.   [6] Ibid., 4 April 1797.
[7] Ibid., 5, 10 April 1797.   [8] Ibid., 8 April 1797.
[9] *Messager du soir*, 8 April 1797.

III

The heaviest burden of the royalist campaign was sustained by Wickham, d'André and Despomelles. The British minister had anticipated the great opportunity which the elections presented to the royalists and had promised d'André sufficient funds to finance a large-scale campaign.[1] Wickham further elaborated upon this theme with an analysis of the psychological mood of the country. For him the majority of Frenchmen were animated by '. . . a marked hatred and contempt for the present Rulers, a secret wish for a change *more or less* effective in the present government [and] a general desire for Peace'. To this, Wickham added that all Frenchmen, regardless of party, were deeply convinced that their country's enemies were intent on its destruction. The Directory derived its real strength not from the successes of the army but from its ability to play upon the widespread fear of the unknown consequences of military defeat. Wickham was therefore insistent that:

We can never succeed in shaking the power of the government until we shall have conquered the good will and good opinion of the people. The gaining of this point becomes more important since His Majesty is pleased to incline towards an honourable peace with France. . . . My conviction that public opinion must be gained is influenced by the belief that the Revolution will not end without leaving a share of the government in the hands of the people and that the state of the continent may soon be such as that the friendship and hatred of that government cannot be considered as matters of indifference.[2]

Wickham's reference to Britain's future in Europe was prompted by the military defeats of the allies in the winter of 1796–7 and Bonaparte's victories in Italy. His failure to establish the counter-revolution by means of internal insurrections also bolstered his confidence in the beneficent effect of the elections. To support his argument that it was possible to hasten the breakdown of the Directory in this way, he maintained that it was too weak to threaten its opponents; that it feared the Jacobins more than the royalists and would therefore continue its anti-Jacobin policy; and that consequently a policy aimed at aggravating

[1] Wickham to d'André, 17 November 1796, F.O. 74/19.   [2] Ibid.

its dilemma and increasing its isolation was the most effective way of hastening its fall.[1] As for the more intransigent royalists, he believed that they would have to choose between acceptance of a constitutional monarchy, which would undoubtedly be the first fruits of this policy, and complete impotence. Basically, however, his views were influenced by the probability of peace and the implications which it held for Britain. He minimized the anti-British sentiments of the constitutionalists on whom he counted most, by pointing out that their appeals for peace would prevent them from demanding outrageous peace terms.[2]

Although Wickham did not underestimate the adverse effect on public opinion caused by the arrest of the agents,[3] he did not conceal his satisfaction at their enforced inactivity during the elections.[4] D'André, armed with Wickham's approval to direct the affairs of a union of royalists and constitutionalists in Paris, reached the capital a short time before the government's discovery of the conspiracy.[5] He did not entirely dismiss the damage caused by the discovery but he did not think that it was irreparable. The Directory would hardly delay or prevent the elections from taking place; instead it would probably exert tremendous pressure in support of candidates whose wealth rested on their purchase of national property.[6]

One of the unfortunate effects of the discovery of the agents was the reaction of Mathieu Dumas' Committee; apprehensive of possible repercussions, it was reviewing its decision to work for the defeat of the Directory and was instead planning to aid it. Fortunately d'André was able to prevent this.[7] He was, however, not successful in his plan to unite all of the Directory's right-wing opponents, since some of the constitutionalist deputies were still somewhat wary of the royalists. For d'André, complete accord between the two rival groups would depend on the restraint shown by Louis and his ministers, and he intimated that the majority of the deputies would not tolerate the presence of the king's agents in Paris. He also noted that the rift on the Right extended to the broad mass of the electorate which, while

[1] Ibid.
[2] Wickham to Grenville, 8 March 1797, no. 3, F.O. 74/20.
[3] Wickham to Grenville, 8 March 1797, no. 2, ibid.
[4] Wickham to Grenville, 8 March 1797, no. 3, ibid.
[5] D'André to Wickham, [?] October 1797, F.O. 27/52.
[6] Wickham to Grenville, 8 March 1797, no. 2, F.O. 74/20. [7] Ibid.

generally anti-Directorial, suffered from the same divisions evident in the *Conseils*.[1] Despite these obstacles he felt that there were many opportunities to remove their worst effects.[2] When Wickham contrasted the 'method, union and vigour' of the opposition in the *Conseils* after d'André's arrival in Paris with its previous confusion and pusillanimity, he was satisfied that a great step forward had been taken.[3] What happened was that for purposes of the elections, d'André succeeded in persuading the constitutionalists clustering around Mathieu Dumas and his Committee that a coalition including all the right-wing opponents of the Directory was advisable. When he reminded them of their previous betrayals by the Directory, they surrendered to his views. Secondly, he emphasized that the king's assurance of moderation was now his avowed policy. The Dumas Committee came round but reserved its right to support its own candidates wherever they came forward.[4]

The *Institut philanthropique* and other organizations originated by the agents, of course, could be of decisive influence in the elections. But how could the *Institut*'s machinery be utilized without submitting to the directives of Blankenburg? A few weeks before the opening of the primary assemblies, a meeting was arranged between d'André's Committee and Despomelles and agreement was reached on exploiting the *Institut*'s facilities in the elections. This decision was important for it determined the lists of candidates in several departments. Moreover, d'André realized his plan without having to submit to the agency to ensure success.[5] The *Institut*, however, had made good progress only in a few departments. Consequently d'André dispatched agents to most parts of France and Belgium, but since there was little time left to prepare the candidacies of '*hommes ardents et actifs*' [confirmed royalists], they decided to risk their chances on the '*honnêtes gens*' [the more moderate royalists].[6] Feverish preparations resulted in the establishment of the *Institut* in several

[1] D'André to Wickham, 19 March 1797, F.O. 74/20.
[2] Wickham to Grenville, 1 April 1797, no. 2, ibid.
[3] Wickham to Grenville, 1 April, 1797, no. 1, ibid.
[4] Wickham to Grenville, 20 May 1797, ibid.
[5] Wickham to Grenville, 20, 24 May 1797, F.O. 74/20; d'André to Wickham, [?] October 1797, F.O. 27/52. Wickham claims that d'André concerted his plans with Despomelles a few days before the convocation of the primary assemblies, but d'André says that the meeting took place six or seven weeks before the first stage of the elections, which is more probable. [6] Ibid.

departments.[1] The entire scheme was financed by Wickham, whose remittances to d'André were increased at the end of March by an additional £30,000.[2]

The members of the *Institut* were active almost everywhere in France; the rebel commanders in western France were especially zealous in propagandizing the areas under their direction. Rochecotte's agents were busy in the department of the Sarthe;[3] Mallet and Bourmont in the Eure, Orne and the Côtes-du-Nord; and Frotté's agents in the Manche and Calvados.[4] Wickham reported progress in the departments of Jura, Ain, Marne, Haute-Saône, Doubs, Isère, Aube, Haut-Rhin and Bas-Rhin.[5] General Willot used all his powers as commander in the south to ensure favourable results in the departments of Bouches-du-Rhône, Vaucluse and Basses-Alpes.[6] Dupont Constant, a Frenchman from the West Indies, and a certain Mailhos directed a precursor of the *Institut* in an extensive region around Bordeaux.[7]

Within these and other departments troops of royalist agents cooperated with the *Institut*, took an active part in the primary and electoral assemblies or, if necessary, were wholly responsible for royalist agitation and propaganda. D'André sent an agent named Foy to the department of the Pas-de-Calais to offer moral and financial aid to the royalist, Cambis.[8] Précy worked with Polissard, who, as an *émigré*, had been denied his seat in the *Conseil des*

---

[1] D'André to Wickham, [?] October 1797, F.O. 27/52. Cf. Caudrillier, *La Trahison de Pichegru*, p. 326. Caudrillier's statement that the *Institut* was founded in 66 departments before the elections is based on a misinterpretation of this document. He saw, it would appear, only the published extracts in C. Ballot, *Le Coup d'état du 18 Fructidor* (Paris, 1906). pp. 167–73.

[2] Wickham to Grenville, 1 April 1797, F.O. 74/20.

[3] A. de Beauchamp, *Mémoires du comte Fortuné Guyon de Rochecotte rédigés sur ses papiers et sur les notes de ses principaux officiers* (Paris, 1818), pp. 149, 178.

[4] Frotté to Dutheil, 5 April 1797, *Dropmore Papers*, iii. 309.

[5] Wickham to Grenville, 8 March 1797, no. 2; Wickham to Grenville, 1 April 1797, F.O. 74/20.

[6] Wickham to Grenville, 8 March 1797, no. 1, ibid. Cf. C. L. Chassin, 'La Trahison du général Willot', *La Révolution française*, xxxii (1897), 403–14 and Reinhard, *Le Grand Carnot*, ii. 225–6.

[7] M. Dupont Constant, *Essai sur l'Institut philanthropique* (Paris, 1823), pp. 45–6. Cf. Lacouture, op. cit., pp. 4, 40.

[8] D'André to Wickham, 19 March 1797, F.O. 74/20. Cf. Caudrillier, *La Trahison de Pichegru*, p. 326, who is incorrect on two points. In the first place, he confuses the Pas-de-Calais with the departments carved out of Belgium, and secondly he attributes an important rôle in the elections to the *Mémorial*, a journal which d'André established only after the elections.

Cinq-Cents, and with Serret, the former lieutenant-general of the *baillage* of Semar, to keep the issues alive in the department of the Haute-Saône.[1] Villecrose, one of Précy's agents, was active in the various departments of Dauphiny. At Lyons[2] the Directory's commissioner, apparently a secret royalist, openly supported the royalists.[3] The former president of the *Parlement* of Besançon, de Vezet, persuaded the marquis de la Champagne to return to the Jura department where he had formerly been a large landowner to lend his support to the royalist candidates.[4] Another of de Vezet's correspondents was Folnais, a member of the military command at Besançon where he was chosen as an elector.[5] Also very occupied in the Jura was Dauphin, who had been Wickham's chief correspondent for that department for a long period, and who was nominated as one of the electors at Lons-le-Saunier.[6] And Pichegru, who was standing for election in the Jura, though simulating aloofness during the campaign, received financial aid from Wickham through a number of his agents.[7]

The royalists employed a number of other expedients in their campaign, foremost among them being the emphasis on religion and the employment of clerical agents. A year before the elections Louis had planned to persuade the *émigré* bishops in Switzerland, Italy, Germany and Great Britain to organize and direct nonjuring priests in four separate areas in France, the object being to increase popular opposition to the Directory.[8] The plan never materialized because of the opposition of some key prelates such as Marbeuf, the former archbishop of Lyons; Dillon, the former bishop of Narbonne; and the former archbishop of Reims, who rejected the king's appeal on the premise that consultation with

[1] Précy to d'Avaray, 7 March 1797, A.A.E., France 590.

[2] Précy to Louis XVIII, 16 March 1797, ibid.

[3] Wickham to Grenville, 1 April 1797, no. 1, F.O. 74/20.

[4] De Vezet to Louis XVIII, 2, 27 March 1797, A.A.E., France 590. Cf. L. Pingaud, 'Le Président de Vezet', *Revue historique*, xx (1882), 282–326, for a biographical sketch.

[5] Wickham to Grenville, 1 April 1797, no. 2, F.O. 74/20; de Vezet to Louis XVIII, 2 March 1797, A.A.E., France 590.

[6] Wickham to Grenville, 1 April 1797, no. 1, F.O. 74/20.

[7] Wickham to Grenville, 22 October 1796, F.O. 74/19; de Vezet to Louis XVIII, 15 March 1797; Fauche-Borel to d'Avaray, 24 March 1797, A.A.E., France 590.

[8] Archbishop of Embrun to Louis XVIII, 2 March 1796; bishop of Agen to Louis XVIII, 5 March 1796, A.A.E., France 589.

the Papacy was essential.[1] Later that year la Vauguyon even suggested that efforts be revived to have the Papacy declare a war of religion against the Revolution.[2] This project also made no progress.

Notwithstanding the rejection of the larger plan, a number of *émigré* bishops promised in February 1797 to instruct the priests in their former sees to support the candidates designated by the king's agents.[3] The Midi was an area of such clerical campaigning. The abbés Bréluque and Lambert were busy at Besançon.[4] From Lyons Imbert-Colomès sought the aid of Marbeuf and the abbé Linsolas in support of the candidacy of Camille Jordan and that of his own.[5] At Vesoul and other towns in the department of the Haute-Saône the abbé Chaffoy gave freely of his time.[6] To his care was entrusted the printing of a number of pamphlets[7] at Fauche-Borel's printing establishment in Neuchâtel[8] and their distribution in Franche-Comté and Champagne. Another industrious priest was d'André's close friend, the abbé de Lacombe, to whom the bishop of Clermont, acting together with Précy and de Vezet, assigned the province of Dauphiny.[9] So numerous were the clerical and non-clerical agents in these areas that the abbé de la Marre insisted that more attention would have to be given to Paris and central France.[10] De la Marre himself was responsible for sending *émigré* priests into Franche-Comté to aid in the election campaign.[11] But the clerical campaign at Paris was weakened by the resistance of its former archbishop.[12]

However, if the archbishop of Paris refused to permit the priests of his former bishopric to take an active part in the

[1] C. Ledré, *Le Culte caché sous la Révolution. Les Missions de l'abbé Linsolas* (Paris, 1949), p. 247.

[2] La Vauguyon to d'Antraigues, 27 October 1796, A.A.E., France 609.

[3] Bishop of Clermont to la Vauguyon, 6 February 1797, A.A.E., France 590. The bishops named by Clermont numbered fourteen, including those of Paris, Chalons-sur-Saône, Poitiers, Embrun, St. Claude and Valence.

[4] De Vezet to Louis XVIII, 2 March 1797, ibid.

[5] Imbert-Colomès to d'Avaray, [?] March 1797; de Vezet to Louis XVIII, 15, 20 March 1797, ibid. Cf. Ledré, op. cit., p. 249.

[6] De Vezet to Louis XVIII, 15 March 1797, A.A.E., France 590.

[7] De Vezet to Louis XVIII, 27 March 1797, ibid.

[8] Fauche-Borel to d'Avaray, 13 April 1797, ibid.

[9] De Vezet to Louis XVIII, 20 February 1797; Précy to Louis XVIII, 16 March 1797, ibid.

[10] De Vezet to Louis XVIII, 6 April 1797, ibid.

[11] Desportes to Delacroix, 3 April 1797, A.N. F⁷6371.

[12] De Vezet to Louis XVIII, 2 March 1797, A.A.E., France 590.

elections, he joined the bishops of Clermont, Chalons-sur-Saône and other prelates in sending personal messages from Louis to their congregations.[1] Among these messages was Louis' important address of 10 March to his prospective subjects. Its tactful promise of clemency and moderation marked a retreat from the dogmatic and vengeful language of the Verona Declaration.[2] It appeared in the Parisian newspapers and was also distributed widely in pamphlet form.[3] In addition to the new proclamation, a number of pamphlets made their appearance. Some were the work of Fenouillot, the former *avocat* from Besançon, who had been involved in the negotiations with Pichegru.[4] De Vezet praised one of them, *Crime veille et vous dormez*, adding that Fenouillot was producing pamphlets at the rate of one a day;[5] one of them created a sensation at Besançon where the police issued a warrant for his arrest.[6]

IV

The proceedings in the Paris primary and electoral assemblies were dominated by the royalists and their friends. For example, the officers of the primary assembly in the Grenelle section were Trie, Quatremère de Quincy, the baron de Choiseul (a former ambassador at Turin), and the marquis de Seisseval.[7] According to Peltier, editor of an *émigré* paper in London, the presidents and secretaries of the primary assemblies were chosen from among the electors of the 1795 elections and were, in the main, lawyers, merchants and bankers.[8] The agents of the Directory confirmed this by reporting that the majority of the officials chosen to supervise the elections were the same men who had been prominent in 1795.[9] The electors named included Dufresne de Saint-Léon,

[1] De Vezet to Louis XVIII, 27 March, 10 April 1797, A.A.E., France 590.
[2] See Buchez and Roux, op. cit., 245–6.
[3] Wickham to Grenville, 12 April 1797, F.O. 74/20. On the whole Wickham was pleased with the moderate tone of the new declaration but he regretted its references to the activities of royalist agents.
[4] Fauche-Borel to d'Avaray, 24 March 1797, ibid. Montgaillard later disclosed to the Directory that Fenouillot had been 'hired by Wickham to distribute these vulgarly written sheets', A.N., AFIII44.
[5] De Vezet to Louis XVIII, 27 March 1797, A.A.E., France 590.
[6] Fauche-Borel to d'Avaray, 13 April 1797, ibid.
[7] Peltier, op. cit., xii. 438, 441.
[8] Ibid.
[9] Aulard, op. cit., iv. 18.

director of the Treasury under Necker; Chaumont de Lamillière, a former *intendant* of finances; the journalists, Lacretelle *jeune* and Suard; the abbé Sicard, the famous teacher of deaf and dumb children; Hennin, a former senior clerk in the foreign ministry; the brother of Barthélemy, the minister in Switzerland; Desmeuniers, a member of the Constituent Assembly; Devaynes, a former official in the ministry of finance; Boscheron and Popelin, who were lawyers; Fieffe, a notary; Desbonnières, a lawyer once in the service of Artois; Plantigny and Geoffroy de Chamois, former counsellors to the *Parlement* of Paris.[1] On this point, Mallet du Pan's observations are pertinent, for the social composition of the assemblies in most parts of the country seems to have been the same as in Paris: 'The reports of the proceedings of fifty-six primary assemblies in various departments reveal the presence of crowds of electors drawn from the nobility, the class of *chevaliers de Saint-Louis*, the former magistracy, and public officials who remained faithful to the monarchy.'[2] It was therefore not surprising that opinion in Paris was that the republicans had simply been overwhelmed.[3]

The results of the elections have been studied for the first time with the care they deserve by M. Suratteau.[4] What is most revealing is that of the 269 successful candidates, 228 were men who had never been members of a revolutionary assembly; the remainder had been deputies to the Constituent, Legislative, and local assemblies.[5] Indeed, in the Seine department several *feuillants* were defeated for being too moderate and insufficiently clerical in sentiment.[6] It may also be that the electors' preference for candidates who were innocent of previous association with the Revolution reflected a wish to bury the past and start anew. Moreover, the owners of national property, anxious to appear as '*honnêtes gens*'—as an integral part of the society of notables to which they aspired—were particularly attracted by the anti-Jacobin propaganda of the royalists and were perhaps even willing to accept a monarchy that promised to respect wealth, whatever its origin. The nature of the royalist campaign was precisely designed to

[1] Peltier, op. cit., xii. 507; *Quotidienne*, 28 March, 11 April 1797.
[2] *Correspondance de Mallet du Pan*, ii. 262, 5 April 1797.
[3] Aulard, op. cit., iv. 26, 28, 31, 33, 37.
[4] Suratteau, loc. cit.
[5] Ibid., 39–40.
[6] Ibid., 47.

attract this kind of support. It is beyond dispute that Wickham's fears of the consequences of the arrest and trial of Brottier and his colleagues were groundless, for the electors did not believe in the reality of the royalist conspiracy, while they did respond much more than the Directory had intended, to the seriousness of the Babeuf conspiracy.[1]

The massive blow which the Directory suffered and the extent of the royalist victory can also be gauged by glancing at some of the more important new deputies. It should first be noted that 63 of the 97 departments (including those in Belgium and Luxembourg) returned 182 deputies with counter-revolutionary tendencies.[2] Their accession to the *Conseils* converted a minority into the majority which the royalists had laboured to create. Symbolic of the electors' preferences was the almost total repudiation of the 216 Conventionals; only eleven were returned, and of these, five were anti-government: Boissy d'Anglas; Sallèles; Gumery; Pénières-Delzors; and Dabray. Such well-known men as Emmery, once president of the Constituent Assembly, and Quatremère de Quincy and Tarbe, members of the Legislative, were among the thirteen deputies from preceding assemblies who would be caught in the Directory's round-up of suspects after Fructidor. The newcomers to politics included intellectuals: Vauvilliers, the Hellenist scholar who had been implicated in the Brottier conspiracy; Marmontel, the academician, also involved in the same plot; Maine de Biran, who had a great reputation as a philosopher; and Royer-Collard, the future 'doctrinaire' of the Restoration assemblies. The notables of the *ancien régime* were doubtless pleased with the election of Claret de Fleurieu, navy minister for several months in 1790 and 1791; Desbonnières, who had been in Artois' service; and Bourlet, a former *intendant* in Artois. Even *émigrés*, on the active list, like Gigault-Crisenoy, or on the list under revision, like Grégoire-Derumare, won election. The army was well represented in the persons of general Willot, who had extended his protection to the White Terrorists in Marseilles; adjutant-general Normand, who turned to the Right after participating with Hoche in the pacification of the Vendée; MacKurtain de Kainlis, a *commissaire des guerres*; general Ferrand, whose involvement in the projected insurrection in the Doubs department in 1795 had earned him a short prison term;

[1] Suratteau, 54.　　　　[2] Ibid., 45.

and, of course, general Pichegru. Villaret-Joyeuse, spokesman for the wealthy West Indian planters, was the royalists' most conspicuous recruit from the navy. More astonishing was the election of such avowed rebels from the Chouan country as Pavie de l'Eure and Piet. Imbert-Colomès stood for election and was returned by the voters in the Rhône along with his fellow deputy, Camille Jordan, who had achieved notoriety as one of the leaders of the Lyons uprising in 1793. These are only a few of the more impressive names which were to adorn the debating halls of the Legislature.

The choice of the electorate was greeted enthusiastically by Wickham and Mallet du Pan, but for different reasons. The latter rejoiced that known republicans had been successful only in ten departments, while those elected in the rest of France were not royalists attached to the dogmas of the *ancien régime* but moderate constitutionalists. He hoped that 'the general idea of this new third will be to rebuild the monarchy stone by stone, even, if necessary, by means of the Constitution itself, and without running the danger of setting off revolutionary violence'.[1] Wickham's analysis of the results differed only slightly from that of the famous *émigré*. Attributing success to d'André's skilful manipulation of the competing groups of royalists, the work of the *Institut*, and the propaganda of the press, he was pleased that such moderates as Talleyrand, Montesquiou, Roederer, Garat and Desmeuniers had been rejected.[2] Mallet, too, regarded the defeat of the *fayettistes*, as he termed the followers of Dumas, Dumolard and Pastoret, with favour. But while Wickham saw the results as a repudiation of the framers of the Constitution of 1791, Mallet thought of them as an endorsation of the more conservative constitutionalists. The observations of the two men were not really irreconcilable; while Wickham was pleased by the rejection of those constitutionalists whom he believed to be notoriously anti-British,[3] Mallet's analysis was governed by his belief that even the royalists had discarded their ancient prejudices and had not, on the whole, supported the most notorious counter-revolutionaries.

[1] *Correspondance de Mallet du Pan*, ii. 265, 19 April 1797.
[2] Wickham to Grenville, 20 May 1797, F.O. 74/20.
[3] But C. Ballot (*Les Négociations de Lille* (Paris, 1910), p. 110) places the unsuccessful candidates whom Wickham names above in the pro-British, pro-peace camp.

If the results were agreeable to the royalists, they were most disconcerting to the Directory. Reubell proposed the annulment of the election and the proclamation of a new one for 20 May under *proper* supervision. This time all the *émigrés* and refractory priests would be prevented from voting and a strict censorship of the press imposed.[1] These suggestions were opposed vehemently by Carnot and Le Tourneur, who won over the wavering La Revellière at a meeting of the Directory on 4 April.[2] Somehow the *Quotidienne* got wind of the altercations and published them with the obvious purpose of stressing the divisions within the Directory.[3] Carnot's views were those of a moderate republican converted to the idea of legislative supremacy.[4] For the moment, he, Le Tourneur and, to a lesser extent, La Revellière, were the Directors believed by the royalists to be most sympathetic to their cause. But there was still an undercurrent of apprehension in the capital: reports that the Directory was planning a show of force in the working-class faubourg of Saint-Antoine circulated a few days after the Directory's stormy session.[5] Wickham's fears that violence would erupt vanished after he received obviously genuine news that the Directory's decision not to employ force 'was the result of much debate and difference'.[6]

The elections, the second held under the terms of the Constitution of the year III, continued the shift to the Right registered by the 1795 elections. This was due, as we have seen, to the impact of counter-revolutionary propaganda. That there were other reasons for the rout of the Directory is also evident; it would be an oversight to ignore the basic longing for peace, the run-away inflationary pressures, the general political instability, the disillusionment with a government that appeared to lack cohesion and purpose. In short, the revolutionary *élan* that had attracted loyalty and sacrifice had disappeared, leaving in its wake a desire for stability, a longing that the royalists and their allies exploited in their appeals to the electorate. They had assessed the groundswell of opinion against the Directory correctly.

Success was apparent to Wickham even before the final results

---

[1] R. Guyot, *Documents biographiques sur J. F. Reubell, membre du Directoire exécutif* (Paris, 1911), p. 118. Cf. G. D. Homan, 'Jean-François Reubell', *French Historical Studies*, i. (1960), 426.

[2] La Revellière-Lépeaux, *Mémoires*, i. 380. [3] *Quotidienne*, 8 April 1797.
[4] Reinhard, *Le Grand Carnot*, ii. 228–9. [5] *Quotidienne*, 9 April 1797.
[6] Wickham to Grenville, 12, 15 April 1797, F.O. 74/20.

were known. His praise of d'André's plan was unlimited: '. . . This is the only plan I have seen that had as its basis at the same time, the real situation of affairs both at home and abroad and that was conformable to the general spirit and opinions of the people.'[1] He predicted that the months ahead held the key to the future, either in the form of '*Royalty* or a military *Tyranny* fairly established'.[2] How could the former eventuality be assured? Wickham was certain that the greatest source of danger to a restoration was the pure royalist party itself. There was no escaping the fact 'that the Monarchy was entirely and exclusively in the hands of the Third Estate'.[3] It was to that Estate, Wickham declared, 'that the King ought to address himself with confidence . . . for the true interests of the King himself as well as those of the Nobility (I might add also those of Europe) [are] much safer in their hands than in those of the ancient court, or of the old nobility of France exclusively'.[4] This had always been his view, Wickham wrote in oracular fashion to Grenville, but how was it possible to penetrate the twisted thinking of the men around Louis, none of whom appreciated 'the secret springs and causes by which the Revolution had been brought about and supported or . . . any clear notion of a popular assembly or a mixed government?'[5] Their blindness to the demands of conditions worried Wickham. The monarchy could be restored, but only if Louis and his court finally became aware of the great fears their encouragement of conspiratorial means inspired among their potential and actual partisans among the deputies. Would Louis come to his senses and allow his real friends in Paris to prepare the way for his return? Or would he revive his attempts to direct affairs through his agents in France, thereby provoking old suspicions of collusion between the monarchists in France and the *émigrés* and between the *émigrés* and the foreign invaders? If so, the Directory would, Wickham implied, reap the rewards.

[1] Wickham to Grenville, 1 April 1797, no. 1. ibid.
[2] Ibid.
[3] Wickham to Grenville, 15 April 1797, ibid.
[4] Ibid.
[5] Wickham to Grenville, 12 April 1797, ibid.

9

AN EXERCISE IN FUTILITY

THE arrest of the agents virtually marked the eclipse of the agency's activities in Paris. The repercussions of the disaster were felt at Blankenburg, London and Berne. In Blankenburg Louis and his advisers, puzzled and dismayed, tried to save the situation by issuing new orders to make the agency a more responsible body. In London Dutheil attempted to convince Grenville that the exposure of the agency would not paralyse royalist objectives in Paris and that financial support should therefore be continued. In Berne Wickham was, on the whole, relieved that the agency which he had long considered to be obstructive was now out of the way. And in Paris the agents who had escaped the Directory's net became involved in a series of stale and sterile struggles arising from the question of 'succession'.

Feeling certain of acquittal, and unwilling to relinquish his control over the members of the agency who had avoided arrest, Brottier managed to consult with his fellow-prisoners and decided to entrust its affairs to three men.[1] They were Sourdat who had been assisting la Villeurnoy in his work,[2] Bachet, a newcomer, and the abbé d'Esgrigny who, at the time of the arrest, was working for Rochecotte in the Le Mans region.[3] It was to the latter that Brottier turned to take over the agency's affairs pending d'Esgrigny's arrival in the capital. Rochecotte's intimate connections with the prisoners and his organization of the military cadres to the west of Paris made him the logical choice.[4] As interim director, his primary concern was to ensure the continued

---

[1] Brottier's précis, 15 July 1797, A.A.E., France 611.

[2] D'Antraigues to la Vauguyon, 22 February 1797, A.A.E., France 610.

[3] See Beauchamp, op. cit., pp. 86, 177. Before the Revolution, d'Esgrigny was *commandataire* of the abbey of Daudeauville in the Boulonnais. When the old regime fell, he sought refuge in London and gained from the bishop of Arras the honorific title of vicar general. In 1795, while on a mission in France for the bishop, he was taken prisoner. In the following year he found a protector in the person of La Revellière-Lépeaux's sister who lived in Angers. See Sangnier, op. cit., pp. 95–6.

[4] Rochecotte to Dutheil, rec'd 1 March 1797, A.A.E., France 626 and F.O. 27/51.

flow of British funds; and for this purpose he quickly dispatched to London François and the vicomtesse d'Esson, his mistress who had nursed the wounds he had sustained in a skirmish with republican troops in 1796.[1] The carefully disguised emissaries reached London towards the end of February; François went on to Edinburgh to confer with Artois, while Madame d'Esson remained in the capital as a guest of Dutheil.

Dutheil tried to assure Grenville that the agency's activities had not been disrupted.[2] Grenville was not convinced. Before the arrest, he had entertained cautious hopes about the agency's project. The *Institut philanthropique*, with its stress on a legal and non-violent approach, would, he had thought, be a most effective vehicle to promote royalist propaganda in the election campaign. He had been prepared to overlook the past record of the agents in the knowledge that they would be closely supervised by Wickham, and he had been confident that a resounding electoral success would intensify the crisis and lead to the fall of the Directory. He was consequently deeply disappointed when he learned of the arrest, and his first impulse was to inform Dutheil that the ministry could no longer be bound by its financial promises.[3] There was an additional reason for Grenville's refusal to meet the demands of the agency. The financial position of the British government was perilous. Even when the Cabinet had first agreed to increase the flow of funds to the agency in January, Grenville had noted that 'our financial resources [are] not . . . unlimited or inexhaustible as at first sight would appear to be'.[4]

By the time François returned to London on 21 March, with a request to allow Artois to join Frotté's army in Normandy after the elections,[5] Britain's finances had further deteriorated; so had the fighting front; the rapid advances of Moreau and Hoche in Germany and Bonaparte in Italy had swept over the Austrian armies and left them in a complete state of confusion. Everything pointed to Austria's imminent withdrawal from the war with the likelihood that Britain would have no choice but to sue for peace. These factors set the mood for Grenville's meeting with Dutheil at the end of March; he was impatient with Dutheil's

[1] Beauchamp, op. cit., pp. 92, 98–9.
[2] Dutheil to Grenville, 1 March 1797, F.O. 27/51.
[3] Minute of Grenville, 30 March 1797, *Dropmore Papers*, iii. 305.
[4] Grenville to Windham, 5 February 1797, Add. MSS., 37846.
[5] Dutheil to Grenville, 22 March 1797, F.O. 27/51.

apologia[1] for the agents, but agreed to await the results of the elections before withdrawing funds from the agency.[2]

Dutheil had taken great pains to assure Grenville that the outcome of the elections would in no way be compromised by the arrest. His prediction was justified, but his roseate picture of a flourishing agency was not. He was not really aware of the chaotic state into which the agency had degenerated. Brottier's decision to entrust matters chiefly to d'Esgrigny and Rochecotte immediately encountered the opposition of Despomelles, who complained to Louis that, but for his efforts, the agency would not have been founded.[3] Similar complaints, alleging that Rochecotte's appointment had been pre-dated to give him priority, reached Wickham at the same time.[4] Meanwhile Sourdat, alienated by Brottier's complete disregard of his advice, supported Despomelles' claims. In a long memorandum addressed to the king in the middle of March, he assailed Brottier's arbitrary delegation of powers, and hinted that Brottier might even be in league with the Directory. He believed, moreover, that while he could not know the trustworthiness of d'Esgrigny and Rochecotte, there was no reason to suspect Despomelles. The king was also reminded that Despomelles' *Institut* had been accepted as the basis of all royalist plans and should, because of the urgency of the elections, remain the focal point of the counter-revolution. The implication was that the agency would suffer only minor dislocations if Sourdat and Despomelles were permitted to direct it; to entrust it to a newcomer would endanger the *Institut*.[5]

Sourdat then went on to suggest a new plan, namely to sound the opinions and sentiments of the Directory. He notified Louis that the constitutionalists were exerting all their efforts to discredit the agency for the purpose of creating a situation in which the king would owe his throne to them. To avoid this he asked Louis to grant him powers to negotiate with the Directory and authority to recruit new members for the agency. He put forward

[1] Dutheil to d'Avaray, 31 March 1797, A.A.E., France 611.

[2] Minute of Grenville, 30 March 1797, *Dropmore Papers*, iii. 305–6. See also Grenville to Buckingham, 20 March 1797. 'What the result [of the election] will be, I believe nobody knows, and it is therefore in vain to guess.' *Memoirs of the Court and Cabinets*, ii. 367.

[3] D'Antraigues to la Vauguyon, 8 March 1797, A.A.E., France 610.

[4] Unsigned and undated letter in Wickham's despatch to Grenville, 8 March 1797, F.O. 74/20.

[5] Sourdat to Louis XVIII, [14?] March 1797, A.A.E., France 590.

his own name and those of Despomelles; de Ramath, a former member of the *Parlement* of Aix; Desportes, a former *maître des requêtes*; Doucé, a former *conseiller au Parlement*; and de Grosbois, first president of the *Parlement* of Besançon. As it was impossible to keep out d'Esgrigny and Bachet, they were also included; but a request was made for a new director—a person whose prestige and military rank would serve to give the agency unity.[1]

The king had already taken his own measures. He had empowered La Trémouille to solicit funds from the British government for the reconstruction of the agency. La Trémouille lost no time in making his way to London where he conferred with Dutheil.[2] The future of the royalist cause rested with the British government, but Grenville had been most unreceptive at the end of March. What was to be done? Dutheil asked the bishop of St. Pol to seek the intervention of the marquis of Buckingham, Grenville's brother.[3] He then made his own request to Grenville but received no answer. Grenville agreed with Wickham[4] that Britain's future interests would best be served by resisting the agents' appeal for funds other than for the purpose of maintaining their correspondence and procuring intelligence.[5] However, he could not put off an interview with Dutheil and la Trémouille, and on 28 April he agreed to see the former. Dutheil was in a buoyant mood; he apparently believed that the ministry was prepared to grant la Trémouille fifty thousand louis a month![6] Dutheil's ingenuousness grew out of the myth current among Britain's friends and enemies alike that the British Treasury was bottomless. His naïveté was somewhat punctured by Grenville's refusal to commit the ministry to such a sum.[7] But he did impress Grenville with the fact that the election results had exceeded all expectations; indeed the royalists had not overestimated the latent support for the king in the country. He could not possibly conceive that the ministry would forsake them just when success appeared certain. La Trémouille, who saw Grenville the next

[1] Ibid.

[2] Dutheil to Grenville, 16 April 1797, A.A.E., France 626 and F.O. 27/51.

[3] Buckingham to Grenville, 13 April 1797, *Dropmore Papers*, iii. 313. Cf. Grenville to Buckingham, 28 April 1797, *Memoirs of the Court and Cabinets*, ii. 376.

[4] Dutheil to d'Avaray, 18 April 1797, A.A.E., France 611; Wickham to Grenville, 8 March 1797, F.O. 74/20.

[5] Grenville to Wickham, 18 April 1797, ibid.

[6] Dutheil to d'Avaray, 28 April 1797, no. 1, A.A.E., France 611.   [7] Ibid.

day, embellished Dutheil's account, but had to be content with a promise that the ministry's position was subject to revision.[1]

The motives behind Grenville's attitude were twofold. In the first place, he had all the time agreed with Wickham that the agency's impulsiveness had lost it all claim on the government's confidence.[2] He also saw no reason to pour money out on a scheme which would only duplicate Wickham's own plans. The victory of the royalists at the elections not only confirmed his faith in Wickham, but also proved that a great deal could be accomplished without having to rely on the agency. This had been Wickham's belief since the late summer of 1796 and it had borne its first fruits. Grenville now looked forward to the time when Wickham's direction of d'André's efforts would achieve an even more startling metamorphosis of French politics.[3] British funds were heavily invested in this project and given the deplorable state of British finances, Grenville hesitated to ask the Treasury to bear the strains of a further demand.

II

Louis and his ministers arrogantly ascribed the success of the elections to their own agents and dismissed as inconsequential the influence of Wickham's liberal use of funds and d'André's organizing abilities. They therefore saw no reason to postpone the setting up of a Council in Paris along the lines suggested by Sourdat. Obviously they did not doubt that London would grant the necessary funds. What they had in mind was a most elaborate affair; they intended to make the Council even more important than the defunct agency. It is even evident that they wanted it to function openly!

The important functions which your Majesty will attribute to this Council and the recent troublesome incident [the discovery of the

[1] Dutheil to d'Avaray, 28 April 1797, no. 1, A.A.E., France 611.
[2] Wickham to Grenville, 8 March 1797; Grenville to Wickham, 18 April 1797, F.O. 74/20.
[3] Grenville to Wickham, 5 August 1797. Though written in August, this despatch reveals that Grenville had supported Wickham's and d'André's plans since the spring: 'The moment that all idea of acting on the frontier or in the interior by force . . . was abandoned, I of course had to inform you of it. But the reasons for that resolution do not apply to operations in which d'André is concerned and which seems more likely to be more useful than the other plans have been.' *Correspondence of William Wickham*, ii. 44.

agency] make the adoption of this title [Council] indispensable. The designation of agency recalls to Frenchmen that truly appalling period of the revolutionary government which various agencies, infinite in number, have served and supported so well.[1]

Wickham aptly described their plan as ludicrous and was unable to resist adding: '[It is] just as if Paris and France were in a state of peace and the King really on his throne.'[2]

The Council was to be controlled by seven deliberating members. Its chief official, the president, would carry on all correspondence with the king, Artois and Condé, and transmit their orders to the other members and to the king's 'military commanders'. These duties were to be la Trémouille's. As a check against the president, Sourdat was to be authorized, as secretary, to scrutinize all his decisions. As the military expert, Despomelles was to be given the responsibility of organizing military commands, selecting their commanders, purchasing arms and, if necessary, promoting military sedition. Correspondence with the military commanders was to be the main duty of a fourth member,[3] who would also direct royalist propaganda, dispatch pamphlets and journals to all parts of France and increase the Council's financial resources by soliciting funds from supporters of the monarchy. The reconstruction of the *Parlements* and other pre-revolutionary organs of justice were to be put into the hands of a fifth man, and the re-organization of provincial and municipal administrative bodies was made the responsibility of a sixth member. The last officer of the Council was its treasurer. Each of the members was to have a second who would be able to assume the duties of his partner if any emergency arose. However, only the seven senior members were given deliberating powers. The Council was to be aided in its operations by eight military officers, four having the rank of colonel, whose main concern would be to give regular personal accounts to the king and Artois, and the other four, having the rank of lieutenant, would serve as liaison officers between the various military commands.

Plans were also made to extend the activities of the Council. Priority was given to the dissemination of propaganda favouring

---

[1] Conseil du Roi à établir à Paris, no date, A.A.E., France 617.

[2] Wickham to Grenville, 24 May 1797, F.O. 74/20.

[3] This section in the plan was obviously based on Rochecotte's experience in establishing military commands as part of the *Institut* scheme. See above, pp. 103, 109.

the monarchy, in which the tolerance, moderation, wisdom and clemency of the king were to be stressed. Secondly, the Council was instructed to assure the officers of the republican armies full recognition of their rank and service if they joined the cause. The same promise was to be given to conscripts who deserted. Thirdly to those whom the Revolution had widowed and orphaned assurances of the king's generosity were given; and to all public functionaries who had not shared in the worst excesses of the Revolution as well as to 'misguided Frenchmen' was promised the king's pardon. Finally, the Council was directed to make overtures to members of the *Corps législatif*, to the ministers, and to the Directors.

On the surface, the plan seemed logical and appeared to take into account any exigency. However, it possessed several defects. It would inevitably run into difficulties, because Louis and his advisers intended to deny Wickham his proper rôle in the Council. Insistence on constant consultation with Blankenburg was bound to sacrifice initiative; failure to make provisions for the *Institut* was either the result of a gross inability to assess its value or a transparent proof that Louis was dissatisfied with its emphasis on the parliamentary approach to the counter-revolution; stress on the military side of royalist activity did not conform to the wishes of the majority of Louis' supporters in the *Conseils*; and the revival of many administrative anomalies which the Revolution had swept away was another demonstration of gross ignorance of the hard facts of politics.

Louis and his ministers sent their plan to Paris in the care of Mesières; the abbé de la Marre was to follow to help organize the new Council, but his departure for Paris was delayed until late in May. In the interval Wickham convinced him that the Council would hinder rather than promote the work of the royalists in Paris.[1] Just then Bayard returned from Paris with a plea from d'André to the king to set aside his plans and to put his trust in the *Institut* and the arrangements made with the deputies.[2] Précy's powers of persuasion were even greater.[3] Their combined pressure was overwhelming. Louis admitted his failure to give due weight to reports from Paris, and told de la Marre to

---

[1] Fauche-Borel to d'Avaray, 11 May 1797, A.A.E., France 591.
[2] Wickham to Grenville, 24 May 1797, F.O. 74/20.
[3] Précy to Louis XVIII, 31 April 1797, A.A.E., France 590.

delay the organization of the Council until he received new instructions.[1]

Meanwhile, notwithstanding Grenville's denial of funds to the agency, la Trémouille remained in London, hoping to persuade him to reconsider his decision. The cause of the royalists seemed to be slipping away, overwhelmed by events in England, Ireland and on the continent. The mutiny of the fleet in various ports alarmed the government and accentuated the fears of a French invasion. Ireland, seething with the hatred of suppressed revolutionaries, demanded the almost undivided attention of the ministry. Austria had already withdrawn from the conflict and made the pressure for a general peace practically irresistible. Britain was rent within and on the brink of economic breakdown. Peace appeared to be the only solution but the ministry was divided on this question. Grenville and Windham were in the small and isolated war party against Pitt and the other members of the Cabinet.[2] La Trémouille and Dutheil were not oblivious of these facts. The former deplored his absence from Paris but was determined to employ 'extreme measures to meet the contingencies which the advent of peace would create'.[3] The latter was hopeful that the 'present situation in England [would] not stand in the way of the ministry making good any of the hopes that it had given us'.[4]

The complete disarray of the agency added to the uncertainty. François wrote that d'Esgrigny was incapable and that he and Rochecotte did nothing but slander their predecessors.[5] Apparently they had become Brottier's bitter enemies, thus detonating a new series of altercations.[6] The only way to restore order, Dutheil felt, would be to repudiate the imprisoned agents.[7] Then Duverne inopportunely informed Grenville, in a letter which he managed to send from prison, of the sorry state of the agency's affairs. This neglect of elementary precautions completely exasperated Dutheil who had taken extraordinary pains to conceal

[1] Wickham to Grenville, 24 May, 30 June 1797, F.O. 74/20.
[2] Grenville to Buckingham, 5 May 1797, *Memoirs of the Court and Cabinets*, ii. 377–8; Cf. Grenville to George III, 16 June 1797, *Dropmore Papers*, iii. 329–30. See also *Diary of William Windham*, p. 355.
[3] La Trémouille to Louis XVIII, 12 May 1797, A.A.E., France 591.
[4] Dutheil to d'Avaray, 19 May 1797, A.A.E., France 611.
[5] François to Dutheil, 25 April 1797, ibid.
[6] François to Dutheil, 2 May 1797, ibid.
[7] Dutheil to d'Avaray, 12 May 1797, ibid.

the true state of the agency's circumstances from the ministry.[1] It was an essential feature of his negotiations with Grenville to say nothing which would arouse the latter's suspicions. To admit the weakness of the agency would be fatal. Thus, in his efforts to gain a second hearing from Grenville, he sent him information from Frotté about the opportunities to improve the military position in Normandy.[2] And to prove that the agency still had links with the public offices in Paris he presented the Foreign Office with authentic intelligence of the Directory's Irish agents,[3] its plans for another invasion of Ireland and its colonial projects in Spanish and Portuguese America.[4] He then informed Grenville that la Trémouille could not defer his departure for Paris any longer,[5] and once again sought Buckingham's intervention with Grenville.[6] He and la Trémouille were finally granted interviews on 2 and 3 June. Grenville was distraught over the gravity of the situation in Ireland and intimated that his government was contemplating making overtures for peace.[7] The agency could count on £1,000 to defray the expenses of its correspondence with London, but no more would be forthcoming once peace negotiations were underway.[8] Dutheil and la Trémouille were dejected but succeeded in having the sum increased to 10,000 louis.[9]

The prospect of peace nevertheless meant the end of the counter-revolution. There was nothing for it but to exploit every opportunity to wreck the peace talks. Before la Trémouille left for France, he agreed with Dutheil that he would use his influence in the *Conseils* against the formulation of conditions which would be acceptable to Britain.[10] Their understanding of the situation was seriously distorted for the majority in the *Conseils* was clamouring for peace.

[1] Dutheil to d'Avaray, 23 May 1797, F.O. 74/20.
[2] Frotté to Dutheil, 28 April 1797, F.O. 27/51.
[3] Note sent to Dutheil, 18 May 1797, F.O. 27/51 and A.A.E., France 626.
[4] Dutheil to Grenville, 22 May 1797, F.O. 27/51. Cf. Dutheil to d'Avaray, 23 May 1797, A.A.E., France 611. The reports included one drawn up by Carnot on 27 January 1797 and another drafted by Truguet on 26 December 1796.
[5] Ibid.   [6] Dutheil to d'Avaray, 12 May 1797, ibid.
[7] Grenville to George III, 31 May 1797, *Dropmore Papers*, iii. 327. The note asking the Directory to consider the desirability of peace negotiations had already been drafted.
[8] Dutheil to d'Avaray, 2 June (2 notes), 3 June 1797, A.A.E., France 611.
[9] Dutheil to d'Avaray, 9 June 1797, ibid.
[10] Dutheil to d'Avaray, 20, 21 June 1797, ibid.

La Trémouille's long absence from Paris at so critical a time was unfortunate for the agency. There were, when he arrived, three factions among its survivors. The first and most disconcerting found its headquarters in the Temple, behind whose walls Brottier took infinite pains to retain his control over his former subalterns. The second comprised Rochecotte and d'Esgrigny who wished to free themselves from Brottier's annoying interference. The leader of the third faction was Despomelles who was on friendly terms with Wickham and secure in his attachment to d'André. La Trémouille's only course was to assert his authority, repudiate Brottier and Duverne, and re-establish the Council. Theoretically he could do so, but he realized that he would have to wait until Blankenburg sent new indications of its faith in him.

In granting the agency further funds Grenville did not intend that it should extend its operations; he merely wanted to ensure its survival long enough to procure intelligence. But Dutheil still had most of the £20,000 which he had received as the first instalment of the total sum promised to Duverne.[1] It was therefore possible to establish the new Council on a solid footing. He had no inkling of the efforts to disband it. On the contrary, his reports led him to assume that it was already functioning and only awaiting la Trémouille's return.[2] Because of the time lag between Blankenburg and London, he could not know that Louis had already agreed to suspend it. When, however, Louis learned that London had granted la Trémouille additional funds, he assumed that Grenville approved of the Council, renewed the plans to establish it, and accused Wickham of pursuing a policy contrary to the wishes of his own government.[3]

This time its destinies were to be entrusted to five key agents: Despomelles, who would concern himself exclusively with the *Institut*; Sourdat with the internal affairs of the Council; Bayard with the securing of intelligence; and la Trémouille with its overall plans. Even d'André, who was to devote his time to improving his contacts with the *Conseils*, was included. In addition a subsidiary agency was to be set up in Switzerland comprising de Vezet, Précy and de la Marre to serve as a connecting

---

[1] Dutheil to d'Avaray, 2 June 1797, no. 2, ibid.
[2] Dutheil to d'Avaray, 9, 16 June 1797, ibid.
[3] Saint-Priest to Wickham, 15 July 1797, F.O. 74/21.

link between Paris and Blankenburg.[1] The new plan seemed an improvement over the old as it recognized the work of the *Institut* and found a place for d'André. But it was designed to achieve the same purpose. It is clear that Louis intended to direct the Council, make d'André subordinate to it, and force Wickham to adjust himself to it. Not only was the plan an implicit criticism of Wickham's policy, but it also threatened to undo d'André's work. There was no hesitation in de Vezet's approval of Louis' reversal of policy. He had been one of Wickham's and d'André's staunchest opponents, and had even suggested that the king undertake a direct correspondence with Pichegru.[2] Louis accepted the suggestion and entrusted de Vezet with the task.[3] At the same time he asked Fauche-Borel to continue his attempts to resume his contacts with the wary general.[4] But Pichegru refused to respond to the new advances. So Fauche-Borel resolved to appeal to him personally;[5] Wickham took steps to prevent his departure,[6] but in August the crafty agent succeeded in crossing the frontier.

Pichegru was not the only important royalist whom the ministers at Blankenburg wished to subject to their control. They sent Folnais, who had been so useful in the elections, to Paris to ascertain whether a number of deputies would be willing to correspond with the king. His encounters with a few of the deputies, even those most loyal to Louis, were most discouraging. Apart from receiving promises of continued devotion from Job-Aimé and Imbert-Colomès,[7] most of them insisted on an instant declaration of royal pardon and clemency.[8] Despite Folnais' accurate reports, de Vezet, who never questioned the tact or timing of Blankenburg's decisions, was determined to improve the existing channels of communication between some of the deputies and himself.[9] Among Louis' devoted agents only Précy saw the implications of his insistence on renewing the question of the Council. His intervention in May had been

[1] Saint-Priest to Wickham, 15 July 1797, F.O. 74/21.
[2] De Vezet to d'Avaray, 1 May 1797, A.A.E., France, 591.
[3] De Vezet to Louis XVIII, 7 May 1797, ibid.
[4] Fauche-Boral to d'Avaray, 11 May 1797, ibid.
[5] Fauche-Borel to d'Avaray, 1 June 1797, ibid.
[6] Fauche-Borel to d'Avaray, 11 July 1797, ibid.
[7] Précy to Louis XVIII, 3 July 1797, ibid.
[8] De Vezet to d'Avaray, 10 July 1797, ibid.
[9] Ibid.

decisive in dissuading the king from pursuing his plan to create it. Once again he tried to use his influence to abandon it for good. He claimed that de Vezet's attempts to force the deputies to seek authority directly from the king would undermine d'André's position,[1] and that further concessions to the constitutionalists would strengthen, not weaken royalist sentiment.[2] But he could not openly oppose the king's decision; reluctantly he gave his word to help de Vezet establish the intermediary agency in Switzerland. But while the latter was enthusiastic,[3] the former continued to insist that the Council in Paris would estrange the deputies, citing as proof the deputies' refusal to confide in la Trémouille.[4]

To avoid a rupture with Louis and his ministers, Wickham asked d'André to reach an understanding with la Trémouille and the other agents in Paris,[5] but he refused to sanction the establishment of the Council. He was willing to consider la Trémouille's offer to work within the larger framework of d'André's plan, but he was not prepared to sacrifice his long-term policy to the contorted intrigues of diehard royalists.[6] Because of this, the creation of the Council was only a remote possibility. D'André was afraid of alienating the moderates; Despomelles' *Institut* depended on British money for its life. In the end, as we shall see, d'André, Pichegru and a few of the other royalists were happy to receive la Trémouille's aid. But by then it was too late.

[1] Précy to Louis XVIII, 3 July 1797, ibid.
[2] Précy to d'Avaray, 12 July, 25 August 1797, ibid.
[3] De Vezet to Louis XVIII, 9 August 1797, ibid.
[4] Précy to d'Avaray, 23 August 1797, ibid.
[5] Wickham to Grenville, 27 August 1797, no. 2, F.O. 74/21.
[6] Précy to d'Avaray, 2 September 1797, A.A.E., France 592.

10

CONSTITUTIONAL PROCESSES
DOOMED

THE submergence of the Directory's partisans at the elections exhilarated Wickham and d'André; their estimate of conditions in France had been sound. Yet instead of easing their minds the results ironically created new tensions. The uneasy coalition of the shifting group of constitutionalists—Dumas' Committee taking the lead—and the pure royalists, began to disintegrate immediately after the elections. The electors' preference for the more pronounced royalists heightened the sense of insecurity felt by the constitutionalists; as a result, many of them thought it politic to throw their weight behind the Directory. Wickham could not but deplore this turn of events and, to increase his worries, the Paris agency was threatening to undo the work of the *Institut*. More than that. The prospect of the agency's revival was certain to alienate the deputies. To arrest the divisions among the right-wing deputies and to keep a firm control over the agency's affairs were the immediate concerns of Wickham and d'André.

Although it is not possible to determine the exact membership of the Dumas or Directorial Committee (so dubbed by Wickham), we do know that it included some of the best known deputies in the Legislature: Portalis, Siméon, Cadroi, Dumolard, Gilbert-Desmolières, and Duplantier. Their colleagues, Barbé-Marbois, Lebrun and Emmery were probably not unsympathetic, and, as we saw, Lemerer, Larivière, Thibaudeau, Durand de Maillane, and Mersan were also connected with the group. Moreover, such deputies as Tronson Ducoudray, Pastoret, Vaublanc, and Boissy d'Anglas were associated with these men.[1] And there were undoubtedly a large number of royalists of all shades of opinion who attended the meetings at Clichy which the Dumas group dominated. To Dumas and his colleagues it appeared that the government was in danger of being challenged and overthrown by the more extreme royalists. That danger was intensified by

[1] Barras, *Memoirs*, ii. 606.

the torrent of royalist propaganda let loose during the election campaign. Who knew but that the Directory would use this pretext to apply coercive measures against the *Conseils*, and end forever all hope of tempering the regime? Remote or not, this contingency drove Dumas and his faction to resume a tacit alliance with the Directory: according to Bayard and d'André, Dumas was actually very close to Carnot. In exchange for the Directory's promises to remove the vestiges of revolutionary legislation, the Directorial Committee was prepared to win support for it in the *Conseils* and in the press.[1]

At best the terms of the entente were tenuous. The Directorial Committee demanded the Directory's promise to live by the provisions of the Constitution; to repeal all the revolutionary laws, particularly the Law of 3 Brumaire;[2] to dismiss at least two of the following ministers: Truguet (minister of the marine), Merlin de Douai (minister of justice), and Delacroix (minister of foreign affairs); to favour its candidates for important government and military posts; and to arrange the release of Lafayette and his fellow prisoners. Dumas was said to have put forward these demands to Carnot, who had pledged his support in return for aid against the more determined royalists. It was Wickham's feeling that Carnot had no intention of honouring his promise, and that the unity of Dumas' party was more apparent than real. Though he was not averse to this tactical *rapprochement* with the Directory—he agreed with d'André that the unity of the Directors could not be easily broken—he gloomily predicted that they would betray the Dumas Committee.[3] D'André, to be sure, would have preferred a war of attrition but claimed that the newly elected deputies were not psychologically prepared.[4]

Not that d'André made no attempt to encourage a policy of direct opposition. He approached a great many of the new

[1] Wickham to Grenville, 20 May 1797, F.O. 74/20.

[2] The law of 3 Brumaire an IV (25 October 1795), passed during the dying hours of the Convention, forbade all those implicated in the agitation of Vendémiaire from exercising legislative, municipal and judicial functions. Included in this proscription were *émigrés* whose names were still on the lists, and their relatives. The law required that all persons included in these categories leave France. Finally, the laws of 1792 and 1793 which were directed against the non-juring clergy, stipulated deportation or imprisonment as the maximum penalties, and were to be rigidly enforced.

[3] D'André to Wickham, beginning of May 1797; Wickham to Grenville, 25 May 1797, F.O. 74/20.

[4] D'André to Wickham, [?] October 1797, F.O. 27/52.

deputies who were arriving to take up their seats in the *Conseils*. Instead of firmness and courage he discovered lethargy and weakness, but mainly fear—fear that the Directory's military advances would consolidate its power in France and in Europe.[1] The deputies were equally certain that it would not hesitate to call upon the Jacobins for aid if the right-wing attacks against its authority gained in momentum.[2] Wickham was scornful of them, contrasting their mediocrity with the statesmanship displayed by Mirabeau and d'André in the Constituent Assembly.[3] And d'André regretted his own defeat in the elections, suggesting that membership in the Legislature might have increased his influence: 'Perhaps I would have been able to persuade them to act more decisively,' he wrote after Fructidor.[4]

So it was that d'André was forced to adjust his goals to the deputies' temporizing policy in the belief that its dangers would become obvious with time. For the moment, he and his closest confidants intended to promote British aims in the forthcoming peace negotiations so long as French interests were not compromised. Their second objective, not essentially dissimilar to the cardinal point of the Dumas plan, was the repeal of revolutionary legislation. It was their conviction that the simultaneous agitation for peace and the elimination of the revolutionary aspects of the regime would ensure the peaceful revival of the monarchy. To bring to bear the weight of public opinion upon the Directory d'André advised an intensification of royalist propaganda; and for this purpose founded a new journal, the *Mémorial*, to which Mallet du Pan, La Harpe, the abbé Fontanes and Richer-Sérisy promised to contribute, and for which Wickham was prepared to contribute[5] at least £10,000 a month.[6]

---

[1] Wickham to Grenville, 24 May 1797, F.O. 74/20.

[2] D'André to Wickham, 29 July 1797, ibid.

[3] Wickham to Grenville, 27 June 1797, ibid.

[4] D'André to Wickham, [?] October 1797, F.O. 27/52. The duc de Castries mistakenly assumes that d'André was a member of the lower chamber. See volume iii of his *Le Testament de la monarchie* (Paris, 1958–62), 218.

[5] Wickham to Grenville, 25 May 1797, F.O. 74/20. Later, Wickham revealed d'André's disappointment with the editors of the *Mémorial*: 'D'André had at first undertaken the direction of the *Mémorial* but his associates being men of letters were soon found to be quite unmanageable.' Wickham to Grenville, 27 August 1797, F.O. 74/21.

[6] Wickham to Grenville, 24 May 1797, F.O. 74/20. Wickham also promised to provide an emergency reserve fund of £50,000.

There was a great deal of activity in the *Conseils* even before the new session of the Legislature opened. In the first flush of enthusiasm after the elections, a number of proposals, indicating a further move to the Right, were made. On 24 April an undisguised attack on the events leading to the 10th August was made by the Girondin, Dusaulx[1]. On the 27th Boissy d'Anglas condemned the harshness of the *émigré* laws.[2] On 3 May Dumolard denounced the Directory's interference in the course of justice in the department of Indre-et-Loire where a Chouan's acquittal had been annulled.[3] On 5 May Dumont de la Charnaye pointed out that the Directory was arbitrarily dismissing civil servants of 'suspect' political views.[4] On the 15th the deputies rejected legislation to increase the number of judges on the *tribunal de cassation* as an egregious measure by the Directory to curry favour with the judiciary.[5]

On 19 May, the day before the opening of the new session, the Clichyens, including the Dumas group, d'André's party and many of the new deputies agreed to support Pichegru's election to the presidency of the *Conseil des Cinq-Cents*. His election, the next day, was almost unanimous; even Thibaudeau's proposal to elect the republican general Jourdan as secretary of the *Conseil* failed. The royalists carried their offensive to the *Conseil des Anciens* by electing as its president Barbé-Marbois, a member of the Dumas Committee who had been a high functionary under the *ancien régime*. This was followed by a successful motion demanding the readmission of the deputies who had been suspended from their functions as *émigrés*, relatives of *émigrés*, and suspects during the Vendémiaire uprising. The deputies, who thus took their seats—Job-Aimé, Mersan, Polissard, Gau, Ferrand-Vaillant and Lecerf—constituted a weighty addition to the already swollen ranks of the Right. At the same time, Barère was prevented from taking his seat on the grounds that the law of 3 Brumaire invalidated his candidacy! The day was climaxed by the appointment of a commission in the lower house to consider the repeal of 'unconstitutional' laws.[6]

---

[1] *Réimpression de l'ancien Moniteur*, xxviii. 680.   [2] Ibid., 683.

[3] Ibid., 688. Cf. *Procès-verbal des séances du Conseil des Cinq-Cents, 14 floréal, an V*, pp. 321-2.

[4] *Réimpression de l'ancien Moniteur*, xxviii. 690.

[5] Ibid., 706.

[6] *Procès-verbal des séances du Conseil des Cinq-Cents, 1 prairial an V*, pp. 2-111.

The dice were loaded heavily in favour of the Directory's opponents. Nevertheless the Directors prevented them from making the final assault—on the Directory itself. During the elections, the *Quotidienne* had demanded that the drawing of lots to determine the retirement of one of the Directors be conducted in public.[1] As the date of the election approached, Reubell and Barras were exploring expedients to prevent the elevation of a royalist. Reubell, only reluctantly supported by Barras, proposed a secret lot, and that the Director choosing the negative ballot resign immediately without a public announcement of the fate of the balloting. This proposal was not, strictly speaking, unconstitutional: the lots would be drawn, but the resignation would be made to appear as voluntary rather than as the result of the fulfilment of the constitutional provision regulating retirement from the Directory; moreover, the Constitution did not forbid voluntary retirement. If the resignation of a Director took place before the expiry of his term of office, the outgoing members of the Legislature would have the duty of electing his successor; thus the election of a republican would almost be a certainty and the plans of the new members of the Legislature who would not yet have taken their seats would have been thwarted. Carnot and Le Tourneur opposed this adroit scheme and at the last minute were joined by La Revellière[2] and Barras, who succumbed to the argument that the Directory should face its opponents boldly.

On 10 May the *Conseil des Cinq-Cents* requested that the Directory's proceedings in this important matter be conducted in public.[3] A debate ensued and continued until 14 May when the *Conseil* voted to compel the Directory to choose by lot in the presence of the assembled Legislature.[4] The next day the proposal was returned to the Legislature as contrary to the Constitution. However, because of the threatened resignations of Carnot and Le Tourneur, the other Directors agreed to submit to the demands of the deputies. The victory was short-lived, for the

[1] *Quotidienne*, 29 March 1797. Section 137 under Title VI of the Constitution reads: 'The Directory shall be renewed in part by the election of one new member annually. During the first four years, the order of retirement of those first elected shall be determined by lot.' There was nothing in the Constitution prescribing a public or private ceremony.

[2] La Revellière, *Mémoires*, ii. 43–4; Barras, *Memoirs*, ii. 511–12. Cf. G. Robison, *Revellière-Lépeaux, Citizen Director 1753–1824* (New York, 1938), pp. 133–4.

[3] *Reimpression de l'ancien Moniteur*, xxviii. 700.

[4] Ibid., 706.

lot fell on Le Tourneur who was believed to be sympathetic to the royalist cause. The only Director upon whom the royalists believed they could now rely was Carnot—and even this was far from certain. Furthermore, even if a royalist sympathizer took Le Tourneur's place, a royalist majority on the Directory would rest on the possibility of gaining support from one of three confirmed republican incumbents: Barras, La Revellière and Reubell. But first the royalists had to muster enough votes to elect Le Tourneur's successor. There were a number of possible candidates. It was known that Carnot preferred Cochon, the minister of police.[1] His devotion to the Republic was known to be in doubt.[2] Bénézech, the minister of the interior, whom many believed to be a royalist, was also considered for the post. The more extreme royalists, led by Vaublanc, tried to gain support for general Beurnonville.[3] Cochon and Bénézech were rejected as having compromised their standing by serving the Republic, and Beurnonville was thought to be too extreme. The majority favoured Barthélemy, the minister to Switzerland, and the choice was approved by Wickham. He was duly elected on 26 May, taking his place alongside Carnot. He made an effort to win Carnot's confidence, but encountered a cold reserve that shook his composure.[4] Carnot was not unwilling to accept Barthélemy as his only friend in the Directory but doubted his ability to render great assistance in the inevitable altercations with the other Directors.[5]

With Barthélemy safely lodged in the Directory, d'André and Wickham hoped to form a royalist or semi-royalist majority in the executive branch of the government.[6] Barthélemy's first

---

[1] *Mémoires sur Carnot par son fils* (2 vols., Paris, 1893), ii. 105; *Mémoires de Barthélemy 1768–1819*, p. 178; report of a conversation between Bornes and Carnot, *Dropmore Papers*, iv. 144.

[2] Wickham to Grenville, 30 April 1796, *Dropmore Papers*, iii. 198. He had also sold secrets to Wickham's agents in 1795, though this was not generally known.

[3] Vaublanc, *Mémoires*, ii. 386–7; I. E. Delarue, deputy to the *Conseil des Cinq-Cents*, one of the *inspecteurs de la salle*, and future victim of the *coup d'état* of Fructidor, insisted that the post called for a man of resolute will. The other candidates, Kléber, Masséna, Augereau and Bougainville were not seriously considered. See his *Histoire de dix-huit fructidor* (Paris 1821), pp. 261–2.

[4] Bathélemy, *Mémoires*, p. 177.

[5] Carnot, *Mémoires*, ii. 107. Cf. La Revellière, *Mémoires*, ii. 45.

[6] D'Aubigny, whom Wickham described as a former *intendant* of the post office, was the first to act as intermediary between the majority in the *Conseils* and the new Director. A police report of 9 December 1795 confirms that d'Aubigny was frequenting secret royalist meetings, A.N., $F^7 3688^4$.

impressions of the Directors were disheartening, for he feared that unless the deputies assumed a clear line of conduct, they would be beaten at their own game. He also chafed at his isolation and complained that his freedom of action had been curtailed by the Directory's decision to consider all ministerial affairs jointly.[1] Thenceforth although each Director would still retain responsibility for the administrative policies of particular ministries, no important decisions were to be taken without discussion by the full membership of the Directory. While Barthélemy's opinions were thought to be pro-royalist, there was considerable doubt concerning Carnot's. But there was a widespread feeling that his voice would be raised in favour of the deputies on all important questions. D'André, who had a meeting with Barthélemy, was reasonably certain that his tact and mild character would captivate Carnot. One more Director would then be needed to form a majority. This problem was to occupy the royalists in the succeeding months.

II

Another thorny problem which had caused d'André and Wickham considerable concern before the elections and had been temporarily solved during the election campaign, but was now threatening to break the bonds that had contained it, was the attitude of Blankenburg to their plan and to the agency. Wickham objected to Louis' re-organization of the agency for many reasons. The reconstitution of the agency as a Council, though wise from an administrative viewpoint, was unnecessary, because its most valuable feature, the *Institut*, had already produced results, and d'André and Despomelles, who planned to expand it, were opposed to external control. Furthermore, the establishment of a royalist Council in Paris, with its emphasis on military operations and its reliance on Chouans, would only serve to frighten and alienate the deputies. Wickham felt that the plan to set up a Council was symptomatic of the royalists' profound lack of understanding of the main forces at work in France.

[1] Wickham to Grenville, 27 June 1797, F.O. 74/20. In his *Mémoires*, p. 182, Barthélemy says that he welcomed this innovation in procedure which prevented, he claims, the Directors from making decisions secretly. Wickham believed, on the other hand, that Barthélemy was against a change which would make it possible for the majority in the Directory to veto his proposals and those of Carnot.

He deprecated Blankenburg's flagrant acknowledgement of its agents, blatantly advertised in Louis' Declaration of 10 March,[1] as an example of a complete divorce from reality.[2] Louis still refused to realize that his fate rested not with the vestiges of the former privileged orders but with the new notables, the men of the Third Estate.[3] The benefits of a close working alliance between the constitutionalists and the royalists were incontrovertible; that unity must not be jeopardized.

Wickham and d'André had a powerful supporter in Précy, who was impressed by the value of the *Institut*, and credited its success to 'M. Wickham's careful preparations and funds'.[4] He made much of d'André's sincere attachment to the cause: 'D'André is important for Your Majesty's service [because] he has an incomparable knowledge of all the intrigues and all the parties ...'[5] He declared further that Wickham's generosity stemmed from his confidence in d'André's policy of acquiring 'new partisans for Your Majesty'.[6] These observations were meant to convert Louis to unequivocal support of Wickham's plans. Précy's intervention,[7] though encountering determined opposition from other royalist agents, of whom de Vezet[8] was the most intractable, was an important factor contributing to Blankenburg's reappraisal of its decision to establish the Council. By the middle of June, the Council was set aside (so far as Wickham knew), allowing d'André an unchallenged direction of royalist affairs at Paris.

Among the deputies upon whose assistance d'André felt he could rely, there were at least 200 firm royalists whose adherence to Louis was dictated by expediency rather than devotion. Although the question of the monarchy remained a divisive factor, support for Louis was a less explosive question than formerly. Still the deputies on the Right could not be expected to support a restoration which was incompatible with the new ideas of liberty. Their number could be increased if the more moderate constitutionalists, numbering some 350, could be shown the

---

[1] See above, p. 156.

[2] Wickham to Grenville, 12 April 1797, F.O. 74/20.

[3] Wickham to Grenville, 15 April 1797, ibid.

[4] Précy to Louis XVIII, 31 April 1797, A.A.E., France 590.

[5] Précy to Louis XVIII, 4 May 1797, A.A.E., France 591.

[6] Ibid.

[7] Précy to Louis XVIII, 17 May, 8 June 1797, ibid.

[8] De Vezet to d'Avaray, 19 June 1797, ibid. De Vezet even hinted that Précy's devotion to Wickham exceeded his loyalty to the king.

folly of trusting the Directory.[1] The creation of a legislative majority was not the only aim. Important, too, were the reorganization of the national guard, the planting of royalists in departmental administrative posts, an intensified campaign to extend the *Institut* to every department and, above all, the shaping of public opinion.[2]

By the middle of June the features of Wickham's and d'André's plan were clearly discernible. The counter-revolution would be fought from concealed positions. Even if a more vigorous policy were possible, it would not obviate the need to restrain the more impatient royalists. The way seemed to be clearing for a slow but mounting attack on the Directory. The paramount questions were whether legislative resistance to the Directory could be stiffened, and whether the impulsive decisions of Blankenburg could be repressed.

Having made such rapid progress in founding *Instituts* in several departments before the elections, d'André and Despomelles began seriously to consider adding to their number. The departments in which the *Institut* struck roots was increased to seventy by September. In some, such as the Bouches-du-Rhône, Vaucluse, Gironde, Ardèche, Seine-Inférieure—these are the only departments to which d'André directly referred—great headway was made.[3] On the other hand, according to a police report, there were branches of the *Institut* in at least thirty-one departments.[4] The departments in which royalist agents were very active (in some cases the police report names them) may also be considered as having had *Instituts*.[5] The *Institut* must surely have been established in the area under Rochecotte's control to which Despomelles had applied its principles first. This area included another eight departments.[6] Together with the five mentioned by

[1] Wickham to Grenville, 27 June 1797, F.O. 74/20.

[2] Wickham to Grenville, 30 June 1797, ibid.

[3] D'André to Wickham, [?] October 1797, F.O. 27/52.

[4] A.N., F⁷6259, cited in Lacouture, op. cit., p. 41. These were the Rhône, Ain, Isère, Mont Blanc, Drôme, Hautes-Alpes, Basses-Alpes, Var, Landes, Gers, Basses-Pyrénées, Hautes-Pyrénées, Pyrénées-Orientales, Ariège, Haute-Garonne, Tarn, Loire, Puy-de-Dôme, Creuse, Haute-Vienne, Charente, Charente-Inférieure, Dordogne, Corrèze, Cantal, Haute-Loire, Lozère, Gard, Aveyron, Lot and Lot-et-Garonne.

[5] See above, pp. 152–3. These were the Pas-de-Calais, Calvados, Eure, Orne, Manche, Côtes-du-Nord, Sarthe, Marne, Aube, Haute-Saône, Bas-Rhin, Haut-Rhin, Doubs, Jura—numbering fourteen.

[6] These departments were the Oise, Seine, Seine-et-Marne, Seine-et-Oise, Yonne, Loiret, Indre-et-Loire and Eure-et-Loire.

d'André, fifty-eight departments had functioning *Instituts*—only twelve short of the number claimed by the royalists.

Strangely enough the departments in which there was little or no *Institut* activity were those in Brittany and in the Vendée (the Côtes-du-Nord was the exception).[1] Perhaps d'André felt that the deep royalist feeling of those areas would make the *Institut* superfluous. Another region where it was not established was the broad belt of departments from the west almost to the extreme east across the middle of France. There seems also to have been little penetration of the departments bordering on Belgium. The heaviest concentration seems therefore to have been in the south where nearly every department was affected. Next came the departments to the immediate west and north of Paris in the provinces of Orléanais, Maine and Normandy. Finally there were the departments bordering Switzerland and the two departments of former Alsace.[2]

The expansion of the *Institut* was perhaps the least difficult part of d'André's programme. More intractable was the rallying of a large and cohesive legislative majority sufficiently in agreement on basic principles to embarrass, weaken and finally wear down the resistance of the Directory. The first few days of the new Legislature had seen a certain amount of resolution, but would it continue? Would the constitutionalists throw off their fear of the royalists? They wanted to travel the middle road without being crushed by either of the extremist groups. When would they lose their illusions, join the royalists and force through a constructive anti-Directorial policy? Could a united front materialize?

We can assess the nature of the division between the two groups by analysing proceedings in the *Conseils*. At the close of the previous legislative session, the deputies had been examining the practice, then widespread, of *émigrés* from the West Indies receiving American certificates of residence and returning to their plantations, thus avoiding the application of French laws on their

---

[1] Cf. Chassin, *Les Pacifications de l'Ouest 1794–1800*, i. 40. Chassin writes: 'In sum, the region of the Vendée had not fallen into the trap of the *Institut philanthropique*.'

[2] Wickham had been carrying on a correspondence with Herrenberger, the former mayor of Sélestat, since 1795. Herrenberger to Wickham, 5 September 1795, F.O. 74/11. Bacher, an Alsatian and first secretary in the French embassy in Switzerland, named Herrenberger as Wickham's chief agent in Berne. Bacher to Delacroix, 1 August 1796, A.N., AFIII51A, dossier 187.

property and themselves.[1] Behind this question was the much more important one of the abolition of slavery in the Indies, economically injurious to a handful of wealthy plantation owners who found support from a good number of deputies. On 29 May, after the new session opened, Vaublanc, himself a wealthy proprietor from San Domingo, raised the matter again, demanding a review of the entire West Indian problem. He was supported by Villaret-Joyeuse, Doulcet de Pontécoulant, Bourdon(!) and Tarbe. On 4 June Tarbe violently attacked the Directory in a critical review of the Republic's colonial policies. Instead of sustaining this level of criticism, Thibaudeau and Pastoret, two of the more vocal constitutionalists, attacked Tarbe for having maligned the good name of the Republic.[2] Thus, the union of the Directory's opponents, which had won the elections and elected avowed royalists to high positions, had been succeeded by an open demonstration of discord, consoling to the government but distressing to d'André and Wickham.[3]

After this sorry spectacle d'André resigned himself to an attempt to accomplish at least two things: the abrogation of the more offensive revolutionary laws and the placing of French finances on a sound footing.[4] In his opinion the root of the trouble was the constitutionalists' lack of security. It would vanish if Louis made them a specific offer guaranteeing their political future. Wickham was more optimistic, convinced that on issues of greater importance they would conceal their differences with the royalists. Both, however, hoped that time would heal the breach; an all-out attack on the Directory would have to be deferred until after the elections of 1798.[5] For the moment Wickham's assessment was only partially justified. On 27 June the *Conseil des Anciens* succeeded in having the law of 3 Brumaire, the *bête noire* of the royalists, declared null and void.[6] But the blow quickly followed. As a proof of their impartiality, the constitutionalists, led by Thibaudeau, prevented the royalists from debating the repeal of the law of 4 Brumaire. Its abrogation

---

[1] *Procès-verbal des séances du Conseil des Cinq-Cents, 4 floréal an V*, pp. 85–106.

[2] Sciout, op. cit., ii. 503–15; cf. *Réimpression de l'ancien Moniteur*, xxviii. 718, 721, 723.

[3] Wickham to Grenville, 27 June 1797; D'André to Wickham, 29 June 1797 F.O. 74/20.

[4] Ibid.   [5] Ibid.

[6] *Procès-verbal des séances du Conseil des Anciens, 9 messidor an V*, pp. 90–4.

would have reimposed on the Jacobins those political disabilities that a grateful Convention had removed in October 1795 in appreciation for their aid against the Vendémiaire insurrectionaries. Thus, while removing one set of discriminatory laws, the constitutionalists vitiated royalist efforts somewhat by making it easier for the Jacobins to continue their attacks.

The royalists' most audacious scheme had as its aim nothing less than the paralysis of the Directory. In the lower chamber, Gilbert-Desmolières took the first step when he presented the report and recommendations of the committee on finance of which he was chairman. His proposal would have curtailed the Directory's control of the state's finances by vesting it in the *Conseils*, thus making the committee of the national treasury, established by the Constitution of 1795, dependent on the Legislature. To be sure, the Constitution empowered this committee to collect taxes and to pay the debts of the state on the order of the appropriate legislative committee, the Directory and the minister of finance. But Desmolières' recommendation would have made the committee of the national treasury subservient to the *Conseils*. The gravity of this threat to the Directory cannot be overestimated, for it could have deprived the government of the means with which to govern and to carry on the war. The royalists planned in this way to hasten the restoration and help Austria and Britain immeasurably in their negotiations with France.[1] Desmolières' resolution was passed in the *Conseil des Cinq-Cents* on 18 June,[2] but it was so extreme that the constitutionalists in the upper chamber rejected it on the 27th.[3] There was evidently little agreement among the deputies on the Right.

The same lack of unity was evident in the debates of the *Conseil des Cinq-Cents* on the church. The laws of 1792 and 1793 against the refractory clergy were abrogated on 4 July with Camille Jordan and Dubreuil taking an active part in mobilizing opinion for the resolution. There was, however, a violent scene between Larivière, who was president of the *Conseil* that day, and Thibaudeau, who questioned the former's impartiality in the debates.[4] Moreover, the royalists lost their opportunity to make

[1] Lefebvre, *La Révolution française*, p. 463.
[2] *Procès-verbal des séances du Conseil des Cinq-Cents, 26–30 prairial an V*, p. 666.
[3] *Procès-verbal des séances du Conseil des Anciens, 9 messidor an V*, pp. 100–7.
[4] A. C. Thibaudeau, *Mémoires sur la Convention et le Directoire* (2 vols., Paris, 1824), ii. 184–5.

this a complete victory when, as a consequence of constitutionalist pressure, the *Conseil* voted by a slender majority of six to force the clergy to take an oath of allegiance to the Republic.[1]

Outside the legislative halls the constitutionalists attempted to gain a majority in the Directory and to have their friends appointed to the key ministries. Dumas and Carnot were on good terms even before the elections.[2] After the elections their friendship grew and Carnot began the practice of discussing policy with such members of the Dumas group as Portalis, Tronson Ducoudray, Thibaudeau and Siméon.[3] Barthélemy was posted on opinion in the Legislature by Barbé-Marbois and Desmolières.[4] D'André and Wickham encouraged these tactics in the expectation that Barthélemy would smooth the process of winning over Carnot.[5] The royalists made their own sorties: Willot, Vaublanc and Villaret-Joyeuse saw Carnot frequently.[6] Carnot, himself, welcomed and encouraged these visits, making vain attempts to mitigate the harshness of the legislative attack on the Directory.[7] There was no doubt about Barthélemy's loyalties, and Carnot's were wavering. How could one more Director be brought into the fold? Reubell's hatred of the royalists precluded approaching him. There remained only Barras, the opportunist, and La Revellière whose opinions, apart from his fervent support of theophilanthropy, were not too well-known. If one of them agreed to join Carnot and Barthélemy, it would be possible to transform the ministries.

La Revellière's detestation of Barras as a profligate and his repugnance for Reubell was no secret. Neither was his healthy suspicion of the royalists, but he was still undecided about the proper course to follow.[8] A few deputies, notably Portalis and Tronson Ducoudray, tried to bring him round by pledging the good behaviour of their colleagues. Carnot, whose opportunities were greater, also made an attempt to convince his intransigent

[1] *Réimpression de l'ancien Moniteur*, xxviii. 746.

[2] Wickham to Grenville, 20 May 1797, F.O. 74/20.

[3] Carnot, *Mémoires*, ii. 110; Barthélemy, *Mémoires*, p. 191; *Souvenirs du lieutenant-général comte Mathieu Dumas de 1770 à 1836* (3 vols., Paris, 1839), iii. 104.

[4] Barthélemy, *Mémoires, p.* 185.

[5] Wickham to Grenville, 27 June 1797, F.O. 74/20.

[6] Reinhard, *Le Grand Carnot*, ii. 230; Barthélemy, *Mémoires*, p. 209; Vaublanc, *Mémoires*, ii. 398-9.

[7] Carnot, *Mémoires*, ii. 111.

[8] Robison, op. cit., pp. 134-5.

colleague of the value of co-operation with the deputies.[1] But La Revellière believed that their ultimate aim was the destruction of the Directory's constitutional powers.[2] His final rejection of their overtures was due to his anticlericalism which had suffered a set-back in the *Conseils*.

Proposals were made at the same time to Barras. Immediately after the elections he was thought by many royalists to be ready to embrace their cause.[3] But this clever intriguer, thinking only of his own safety, not only negotiated with the deputies and Louis' agents but also with Reubell and La Revellière. Barthélemy was asked to use his influence with him but was politely rebuffed.[4] Barras was also frank in ascribing royalist motives to the visit of Dumas and Villaret-Joyeuse, who enjoined him to support their favourite candidates for the chief ministries.[5]

III

By this time, Barras, Reubell and La Revellière could not doubt the gravity of the dangers to the Republic. To meet the peril Barras sought Bonaparte's promise of military assistance in the event that the Directory decided to use force against the deputies. Once again Barras was asking Bonaparte to repeat his rôle as defender of the Republic, as during Vendémiaire. His emissary to the general was the deputy, Fabre de l'Aude, who reached Bonaparte's Italian headquarters at Montebello in time not only to receive his pledge of support but also to be entrusted with a copy of a memorandum revealing Pichegru's treasonable nego-tiations with Condé and Wickham.[6] The original memoran-dum had allegedly been drawn up by d'Antraigues, Bonaparte's prisoner since his arrest[7] at Trieste on 21 May by general Bernadotte

---

[1] La Revellière, *Mémoires*, ii. 86.

[2] Ibid., 86–91. Wesley, who was in Lille assisting Malmesbury in the negotiation of peace terms with the French, heard that Carnot had appealed to La Revellière. See memorandum of Mr. Wesley, 31 July 1797, *Dropmore Papers*, iii. 340.

[3] Report of Doulcet de Pontécoulant's conversation with Wickham, Wickham to Grenville, 29 October 1797, F.O. 74/21.

[4] Barthélemy, *Mémoires*, p. 219.

[5] Ibid., pp. 238–9; Thibaudeau, *Mémoires*, ii. 209; Dumas, *Souvenirs*, iii. 107; Barras, *Memoirs*, ii. 567–8.

[6] See Fabre de l'Aude's *Histoire secrète du Directoire* (4 vols., Paris 1832) of which a full chapter in the third volume is devoted to this episode.

[7] See a recent account of d'Antraigues' arrest by A. Ollivier, *Le Dix-huit brumaire* (Paris, 1959), pp. 42–62, 76–91.

some five days after his flight from Venice in the company of the Russian minister, Mordvinov. On 10 June, Bonaparte forwarded to the Directory the dossier of d'Antraigues' interrogation, the original memorandum, and the more important of the documents found in the comte's portfolio of papers.[1] Fabre did not, as he recalls in his *Histoire*, reach Paris until some time between 20 and 25 June, and Bonaparte's message and its enclosures probably reached the capital at about the same time.[2] Thus by the end of June Barras and his two closest colleagues, Reubell and La Revellière, had evidence of a particularly damaging nature; could there be any greater proof of Pichegru's treason than that given them by Bonaparte? A formidable weapon had been sent to them, almost fortuituously.

Bonaparte's relations with d'Antraigues must be examined if we are to understand his motives in taking extraordinary measures to obtain such momentous evidence, evidence which he hoped would be as useful to him as to the Directors. When d'Antraigues was arrested, the world which he had known and cherished and wanted to preserve by every stratagem, was fast being transformed into its very opposite. In desperation, having lost his position at the Spanish embassy when Spain withdrew from the war, he not only sought accreditation as a counsellor at the Russian embassy in Venice,[3] but later, after Grenville's cold reception to his request for British asylum, took the more drastic step of becoming a naturalized Russian. He also tried to open as many paths to meaningful survival by extending contacts with officials in Austria and Naples, as well as maintaining his friendship with Drake. In the critical months before Bonaparte's inevitable move towards Venice, d'Antraigues, facing a bleak future, nevertheless continued to exert what influence he could in the circles of the counter-revolution, principally through Drake.

The last episode in d'Antraigues' relations with Drake centred on his attempt to win Bonaparte for the cause. In the spring of 1796, Du Vernegues, the royalist representative in Genoa, formed a clandestine communication with one of the generals in Bonaparte's army, and immediately informed Drake in sibylline tones

[1] *Correspondance de Napoléon* (32 vols., Paris 1858–70), iii. 143.
[2] Barras' description of his reaction to the revelations sent by Bonaparte is dated between 23 and 25 June, *Memoirs*, ii. 548–58.
[3] Pingaud, op. cit., p. 104.

of his hopes.[1] Although Du Vernegues did not refer to the general by name, it is probable that the general in question was the mysterious Boullard, who figures in Drake's correspondence.[2] Boullard gave Drake what the latter described as a great deal of useful intelligence: he informed him that many officers in Bonaparte's army were disposed to support Britain and the royalists but refused to commit themselves because of their belief in Britain's betrayal of Pichegru.[3] Boullard was also friendly with Gamon, whose ideas on restoring the monarch he shared;[4] and Gamon was apparently planning to secure Boullard's appointment as commander at Lyons.[5] A short time later Louis XVIII approached d'Antraigues to 'convert' Bonaparte and the principal officers of his army, and for this purpose to work with Drake.[6] Nothing came of this mission. Boullard, who approached Marmont (at this time one of Bonaparte's aides-de-camp), soon realized that Bonaparte was unsympathetic to the royalist cause, and an Austrian officer who had been delegated to sign the capitulation of Mantua returned with the same impression.[7]

Despite M. Godechot's careful researches, Boullard's identity remains unknown.[8] But there need not be any caution in suggesting that d'Antraigues, Drake, Du Vernegues, and other royalists did establish some form of communication with officers in Bonaparte's army, and that an attempt was also made to subvert the future emperor himself. D'Antraigues' apprehension by Bernadotte proved to be a lucky accident for Bonaparte, for the comte's confiscated papers included a lengthy report of his conversation with Montgaillard, an account which was long believed to be the basis for the famous memorandum that Bonaparte sent to Paris.[9] Montgaillard had come to Italy at the close of 1796, ostensibly seeking money in payment for his effort to

---

[1] Du Vernegues to Drake, 22 April 1796, Add. MSS., 46835.

[2] Drake to Grenville, 23 June 1796, F.O. 28/15.

[3] Drake to Wickham, 3 August 1796, ibid.

[4] Boullard to Drake, 10 August 1796, ibid.

[5] Boullard to Drake, 30 September 1796, ibid.

[6] La Vauguyon to d'Antraigues, 27 October 1796, A.A.E., France 609.

[7] D'Antraigues to la Vauguyon, 1 March 1797, A.A.E., France 610.

[8] See his article, 'Essai d'identification de quelques correspondants du comte d'Antraigues', loc. cit., and also his book, op. cit., pp. 207–10.

[9] In a recent article, R. de Grandsaignes ('L'Affaire du portefeuille d'Antraigues', *Annales historiques de la Révolution française*, xxxiv (1962), 54–69) presents an over-subtle explanation of the motives of Bonaparte and d'Antraigues, and suggests

bring Bonaparte into the royalist camp. In Venice, d'Antraigues listened to Montgaillard's account of his rôle in the Pichegru negotiations (which forms the major part of his recorded memorandum), but he knew him to be a double-agent and a clever mercenary, capable of doing great harm to the counter-revolution.[1] During the conversation, Montgaillard obviously tried to impress d'Antraigues with the importance of his part in the Pichegru affair, in the hope that he would surrender his good sense and some of his money. It is also clear that d'Antraigues subsequently made a record of Montgaillard's efforts to win over the officers under Bonaparte's command and possibly Bonaparte himself. This was not the report, however, that Bonaparte sent to the Directory.

Bonaparte's motives in altering the report are not our chief concern. For our purpose, it is enough to point out that, while out of sympathy with the government in Paris, he was nevertheless reluctant to face its fall with equanimity, for he knew that those plotting its destruction would try to deprive him of his newly-won laurels. The prospect of a royalist victory was abhorrent to him. It was therefore in his interest to lend the prestige and power of his name to the Directors to overcome royalist opposition. What more effective way than to present them with additional and final evidence of Pichegru's treason in the form of an altered report of d'Antraigues' conversation with Montgaillard. Presumably, at Bonaparte's dictation, d'Antraigues deleted all references to the royalist plans to win him over, for although the improbability of his defection was never in question, he could not risk any such allusions to stand, lest the Directors, who had become his unwilling captives in the execution of their military plans and foreign policy, seize the opportunity to dismiss him. Thus the report sent to Paris was designed to serve both his and the Directory's advantage. It also served d'Antraigues' immediate interests, for Bonaparte made good their prior agreement by allowing him to escape from a suspiciously lax captivity.

---

that the altered document sent by Bonaparte to Paris was based, not on d'Antraigues' reported conversation with Montgaillard, but on a report forged by Montgaillard's secretary, the abbé du Montet, who sold it to Bonaparte.

[1] Montgaillard's relations with the Directory's officials were known to Wickham, Wickham to Grenville, 28 December 1796, F.O. 74/19. There is a record of Montgaillard's offer to assist the Directory. See Montgaillard to Lallement, 9 September 1796, A.N., AFIII44.

Upon reading the report of Pichegru's treason, Barras was inclined to dismiss it as unsubstantiated and inspired by Bonaparte's lust for power and suspicion of Pichegru's possible ascendancy.[1] However, a few days later, Carency, now exceedingly adept in the art of betrayal, gave Barras additional secret information. He disclosed not only the presence of d'André in Paris and his links with Britain, but also the names of several deputies who were leading the attack on the Directory's defences.[2] Barras, in turn, informed Reubell and La Revellière, and the three Directors suddenly voted for a new Irish expedition. The real purpose of this decision was to bring Hoche's army of the Sambre and the Meuse to Paris and to use its alleged destination to Brest as a pretext for having it pass within the perimeter of Paris—a direct violation of the Constitution.[3] It is clear beyond doubt that the Directors, fearing Bonaparte's pretensions, preferred to call on Hoche whom they believed to be more reliable. They were, in effect, preparing to dissolve the Legislature by a *coup d'état*.

The deputies were completely in the dark. So was Wickham, who was still under the impression that Barras was about to join Carnot and Barthélemy! Indeed he assumed that the deciding vote in the Directory's resolution to invade Ireland was Carnot's, absolving Barras who, he believed, was siding with Barthélemy against such a plan.[4] The royalists and Wickham remained Barras' unsuspecting victims until the middle of July when he revealed his hand. Until then the deputies believed that everything was running smoothly. As far as they knew, Carnot, Barthélemy and Barras would force the retirement of finance minister Ramel, foreign minister Delacroix, marine minister Truguet, and justice minister Merlin de Douai, and appoint Bourgoing in Delacroix's place and Gaudin in Ramel's. They were sure that the advocacy by Reubell and La Revellière of Talleyrand for the post of foreign minister and of Montesquiou for that of minister of justice would not prevail.[5]

To their complete consternation the unexpected happened. On 16 July the 'triumvirate', as the majority of the Directors were

---

[1] Barras, *Memoirs*, ii. 550.　　　[2] Ibid., 605–8.　　　[3] Ibid., 620.

[4] Wickham to Grenville, 29 June 1797, F.O. 74/20. Later Wickham came to believe that Reubell had masterminded the whole affair. See Wickham to Grenville, 18 August 1797, ibid.

[5] D'André to Wickham, 29 June 1797; Wickham to Grenville, 7 July 1797, F.O. 74/20.

thenceforth dubbed, reassured by Hoche's impending presence in Paris, considered the nominations to the ministries. Reubell and La Revellière were certain, as was Barras, that the royalists' efforts to have men of their choice appointed to the ministries was a stratagem to conceal their ultimate plan to seize the Directory itself. Barras' simile, 'The Royalists are united and crouching in the Trojan horse; the modern Sinons must find a means of getting it into the city',[1] was not wholly appropriate inasmuch as he ascribed to them a greater unity than they in fact possessed. Carnot, serving his turn as president of the Directory, unwittingly served the aims of the royalists by proposing the dismissal of those ministers who did not have the confidence of the Legislature, on the principle that the executive branch of government must be responsive to the will of the Legislature. Reubell objected that Carnot's motion was presumptuous, since the wishes of the legislative majority were not truly identical with those of the people.[2] When the smoke cleared, Carnot, and Barthélemy realized that they had been outwitted as well as outvoted. Truguet and Delacroix were retired; but so were Cochon, Bénézech and Petiet from the ministries of police, interior and war—the three ministers whom the royalists wished to keep in office. Instead the 'triumvirate' voted to extend the terms of Ramel and Merlin. In Cochon's stead they appointed Lenoir-Laroche, a friend of La Revellière and a member of the Club de Salm, the haunt of such notables as Benjamin Constant, Sieyès, Talleyrand, and Madame de Staël. They replaced Petiet by Hoche, Bénézech by François de Neufchateau, Truguet by Pléville-le-Peley, and Delacroix by Talleyrand. The royalists from left to right were almost at their wits' end. Paris was, as one observer put it, thrown 'into an abominable crisis'.[3]

More astounding news followed. The next day Petiet informed the royalists that he possessed authentic information of the approach of Hoche's army.[4] At last the royalists realized the complete meaning of the events of the day before: it had been a curtain-raiser to the main event—a *coup d'état* against the deputies.

[1] Barras, *Memoirs*, ii. 571–2.
[2] Reinhard, *Le Grand Carnot*, ii. 231.
[3] Malmesbury to Grenville, 25 July 1797, F.O. 27/50.
[4] Thibaudeau, *Mémoires*, ii. 214.

IV

Although they were not prepared for an immediate attack, the more realistic members among the royalists anticipated an eventual trial of strength. As president of the military committee of the *Conseil des Cinq-Cents*, Pichegru, though having proved a disappointment as its presiding officer, had promised to exert his influence in counteracting the Directory's 'illegitimate' use of the army to intimidate the *Conseils*.[1] The Directory's armed support could be weakened in another way. It had been part of d'André's plan to re-organize the National Guard not only in Paris but everywhere in France: the entire Guard would not be restored; only the *grenadiers* and the *chasseurs*, drawn from the wealthier and more reliable classes, would be recruited.[2]

But such a manœuvre would take time and time was clearly on the side of the Directory. The re-organization of the ministries and the news of Hoche's troops advancing on Paris had precipitated matters. Some of the members of Dumas' party therefore saw the need to abandon their moderate policy in favour of a more aggressive one.[3] On 18 July the first warning was given by a member of the more extreme royalist group. That day the members of the *Conseil des Cinq-Cents* heard Camille Jordan excitedly denounce the Directory's intention of planning to overawe the Legislature by a display of force. In the evening a number of deputies—Portalis, Siméon, Thibaudeau, Doulcet de Pontécoulant, Dumas, Willot, Pichegru, Villaret-Joyeuse, Vaublanc, Crassous, and Imbert-Colomès—met at Tronson Ducoudray's home to consider a course of action. D'André was also present. Would they be able to match their mood of desperation by cool determination? Portalis and Ducoudray called for the impeachment of the 'triumvirate' and were seconded by Willot.[4] The success of such a move, Vaublanc observed, required Carnot's

[1] Wickham to Grenville, 30 June 1797, F.O. 74/20.

[2] D'André to Wickham, beginning of May 1797; Wickham to Grenville, 27 June 1797, ibid.

[3] Wickham to Grenville, 18 August 1797, F.O. 7421. Cf. Dumas' remarks to Moreau in Pierre, op. cit., p. 36: ' . . . The recall of our friend Petiet at the very moment when he was concerting plans with Pichegru and myself . . . is, in truth, a calamity.'

[4] Thibaudeau, *Mémoires*, ii. 215; Hyde de Neuville, *Mémoires*, i. 181; Wickham to Grenville, 18 August 1797, F.O. 74/21.

co-operation; he said that he would demand an explanation of the troop movements from Carnot, who would have no choice but to reveal everything to the deputies and accuse the 'triumvirate' of having called in Hoche. Then a motion for their impeachment would be put to the deputies.[1] This was to be the first step. Following it, Imbert-Colomès proposed to issue a call to arms; he was certain that it would rally the spontaneous support of the troops.[2]

Immediately objections were heard from Thibaudeau, who asked the incensed deputies if they had sufficient force to form even a nucleus of armed strength against the undoubtedly superior force at the disposal of the Directory.[3] The answer was clearly no, for apart from their plan to re-organize the National Guard, their reliance on a motley and undisciplined crowd of deserters, the doubtful help of the *jeunesse dorée* and a few Chouan leaders, whom the deputies suspected rather than trusted, the *Conseils* would be defenceless against Hoche's troops. Mathieu Dumas then suggested that overtures should be made to win over the guard of the Legislature, and to send detachments to every quarter of Paris to serve as a nucleus of resistance against the regular troops. It was then Pichegru's turn to reject this proposal as too dangerous.[4] The various plans were debated but nothing emerged from these flourishes except an agreement to defer action until the opinions of Carnot, Cochon and Petiet were canvassed.

The next day a delegation of royalists conferred with Carnot, who told them that to his knowledge Hoche's army had orders to proceed to Brest, and that it had violated the constitutional limits of Paris inadvertently.[5] His veracity was above suspicion. The Director, unhappy in his position of conciliator *manqué*, refused to fall in with Vaublanc's idea of impeaching the 'triumvirate'.[6] Petiet and Cochon similarly cautioned against such an extreme measure. Later that day the royalists re-assembled and were joined by Emmery, Lacuée and Lafond-Ladébat. By now, their resolve of the evening before had evaporated. The majority,

[1] Vaublanc, *Mémoires*, ii. 401–2.

[2] Imbert-Colomès: Mémoire sur 18 Fructidor, 11 October 1797, A.A.E., France 592.

[3] Thibaudeau, *Mémoires*, ii. 216.

[4] Ibid., 217, Cf. Dumas (*Souvenirs*, iii. 103) who writes that, despite several efforts to understand Pichegru's viewpoint, he obtained only 'vague replies . . . and I remained convinced that he had not thought out a plan . . .'

[5] Reinhard, *Le Grand Carnot*, ii. 232.

[6] Ibid., 233. Cf. Thibaudeau, *Mémoires*, ii. 217.

Willot, Imbert-Colomès and d'André dissenting, voted to avoid all provocative action until the formation of the National Guard in Paris, Lyons and Bordeaux.[1]

What followed was neither the climax nor the dénouement. The royalists preferred to reconnoitre. Having failed to decide on an exhibition of force, they proceeded to moderate their demands. Following what seems a concerted plan, Pichegru on 20 July rose in the lower chamber to report on the military committee's plan of re-organizing the National Guard. He was interrupted by Aubry, who moved that the deputies demand an explanation from the Directory for the presence of troops within the area proscribed by the Constitution.[2] The Directory replied evasively that their presence was the result of a clerical error which had been made in transmitting the orders to Hoche. But the greatest blow was the discovery that Carnot had signed the Directory's message! Barras had chosen this critical time to reveal to the *entire* Directory the evidence he had accumulated from Bonaparte and Carency of a vast royalist plot in which Pichegru had been involved since 1795.[3] These revelations were enough to frighten Carnot, who was fundamentally anti-royalist.

Carnot, as Director, was unable to cope with the crisis effectively. At his best as a military planner, the problems of government were too much for him, and the talents of a politician were almost entirely lacking in his character. Conservative by nature, he regarded the Constitution as an instrument of perfection, as a means whereby the new class of wealthy men created by the Revolution would bring stability to France. At first he thought that the men of the new third, elected to the upper chamber in 1795, would be his natural allies; but he soon discovered that they were no match for the more determined royalists in the *Conseil des Cinq-Cents*. He laboured to create among the deputies a middle party that would give him effective assistance in his struggle with his colleagues on the Directory. The appointment of Barthélemy was a bitter disappointment, for he considered the former ambassador as excessively temporizing by nature, a frail reed in a time of great danger. Without the assurance of a party

---

[1] Imbert-Colomès: Mémoire sur 18 Fructidor, 11 October 1797, A.A.E., France 592. Imbert-Colomès felt that one of the reasons for this lack of unity was due to the unwillingness of le Normand, one of the *Inspecteurs*, to embarrass his friend, Hoche.

[2] Bouchez and Roux, op. cit., xxxvii. 305.

[3] Reinhard, *Le Grand Carnot*, ii. 233.

friendly to him in the Legislature, and increasingly doubtful of Barthélemy's ability to stand firm, Carnot silently acquiesced in a policy determined by the other three Directors, led by Barras. Indeed, after his term as president of the Directory expired, he retired to the periphery of the power struggle. In the last resort, what drove him to this passivity was his fear that support for the royalists would bring about a restoration that would ultimately crush him; he dreaded the eventuality of becoming the instrument of his own destruction. Essentially he lacked the finesse and subtlety to resist the greater capacities of the masterful Barras.[1]

But the 'triumvirate' was unable for the moment to take advantage of Carnot's shift. When Hoche arrived in Paris, Carnot, as president, summoned him to appear before the Directory. The general, humiliated and angry, learned that the orders to march his troops within the limits of Paris had been sent to him not by the Directory as a body but only by Barras, Reubell and La Revellière. Barras remained silent throughout the interrogation without coming to Hoche's defence. Carnot demanded that the Directory send the troops back to the army of the Sambre and Meuse. The 'triumvirate' refused, insisting that the troops would, at the proper time, proceed to their destination in the west.[2] Not only was Carnot in a minority but Hoche was also the supine instrument of the majority. His troops remained near Paris, demonstrating once more that the Irish expedition had been a mere feint. But the royalists did not rise to the occasion. Willot merely succeeded in having his objection to Hoche's appointment as minister of war supported in the Legislature and approved by the Directory.[3]

Each side then made a further attempt to negotiate secretly with the other. This time, Pichegru tried his luck with Barras and La Revellière, while Barras urged the general to desert the royalists.[4] Both efforts were dismal failures, and the struggle

[1] Bornes' conversation with Carnot sent to the British cabinet, March 1798, *Dropmore Papers*, iv. 144–6. See J. Godechot's evaluation of this important document: 'Carnot au 18 Fructidor', *Annales historiques de la Révolution française*, xxii (1950), 160–2.

[2] Reinhard, *Le Grand Carnot*, ii. 233.

[3] *Réimpression de l'ancien Moniteur*, xxviii. 751. On the ground that he was under-age, Hoche was replaced by Schérer.

[4] Memorandum by Mr. Wesley, 31 July 1797, *Dropmore Papers*, iii. 340. In an interview with Ellis [Malmesbury's agent], Pein, the confidential agent of Maret who was one of the French negotiators at Lille, disclosed that Pichegru was trying to

seemed to have been suspended. But not for long. On 26 July the royalists voted for a more clearly defined perimeter around Paris beyond which troops would be forbidden to pass, as well as for the end of troop movements from one department to another without express permission from the civilian authorities.[1] It was a feeble attack on the Directory but in the circumstances the only possible one. Wickham felt that the opportunity to overpower the Directory had been lost after 18–19 July, but he was thankful that the deputies had not been expelled like the Girondins in 1793.[2]

mediate between the royalists and the 'violent' part of the Directory, that is, the 'triumvirate', especially Barras. Cf. Malmesbury to Grenville, 6 August 1797, F.O. 27/50. Malmesbury reported that Pichegru and Lacuée were also trying to win over La Revellière.

[1] *Réimpression de l'ancien Moniteur*, xxviii. 754.

[2] Wickham to Grenville, 18 August 1797, F.O. 74/21.

II

FRUCTIDOR

AFTER their exhibition of indecision and confusion, the Directory's right-wing opponents found themselves in an extremely dangerous situation which they had in part created. The great question confronting them was whether to pursue a more aggressive policy which meant the creation of an armed force, or to confine themselves to a gradual and constitutional undermining of the Directory. They chose neither alternative, preferring to bask in the impossible luxury of pretending to do both at once. That the issue had already been joined was evident to most observers; the use of force by the Directory appeared imminent. The deputies made only half-hearted attempts to increase their military strength and were even more reluctant to face the contingency of having to use it. The dilemma in which they found themselves was the consequence of a contradictory attitude which had been apparent to d'André from the time of his arrival in Paris. The constitutionalists and even some of the royalists refused to grasp the logic of their own arguments and the logic of experience. It was possible up to a point to attack the Directory within the bounds of the Constitution. But it was wishful thinking to believe that the Directory, once it had realized the implications of the attack, would hesitate to take defensive measures. This became painfully obvious to a few of the more prescient deputies during the critical days of the ministerial changes and the appearance of troops in Paris. There may have been a few deputies who looked on the struggle as an experiment in parliamentary procedure. Yet to think of the hostility, concealed and overt, which characterized the daily debates in the Legislature—debates on issues sharply dividing republican and royalist—as providing the means whereby a stable legislative-executive relationship could be established, was to divorce theory from reality. The differences between the temporizing element, which still refused to re-examine its premises, and its numerically smaller 'action' opponent, remained very much in the forefront of their discussions and were paralysing their efforts.

To the majority of the royalists the most pressing need, even after the unmistakable signs of the Directory's military superiority could no longer be ignored, was to stand firm until the elections of 1798. At the same time they took faltering steps to improve their military position. In the last critical month before the *coup d'état* not even the Directory's provocations could shake them from their lethargy. Their objective, another electoral victory, was months away. It is true that they anticipated another Vendémiaire, but they predicted only a nasty interlude at worst: it would not prevent them from resuming their activities in relative freedom. So we witness the strangely unreal spectacle of their legislative objectives taking precedence over the demands of the moment.[1]

D'André was tormented by the dangers of such a course, but could do nothing to alter it. He found little support for a more active and more aggressive policy. Those deputies upon whom he could rely were leaderless and easily swayed by the arguments of their more moderate rivals. He could consequently not move any faster than his slowest followers. Like them he had his attention fixed both on the next elections and on the need to build a military machine. Unlike them, he and a handful of others made a concrete effort to explore the possibilities of establishing a para-military organization. Notwithstanding his sense of impending disaster, he saw no reason to slacken his supervision of the *Institut*. It was necessary to root it deeply enough to enable it to survive any violent shocks. The use of force by the Directory could not be discounted; neither could the cessation of communications between the royalists and London (he was thinking of the possible consequences of the peace negotiations between Britain and the Directory), nor the resumption of a fiercer struggle between the royalists and the constitutionalists. Whatever happened, the *Institut* should be given the means to carry on the struggle and even win the 1798 elections on its own.[2] More immediately, its members could serve as the nucleus of the re-organized National Guard in the departments.[3]

Wickham also refused to lose sight of the *Institut*'s potential power. Like d'André, he was not blind to the probability of a

---

[1] Delarue (op. cit., p. 269) maintained that the deputies, inhibited by scruples and paralysed by timidity, lost the initiative. Cf. Neuville (*Mémoires*, i. 178) who agreed with d'André that success 'would accrue to the party which took the initiative'.

[2] Wickham to Grenville, 27 August 1797, no. 2, F.O. 74/21.

[3] D'André to Wickham, 29 July 1797, ibid.

coup d'état against the deputies. For that very reason he held that the *Institut* had to be preserved at any cost.[1] He wished, however, to retain the direction of the *Institut* in his own hands without interference from Blankenburg, and decided that this could best be accomplished by continuing to divide its activities between d'André and Despomelles. The former was to be responsible for its management in twenty-two departments, while the latter was to be in control of the others.[2] Those under d'André's direction were to be financed by a portion of the total monthly funds already at his disposal, that is, one-fifth of the monthly grant of £10,000. A like amount was promised Despomelles on condition that it was to be used exclusively for the *Institut*.[3]

D'André's optimistic reports on the *Institut*, drawn up in August a few weeks before the *coup d'état*, were based on his unshaken belief that it was the pre-requisite for electoral success in 1798. He developed an extensive correspondence with the *Instituts*, sending out a large number of *voyageurs* either for the purpose of establishing new branches or to strengthen those already in existence.[4] As the Directory adopted an increasingly belligerent attitude towards the Legislature, and as fear became the normal reflex of the royalists, he began to feel more than ever that safety lay only in a widespread application of the *Institut* principle.[5] The Midi was the area of greatest promise; twenty departments had been thoroughly penetrated and the republicans had been almost completely dislodged from their control of local administration.[6]

A similar grim tenacity was evident in his exertions to create a dependable fighting force to resist the Directory and to seize power if possible. But it was a slow process. After Barras had shown his hand and Hoche's troops were converging on Paris most of the royalists had agreed to defer action until the National Guard had been reformed. They wanted the 'reorganization of the Vendémiaire National Guard',[7] that is, a military body similar

[1] Wickham to Grenville, 18 August 1797, F.O. 74/21.

[2] Wickham to Grenville, 27 August 1797, no. 2, ibid.

[3] Le Clerc to la Barberie, 26 July 1797; le Clerc to Despomelles, 1 August 1797; Wickham to d'André, 15 August 1797, ibid.

[4] D'André to Wickham, 16 August 1797, ibid.

[5] D'André to Wickham, 18 August 1797, ibid., and A.A.E., France 592.

[6] D'André to Wickham, 28 August 1797. Cf. d'André to Wickham, 29 July 1797, ibid.

[7] D'André to Wickham, [?] October 1797, F.O. 27/52.

to the semi-spontaneous formation of the sections in 1795. Pichegru had taken the lead in the discussion on the membership of the Guard on 20 July. It was resumed three days later and continued until 27 July.[1] The *Conseil des Cinq-Cents* voted to restore the Guard by recalling the *grenadiers* and the *chasseurs* and excluding the gunners. The former had been ejected after the fall of the monarchy while the latter were reputed to have become the radical element in the Guard. It was only on 11 August, during the course of the debate in the lower chamber, that Pichegru revealed the full intention of the bill's sponsors. The officers of the Guard would be armed from the national arsenals first; the arming of the rank and file would have to wait. The bill was passed by the *Conseil des Anciens* on the 12th, and was submitted to the approval of the Directors, who, of course, refused to promulgate this transparent attempt[2] to arm the wealthier ranks of society—the same social groups that had marched against the Convention in Vendémiaire.

There was also a plan to increase the fighting strength of the Legislative Guard. It had been suggested by Dumas on 18 July. On 7 August Aubry proposed a measure to increase the Guard's number by adding 300 cavalry troops and 70 gunners entrusting their supervision to the *Commission des Inspecteurs de la Salle*.[3] This body, a five-member Committee with power to guarantee the security of the Legislature, had control over a police force made up of no fewer than 1500 National Guardsmen from all departments, Since this Committee included Pichegru, Delarue and Vaublanc it seemed possible to transform the Guard into a royalist tool. But Jourdan's amendment to Aubry's proposal vitiated the entire project: the new additions to the Guard would have to be taken from the active army and not from any body which the Committee preferred. The upper chamber had the power to remove the amendment, but it debated Aubry's plan too slowly for the comfort of either its friends or opponents. Obviously the Legislative Guard could not be a first line of defence or attack.

Constitutional methods being doomed, the royalists sought

---

[1] *Réimpression de l'ancien Moniteur*, xxviii. 753. On Malmesbury's high hopes for the Guard, see Malmesbury to Grenville, 6 August 1797, F.O. 27/50.

[2] Ibid., 768.

[3] *Procès-verbal des séances du Conseil des Cinq-Cents, 20 thermidor an V*, pp. 470-83. Cf. *Réimpression de l'ancien Moniteur*, xxviii. 762, 764-5.

other means. By 10 August d'André reported that a secret military establishment of 500 men had been organized; 20,000 rounds of ammunition had been manufactured; half of the 20th *régiment de dragons* had been gained; the commander of the *chasseurs à cheval* had promised to countermand any orders to march against the Legislature; and general Richepance, commander of a detachment of troops from Hoche's army of the Sambre and Meuse, was thought to be sympathetic.[1] Further progress in extracting similar pledges of loyalty from the troops stationed in Paris was made in the next few days.[2] By the 18th rifles were being distributed,[3] and by the 28th the ranks of the royalists were augmented with 600 raw recruits from the *jeunesse dorée*.[4] Then a few days before 18 Fructidor this force was strengthened by 14 non-commissioned officers and 350 dragoons from the regiment commanded by Malo (the same officer who had betrayed Brottier, Duverne and La Villeurnoy and who had again changed sides), 50 *chasseurs à cheval*, 1 lieutenant and about 100 troops of the 19th *demie-brigade*. Support from the cavalry depots at Saint-Germain and Versailles was also assured.[5]

But these were not the only measures taken to establish a force capable of resisting the government's troops. D'André also wished the Legislature to suppress the ministry of police or to bring it under legislative jurisdiction; he believed that the *Commission des Inspecteurs* was in the best position to achieve this.[6] As a member of this body, Thibaudeau knew of this plan:

They debated two articles of the Constitution. The one gives to the legislative body the right of policing the debating chambers and the external precincts determined by it; the other allows the Legislature to

[1] D'André to Wickham, 10 August 1797, A.A.E., France 592.

[2] D'André to Wickham, 14 August 1797, F.O. 74/21.

[3] D'André to Wickham, 18 August 1797, ibid., and A.A.E., France 592; Wickham to Grenville, 27 August 1797, no. 2, F.O. 74/21.

[4] D'André to Wickham, 28 August 1797, F.O. 74/21 and A.A.E., France 592. Cf. d'André to Wickham, [?] October 1797, F.O. 27/52.

[5] Ibid. On 26 August, Barthélemy informed Colchen, secretary of the French peace delegation meeting with the Malmesbury peace mission at Lille, that 'there are in Paris 6,000 officers and about 6,000 bandits who have come from the interior'. Cited in M. Reinhard, 'Les Négociations de Lille et la crise du 18 Fructidor d'après la correspondance inédite de Colchen', *Revue d'histoire moderne et contemporaine*, V (1958), 53.

[6] D'André to Wickham, 29 July, 14 August 1797; Wickham to Grenville, 18 August 1797, F.O. 74/21.

review the powers of the police in the commune where it meets. In other words, they wanted the *Conseils* to decree that their policing powers extended throughout Paris or at least to the river's edge—the site of the Legislature—and they proposed Cochon as their inspector . . .[1]

However, apart from the rejection by the *Anciens* on 26 July of the sums requested by the ministry of police as excessive, the *Conseils* failed to introduce such a scheme.[2]

Another of d'André's intentions was to have the *Conseils* press for the dismissal of the officers of the 17th division, who were reputed to be among the most devoted republicans in the army. The idea had come to him when Aubry and Tarbe protested the Directory's dismissal of a number of army officers; Willot was more direct; he pointed out that many officers with royalist sympathies had been discharged. Unfortunately the matter was referred to the military committee[3]—it was thus deferred indefinitely. D'André felt that the question could be re-opened and that the debate might be turned to the advantage of the royalists by demanding the dismissal of officers whose Jacobin sympathies should have been properly suspect to the Directory. But there is no record that the deputies introduced such a measure.

The great majority had still to be won over to the use of force. While the restoration of the monarchy was their ultimate goal, their means, as they had often made clear to d'André, excluded any recourse to extra-constitutional expedients. Most of them, including the most vocal members of the Dumas Committee, wanted to direct the counter-revolution along lines of their own choosing. They favoured a less aggressive attack on the Directory but were finding that it was thwarting most of their efforts. Anger and indignation followed but were quickly succeeded by fear—the fear that the Directory would unleash its armies, submerge and still them forever. Why should they be made to suffer such a fate? After all they were not planning a *coup* against the Directory; only a few impulsive reactionaries had expressed such an idea. They were ploughing the middle-furrow but ran the danger of being trampled into the ground by their lustier rivals. However, they refused to admit this as a real possibility. Besides there were many among them whose monarchical sentiments did

---

[1] Thibaudeau, *Mémoires*, ii. 220–1.
[2] *Réimpression de l'ancien Moniteur*, xxviii. 755.
[3] Ibid., 764.

not run very deep. Without clear convictions they were floundering in a no-man's land, trying to avoid contamination from the harsh world of politics which was then wavering between words and violence.

How could the deputies be prepared to face the implication of their political escapism? Their illusions might perhaps be shattered by presenting them with conclusive proof of the Directory's threats.[1] This is what d'André tried to accomplish. But at first, he could not even rely completely on Pichegru and Imbert-Colomès. They despaired and did nothing.[2] They were failing to take advantage of public hostility to the Directory. Why? The Directory's resources, they claimed, were overwhelming. To d'André, who maintained that the advantage was always with the attacking force, the defensive posture assumed by the deputies was absurd. The Directory was hardly a monolithic body; it had hesitated to use violence on 13–14 August because Reubell and La Revellière had refused to support Barras.[3] Nevertheless time was running out. With the retirement of Carnot from the presidency of the Directory on 23 August and his succession by La Revellière the following day, d'André was certain that the decisive day was fast approaching. It would not be delayed unfortunately because: 'There is not a single man worthy of the name in the two *Conseils*. Perhaps there is no one with the necessary qualities in the whole country.'[4]

There was no such vacillation on the Directory's part. From the middle of July onwards, it published Bonaparte's and Hoche's addresses of loyalty to the Republic. The former sent general Augereau to Paris where he was named commander of the Paris

[1] Wickham to Grenville, 27 August 1797, no. 1, F.O. 74/21.

[2] D'André to Wickham, 16 August 1797, ibid. Malmesbury's secret informant, whose grasp of the situation was excellent, believed that Pichegru was 'no friend to tumult or revolution', Malmesbury to Grenville, 14 August 1797, F.O. 27/50. Malmesbury received this information from Lagarde, the editor of the *Journal de Perlet*, who had been employed in the ministry of foreign affairs during the Terror. At this time he was the Directory's secretary-general, as well as being Talleyrand's confidential agent or at least one of his closest collaborators. Malmesbury paid him 25,000 francs for the information he procured during the negotiations. See Guyot, op. cit., p. 453.

[3] D'André to Wickham, 18 August 1797, F.O. 74/21. D'André's stress on this point is corroborated by La Revellière (*Mémoires*, ii. 127) and Doulcet de Pontécoulant, who reported Reubell's hesitancy to Wickham. See Wickham to Grenville, 20 October 1797, F.O. 74/21.

[4] D'André to Wickham 26 August 1797, F.O. 74/18.

military division on 8 August. On the 20th Hoche's chief of
staff, general Chérin, was appointed commander of the Legislative
Guard. These developments brought cannon, arms and troops
into Paris.[1] While improving its military position, the Directory played the double game of finding pretexts for its decrees
and making lightly veiled threats againts conspirators, royalists,
priests and *émigrés*. On 10 August it admitted that the loyal addresses of the armies were unconstitutional but stated that they
were justified in the light of royalist intrigues and provocation.
This unequivocal defiance of the Legislature was repeated with
renewed force on the 27th when La Revellière publicly promised
to defend the Republic by force. The deputies did nothing but
utter feeble protests.

At the eleventh hour d'André, Willot, Imbert-Colomès, Pavie,
Camille Jordan, Larivière, Pichegru,[2] Royer-Collard, Jarry and a
few others decided to call for support from la Trémouille, the
Chouans and Louis' agents. Until then, fearful that la Trémouille
and his followers would alienate the majority, they had refused
their offers of military assistance. But they also had a definite
aversion for la Trémouille, whose agents were said to be tireless
in proposing military plans but interested only in pocketing the
money needed to put them into operation. Not only were they
undisciplined and uncertain of reinforcements,[3] but Cochon had
warned Pichegru that the Directory's agents had infiltrated their
ranks.[4] The royalists would have preferred to keep la Trémouille
at arm's length but the desperate situation forced them to seek
his aid.

La Trémouille had reached Paris in July, bringing with him the
assurance of funds from the British government. He immediately
began to set up the Council, which Louis had commissioned him
to establish, though the decision had been rescinded at Wickham's

[1] D'André to Wickham, 18, 24 August 1797, F.O. 74/21 and A.A.E., France
592.
[2] Pichegru finally realized the hoplessness of the situation and joined in this last
ditch effort to defend the *Conseils*. Montgaillard, probably uncertain of his own
position *vis-à-vis* the royalists, wrote Pichegru a curious letter on 11 August warning
him that the Directory was aware of his intrigues with Wickham, Condé and
d'Antraigues, A.A.E., France 591. It should be noted that Dumas also threw
his customary caution overboard. See d'André to Wickham, [?] October 1797,
F.O. 27/52.
[3] D'André to Wickham, 10 August 1797, A.A.E., France 592.
[4] Wickham to Grenville, 27 August 1797, no. 1, F.O. 74/21.

urging.[1] Waiting for him were Sourdat, Bachet, d'Esgrigny and François.[2] The abbé de la Marre arrived in August.[3] Frotté,[4] Bourmont,[5] Rochecotte,[6] and their officers filled the hotels of Paris. These included a large number of Vendeans and Chouans: Frotté's younger brother; Suzannet; d'Andigné; Stofflet's successor, d'Autichamp; Bruslart; the marquis de Rivière; Polignac; Puyvert; the Swiss colonel, Pillechody; la Rochejaquelein.[7] Also in Paris was Tryon,[8] the indefatigable emissary from the Vendée to London; general Danican,[9] the commander of the sections during Vendémiaire; Fauche-Borel[10] who had come to keep an eye on Pichegru; and Hyde de Neuville[11] who was involved in minor royalist conspiracies after Fructidor. La Trémouille thus had a substantial following presumably ready to act. Moreover, on 1 August Frotté issued an appeal to the royalists in Normandy to take up arms, and two weeks later extended it to the royalists in Paris.[12]

Because of his unwillingness to revive the old quarrels with Blankenburg Wickham urged d'André to take de la Marre and la Trémouille into his confidence. In this way d'André would be able not only to keep a check on their activities but also to make use of their resources.[13] When d'André informed Wickham that Pichegru and Imbert-Colomès disapproved of la Trémouille's mission, he begged them to co-operate for the sake of unity.[14] By 22 August d'André was able to gain promises of aid from la Trémouille and Frotté.[15] And by the 30th, they were ready to work together with Pichegru and the others.[16]

Even then d'André's views were divided. It was Willot's suggestion that la Trémouille send out a call for more of his

[1] See above, pp. 169, 172.
[2] Montarlot, loc. cit., 105.
[3] De Vezet to Louis XVIII, 9 August 1797, A.A.E., France 591.
[4] Frotté to Grenville, 30 September 1797, F.O. 27/52.
[5] La Trémouille to Louis XVIII, [?] October 1797, A.A.E., France 592.
[6] Beauchamp, op. cit., p. 190.
[7] Sicotière, op. cit., ii. 93; Neuville, *Mémoires*, i. 178.
[8] Note by Windham, 29 November 1797, Add. MSS., 37903.
[9] Danican left for Paris in June. See Fauche-Borel to d'Avaray, 1 June 1797, A.A.E., France 591.
[10] Fauche-Borel to d'Avaray, 21 September 1797, A.A.E., France 592.
[11] Neuville, *Mémories*, i. 178.
[12] Sicotière, op. cit., ii. 100, 102.
[13] Wickham to d'André, 8, 15 August 1797, F.O. 74/21.
[14] Wickham to Grenville, 27 August 1797, no. 2, ibid.
[15] D'André to Wickham, 22 August 1797, ibid. and A.A.E., France 592.
[16] D'André to Wickham, 30 August 1797, F.O. 74/18.

followers to come to Paris. At first d'André objected on several grounds; a hundred more Chouans would not tip the scales; if civil war broke out in the departments their absence might mean the difference between defeat and success; they would probably refuse to serve in the ranks; and they would be easily recognized by the police. However, he gave in to Willot who felt sure that he could mould the heterogeneous group of Chouans, agents, the *jeunesse dorée*, deserters, *émigrés* and the ranks from the different units who had promised their support, into a force of determined fighters.[1] La Trémouille persuaded the Chouan leaders to bury their pride for the sake of the common cause.[2] There was thus available a force with potential striking power.

The royalists tried to keep informed of the activities of the Directory's political supporters. They learned that three separate committees, meeting nightly, were discussing plans to scotch royalist designs. A group of officers was meeting at Barras' home; Sotin, the minister of police who was also an habitué of these soirées, recommended the establishment of a military government. Another group gathered at Madame de Staël's and included La Revellière, Constant, Garat, Sieyès and Daunou. There was yet a third group led by Merlin de Douai, Jean de Bry, Gohier, Menou and Lamarque, an allegedly Orléanist party. All three advised the arrest of at least fifty of the more notorious royalist deputies and the annulment of the elections.[3] A *coup d'état* seemed to be in the making.

D'André, taking the initiative, made a last attempt to win over the majority to a more forward policy. He approached Emmery, one of the members of the *Commission des Inspecteurs*, upbraided him for his acquiescence in the Directory's aggressive attitude and shamed him into promising to speak out against it.[4] If Emmery, who had a large following among the moderates, were to declare his intention to resist the Directory, there would be a fair chance of creating a solid core of opposition. Though Emmery

[1] D'André to Wickham, [?] October 1797, F.O. 27/52.
[2] La Trémouille to Louis XVIII, [?] October 1797, A.A.E., France 592.
[3] D'André to Wickham, [?] October 1797, F.O. 27/52. Cf. Doulcet de Pontécoulant's conversation with Wickham as reported in the latter's despatch to Grenville, 29 October 1797, F.O. 74/21. Doulcet named Jean de Bry, Sieyès, Lamarque, Riou and Chazal as belonging to the party demanding action against the royalists in the *Conseils*; he singled out Merlin de Douai as an Orléanist.
[4] D'André to Wickham, 30 August 1797, F.O. 74/18.

did not rise in the chamber to denounce La Revellière's anti-royalist appeal of the 27th,[1] his colleague, Thibaudeau, made a temporizing one on the 30th, destroying the effect created by an earlier scathing attack made by Duprat.[2] The deputies were again subject to conflicting interpretations of the crisis: while one group took it for granted that an impasse had been reached, the other refused to admit that there was any cause for alarm.[3] On the evening of the 30th, eighty deputies met at the home of Imbert-Colomès to discuss measures to defend the Legislature. But they were still hopeful that there was enough time to weaken the Directory by cogent criticism during the debates. They planned to continue these tactics for the purpose of ending the Directory's military preparations, wresting from it the powers to police the capital, moving the Legislature into permanent session, and declaring that the Fatherland was in danger.[4] But they also decided to carry out a preventive attack on the Luxembourg Palace, the residence of the Directors, the moment there was evidence of an attack against the Legislature.[5]

Despite their resolutions, they revealed an astonishing lack of vigilance in the last few days before the explosion. On 31 August, the five members of the *Commission des Inspecteurs*, Pichegru, Delarue, Vaublanc, Emmery and Thibaudeau received news confirming the Directory's intention to disperse the Legislature by armed might. Nevertheless the majority of the deputies voted in favour of waiting for a confirmatory report before raising the question in the Legislature. Imbert-Colomès, who was present during their discussions, bitterly accused them of continually

---

[1] See above, p. 205.

[2] *Réimpression de l'ancien Moniteur*, xxviii. 791–2, 796–7. Cf. Thibaudeau *Mémoires*, ii. 259–60.

[3] Malmesbury to Grenville, 5 September 1797, F.O. 27/50. In a report to Malmesbury, dated 28 August, Lagarde included Villaret-Joyeuse and Vaublanc among the deputies who advised restraint. Lagarde's report does not square with Vaublanc's own account in which, writing about his close collaboration with Villaret-Joyeuse, he claims that they were among the warmest advocates of a more aggressive policy. See Vaublanc, *Mémoires*, ii. 420–1. In a previous report, dated 3 September, Lagarde mentioned Larivière, Camille Jordan, Boissy d'Anglas and Quatremère de Quincy as being committed to moderation, F.O. 27/50. But according to d'André, Jordan and Larivière belonged to the more forward group. See d'André to Wickham, [?] October 1797, F.O. 27/52. Mallet du Pan's information led him to believe that Vaublanc was in the moderate camp. See *Correspondance de Mallet du Pan*, ii. 339.

[4] D'André to Wickham, [?] October 1797, F.O. 27/52.

[5] D'André to Wickham, 30 August 1797, F.O. 74/18. Cf. Imbert-Colomès: *Mémoire sur 18 Fructidor*, 11 October 1797, A.A.E., France 592.

'digressing from the main point without reaching any conclusions'.[1] La Trémouille also did 'his best to make them see the situation in its true light'.[2] Only Willot, d'André felt, was a truly 'valuable person, but what could he hope to accomplish among that pack of lawyers?'[3]

The next day, 1 September, d'André sent a short note to Wickham, saying that the moment had arrived.[4] On Sunday morning, the 3rd, he wrote that the *Conseils* were preparing to declare themselves in permanent session that very afternoon.[5] The *Inspecteurs* had indeed resolved that Vaublanc would ask on the 4th for an explanation of all the troop movements taking place in the capital. Meanwhile during the afternoon sitting of the Legislature, it was learned that the Directory had issued orders to assemble all the troops in one location. The *Inspecteurs*, led by Delarue, decided to question the constitutionality of this measure, but before they could do so the debates in both chambers were adjourned.

The *Inspecteurs* knew that the blow was coming but they did not know when. Rumours were legion. Malmesbury's secret informant, Lagarde, who received his information from a minister purporting to have heard about the Directory's plan, came nearest the truth. According to him the government would:

Issue warrants of arrest against sixty to seventy members of the *Conseils*, on the basis of the constitutional article permitting the Directory to arrest deputies for flagrant crimes against the state . . .; have them taken from their own homes at three or four in the morning; publish the papers taken from these members as proof of their correspondence with the *émigrés* and of their plans to restore Louis XVIII. All of this would then be presented to the Legislature on the following day, where action would be demanded against these deputies with a

[1] Imbert-Colomès: Mémoire sur 18 Fructidor, ibid.
[2] La Trémouille to Louis XVIII, [?] October 1797, ibid.
[3] D'André to Wickham, 1 September 1797, F.O. 74/21.
[4] Ibid.
[5] D'André to Wickham, 3 September 1797, F.O. 74/21. Cf. D'André to Wickham, [?] October 1797, F.O. 27/52. D'André had been assured on the 2nd, after the arrest of Raffet, the commander of the National Guard of the Butte des Moulins section, that the majority of the deputies would no longer hesitate. Raffet was arrested as a result of information provided by Veyrat, one of Sotin's spies. Veyrat succeeded in winning the confidence of Chauveau, an agent of the royalist counter-police working under the direction of Rovère and Dossonville, a former employee of the Committee of Public Safety. See P. H. Veyrat's *Précis historique, rélatif à la journée du 18 Fructidor*, Brit. Mus. Pamphlet, F. 1199 (9).

further request for the quashing of the last elections as counter-revolutionary. Support for these demands by the government will be made immeasurably easier by the presence and shouts of the soldiers—the best way to intimidate the Assembly.[1]

The royalists' own agents informed them of the outlines of the plan. They expected a *coup d'état* but they waited for the Directory to take the offensive. Admittedly they were outnumbered but their last-minute delays in trying to form a united front in the *Conseils*, where they probably could have found support if they had put their case in dramatic terms, lost them their chance.

The debates having been adjourned until the 4th, d'André assembled all the agents of the *Institut*'s branch in Paris, and after a lengthy meeting directed them to prepare their members for any emergency. They were to return to his house only if they detected signs that the troops in their quarters were being alerted for an attack that evening.[2] In another part of the city, between eight and nine in the evening, about twelve deputies including Willot, Pichegru, Imbert-Colomès and Delarue met at the *Salle des Inspecteurs* in the Pavilion de Marsan. The city appearing quite normal, they felt that the night would pass without incident, and so they dispersed. Delarue and Imbert-Colomès left the Pavilion but Pichegru and Willot remained to spend the night.[3] At nine a deputy, who acted as liaison officer between the *Inspecteurs* and d'André, hurried to tell them that everything was quiet. Just the opposite was the case. The 'triumvirate' had successfully isolated Carnot and Barthélemy; had they been more at home with one another they might have joined forces. It might even be suggested that their failure to halt the trend towards Caesarism—which the victory of the 'triumvirate' implied—matched the lack of realism of the deputies. With no opposition from Carnot and Barthélemy, the 'triumvirate' asked Augereau to carry out his orders. The story is well known; Lagarde's prophecy was almost entirely realized. At four in the morning Imbert-Colomès was roused from a fitful sleep by the sound of cannon,[4]

---

[1] Malmesbury to Grenville, 5 September 1797, F.O. 27/50.
[2] D'André to Wickham, [?] October 1797, F.O. 27/52.
[3] Imbert-Colomès: Mémoire sur 18 Fructidor, 11 October 1797, A.A.E., France 592.
[4] One of Dutheil's agents, who fled Paris in the early hours of Monday morning, said that he did not hear any sounds of cannon, report of 7 September sent to Grenville, F.O. 27/52. Barras (*Memoirs*, iii. 25) said that he gave the signal for the alarm gun to be sounded.

which seemed to be coming from the quays, but it was not till six that he ventured out. By then the bridges and roads leading to the quays had been blocked off. He ran to rouse two deputies who lived in his quarter and they decided to separate, each to discover his own refuge or the means to leave the city.[1] Elsewhere la Trémouille, having previously arranged to meet his officers, gave them orders to return to their posts in the departments and commanded Frotté to leave for London and Bourmont to set out for Edinburgh.[2] D'André was able to assemble only thirteen of his agents; the rest had fled. Again there was nothing he could do but instruct the agents of the *Institut* to continue their work and correspondence.[3] He then also went into hiding, making his way to Switzerland by slow stages. Others were able to evade arrest in a similar manner.

The rest were not so fortunate. Pichegru and Willot were rudely awakened by Augereau and taken prisoner. Though Carnot fled, having been informed in time, Barthélemy refused to take measures for his own safety.[4] Orders of deportation were issued against forty-two deputies in the *Conseil des Cinq-Cents* and eleven in the *Anciens*; the two Directors, Carnot and Barthélemy; Cochon, the former minister of police; Brottier and la Villeurnoy (Duverne, who was also included at first, having given away the agency's secrets, was released); Dossonville; Ramel, who had betrayed the agents in January and was now reaping the rewards for his loyalty; the newspapermen, Suard and Mailhe; and generals Morgan and Miranda, the latter as an alleged British spy.[5]

II

Polissard, one of the fortunate few who found refuge in Switzerland, analysed the political opinions of forty of the fifty-three deputies whose names appeared on the deportation lists. He divided them into four categories: the pure royalists; those who

[1] Imbert-Colomès: Mémoire sur 18 Fructidor, 11 October 1797, A.A.E., France 592.
[2] La Trémouille to Louis XVIII, [?] October 1797, ibid. La Trémouille remained in hiding until 26 September, finally managing to clear Calais with François a few days later.
[3] D'André to Wickham, [?] October 1797, F.O. 27/52.
[4] Bornes' conversation with Carnot [?] March 1798, *Dropmore Papers*, iv. 144–6.
[5] Of these, only seventeen—Murinais, Job-Aimé, Aubry, Tronson Ducoudray, Desmolières, Rovère, Bourdon de l'Oise, la Villeurnoy, Brottier, Ramel, Willot,

had wanted the Legislature to go into permanent session; the constitutionalists; and a minority about whose views he could not comment with too much certainty. According to him twenty-one belonged to the first group, three to the second, four to the third and twelve to the last. He believed, however, that at least four in the last category properly belonged to the pure royalist party.[1] He failed to analyse the views of Pichegru, Willot, Aubry, Delarue, Desmolières, Rovère, Duprat and Barbé-Marbois; the first seven were definitely pure royalists and the last, a constitutionalist. Of a total of forty-eight whose political leanings can be checked, thirty-two were thus very probably members of the extreme royalist party—or two thirds.

But the Directory threw its net wider still. It annulled the elections in forty-nine departments and validated those which the Legislature had overruled. Altogether 140 deputies lost their seats.[2] Yet had the Directory's surveillance been more thorough, the number of expelled deputies would have been greater, since the agents of the *Institut* were active in fifty-eight departments.[3] The Directory could not have been aware of the great inroads it had made. Moreover, of the forty-nine departments affected, there were *Instituts* only in thirty-seven. The Directory thus annulled the elections in twelve departments where the *Institut* did not exist, and failed to annul them in twenty-one where it did. Its decrees paradoxically omitted many departments where royalism had made most headway. This was particularly true of the south where the elections of the following departments were allowed to stand: Doubs, Jura, Isère, Drôme, Hautes-Alpes, Basses-Alpes, Gard, Lozère, Landes, Gers, Basses-Pyrénées, Hautes-Pyrénées, Pyrénées-Orientales, Haute-Garonne, Charente-Inférieure, Lot, Lot-et-Garonne, Creuse, Haute-Vienne, Corrèze, Cantal. While it is true that the deputies elected by the departments of Hautes-Pyrénées and Charente-Inférieure were partisans of the Directory, it could by no means be certain that the local administrative agencies would give their support. On the other

---

Delarue, Pichegru, Barthélemy, Barbé-Marbois, Dossonville and Lafond-Ladébat— were actually deported, the rest evading arrest. Of the deportees, the last eight succeeded in escaping in June 1798. Job-Aimé was pardoned in December 1799.

[1] Précy to Louis XVIII, 16 October 1797, A.A.E., France 592.

[2] A. Kuscinski, *Les Députés au Corps législatif de l'an IV à l'an VII* (Paris, 1905), pp. 191, 204.

[3] See above, pp. 182–3.

hand, it was acting on good information in not annulling the elections in the Vendée where the *Institut* had little or no roots.[1] Malmesbury was therefore probably right in concluding that 'the royalists have almost universally escaped, and continue to form a considerable, though an inert and passive body in the Councils'.[2] The press suffered the severest repression. Forty-two journals, Parisian and departmental, were banned on 12 September.[3] Richer-Sérisy, Fiévée, Marnésia, Dussault, Langlois, Beaulieu, Bertin d'Antilly, the Bertin brothers, Lagarde, Poncelin de la Roche-Tillac, Jardin, Michaud, Nicole, Lacretelle, Suard, Mailhe, Durand-Molard, Gallais, Fontanes, Vauxcelles, Ladevèze and other journalists not so well known, all of whom had been pleading the royalist cause since Thermidor, lost their newspapers. Some had their names placed on the deportation lists while others were imprisoned; but most were able to avoid arrest. The majority later took advantage of Bonaparte's amnesty and returned to Paris either to edit sycophantic journals or to assume administrative posts under the Consulate and the Empire. The Restoration took care to honour most of these chameleons of opinion.

Until the very last Wickham had feared that 'the jealousy which several of the members entertain of the plan of the pure royalists seems to preclude any solid union among them until, at any rate, the elections, to which period I feel we will never get without an explosion of some sort, and success will be with the party that attacks first'.[4] A month after the sudden purge he hesitated to assess its consequences but believed that 'something of this kind had to happen to unite friends of order and good government and to put an end to the dissension which made unity of conduct impossible'.[5] Obviously he still hoped that a formidable royalist party would begin its operations again in the not distant future. He realized how exaggerated his hopes had been and still were after seeing and talking to d'André[6] and Doulcet de Pontécoulant.[7]

[1] Ibid.
[2] Malmesbury to Grenville, 9 September 1797, F.O. 27/50.
[3] *Réimpression de l'ancien Moniteur*, xxviii. 815.
[4] Wickham to Grenville, 10 September 1797, F.O. 74/21.
[5] Wickham to Grenville, 4 October 1797, ibid.
[6] Wickham to Grenville, 15 October 1797, ibid.
[7] Wickham to Grenville, 29 October 1797, ibid.

III

There are two views, not sharply distinct from one another, concerning the causes of the *coup d'état* of 18 Fructidor. French historians have been debating the question ever since Mallet du Pan only a few short weeks after the disaster contemptuously dismissed the allegation of conspiracy:

This alleged conspiracy, for which the 'triumvirate' held the *Conseils* responsible, is a fiction similar to those invented by Robespierre. It is true that in their plans and in their conviction of the need to defend their inviolability against the outrages of the Jacobin faction, the *Conseils* were adopting certain measures of force; but the event proves that they were fools in hesitating to apply them.[1]

For Mallet du Pan, a true conspiracy had to be led by men prepared and unafraid to use force. The historians Caudrillier,[2] Aulard,[3] Mathiez,[4] and Lefebvre[5] disagree with Mallet du Pan. Meynier,[6] however, for reasons similar to those of the Genevese writer, denies the reality of the Anglo-royalist conspiracy. He claims that it was rather an Anglo-royalist *entente* which was formed to change the government by legal means: the royalists naïvely believed that they could re-establish the constitutional monarchy of 1791 by a simple decree. Thus they pursued a defensive and moderate but ineffectual policy. It was destined to fail in the face of the armed force at the disposal of the 'triumvirate'. In justification of the *coup d'état*, the Directory naturally exaggerated the ramifications of the conspiracy. What really happened was that a minority of the royalists, in agreement with Wickham as their paymaster, but with many unsuspecting deputies as their dupes, attempted to effect a constitutional restoration of the limited monarchy. Meynier's thesis is contested by Lefebvre. The royalists could not have had any illusions as to the fate of constitutional revision, for the Constitution made it almost impossible. Even if the opposition was sincere in

---

[1] *Correspondance de Mallet du Pan*, ii. 343.

[2] Caudrillier, *La Trahison de Pichegru*, passim.

[3] Aulard, op. cit.

[4] Mathiez, *Le Directoire*, ch. xiv.

[5] Lefebvre, 'Réponse à M. Meynier', *Annales de la Faculté des Lettres de Strasbourg*, x (1931), 49–52.

[6] A. Meynier, *Le Dix-huit Fructidor an V* (Paris, 1927).

its attachment to the Constitution, could an agreement with a government at war with France be regarded in any other light than a counter-revolutionary conspiracy?

There can be no doubt that a plot to overthrow the Directory did in fact exist. That it was confined to a minority does not alter the picture materially,[1] especially when that minority had acquired the support of even Dumas. Moreover, he had in his possession proof of Pichegru's treason and Moreau's potential treachery.[2] Without arguing the justice of the Directory's *coup d'état* or whether it possessed proof of a conspiracy, there is no questioning the fact that the leaders of the anti-Directorial group did their utmost to convince the majority of confused and frightened royalists that a blow against the Directory was necessary. That they failed and were forced to assume a defensive position, going so far as to agree to an attack on the Luxembourg Palace if the Directory attacked the deputies first, is additional proof. Even though Pichegru and Imbert-Colomès waited until the last moment to accept la Trémouille's aid, the view that a conspiracy did exist is incontestable. Moreover, a successful defence might have led to the victory of the royalists and the eventual restoration of the monarchy.

That is the most probable reason for the hostility of the majority in the opposition—the constitutionalists and even a few of the undecided royalists—to a more aggressive action. They realized its implications only too well. Lacking a definite assurance that their political future would be safeguarded under a restored monarchy, opposed to pre-revolutionary ideas and institutions which they suspected would be reaffirmed and re-established, sincere parliamentarians as some of them undoubtedly were, they were unwilling to lend their support to a programme which courted so much danger. In this respect, it is true that they preferred to follow a moderate, constitutional and defensive

[1] Reinhard adverts to the Right's lack of realism and fears during the frantic weeks before Fructidor as proof that there is no clear evidence of a plot against the Directory. But this is to view the Right as a bloc and to overlook that, however weak it was, one segment of the Right was prepared to pursue more aggressive action. See Reinhard's article on the Lille negotiations, loc. cit., 53.

[2] See J. Godechot, 'Moreau et les papiers de Klinglin', *Annales historiques de la Révolution française*, ix (1932), 309–24. The same writer deals at length with Pichegru's and Moreau's encouragement of royalist propaganda in their armies. See his 'Les Insurrections militaires sous le Directoire', ibid., x (1933), 129–52, 193–221, particularly 134 and 148.

policy. And their numerical strength forced the more resolute royalists to follow suit. It is also true that the latter adhered to legislative procedures until the very last day, but it is equally undeniable that they had agreed on the use of violence as an alternative. It is therefore a mistake to insist that the majority was made up of unsuspecting deputies who were unaware of the objective of their more forward colleagues. It was precisely because they feared the restoration of an unreformed monarchy that they opposed a closer working alliance with the confirmed royalists. In a positive sense, they were not a party to the conspiracy against the Republic; but in a negative sense they helped contribute to the political instability and made the *coup d'état* possible. Unfortunately their inflexible stand, based on principles about which they themselves were not too certain, did not save them from avoiding that which they most dreaded—political suicide.

12

TOO LITTLE AND TOO LATE

FRUCTIDOR is a turning point in the history of the Revolution. For the third time since Thermidor, the government success-fully used the army against its foes, and the army was the decisive factor in Fructidor as in Vendémiaire and in Prairial. The conse-quences were devastating for the royalists, the Revolution and the peace of Europe. With withering scorn and irony, Mallet du Pan ridiculed the Directory in its pose as the saviour of the Republic and of the Constitution: Fructidor had really under-mined the Republic and the Constitution by destroying the basis of popular sovereignty and national representation.[1] A dictator-ship seemed inevitable, for the puny men responsible for France's destiny were actually its puppets. No one was any longer the master of events. On the contrary, France and Europe were at the mercy of '*la force des choses*'.[2]

Neither Reubell, nor Bonaparte, nor Sieyès, nor Merlin is in control of the nation; the Revolution is. It is an irresistible movement acting on men and events; it is like the force of gravity to which they must respond.[3]

Fructidor was not only the end of peace, justice and good faith in Europe; it had given the Revolution an irrepressible momentum. The men who had almost held power in their grasp had let it elude them at the crucial moment. After all, it had been an illu-sion to expect the deputies, blinded by the chimera of constitu-tionalism, to act with resolution.[4]

La grande nation was on the march. Malmesbury, the inveterate trouble-shooter, had been in France on the eve of Fructidor— the second time within a year trying to negotiate peace. Even before the fateful day, he had been painfully aware that the future of Britain and Europe depended wholly on the outcome of the struggle between the Directory and the *Conseils*.[5] The Directory's

[1] *Correspondance de Mallet du Pan*, ii. 351.
[2] Ibid.   [3] Ibid., 387.   [4] Ibid., 339.
[5] Malmesbury to Grenville, 25 July 1797, F.O. 27/50.

victory put an end to Britain's hopes for a more tractable French policy. It drew from Grenville a comment remarkably like Mallet du Pan's. He denounced the 'imbecility of the Councils, . . . particularly . . . those who conducted what was called the moderating system in the *Conseil des Anciens*'.[1] The price of peace with the Directory meant a continent

abandoned without defence of any kind to these monsters, of the Netherlands, Holland and Italy left in their hands, of Germany revolutionized, and of the little hope we can have of any permanent tranquillity in the midst of all this wreck and convulsion of everything around us. . . . If this country could but be brought to think so, it would be ten thousand times safer . . . to face the storm, than to shrink from it.[2]

The rupture of the Lille negotiations intensified Grenville's uneasiness that the Revolution was moving ineluctably towards the domination of Europe; but now that peace was remote, France must be pushed back to her pre-war frontiers.

That the struggle with *la grande nation* would be an uneven one was almost immediately demonstrated by the Directory's demand to the Swiss Cantons that they expel Wickham for his part in anti-French intrigues. In the face of this, Wickham felt that rather than run the risk of being the cause of dissension between Switzerland and France, it would be best to retire from his post and to leave as chargé d'affaires his secretary, James Talbot, one of Malmesbury's aides in the 1796 peace mission to France. Wickham instructed Talbot to reduce the expenses of maintaining the mission's liaison with the agents in France.[3] Before departing he saw to it that the victims of the *coup* who had fled to Switzerland were given the means to renew their opposition to the Directory.[4] His withdrawal from Switzerland was a recognition not only of the desperate weakness of the royalists, but also of the considerable energy which the Revolution still possessed, a force that could not be halted without tremendous power. Could the necessary power be created? This was the

---

[1] Grenville to Malmesbury, 11 September 1797, *Dropmore Papers*, iii. 372.
[2] Grenville to Pitt, 8 October 1797, ibid., 378.
[3] Wickham to Grenville, 10, 13, 21 October 1797, F.O. 74/21.
[4] Wickham to Grenville, 4 October 1797, ibid.; Précy to d'Avaray, 10 October 1797, du Lac, op. cit., pp. 288-9. Wickham gave the deputies five hundred louis.

problem to which the British government addressed itself in the following three years. Yet, the solution of that problem was already predetermined by the happenings of 1797 which culminated on 18 Fructidor. The succeeding period, though of great interest, is, in every sense, a dénouement. If ever the royalists approached victory, it was in the days before September 1797. All that happened afterwards flowed mercilessly from that date, as if dictated by a wrathful classical deity avenging itself upon the frailties of man. To be sure, the British were not backward in breathing life into a fresh coalition and were fertile in devising new projects, military and conspiratorial, to bring down the Republican edifice, but rivalries within the Cabinet, failure to co-ordinate plans, and the same suspicions among the allies proved fatal to the new design.

II

Talbot's mission to Switzerland survived Wickham's by little more than a month. In February 1798, he took up residence near the German frontiers of Switzerland, but maintained his connections with Wickham's agents and important Swiss *émigrés* who were intent on opposing the Confederation's absorption by France. The chief of these was Steiger, the *avoyer* or first magistrate of Berne. Wickham, assuming his new post as under-secretary of state in the Home Office under Portland's direction, had great confidence in Talbot's abilities to perform his duties 'with equal industry and discretion'.[1] As events were to show, Talbot's industry was greater than his discretion. His chief contribution to the counter-revolution was to recommend a modified version of the plan put to the test before Fructidor. The modification consisted in lulling the Directory into a false sense of security by encouraging the deputies who would be returned in the 1798 elections to co-operate with it. Behind the smokescreen, a small but resolute group of deputies could plan a *coup d'état* with the connivance of the army.[2]

While Talbot was eagerly exploring this theme, d'André and Précy were trying with mounting desperation to revive the

[1] Wickham to Grenville, 29 December 1797, *Correspondence of William Wickham*, ii. 68.
[2] Talbot to Grenville, 18 November 1797, *Dropmore Papers*, iii. 397-9.

spirit of resistance among those deputies[1] who had found a refuge in Switzerland. In answer to Précy's appeal,[2] they met at Yverdon but, after agreeing to publish a protest against the *coup d'état* and await Louis' orders, they did nothing more; they were, they recognized, powerless.[3] Without funds and without Wickham's directions, Précy and d'André were in no position to inject new life into the counter-revolution. All they could do was trust in Britain to renew her commitments.[4] Both agents felt—Précy more so than d'André—that the elements of opposition to the Directory, especially in the areas neighbouring Switzerland, could be fanned to life only when the Swiss Cantons took the initiative by an invasion of the Midi. Even if this were possible—the lack of funds and the irresolution of the Cantons made it extremely doubtful—the presence of large numbers of French troops in the crucial departments made the enterprise extremely risky.[5]

In London, Wickham recommended financial assistance both to the Bernese and to the deputies, most of whom had by this time moved on to Swabia.[6] The imminence of the Directory's extension of power to Switzerland governed Grenville's instructions[7] to Talbot. Steiger was promised a sum of £5,000 monthly, which would be increased to £200,000 or more a year if Berne resisted the French. In the latter contingency, military measures with the royalists should be concerted. If, on the other hand, the Swiss reached an agreement with France guaranteeing their independence, it would still be a vital part of Britain's policy to provide funds to the royalists both to maintain their correspondence with the interior of France and to finance their election campaign.[8] Even before this, Grenville gave his approval to a grant of £20,000 for d'André's use,[9] and, in his formal instructions, he authorized Talbot to draw on an additional £10,000 for

[1] The following deputies succeeded in making their way to Switzerland: Bornes; André de la Lozère; Camille Jordan; Polissard; Lemerer; Imbert-Colomès; Couchery; Doulcet de Pontécoulant; Vauvilliers.

[2] Précy to d'Avaray, 10 October 1797; Précy to Louis XVIII, 16 October 1797, du Lac, op. cit., pp. 288–90.

[3] Talbot to Grenville, 8 November 1797, F.O. 74/21.

[4] Précy to d'Avaray, 6 January 1798, du Lac, op. cit., pp. 292–3.

[5] Précy to Wickham, 11 January 1798; d'André to Talbot, 27 January 1798, F.O. 74/22.

[6] Wickham to Grenville, 29 January 1798, ibid.

[7] Grenville to Steiger, 13 February 1798, ibid.

[8] Grenville to Talbot, 14 February 1798, ibid.

[9] Talbot to Grenville, 6 February 1798, ibid.

the same purpose. The sums were hardly as munificent as those that had formerly been granted Wickham and their free use was conditioned by the caution that they ought not to be wasted.

Talbot reached Ulm on 2 March and arranged for the delivery of Grenville's greetings to Steiger.[1] A few days later, he met with d'André, Précy and de Vezet in the privacy of the abbey of Salmansweiler in Ulm. There the agents reconstituted themselves as the Swabian agency and agreed that there was little prospect of a favourable change in France because of the completely demoralized state of the royalists.[2] In the light of these circumstances and the failure of the larger Swiss Cantons to resist the French advance under generals Brune and Schauenberg—Berne capitulated to the French on 5 March and Steiger fled to Germany —Talbot would not promise the agents any funds beyond the £20,000 Grenville had authorized for d'André. So strongly did Talbot feel that the agents' request for more funds for the election campaign would be 'a waste of money', that he did not hesitate to make the remarkable suggestion that 'violent Jacobins should be elected' as 'their gaining the preponderance would possibly produce a convulsion of which some advantage might be taken'.[3]

Conditions seemed unlikely to change, and so critical did the British think the situation in Switzerland that Grenville despatched Jolivet, a partner in the Swiss bank, Messrs. Schmitz Meyer in London, and a son of the counsellor of Geneva, with a promise of £150,000 to the Bernese if they chose to renew resistance to the French.[4] Colonel Malcolm was also sent to offer his services.[5] During the next few months, however, the French advance and the almost wholesale capitulation of the Swiss obviated any immediate use of the funds which was Berne's for the asking. The large Cantons, including Berne, acquiesced in the Directory's ultimatum to accept the new constitution

[1] Talbot to Steiger, 5 March 1798; Talbot to Canning, 6 March 1798, ibid.
[2] Précy to d'Avaray, 18 February 1798, du Lac, op. cit., pp. 296–7. Their decision was partly based on Royer-Collard's (he had travelled to Germany to see the refugee deputies) pessimistic account of the political situation.
[3] Talbot to Canning, 13 March 1798, F.O. 74/22.
[4] Grenville to Talbot, 29 March 1798; Wickham to Banneret Fisher, 29 March 1798, ibid.
[5] Grenville to Talbot, 29 March 1798, ibid.

transforming Switzerland into a unitary republic. The smaller Cantons (chiefly Catholic and economically underdeveloped) resisted in the hope that the mountainous terrain would wear down the French troops. But they, too, submitted; a brief uprising in the Upper Valais suffered the same fate. Thus by the end of May, the French appeared to be in control of the Cantons. Although Talbot wondered, on the eve of the struggle between the little Cantons and the French, whether he should offer them assistance, he hesitated for fear of compromising his government 'in so desperate a cause',[1] and, in this decision, he was commended by Grenville who wished to avoid a senseless slaughter; nor would he sanction it in the future unless the Swiss could count on Austrian military help. Talbot's attitude was thus in perfect harmony with Grenville's. He managed to see Steiger at Wurzach, where they agreed to encourage a policy of underground warfare against the French. Steiger then left for Vienna to seek aid from the Austrian high command.[2]

The enemies of the Directory were marking time everywhere. In anticipation of the 1798 elections, the Directory took special care to arrange for the return of deputies who were neither Jacobins nor independents.[3] By its firm supervision of the press, preparation of official lists of candidates, and the despatch of government servants to key electoral areas, the Directory hoped to produce favourable results. Despite all these precautions, the government was alarmed by the success of candidates who were too much associated with Jacobinism for its taste; accordingly it replaced fifty-three of the newly elected deputies with others who would do their bidding and left an equal number of seats vacant. This—the *coup d'état* of Floréal—the royalists saw as a prelude to a great surge of opposition from the discomfited Jacobins; if d'André is to be believed, they actually approached the royalists to unite in a common struggle against the Directory.[4] Similar information reached Talbot, who thought that this would be good strategy.[5] D'André was more cautious.[6] Nevertheless both agreed that legislative co-operation between the two parties might

[1] Grenville to Talbot, 24 May 1798, F.O. 74/22.
[2] Talbot to Canning, 19, 27 May 1798, ibid.
[3] See Lefebvre, *La Révolution française*, pp. 488–9.
[4] D'André to Canning, 14 June 1798, F.O. 74/22.
[5] Talbot to Canning, 17 June 1798, ibid.
[6] D'André to Canning, 14 June 1798, ibid.

produce positive results. How? By some strange mode of reasoning, they predicted that the Directory would launch a full-scale campaign against the Jacobins rather than the royalists in order to extricate itself from the impossible position of being thwarted by both. If this happened, the royalists would derive 'the advantage of being delivered from one of [their] enemies'.[1]

However muted the enemies of the Directory were, for a time the situation in Switzerland gave Talbot some cause for hope. The Helvetic Councils on 12 July asked their citizens to take an oath swearing to uphold liberty and equality; Steiger appealed to the Swiss to refuse. He thus helped to launch a new wave of resistance among the people of the smaller Cantons. The Cantons of Schwyz, Uri, and Unterwalden renewed their agreement for mutual defence and were prepared to fight at the first sign of the French penetration of the Mont St. Gothard pass into the Milanese. The mountaineers of Lucerne, Soleure, Fribourg, Berne, Glarus and Upper Valais were, Talbot reported, also at boiling point.[2] He was also assured by Hotzé, the Austrian commander, that Austria was planning a renewal of hostilities; and he had similar news from Sir Morton Eden in Vienna.[3] Meanwhile fighting broke out in Schwyz and in the town of Stanz in Unterwalden on 18 August. Shortlived in the former, it persisted in Stanz, but stood little chance of success or of spreading to the other Cantons because of the obvious superiority of the French under Schauenberg. Talbot's news had prompted Grenville to promise £400,000 for the service of the Swiss army under Hotzé's command.[4] But by that time, the fighting spirit in the Cantons had been crushed; potential opposition to France remained only among the people of the Grisons, Switzerland's ancient ally. The struggle in Switzerland was over for 1798.

In expectation of prolonged Swiss resistance, Talbot had taken steps to perfect communications with the royalists in the Midi and in Paris. The same reasoning, which had induced Wickham in 1795 to provide funds and arms to the insurgents in the Lyonnais area, inspired Talbot, but he went further. Like Wickham, Talbot conceived of a simultaneous penetration of France

[1] Talbot to Canning, 12 July 1798, ibid.
[2] Talbot to Canning, 30 July 1798, ibid.
[3] Talbot to Canning, 1 August 1798, ibid.
[4] Grenville to Talbot, 12 September 1798, ibid.

from the west, the east and the south. Theoretically, this was sound, but, as he himself admitted, uncertain in the light of Austrian inactivity and the Vendée's tranquillity. Nevertheless since a new coalition was in the offing, it was necessary to prepare the interior of France for a great insurrection.[1]

An examination of his plan will indicate how far Talbot was prepared to commit his government. The plan was worked out with the assistance of d'André, who may be regarded as its most vehement defender. The moment the armies of the coalition advanced, the royalists in the interior, provisioned beforehand with arms and funds, would move towards a general uprising and the seizure of power. In case the war was not renewed, the overthrow of the Directory could be achieved by lulling the Jacobins into a working alliance with the royalists: d'André argued that the inevitable beneficiaries of such an arrangement would be the royalists. In addition, every effort should be made to gain control over the army so as to deprive the Directory of its only shield.[2] Working together with d'André's Swabian agency was its counterpart in Paris, headed by Royer-Collard, the abbé de Montesquiou (whom d'André had known as a fellow-member of the Constituent and in Paris during the previous year), Clermont-Gallerande, and Becquey, an opportunistic but fanatical royalist. It is apparent that they were counting on the allegiance of army officers in and about Paris and were deviously encouraging the Jacobins to plan a *coup de main* against the Directory.[3] While pursuing this objective, they were also organizing resistance in Paris itself, applying the principles of the *Institut* in a modified form, as the following excerpt from one of their letters indicates:

The most perfectly planned organization in the departments should have no other purpose than that of supporting and underlining the movement which is going to erupt here [Paris] . . . I have been successful in gathering together a number of courageous men who, during different periods of the Revolution, made a name for themselves for their resistance. I have extended this work, little by little, to thirty-seven sections and I am going to do more. Only four of my friends know the plan in its entirety. Each of them is in touch with a basic

[1] Talbot to Canning, 30 July 1798, F.O. 74/22.
[2] D'André's note, no date, in Talbot's despatch to Canning, 30 July 1798, ibid.
[3] Letters from Paris, 15, 16, 17, 19 July 1798, ibid.

group made up of the leaders of subsidiary groups; these in turn are subdivided into other groups. I have preferred to seek men who are not prompted to intellectualize, men who are motivated by habit, memory, emotion and by a violent hatred for the *status quo*.[1]

Obviously the agents in Paris were counting on blind hatred of the Directory to produce an explosion; they planned nothing less than a bloodbath with no ideological overtones. If funds were made available, the Swabian agency's man in Lyons promised that by October the southern, eastern and western departments would also be in a state of readiness.[2]

It was not until the end of the year and the beginning of the new that the full impact of Talbot's thinking struck Grenville. There could be no argument with the efforts to form connections with superior officers in the French army: Talbot reported that the commanders at Bordeaux, Toulouse, Huningen and Sélestat promised to surrender their fortresses; that the second in command at Befort was co-operating enthusiastically; that the commanding officers at Besançon and Strasbourg were wavering; and that Bernadotte, too, was prepared to join the cause. Nor could there be any criticism of the tightening of communications from Besançon to La Rochelle by way of Lyons, Toulouse and Bordeaux.[3] For what purpose were these preparations being undertaken? Nothing less than the forcible overthrow of the government and the assassination of the Directors! This was revealed in Talbot's report of his talks with Royer-Collard who came to Augsburg to concert details with the Swabian agency and the deputies who were still in hiding in the area.[4] Talbot was greatly impressed by Royer-Collard's 'just reasoning'. There was, he said, a general yearning for the 'restoration of the ancient monarchy', which would restore finances, reform the tax system and end the requisitions and conscription.[5] It was essential, more than ever before, to reap the advantage of this wholesale disaffection; nearly all would be in readiness for a *coup de main* in the spring of 1799. Eager to participate was the commander of troops stationed in the neighbourhood of Paris, as well as nearly

[1] Letter from Paris, 21 July 1798, ibid.
[2] Letter from Lyons, [?]July 1798, ibid.
[3] Talbot to Canning, 3 November 1798, ibid.
[4] Talbot to Canning, 25 November 1798, ibid.
[5] A new general conscription law had been passed on 23 September 1798.

300 officers in Paris who, at the appointed moment, would converge on the Directory's official residence (the Luxembourg Palace), do away with the Directors, sound the tocsin, assemble the sections, declare for the king, send messengers to the departments, and abolish the *Conseils*. A provisional government headed by Royer-Collard, Jourdan des Bouches-du-Rhône, and Quatremère de Quincy would then be established to await the arrival of Louis. The cost of the entire operation would come to 1,000,000 livres or about £40,000.

With the formation of a second coalition almost a certainty at the end of 1798, the headlong rush of Neapolitan forces towards Rome and Leghorn, the revival of stirrings in Switzerland, and signs of insurrection in the Netherlands, Talbot asked Grenville in December to transport arms to the insurgents in southern France and in the Bordeaux region.[1] A short month later, a note of dejection crept into Talbot's news.[2] It was occasioned by the complete rout of the Neapolitans, Austria's inactivity and indifference to the fate of the insurgents in the Netherlands, and the disappearance of any hope of armed resistance in Switzerland, all of which had thrown the great plans in Paris into, what Talbot hoped was only temporary disarray. He was prepared, in the new circumstances, to 'try to cause a diversion . . . by . . . risings in different parts of France': the *élan* of the insurgents in the departments of the Hautes-Pyrénées, Charente-Inférieure, Ariège, Basses-Alpes and Lozère should be exploited. More important than the enthusiasm of these departments was their strategic value. Forces could be organized in the Basses-Alpes to cut off French communications with Italy; those in the Hautes-Pyrénées and Charente-Inférieure—especially in the latter—could facilitate communications with the Vendée and with Britain; while those in the Ariège could serve as a central point between the insurrections in the Basses-Alpes and Lozère, which were in close proximity to the Lyonnais and the eastern frontiers of France. D'André estimated that the cost of establishing these forces would come to some £18,000,[3] for which sum Talbot drew on Grenville's account. He did not venture to pass judgement on Précy's more elaborate proposal to make an initial outlay of over

[1] Talbot to Canning, 9 December 1798, F.O. 74/22.
[2] Talbot to Canning, 2 January 1799, F.O. 74/23.
[3] D'André's estimate, no date, ibid.

£1,000,000 for the purpose of putting thirteen departments on a substantial war footing under the direction of the *Institut*.[1] The news of Talbot's support of a *coup de main* in Paris drew from Grenville a severe reprimand;[2] Talbot correctly interpreted it as marking the end of his mission. Grenville suggested that Talbot had been the ingenuous tool of the Swabian agency and rejected as puerile and unrealistic any attempt against the lives of the Directors. He reminded Talbot that the chief purpose of his mission was to lay the 'foundations of future co-operation with the efforts of the Swiss in case Austria renews the war', and that 'insurrections [in France] would only be desirable if they afforded a diversion of republican forces employed in Switzerland'. Finally he advised Talbot to recover the funds that he had distributed and to give up any notions of 'gaining individuals of whatever rank or description in the interior of France at the present moment, without a distinct view of the point both of time and place at which their services may be made applicable to Switzerland'. Poor Talbot was at a loss to understand the reasons for his superior's anger. In a comparison of the situation in France before and after Fructidor, he justified his actions by recalling that the organization of a military force seemed necessary because its absence before Fructidor had been the cause of royalist failure.[3] In March he was transferred to Stockholm as secretary of the British legation and colonel Robert Craufurd was sent to Switzerland to prepare the Swiss resistance movement in collaboration with the Austrians who had just joined the second coalition.[4] Two months later, Wickham was plucked from his office in the Home Office to begin his second rendezvous with the royalists.

III

The revival of the coalition in 1798–99 reopened the prospect of the final defeat of revolutionary France. Although Naples was eliminated from the hostilities almost at the outset, the British once again put tremendous reliance on generously subsidizing the arms of Russia and Austria. The war, this time, was not to

[1] Précy's 'Etat approximatif des dépenses nécéssaires pour chaque département', no date, ibid.

[2] Grenville to Talbot, 25 January 1799; 25 January 1799 (marked separate), ibid.

[3] Talbot to Grenville, 19 February 1799, ibid.

[4] Grenville to Talbot, 15, 21 March 1799, ibid.

be pursued along conventional lines alone. Grenville and Pitt believed—with considerably more conviction than in 1793—in the necessary conjunction of military efforts with those of the underground, not only in France, but also in Holland and Switzerland. Wickham's second mission on the continent must be seen as part of Britain's scheme for the final destruction of the nascent *grande nation*.

On the surface everything pointed to a successful final assault upon France. The spring of 1799 saw the expulsion of the French from northern Italy by Austrian and Russian forces, and by the end of the summer only Genoa remained in French hands. In June, Masséna's forces were defeated at the first battle of Zurich. There was no guarantee, however, of continued military success, for diplomatic strains in the coalition, present from the beginning, asserted themselves during the summer. The chief difficulty arose from Austro-Russian rivalry—each distrusted the other's pretensions in Italy and Switzerland—and Austria's complacency in the campaign, which was prompted by the easy reconquest of Italy and archduke Charles' advance on the Rhine in the direction of Alsace.[1]

Although Austria's day-to-day diplomacy and military plans were unfathomable in their apparently meaningless oscillations, at least the Russians lived up to their promise to pursue the Swiss campaign. Following the British plan, it was hoped to throw the French back and undertake preparations for an invasion of Franche-Comté. Grenville, of course, put his faith in Austro-Russian collaboration, but he could not deceive himself as to the jealousies and intrigues of Vienna. He consequently placed the bulk of his hopes in a good understanding with the Russians, with whom his government was also planning an invasion of Holland. It was this need for Russian good will that explains his adamant insistence on the Dutch plan in the face of repeated criticism from Windham. The success of the British plan depended, in Grenville's view, on a simultaneous impact upon France from Holland, Franche-Comté, and, to a lesser extent, from the action of the royalists in the west; Windham would have preferred Britain to commit her forces entirely to the Vendée. The core of British strategy had therefore three segments; each requires separate examination.

[1] *Cambridge History of British Foreign Policy*, i. 293.

The chief objectives of Wickham's second mission were, in collaboration with Hotzé, Steiger and Craufurd, to consult with the Russian and Austrian representatives in Switzerland on the best means of restoring its former rulers. The possibility of insurrection in eastern and southern France[1] was to be explored as well, in order 'to resist the Directory' and 'to co-operate with the allies . . .'[2] The last admonition meant that Grenville would countenance full-scale assistance to the royalists only in the event of certain military advance by the allies; but the royalists must be given every inducement to take up arms when the grand push into France became a reality.

From Schaffhausen, on 29 June, two days after his arrival, Wickham informed Grenville of the near impasse in the progress of the allied plans. It was apparent that Charles and Thugut were at odds, making it impossible to concert plans for the liberation of Switzerland.[3] The simple fact was that Charles could not make decisions without instructions from Vienna; however well-disposed he was towards the efforts of the smaller Swiss Cantons to act against the French—the result of Wickham's skilful briefing —he was unable to move on his own.[4] What Wickham also found irritating was the reluctance of the more important Cantons to support the allies because they preferred their new governments and feared the revival of the old. The Swiss, of course, had good cause to remember their grievances under the old regime; but Wickham was certain that Austrian agents were deliberately restraining them from acting until they were given the signal from Vienna. The implication was that Austria was waiting for the appropriate moment to occupy, subdue and incorporate Switzerland into her dominions. Only the presence of Russian troops could undo Austria's designs.[5] By the end of July, Wickham reported that he found it impossible to arrest the course of events. Expatiating at length on the demoralized state of the Cantons, on the inroads of Jacobinism among the 'lower classes in the commercial area', and popular disillusionment with their

---

[1] Grenville to Wickham, 6 June 1799, *Correspondence of William Wickham*, ii. 104–7.
[2] Grenville to Wickham, 6 June 1799, separate and secret, F.O. 74/24.
[3] Wickham to Grenville, 29 June 1799, *Correspondence of William Wickham*, ii. 110–15.
[4] Wickham to Grenville, 6 July 1799, ibid., 120–5.
[5] Wickham to Grenville, 6 July 1799, F.O. 74/24.

governments in the little Cantons, he saw no prospect of vigorous Swiss action.[1]

Nothing would swerve the Austrians from pressing their advantages before those of their allies. To be sure, a successful Anglo-Russian invasion of Holland would probably lead to the defeat of the French in Belgium. But how much better if the campaign could be pressed on as many fronts as possible. To this end, Grenville substituted Lord Minto for Morton Eden at Vienna to speed Austria's movements in Switzerland. But Austrian assurances were beginning to sound hollow, and, indeed, on the very day that Wickham learned of Whitehall's decision to send major-general Lord Mulgrave to confer with Charles,[2] Vienna decided to abandon the Swiss invasion and instead attempt the capture of Mainz. Mulgrave's mission to Switzerland was intended to impress Charles with the utter seriousness of Britain's intentions. Moreover, the king had given approval to Artois' preparations to enter Lyons following a successful campaign.[3] That the government had journeyed far from the objectives of 1793 may be seen in Grenville's remarks to Mulgrave: '. . . Europe can never be really restored to tranquillity but by the restoration of monarchy in France.'[4] And since the contemplated Austrian operation against Mainz would never accomplish this, it was important to convince Charles of the folly of diverting his forces from the only area—Lyons—that could.[5]

Grenville's feverish efforts to force the Austrians to a sense of their responsibility were matched by Wickham who was not at all sanguine. For him Austrian deviousness meant the loss of Switzerland to the French. It provoked from him a volcanic denunciation of Austria's deceptions from which he had suffered during his first mission:

. . . During the whole course of my former mission, no measure tending either to give honour, security, or stability to Switzerland, or to bring forward any of the French Princes, or to restore Royalty in France in the person of the lawful claimant to the Crown was ever proposed

[1] Wickham to Grenville, 28 July 1799, F.O. 74/24.
[2] Grenville to Wickham, 30 July 1799, ibid.
[3] Ibid.
[4] Grenville to Mulgrave, 5 August 1799, Dropmore Papers, v. 243.
[5] Grenville to Mulgrave, 7 August 1799, ibid., 251–8.

by His Majesty's Government that was not received with a certain quantity of fair words and afterwards effectively counteracted. . . .[1]

Austria's intransigence was not the only source of British concern. The Russians refused to countenance the departure of Artois for the battle area,[2] but Grenville sought Paul's support, adducing as evidence of its propriety George III's acquiescence.[3] Thus everything was being done to persuade the allies of the reasonableness of Britain's representations. While Charles contrived to prolong his stay in Switzerland until early September, the consequences of his withdrawal to the Rhine, Wickham predicted, would assure a French victory.[4] Grenville's plea that Wickham do something to halt the inevitable was a cry of deep despair.[5] By the end of September, Zurich was again in French hands. Suvarov's penetration of the Grisons in early October marked not the resumption of the campaign against the French but its end, for Suvarov swore never to fight alongside the Austrians again.

Throughout this period, the British continued their preparations for a combined Anglo-Russian invasion of Holland; they also gave some attention to the project of lending assistance to the royalists in the Vendée region. There was a struggle in the Cabinet over the objectives and advantages of each. From its inception, Grenville, supported by Pitt, regarded the Holland invasion as the first step in breaking France's mastery over the north-east, and he fully expected the Dutch to welcome the invaders as their liberators. The Dutch operation was, of course, part of the grander scheme of inflicting blows upon France at her weakest points: Holland was seen as a fresh foyer of the counter-revolution which could be added to that in France and Switzerland. From this conception, Windham demurred, and Dundas took violent exception to anything that went beyond purely military considerations. Their dissensions provide indirect but

---

[1] Wickham to Grenville, 15 August 1799, F.O. 74/24.
[2] Grenville to Wickham, 18 August 1799, *Dropmore Papers*, v. 291.
[3] Grenville to Whitworth, 27 August 1799, ibid., 326-7. George III approved the plan to re-establish the monarchy, to announce to the French that the allies would not seek territorial indemnities at their expense, and to confine France within her pre-war boundaries.
[4] Wickham to Grenville, 28, 31 August 1799, *Correspondence of William Wickham*, ii. 182-5, 191-4.
[5] Grenville to Wickham, 5 September 1799, F.O. 74/24.

fresh evidence for the failure of the Dutch plan. It should be noted that by pressing for its acceptance Grenville provided a trial run for the execution of the policy that proved successful in 1814.

The principal source of controversy between Grenville and Windham arose not from any basic disagreement; Grenville had by 1799 become a counter-revolutionary, a far cry from his reticence of the early war years. Their differences stemmed from opposite views of priority. Grenville's was the larger conception, for he saw the need to obtain allies and to attack France on several fronts, but he was again gambling on allied collaboration, when there was little evidence of its existence, and on the coherence and steadfastness of the western royalists, in whom he placed too much confidence. Windham had little faith in the allies, and apprized much more cogently the needs and fears of the royalists. Yet his vehement acceptance of the royalist position tended to becloud the points upon which he and Grenville were in real agreement. Grenville did not take issue with Windham's stress on the need to restore the monarchy—a fact which the latter's febrile reasoning was always inclined to overlook—but he knew that to trust in the exertions of the royalists alone was a mirage.

Windham's arguments are remarkably similar to those of d'Antraigues'; and it is not surprising that they resemble Burke's, for he was, it is pertinent to recall, Burke's most faithful disciple. From the start of the second coalition, Windham threw doubt on its success. He could not see the military conquest of France as marking the end of the Jacobin threat. 'Nothing is a cure,' he wrote Grenville, 'for the evil of the time but a counter-revolution, . . . and that can never be effected by mere external force.'[1] To expect the French to divest themselves of their republican shackles in the face of external invasion was ludicrous. They would, on the other hand, do so if they could count on a public declaration from the powers of their respect for the territorial integrity of France. If the allied efforts succeeded, it would be mandatory for the government to undertake the capture of Quiberon and Noirmoutier.[2] For Pitt were reserved the caustic shafts of Windham's rhetoric. Making the same points as

[1] Windham to Grenville, 2 May 1799, Add. MSS., 37846.
[2] Windham to Grenville, 7 May 1799, ibid.

in his letters to Grenville, he added the following illustrations to strengthen his arguments:

. . . Reduce France as much as you please . . . unless you can cover it with Russian and Austrian garrisons, and reduce it to the state of Po'd [Poland], while a bit remains, existing in the form of a Jacobin Republick, [*sic*] I have no idea other [than that] the poison from there . . . will not corrode and infect all Europe. . . . The Coalition alone singlehanded never can effect it [the counter-revolution]. A man might as well expect to get a child singlehanded and without the concurrence of a female, as the combined powers . . . [can expect] to establish a good government in France, without the aid of the Inhabitants of that country.[1]

As preparations were being made for the invasion of Holland during July and August, Windham redoubled his efforts to wrest from his colleagues a definite promise to the insurgents in the Vendée; he protested their refusal to do so for fear of precipitating a premature explosion in the region. It was much the better part of wisdom to extend them aid so that they could defend themselves if the Directory suddenly hurled its forces against them.[2] It was too much to expect the Vendeans to remain passive once the allies moved on to Lyons, especially as the allied offensive would force the Directory to drain the Vendée of troops in defence of France's eastern frontier. Windham's disapproval of the Dutch expedition was obvious but to no avail; he asked only that the forces destined for Holland be transferred to the western coasts of France upon the completion of the Dutch conquest. Grenville's hopes for a counter-revolution in Holland,[3] he was certain, would not only fail, but also 'destroy in the bud an army which could be better used in western France'.[4]

On 26 August, as admiral Duncan's invading force was nearing the Helder where it landed the next day, Grenville explained to Windham that the Dutch plans had been a necessary condition of the negotiations with Russia. As for the proposal to land a British army in western France, Grenville pleaded a poverty of

---

[1] Windham to Pitt, 22 May 1799, Add. MSS., 37844.
[2] Windham to Pitt, 24 July 1799, ibid.
[3] Grenville to Thomas Grenville, 30 July 1799, *Dropmore Papers*, v. 212.
[4] Windham to Grenville, 10 August 1799, Add. MSS., 37846. Auckland drawing upon his experience as ambassador at The Hague, deprecated Dutch energy and predicted failure. Auckland to Beresford, 23 August 1799, Add. MSS., 34445.

men and arms,[1] a plea which was not without foundation. At the back of his mind, there was another reason for the urgency of the Dutch expedition; if successful, it could be a preliminary to an invasion of Belgium. Austria would thus be induced to take a more active part in the Swiss campaign in the hope that Britain would return Belgium to her.[2] The capture of the Dutch fleet elated Grenville.[3] He was now fairly confident of a full victory in Holland and began to examine the possibility of reactivating the war in the Vendée.[4] Yet he was not ready to approve a western expedition until the end of the campaign in Holland and on France's eastern borders clarified the advantages of a campaign in Vendée as opposed to one in Belgium.[5] Apart from considering more carefully the expense of outfitting an army for service in the Vendée, Pitt's views were similar to his foreign secretary's.[6] Dundas, on the other hand, was aghast at the suggestion; he had to think of forming an army which could not be ready until the spring; besides he preferred another strategy altogether—a combined Anglo-Russian landing on the southern coasts of France, a campaign in Belgium, and possibly an invasion in the area of Brest.[7] Dundas's reminder of the paucity of British land forces re-enforced the futility of planning any thrust at any point on the continent without patching up the coalition. It was to this question that Grenville addressed his efforts, but by the end of October there could be no doubt that the grand scheme envisaged for 1799 was ending in disaster. In the last days before the rout of the allies in Switzerland, he still spoke of collecting a force of 100,000 men under Suvarov,[8] but by mid-October there were no straws left to clutch. Grenville learned from Minto what he had long known: Thugut's territorial aims, if satisfied, were not inconsistent with his recognition of the French Republic; Thugut, moreover, had no faith in the royalists, and believed that even if by some remote chance their counter-revolution succeeded, their endless quarrels would reduce French

---

[1] Grenville to Windham, 26 August 1799, Add. MSS., 37846.
[2] Grenville to Dundas, 27 July 1799, *Dropmore Papers*, v. 198–9.
[3] Grenville to Auckland, 2 September 1799, Add. MSS., 34445.
[4] Grenville to Windham, 2 September 1799, *Dropmore Papers*, v. 346–7.
[5] Grenville to Windham, 5 September 1799, ibid., 359–60.
[6] Pitt to Grenville, 10 September 1799, ibid., 380.
[7] Dundas to Grenville, 20 September 1799, ibid., 414–16.
[8] Grenville to Wickham, 29 September 1799, ibid., 433–4.

power to the benefit of Europe.[1] The game had been played and lost in Switzerland and the Dutch invasion had suffered the same fate because of bad timing and the passive attitude of the Dutch.

Failure in the east did not deter the royalists in the western provinces from undertaking sporadic attacks against the troops of the Republic. From the middle until the end of October, the Vendeans advanced and, while not in sufficient strength to hold Mans, Nantes, Saint-Brieuc and a few smaller places, revealed that they could seriously irritate and embarrass their opponents.[2] It was reasonably certain that the rebels would not be able to hold out against the superior forces of the Republic. This Windham knew too well and he made an impassioned request for assistance to be sent to the only 'people who . . . rise first, and trust to support afterwards'.[3] Pitt, believing in the ability of the royalists to resume the offensive, immediately ordered the despatch of 27,000 rifles to the troubled area.[4] And Grenville, reviewing accounts of what were described as a wholesale rising in the north-west, was at one with Pitt and Windham on the need to send money, arms and stores to the rebels so that they might rise in the spring.[5] Much as his brother, Buckingham, urged a winter campaign in Normandy,[6] Grenville knew from Dundas that this was not possible. The immediate future appeared bleak especially after Bonaparte's successful *coup d'état*. So long as the 'Jacobin principles . . . remained unshaken', Europe would be at the mercy of the French.[7] All therefore should be done to exploit every soft point in the French armour.

IV

The north-west of France seemed to be that point, and it was to Wickham that Grenville turned again to support the government in its last venture against France before the peace of Amiens.

---

[1] Minto to Grenville, 25 September 1799, *Life and Letters of Gilbert Elliot*, iii. 93.
[2] Lefebvre, *La Révolution française*, p. 534; Godechot, *La Contre-Révolution*, pp. 374–375.
[3] Windham to Pitt, 30 October 1799, Add. MSS. 37844.
[4] Pitt to Windham, 1 November 1799, ibid.
[5] Grenville to Minto, 1 November 1799, *Dropmore Papers*, vi. 1–2.
[6] Buckingham to Grenville, 5, 9 November 1799, ibid., 9, 14.
[7] Grenville to Dundas, 25 November 1799, ibid., 47.

Grenville's disappointments of the year were confided to Wickham in certainly the most intimate of his private letters.[1] Nothing illustrates better his emotional state than his reaction to the hopes and terrors of the previous months: 'It was very reluctantly that I abandoned the hope that Suwarow [*sic*] was really the instrument destined by Providence to rescue us from all the mischief to which we have been exposed. But this delusion like others is dissipated . . .' Turning to the immediate future, he felt that but for 'the windings of a policy so perverse and crooked that my mind is utterly unable to follow them', Austria had the capacity to make the next (Grenville thought of it also as the last) campaign decisive; if it failed, Britain had the resources and the will to pursue the war alone. The coalition could, in this period of political and military uncertainty in France, deliver a mortal blow to Bonaparte, who would have a difficult time trying to consolidate his power in France and prosecute the war at the same time. The new government in France would therefore likely look to peace negotiations as a temporary expedient, and an Austrian response to such overtures would end all chance of defeating the French for years to come. With Austrian and Russian co-operation what could not be accomplished by an 'immense effort next year against France itself in support of the royalists' in the north-west? It was to further this objective that Grenville asked Wickham to encourage and aid the insurrectionary movements in the east and south of France. The project in contemplation was identical in outline and purpose to that of 1795. Success, in no small measure, Grenville wrote, depended on Wickham: 'You will see by my despatches how great a latitude I have thought myself justified in giving you on that subject. We have had experience enough of each other to make us both feel secure, I in giving it, and you in using it.' To Wickham he also entrusted the opening of a negotiation with general Masséna, who, British intelligence reports suggested, resented, as did most of the military, the ascendancy of Bonaparte.[2] Although the records have yielded nothing on the consequences of this last instruction, they are very rewarding in respect of the others.

As always, Grenville relied on Wickham for a probing interpretation of intelligence available to him. On two vital matters

---

[1] Grenville to Wickham, 30 November 1799, *Dropmore Papers*, vi. 52-4.
[2] Grenville to Wickham, 29 November 1799, F.O. 74/25.

Wickham was able to assure him: Austria was determined to remain in the war provided Britain gave her additional subsidies; and Bonaparte was equally determined to carry the war to Italy and central Europe.[1] Wickham had been extending assistance to the Midi since August when it still seemed possible to hope for an Austrian advance to Lyons. With the help of Précy and d'André, he succeeded in re-establishing a correspondence with Lyons, Marseilles, Besançon and Paris;[2] but although he was financing royalist preparations in the south of France, the insurrections of August which broke out in the Toulouse region under the direction of ex-general Rougé and the comte de Paulo came too soon and were swiftly suppressed.[3]

One consequence of Masséna's victory at Zurich was the rupture of Wickham's communications with the interior of France. He took immediate steps to repair them with help from the archduke Charles. While, of course, the royalists had always to be maintained in a state of readiness, Wickham now felt that the time had come to raise a corps of French deserters and young Frenchmen evading French conscription.[4] The idea had been proposed by d'André and Précy, as well as Willot and Pichegru both of whom had joined Wickham after escaping from their South Atlantic prison in Guiana. On the assumption that Thugut might be persuaded to sanction this project, Wickham was prepared to devote £240,000 to raise a corps of some 8,000 men for service in the Austrian army under Pichegru's immediate command. This body of men, carefully screened and educated in the principles of counter-revolution—brainwashing would be a modern equivalent—could come under the command of the comte d'Artois once Pichegru made good his entry into France. More than one such corps was being planned. Précy would leave for Lyons in March 1800 to command the insurgents assembled there; and Willot, departing for Turin a month earlier, would mount his preparations in Provence at a cost of £125,000.

Thugut censured the idea of using Pichegru. Wickham did not, however, abandon the entire plan. Thugut's objection to the use

---

[1] Wickham to Grenville, 13 December 1799, *Correspondence of William Wickham*, ii. 365–80.

[2] Wickham to Grenville, 25 December 1799, ibid., 400–8.

[3] On the insurrections at Toulouse and the south-west, see Lacouture, op. cit.

[4] Wickham to Grenville, 13 December 1799 (separate from the despatch of same date cited above), F.O. 74/25.

of the Pichegru corps as part of the Austrian army stemmed from his similar reluctance to employ Condé in 1795-6; he was not willing to see the regular army cluttered with nondescript troops and he was, above all, opposed to any royalist undertaking that might hamper his larger diplomatic aims. Significant is Wickham's acceptance of Thugut's veto. Experience had taught him that Austria's decisions were never overruled.[1] On the other hand—and this is what Wickham gambled on—Thugut could raise no objections to stimulus being given to internal insurrection. It was this modified version of his original plan that Wickham now brought forward. The rôles of Willot and Précy assumed major importance, while Pichegru's receded into the background.[2] The project, in many of its aspects, was similar to that proposed in 1795, and was founded on the assumption that the Austrian forces would take the offensive in the spring, both in Italy and along the Rhine. Provence was to be the scene of Willot's endeavours; in preparation for his arrival, several officers would take command of the various insurgent bands. All of them would come under Willot in March after he had arranged with the Austrian head-quarters in Piedmont for the establishment of the necessary channels of communication. An important part of Willot's operations would depend on the landing of arms and ammunition by the British Mediterranean fleet. Précy would meanwhile collect a force of deserters and conscripts in the mountains of Vivarais near Mende and in the forested area south of Moulins. Franche-Comté, the area of Pichegru's preparations, was the least certain, because of the heavy concentration of Republican troops. Not overlooked either was a proclamation announcing the benevolent aims of the coalition and the liberal intentions of the princes.

Whitehall, at the end of 1799 and early in 1800, was responding to the pressure of events beyond its control. It would be mistaken to suppose that the Cabinet knew how formidable was Bonaparte's strength, skill and luck. To be sure, Pitt, Grenville, Dundas and their colleagues were not foolish enough to underestimate Bonaparte's military exploits, but neither did they forget his exhibition of weakness in the Egyptian expedition. They tended to regard his political ambitions as those of a usurper, no different from the men

---

[1] Wickham to Grenville, 13 December 1799 (separate), *Dropmore Papers*, vi. 72–4.

[2] Wickham to Grenville, 25 December 1799, *Correspondence of William Wickham*, ii. 400–8.

who had led France into Revolution and war. So long as France was a victim of internal convulsions, there could be no peace, and peace was only possible with the restoration of the monarchy. This view was not only Windham's; it was shared by Grenville, and, in a lesser degree, by Pitt and Dundas. In these circumstances, Bonaparte's peace overtures in December were bound to be rejected, and measures to prosecute the war went ahead. The Cabinet proceeded with its plans for an invasion of the north-west, unaware that Bonaparte's amnesty to the royalists in December and their capitulation in February would make them superfluous.[1] It is nevertheless of interest to examine the plans of the Cabinet, since they disclose the same division of opinion which prevailed before the Dutch invasion and, by their impingement on Wickham's plans in the south of France, were one of the causes of failure in that theatre of operations.

Supplies to the western royalists were to precede the despatch in March of a force headed by Artois to the coast near Brest. Pitt estimated that 15,000 to 40,000 men would constitute a good invading force; and he felt confident that a further reserve of 20,000 could be mustered. His expectation was that such a force would be numerically superior to the enemy's; it would also inspire the royalists with the will to fight, not only in the immediate area of combat, but throughout the northwest, west and south, especially if the Mediterranean expedition could be scheduled for the same period.[2] But doubts almost immediately began to assail Pitt. The difficulty of establishing and maintaining communications with the royalists, general Grey's criticism of a venture dependent on 'tailors, conscripts, and deserters', and Dundas's last-minute proposal to use Belle Ile, instead of Brest, as a landing point made Pitt reconsider.[3] Bonaparte's pacification of the west ended the speculations.[4]

The spring campaign was now not far off. At once Grenville sent Wickham a series of despatches that demonstrate his determination to transfer the bulk of his country's efforts to the Mediterranean region. Grenville also revealed his deep affection for, and trust in, his envoy. He gave Wickham full authority to

[1] See E. Gabory, *Napoléon et la Vendée* (Paris, 1914), pp. 59–71.
[2] Pitt to Grenville, 22, 23 December 1799, *Dropmore Papers*, vi. 84–5.
[3] Pitt to Grenville, 29 December 1799, 2 January 1800; Grey to Pitt, 16 January 1900, ibid., 89, 94–5, 98–9.
[4] Grenville to Minto, 8 February 1800, ibid., 119.

proceed with his plans in the southern departments and made £500,000 available for this purpose.[1] He promised that a force of 15,000 to 20,000 troops under lieutenant-general Stuart would be sent to the Mediterranean to second Willot's efforts along the Riviera.[2] 'Everything now hangs', Grenville wrote, 'on your activity and exertion; but do not overwork yourself, for, if you are forced to stop, the whole machine must stand still'.[3] In an earlier despatch, his usual reticence was broken by a tribute to Wickham that was certainly a rare communication between a foreign secretary and one of his ministers: 'The value of your suggestions has been inestimable to me, and whatever be the result, I shall never forget the obligations I owe to you for them.'[4] And upon receiving from Wickham a further account of the southern preparations, Grenville's praise soared: 'What you have done has been done in the same masterly style which distinguishes your work from that of all other artists in the same line.'[5]

Willot, as we have seen, was the key figure in Wickham's project,[6] which he insisted on regarding 'rather as a diversion in favour of the Arms of the Allies than an attempt to revive and establish the Royalist Party in the South'; he felt that the blow delivered to royalist morale by the pacification of the Vendée had been overwhelming. Stimulating an insurrection in Franche-Comté was thus totally out of the question. Should, however, Willot succeed in leading a force of deserters and conscripts and Piedmontese 'Barbets'[7] into Provence and Dauphiny, he would be able to count on some assistance from rebel bands organized in the Vivarais and Forez regions under Précy.[8] This, Wickham regretted, modified his original plan of creating links with the Vendean rebels via the royalist organizations in Toulouse and Bordeaux. Willot's operations were clearly to be diversionary, and his potential forces were

[1] Grenville to Wickham, 11 February 1800, no. 2, F.O. 74/29.
[2] Grenville to Wickham, 11 February 1800, no. 1, ibid.
[3] Grenville to Wickham, 11 February 1800, *Dropmore Papers*, vi. 123.
[4] Grenville to Wickham, 8 February 1800, ibid., 119-20.
[5] Grenville to Wickham, 28 March 1800, ibid., 186.
[6] Wickham to Grenville, 28 February 1800, F.O. 74/29.
[7] The 'Barbets' were people of the mountains and valleys of Nice, Tende and adjacent areas, whose hatred of the Republic was inspired by its harsh treatment of them. Their name derives from the fact that, while serving in the militia, they cultivated beards. Their favourite methods of harassing the French armies was by stopping convoys of food, arms and money. This description is taken from *Papiers saisis à Bareuth et à Mende, département de la Lozère* (Paris, an X), pp. 24-35.
[8] See du Lac, op. cit., p. 328.

irregulars, to be ready for action on the wings and rear of the French army. The first objective of his band was to carry out 'partisan warfare, attacks on convoys, weak army detachments and army stores', and 'to intercept recruits and supplies drawn by the army from the interior'.[1] When this aspect of guerilla warfare was well under way, the second objective would be to descend into the Rhône valley, take up fortified positions at Pont St. Esprit, establish communications with Languedoc, Vivarais and Lower Provence, cut those of the Army of Italy, and, with the aid of the royalists, seize at least one of the southern coastal towns to ease the landing of British troops. Without the consent and co-operation of the Austrian command in Italy, the plan could not be achieved. And so Wickham sent Willot to Turin to confer with generals Mélas and Zag, Thomas Jackson, the British envoy, and Lord Keith, the commander-in-chief of the Mediterranean fleet.[2] D'André had already, in January, commissioned the Marut brothers, at one time in the employ of the Lyons police, to begin recruiting the 'Barbet' partisans;[3] and the marquis de Puyvert was busy making preparations for Willot's passage into Provence.[4]

For Wickham this was a time of acute worry.[5] It was not until 21 March that Willot received full powers to act from Louis. To be sure, Louis' grant of authority to Willot to promise a more-or-less sweeping amnesty, and to disturb as little as possible the existing French administrative establishment[6] was all that could be desired, but the delay in its arrival added to the suspense. A further delay was occasioned by Thugut's insistence that Willot confer with him in Vienna before moving on to Turin. Consequently Willot did not reach Turin and was unable to see the Austrian generals before the end of April. Long before this, Wickham, having received reasonably accurate intelligence of the French build-up on the Rhine and in Italy, cited Moreau's strength at 100,000 men and Masséna's in Italy at 30,000.[7] These armies,

---

[1] Appercu présenté à M. le baron de Mélas par le général Willot, no date, F.O. 67/29.
[2] Wickham to Jackson, 24 February 1800, ibid.
[3] *Papiers saisis à Bareuth* . . .
[4] Barruol, op. cit., pp. 268–70.
[5] Wickham to Grenville, 26 March 1800, F.O. 74/29.
[6] Lettres patentes du Roi, portant nomination d'un commandant en chef dans les provinces du Midi, 23 February 1800, F.O. 74/30.
[7] Wickham to Grenville, 24 March 1800, F.O. 74/29. These are the actual figures as recorded in Bonaparte's correspondence, *Correspondance de Napoléon I*, vi. 196, 229.

together with Bonaparte's own reserves at Dijon and those of the army of the Interior and in Holland, convinced Wickham that the First Consul was intent on gaining a 'decisive victory to excite France'.[1] There could thus be no doubt that the start of the campaign was near at hand; additional information, received by means of a correspondence initiated by d'André with persons close to the Consuls, told of the political intrigues against Bonaparte—more proof of his need to still his opponents with a resounding victory.[2]

The Austrian generals at first showed scant concern for Willot. Mélas refused to authorize his lieutenants to co-operate with him, and it became apparent that once the Austrians had pushed the French beyond the Var, they intended to take up defensive positions and not pass the French frontier.[3] This completely nullified Willot's project, for it depended on Austrian assistance in penetrating the frontiers into Provence. His hopes were thus extinguished from the beginning, though he seems to have had some luck at the end of May in gaining consent for his preparations.[4] But within a few days Bonaparte entered Milan, and, with the timely arrival of general Desaix, he defeated Mélas at Marengo on 14 June.

The Austrians, though they must bear the major portion of responsibility for their defeat,[5] cannot alone be charged with negligence. It is possible that more intelligent collaboration in the British Cabinet would have changed the picture, at least in Italy. But this was lacking. The ministers could not agree where to concentrate the country's fighting strength: in the Mediterranean theatre or in operations off Belle Ile. Throughout April this problem nearly sundered the Cabinet. Grenville asked for a quick despatch of forces to the Mediterranean; Dundas argued for a two-part offensive; Windham supported the latter, but actually favoured the Belle Ile expedition alone;[6] and Pitt showed more

---

[1] Wickham to Grenville, 26 March 1800, F.O. 74/29.

[2] Ibid. Cf. Wickham to Grenville, 16 August 1800, F.O. 74/30. Most of these persons were among those proscribed at Fructidor, and Wickham believed that one of their confidants was Consul Lebrun who, before assuming that office, had professed loyalty to Louis. Lefebvre (*Napoléon* (Paris, 4th ed., 1953), pp. 91-2) refers to the activities and hopes of Bonaparte's enemies in Paris.

[3] Jackson to Grenville, 11 May 1800, F.O. 67/29.

[4] Jackson to Grenville, 2 June 1800, ibid.

[5] Dundas to Grenville, 20 May 1800, *Dropmore Papers*, vi. 236-7. Cf. Lefebvre, *Napoléon*, p. 95.

[6] Windham to Portland, 31 March 1800, Add. MSS., 37845.

confidence in Dundas than in Grenville. Indeed, Grenville was quite isolated in the verbal contest. Dundas wished to delay the Mediterranean operations until Sir Charles Stuart saw Wickham and received assurances from the Austrians that they would carry out the provisioning of 15,000 British troops in the south of France.[1] Grenville retreated bitterly with the complaint that precious time had been wasted trying to ascertain Austria's capacity to provision the troops; he now pressed Dundas to end the indecision.[2] To Pitt he wrote that if it was found necessary to reduce the size of the Mediterranean force, it would be infinitely better to abandon it altogether in favour of one large assault in western France.[3] All the while, Grenville urged haste so that he could inform Wickham of the Cabinet's decision. By May, Wickham learned that Sir Ralph Abercrombie's Mediterranean expedition would arrive too late to be of any use.[4]

The last great chance to halt Bonaparte before he consolidated his dictatorship was clearly grasped, but confusion and panic had caught the government in their grip. The hectic consultations and the incessant reconsiderations were fatal. After it was all over, Wickham refused to waste time 'in regrets'; he had had his fill of them for some six years.[5]

Within a year the Pitt ministry resigned, and its successor began peace negotiations with a triumphant Bonaparte. Wickham returned home and in 1802 assumed the post of chief secretary for Ireland. The French remembered him long afterwards as their most dangerous foreign adversary on the continent; the police records amply testify to his 'Machiavellian cunning and largesse'. Bonaparte, the man of destiny, had transcended *'la force des choses'*. Mallet du Pan's prophecy had been fulfilled.

[1] Dundas to Grenville, 9 April 1800, *Dropmore Papers*, vi. 193–4.
[2] Grenville to Dundas, 10, 11 April 1800, PRO 30/8/140.
[3] Grenville to Pitt, 11 April 1800, ibid.
[4] Grenville to Wickham, 29 April, 20 May 1800, *Dropmore Papers*, vi. 209, 232–3.
[5] Wickham to Grenville, 14 August 1800, F.O. 74/31.

13

CONCLUSION

HISTORIANS have long interpreted the period from Themidor to Brumaire in terms of a weakening of the revolutionary spirit. This evaluation has passed into the history books as an orthodox cliché. Yet, despite the reaction which gathered momentum after the first crude attempts to dismantle the revolutionary dictatorship, despite the increasing number of concessions to the Right, and despite the revival of royalist propaganda, the spirit of the Revolution and its achievements could not easily be eradicated. France still remained the embodiment of revolution, however muted its ideals had become. The one capital and inescapable fact is that the counter-revolution, though never to experience greater and better opportunities than during the period under review, was embattled with the residue of an experiment which continued to exhibit signs of vitality.

But the cliché, though necessarily qualified, still holds. In the aftermath of Thermidor the protagonists of the counter-revolution firmly believed in the approaching destruction of the Revolution. For all around them they saw—or chose to see—signposts pointing to its imminent disintegration. Was not the Robespierrian dictatorship being succeeded by a regime in which opportunism had replaced principle; and were there not politicians or, more accurately, trimmers, whose concern for their own necks would make them the allies of a resurgent monarchy? The recall of the Girondins and the deputies who had protested against their arrest was welcomed as a prelude to more far-reaching concessions, perhaps to large classes of *émigrés*, including the non-juring priests. The Convention's recognition of religious liberty and its permission to the Church to use unsold confiscated church buildings were other tangible marks of a return to pre-revolutionary forms. And the Constitution of the year III not only departed from revolutionary doctrines, but appeared to be easily transformable into a charter of monarchy. Internal pressure against the revolutionary state continued to mount as the Convention's life drew to a close. Dissatisfaction with the decrees of 5 and 13 Fructidor led directly to the agitation in the primary assemblies in Paris and to the insurrection of Vendémiaire. Though abortive, it acted as a stimulant upon the electorate; at least half of the newly-elected deputies in the new Legislature were royalists or crypto-royalists. The swing to the Right was marked also by the Directory's official policy of repressing the Jacobins. The turning point in the fortunes of the counter-revolution was to be reached, it was expected, after the elections, for should the royalists emerge victorious there would be no legal method of halting the move towards the restoration of the monarchy.

Apart from the positive attacks on the revolutionary government, there were other signs of its weakness. Its enemies were encouraged by the deplorable state of its finances, the continuing inflation, the strain on its resources caused by the demands of war, and the undisguised opposition to conscription.

On the best methods of exploiting these difficulties of the Directory there were, however, differences in the ranks of the opposition. Royalist opinion on the question of the war was not uniform. Some royalists, hoping to see the revival of a coalition strong enough to defeat the Directory, wanted the war to continue. They dreaded the possibility of a peace which would leave revolutionary France secure and free to stabilize her innovations. Such an eventuality would spell the doom of the French monarchy. Other royalists sincerely believed that the revolutionary aspirations of the French people were feeding on the victories won by their generals in the field. Once the victories ceased, once peace and the problem of demobilizing a vast army came to plague the government, the people, it was argued, would cast off their illusions, realize their error and overthrow the government in preparation for the monarchy's return.

While the problem of continuing or ending the war divided the various elements of the counter-revolution, Britain's war aims were not a source of friction among them. Britain's policy was suspect to the pure royalists from the moment of her refusal to recognize Louis XVII, and later, Louis XVIII. To be sure, British recalcitrance on this question did not alienate the constitutionalists, whose fear of a resurrected *ancien régime* dominated their attitude to the problems of the counter-revolution. Nevertheless, they, as well as the pure royalists, felt that Britain's chief objective was the establishment of a stable government in France, preferably monarchist, but not strong enough to threaten the peace of Europe. They were haunted by the fear of seeing France humiliated, dismembered, and at the mercy of a victorious coalition of European powers. Indeed, on the future of France in Europe, the views of the royalists and the constitutionalists were not fundamentally at variance with those professed by the government of the Republic: the expectation that France would suffer division was shared by all Frenchmen.

II

What was to be Britain's policy in this situation? Alliance with the counter-revolution may be said to have been a major aspect of her war policy, though it was not until Thermidor that serious consideration was given to the possibility of supporting the royalists. In the first stages of the war, she sought to defeat France by relying wholly on her system of alliances and on her own efforts. For a time, in 1793, the advances of the rebels in the west and the impressive revolt in Lyons seemed to be making remarkable progress without external intervention or assistance. Britain regarded the civil war as a welcome diversion. But she was too confident in the ultimate success of the coalition to regard the counter-revolution as more than a nuisance value. Indeed, so little did the counter-revolution count in her calculations that, following the capture of Toulon in the late summer of 1793, the government issued a declaration which, while specifying the monarchy as the most desirable basis of government for France, did not preclude the possibility of treating with any other form of polity, so long as it was firmly established and posed no threat to the *status quo* on the continent.

When, however, a year later, the military situation had all but been reversed, the potential threat of the counter-revolution to the Revolution assumed greater importance. Through Wickham, the British government undertook to explore the feasibility of a peace settlement with the Tallien faction which was said to be contemplating the restoration of the constitutional monarchy. This plan, as we saw, led nowhere. Neither did Wickham's scheme to initiate a series of insurrections on the eastern borders of France in conjunction with a combined Austro-Sardinian offensive. The Foreign Office subsidized Condé's *émigré* army in the hope of making it a self-sufficient and effective force fighting alongside the

Austrians. Try as he might, Grenville could not persuade Vienna to grant Condé's corps independent status or to find a place for it in Austria's strategic and diplomatic purposes. In the west of France, the War Office financed and directed the combined British-*émigré* expedition to Quiberon Bay. Though the failure of both royalist efforts seriously upset their plans, it did not destroy British confidence in Wickham's guidance of the royalists. They believed that the challenge of the Parisian sections to the Convention's decrees of Fructidor should be supported, and directed Wickham to grant funds to the Paris agency. This trust in Louis' agents was to prove misplaced. Their success in discrediting the constitutionalists upon whom they laid the blame for the failure of the insurrection of Vendémiaire, their squandering of the funds which had been earmarked for the rebels in the Vendée, together with the utter failure of the projected insurrections in the Midi, forced a major revision in British policy.

The year 1795 proved to be a period of disillusionment and defeat. The Convention had been able not only to disrupt the unity of the coalition, but had also reaped advantages from the discord dividing its enemies. Its successor, the Directory, appeared to have been established upon a solid footing and fully able to absorb new challenges. The British were the first to realize that a revision of their counter-revolutionary methods was necessary before their aims could be achieved. Accordingly they repudiated their previous tactics and directed their attention to the new Legislature, where the minority was pursuing a disguised royalist attack on the Directory. This nucleus of opposition to the new French government was one of Britain's greatest hopes. As long as it carried out its obstructionist tactics, there was every reason to hope for the development of a situation in which the Directory would be forced on the defensive. The struggle, it was calculated, might be decided by the 1797 elections, for there was much evidence that, with financial assistance, the royalists and their allies would become the majority party and end the revolutionary policy of extending France to her 'natural frontiers'.

Meanwhile the Paris agency itself rejected the insurrectional and conspiratorial methods of the past as futile. Impatient, too, with the long delays, which frequent consultation first with Verona and then with Blankenburg demanded, it devised a new approach to its problems. In the first place, it dismissed the uncompromising hostility of Louis and his ministers to the constitutionalist deputies whose policy of legal and legislative opposition to the Directory won its support. Secondly, it initiated a plan designed to ring Paris with concentric circles of royalist organizations ready to take up arms as soon as the political crisis made armed intervention desirable. This plan became the basis for the *Institut philanthropique* with its secret royalist aims but its legal and open methods. Under the direction of the agency the *Institut* became an effective instrument of royalist propaganda in the majority of the departments.

The agency's aims were thus basically similar to the policy that the British government had now decided to pursue; Wickham consequently hoped that Louis and his ministers would bestow their unqualified approval upon it. Working through d'André and his friends in the Legislature, who held that the greatest opportunity for the monarchy lay in a skilfully conducted election campaign, he persuaded Blankenburg to welcome the advances of the deputies who had signified their willingness to subordinate some of their demands for the sake of royalist unity. Holding their differences in abeyance during the election campaign, both wings of the royalist party scored a resounding victory in the primary and electoral assemblies; and, as a result the Legislature came under its domination. Moreover, the new majority looked for support to Barthélemy, who was a royalist all but in name, and to Carnot, whose respect for constitutional procedures made him an enemy of the 'triumvirate'. Henceforth the tactics of the counter-revolution were to be legal and constitutional.

By this time the progress of the counter-revolution had assumed a new significance. The withdrawal of the Austrians from the war at the very moment of the Directory's electoral defeat left Britain in a perilous position; the royalist deputies who would press the Directory for a peace settlement were her last hope. Forced by her growing sense of isolation and by bankruptcy to make overtures for peace, she counted on the royalists in the Legislature to force the Directory to accept reasonable terms. The outcome of the negotiations at Lille thus depended on the consequences of the struggle between the deputies and the Directory. Should the Directory outmanœuvre its opponents, the groups critical of its foreign policy would be silenced, and there would be no obstacle to presenting the British with harsh terms or rejecting peace altogether. Should the deputies, on the other hand, succeed, the British could look forward to a reasonable compromise at the peace conference.

It was for this reason that Wickham opposed Louis' plan to revive the agency. Its emphasis on violence in spite of its apparent conversion to legal methods, its dependence on a motley band of Chouans whose ranks had been infiltrated by the secret police, and its contempt for legal procedure, had alienated the majority of the royalist deputies who were confident in their ability to repeal the more extreme features of revolutionary legislation, and were predicting that their policy of gradualness would inevitably restore a monarchy obedient to their wishes. The restoration would be accomplished without bloodshed, and Louis would be forced to rule as a constitutional monarch or not at all.

For a few weeks this attitude seemed to be the basis of the only wise policy possible and Louis was persuaded to abandon his idea of reviving the agency. But the illusion of being able to carry on normally, as if the Directory had agreed to assist in its own obsequies, quickly disappeared when it took steps to contest the challenges to its power. Even then the majority of the deputies shrank from the use of violence to protect their constitutional rights. They were willing to use all legal means to preserve their power, but they were reluctant to depart from parliamentary practice to ensure it. To the very last they were faced with the horrible choice of having to decide between the use of force which, if successful, might strengthen the position of the pure royalists, or of acquiesence in their own defeat by the Directory. In this dilemma their abhorrence of the doctrines of the *ancien régime* proved greater than their fear of the Directory's retaliatory power. It might be suggested that they believed that in some miraculous way only the most outspoken royalists would suffer and that they themselves would be spared. Despite the last-minute military precautions of the more resolute royalists, the majority revealed their inability to take the necessary action to defend the *Conseils*. The British meanwhile realized that the Directory had snatched the offensive from the royalists—they lacked the resolution that Grenville had mistakenly attributed to them—and watched with growing fatalism the closing stages of the uneven struggle. Their hopes for a favourable peace settlement evaporated when the Directory scattered the deputies like rabbits.

III

One of the characteristics of every counter-revolution is the division which arises between the *émigré* and his non-*émigré* ally. The refugees of every revolution, whether they leave their country during the early days or during the later stages of the upheaval, huddle together in exile, awaiting their deliverance. Differences between them, depending on what specific act of the revolution drove them to seek asylum, arise. One of the most obvious distinctions is the division between those who leave their country voluntarily and those who are involuntary fugitives from violence, persecution, imprisonment or certain death. The voluntary exiles are usually the first to go, the involuntary exiles generally the victims of a forced emigration. The former, the *émigrés* of the first hour, constituted the nucleus of the pathetic armies of the princes. Hoping to enlist the aid of the powers, most of them found refuge in Germany where they were at first received magnificently. They regarded their exile as momentary and optimistically predicted their triumphant return to a France purged of the revolutionary virus. They plotted and schemed to deliver the king from his enforced bondage. But they did not neglect their social customs, for they imported with them all the causes of their decadence. In France they had formed a nucleus of privilege; in exile they lived in the same ostentation. Theirs was not an austere exile. As one of their number has recorded: 'The emigration was in great vogue. . . . The few friends my father had the time to take leave of, especially the women, even his sisters and his mother—congratulated him, as if his departure were a joyous event. The farewells were said as if he would be returning on the morrow.'[1]

The plight of the *émigrés*, their flight from reality and their hate for the new regime which perhaps cloaked a greater self-hatred is best expressed in Alexis de Tocqueville's brief but incomparable analysis:

The *émigrés*, thus, lived in the imaginary enjoyment of their privileges long after these had been lost to them forever. They were always dreaming of what they would do when they would be reinstated in the possession of their estates and of their vassals, without remembering how

[1] J. O. B. de Cléron, comte d'Haussonville, *Souvenirs et mélanges* (Paris 1878).

CONCLUSION

those vassals now made Europe tremble. Their chief anxiety was not
that the Republic might last but that the monarchy should not be
restored exactly in the way it had been before its fall. They hated the
liberal constitutionalists even more than they hated the radical terrorists; they talked only of the just severity that they would exercise
when they returned to power; in the meantime they devoured each
other; in short, they did everything to maintain the hatred felt for
them, and they succeeded in impressing France with the image of an old
regime even more odious than the real one which had been destroyed.[1]

Their idea of the counter-revolution is striking for its puerility
and naïveté. They had not understood the meaning of the Revolution and would never understand it. What they hoped for was
revolutionary excess: the greater the wound, the more quickly
would it heal. Like their spiritual descendants of the Action
française, they welcomed bloodshed as the most desirable means
of purging France of her sins and her undesirables. They were
possessed by one consuming passion: the absolute reversal of the
Revolution and the repression of its leaders.

An unbridgeable gulf arose between them and those partisans
of the monarchy who believed that it was their duty to remain in
France near the king, and to devote their efforts, feeble as they
were, to the re-establishment of order. The extravagances of the
émigrés of the first emigration, their intrigues and plottings, their
demands for vengeance, their hatred and contempt of Louis XVI,
whom they refused to forgive for having retreated before the
enemy, convinced those who had remained that the future of the
monarchy could not be left in the hands of its obvious defenders.

The first émigrés, by maintaining their fossilized dogmas, prevented the development of a permanent royalist opposition both
within and outside France. A basic division between all those who
emigrated and the royalists who remained in France persisted
throughout the Revolution. The constitutionalists were branded
as the advocates of that most pernicious of all theories: a bicameral
legislature based on the British model. The select circle must
therefore be closed to all except those who agreed to swear
allegiance to monarchy in the abstract, for the émigrés theorized
about the monarchy without regard to its true character or institutions. The monarchy was immutable, symbolic and inalienable

[1] A. de Tocqueville, *The European Revolution and Correspondence with Gobineau* (New
York, 1959), p. 138.

and to it they attributed a power independent of time, circumstance and men.

The monarchy's great opportunity came after Thermidor but, having failed to comprehend the nature of the Revolution from its very inception, the *émigrés* were unable to grasp the nature of the reaction. Instead of seizing this chance to repudiate their dangerous ideas, they insisted on making public declarations incorporating and re-enforcing them. Mallet du Pan wisely observed: 'It is as impossible to recreate the *ancien régime* as it is to build St. Peter's in Rome with chimney dust.' The constitutionalists in France had always realized this and were therefore right in wishing to dissociate themselves from the public pronouncements of the *émigrés*. They regretted the Verona Declaration. They deplored the struggle in the Vendée as the work of irresponsible nobles who had blinded themselves to the irreparable harm it was causing the monarchy. They resented the strictures and interference of the smug *émigrés* who were either safe with Louis XVIII or were plotting unsuccessfully in the east and south.

This view was echoed by one of constitutionalism's partisans, Montlosier, from his exile in England:

The Monarchy has sunk with the weight of our rights and privileges, which cling to it for salvation. We must sacrifice our rights and privileges to help it rise to the surface. We are assured that everyone curses the Revolution. Certainly! I believe it. I am only trying to find out if there is not some difference between cursing the Revolution and wishing to restore the old state of things. France wishes only to remain as she is, and to be at peace. . . . The thing is done, the Revolution cursed by all France has spread over the whole of France. We must take this confusion as it is, find our places in it, and convince ourselves that we will not be valued at our former price.[1]

As we have seen, the royalist deputies in Paris and the *émigrés* agreed, with reservations, to co-operate. The *Institut*, though sanctioned by Louis, was actually the inspiration of the Paris agency, which had been attracted by the idea of carrying out a more restrained and moderate royalist campaign. Because the *Institut* was the vehicle of ideas which rejected the absolutist royalist doctrines, and because its spokesmen advocated a programme designed primarily to remove the abuses of the Revolution, it was essentially an instrument of moderate royalism. Its

[1] Cited by Tocqueville, op. cit., pp. 136–7.

importance lies in the fact that, during the election campaign, it supported men of conservative rather than uncompromisingly royalist views, although paradoxically it had come into being with Louis' approval.

Thus after the elections the *Conseils* were made up of men who wanted to achieve the restoration slowly and without resisting the wishes of the majority of Frenchmen for whom certain features of the Revolution had become sacred. All they asked of Louis was to make certain public concessions to the spirit of the Revolution, to rid himself of his most intolerant doctrinaires, and to abstain from conspiratorial methods. A secret royalist force would only endanger them and sacrifice for all time the chances of the monarchy. After much urging Louis agreed to abandon the idea of organizing a royalist cadre in Paris and its environs. But the political atmosphere in which the deputies hoped to pursue their legislative policy was changed when the Directory seized the offensive. This fact the majority, who were not men of action, could not deal with; they hesitated to make use of the clandestine army that had been hastily put together.

Had the deputies misunderstood the nature of the crisis, and was Louis therefore right in having wished to counsel direct action? Despite his tacit acceptance of their policy, Louis and his ministers never made them any public concessions; nor did they depart sufficiently from their stubbornly-held views to assure the French people that the essential conquests of 1789 would be preserved. Royalist pronunciamentoes were definite only in listing the errors of Louis' subjects; they were never specific in outlining an enlightened royalist programme. The legacy of hatred bequeathed by the *émigrés* in their years of exile was too great for its eradication by insignificant and petty promises. Because of these sins of omission, the French could only assume that the restoration would mean the destruction of all innovations, the confiscation of the *biens nationaux*, the revival of the feudal laws and all the other restraining practices of the *ancien régime*. The deputies, in their attempt to make their own aims the faithful reflection of the people's wishes, failed to grasp the terrible dilemma confronting them in the weeks before Fructidor, but Louis was mistaken in having wanted to advise more direct means. For if his counsels had prevailed, the deputies, royalist or constitutionalist, would probably have been forced to delay or alter their attacks on the Directory.

IV

In conclusion, it must be said that because it failed, the counter-revolution was not necessarily doomed to failure from the beginning. Its significance has been generally underestimated. Viewing it as a movement divided against itself, historians have missed the obvious conclusion that it was used by the revolutionaries not merely to impress the population with the threat to the Republic, but that they themselves were genuinely alarmed by it. As long as the counter-revolution was an active force financed by an enemy power they clung to each other for support. The Thermidorians first and then the Directors were nevertheless not inhibited from carrying out their own counter-revolution—short of restoring the monarchy; but for their aggressive anti-Jacobinism to succeed the assistance of the royalist deputies was indispensable; and ironically the Anglo-royalist menace was greatest during their uneasy collaboration. However, with the elimination of the Jacobins, the power gained by the royalists could not be lightly ignored by the Directory. And the military measures it hastily devised immediately revealed the essential weakness of the conspiracy against the Republic. Without foreign support it could hardly have made the progress it did, but that very foreign support was in the crisis fatal to it. Thus, when the decisive moment arrived Carnot, however sympathetic he was to the concept of legislative supremacy, sided with the 'triumvirate' because he could not blink at the undeniable proofs of conspiracy. More decisive were the misgivings of the deputies who, with few exceptions, hesitated to accept the ultimate implications of transforming their verbal onslaughts into real ones.

Although Fructidor represents the true turning point in the history of the counter-revolution, the following period cannot be entirely dismissed as a futile epilogue. For almost three years after Fructidor, the earlier patterns of the counter-revolution as adumbrated by Wickham in 1795 were resurrected; Britain and her royalist allies reverted to their hopes of overthrowing the Republic by a combination of external military pressure and internal insurrection. This time the British conceived of their goals on a grander scale, although as events proved, the means for their execution were hampered by the same weaknesses that had marked their previous efforts. The great paradox is that Grenville was motivated by considerations not dissimilar to those uttered by Burke in the years of his wandering in the wilderness. His earlier disavowals of Burke's uncompromising embrace of the French royalists were replaced by an almost fanatical conviction that the restoration of the monarchy was the only safeguard of European security. While the origins of these views may be found embedded in the Toulon Declaration, it was not until after Fructidor that Grenville made peace contingent upon the restoration of the monarchy. Rather he, as Wickham, had chosen to support the efforts of the royalist deputies because of their attachment to a policy of peace, and, more significantly, because of his hope that Britain would thus be in a better position to determine France's future in Europe. After the Directory's purge of the deputies, a new sense of urgency can be discerned in his approach to the problem. He now saw peace in Europe as necessarily resting on a monarchical base in France. The desperation which marked his efforts to achieve this goal—by supporting Wickham's plans in eastern and southern France, by counting on counter-revolutionary assistance in Holland, and, when that failed, by shifting his attention once again to western France—illustrates his growing realization that time was running out. Will was not lacking, but after Fructidor it weighed little in the balance, for Bonaparte, the despot of Burke's prophecies, had not only the will but the power.

APPENDIX
SECRET SERVICE EXPENDITURES,
1795–1800

ANY attempt to establish with certainty the amounts expended on secret service by the Foreign Office during the Revolutionary war is a hazardous enterprise. It may, however, yield some information regarding the amounts which Wickham and Talbot—and the government as a whole—put at the disposal of the counter-revolutionaries. In the period 1784 to 1792, on the eve of Britain's joining the continental allies against the Convention, the demands upon the Civil List for foreign secret service, as Professor Cobban shows,[1] were decidedly modest, except for the expenditures in 1787–1788 when Sir James Harris, the future Lord Malmesbury, was expending large sums in an effort to restore the fortunes of the Orange party in Holland and defeat the revolutionary faction.[2] Secret service expenditures rose, as is to be expected, after Britain entered the war, although during 1793 and 1794, the rise was far from being spectacular; indeed, for those two years, the Foreign Office's average annual outlays were only slightly above the average of £24,000 a year in the period from 1784 to 1792.[3]

The really significant rise occurred after 1794. Below are cited figures from two sources, from which we may tentatively construct an account of Foreign Office expenditures in the period 1793 to 1801. Although they are not identical with the period of Wickham's and Talbot's missions, they do provide reasonably accurate figures of the amounts expended. Table I indicates the annual expenditures during this period, totalling £841,901 19s. 0¾d. Table II, covering the same period, shows the amounts discharged by the various officials in the Foreign Office and includes a composite sum discharged by the ministers of that office serving in various missions; these amounts total £831,267 10s. 7¼d., which is some £10,000 less than that recorded in Table I. The discrepancy

---

[1] See his article on British secret service in France for the period 1784–92, loc. cit.

[2] Ibid., 233, 237. See also his study on the Harris mission in Holland, op. cit.

[3] Ibid. Cf. the 1793 sum of £21,165 5s. 6d. and the 1794 sum of £29,334 16s. 0d. See Table I.

APPENDIX

revealed by the two tables is relatively minute and need not detain us. What it is important to note is the great increase in the amounts expended by the Foreign Office for secret service, beginning in 1795, the third year of the war.

TABLE I

Expenditures from 24 February 1790 to 20 February 1801

(Source: A.O. 1/2121, Roll 5)

	£	s.	d.
1790	3,165	16	0
1791	13,299	4	3
1792	9,794	9	0
1793	21,165	5	6
1794	29,334	16	0
1795	90,232	6	8
1796	129,951	14	10¾
1797	182,227	17	6
1798	103,469	0	6
1799	159,340	12	11
1800	98,912	11	10
1801	—		
31 Dec. 1800–31 Dec. 1801	1,008	4	0
Total	£841,901	19	0¾

TABLE II

General Account of Monies Issued to the Right Honourable Lord Grenville for Secret Service from 24 February 1790 to 20 February 1801

(Source: A.O. 3/949)

	£	s.	d.
Grenville	16,000	0	0
Nepean[1]	3,780	0	0
Burges	64,541	16	5
Auckland[2]	12,984	15	0
Canning	136,130	10	6
Frere[3]	119,425	17	0
Hammond	100,597	5	9
Foreign Ministers	377,807	5	11¼
Total	£831,267	10	7¼

[1] Evan Nepean (1751–1822), appointed under-secretary of state for war in 1794, and secretary of the admiralty in 1795, a post he held until 1804. He obviously drew some funds for his secret service operations from Grenville.

[2] Auckland expended most of this sum while at The Hague until 1793 when he tried to seek information regarding Dumouriez's intentions in the Austrian Nether-

APPENDIX

Table III lists the total amounts expended on secret service as recorded in the Treasury North and South Account Books of the Foreign Office for the period 1795–9.

TABLE III

(Source: F.O. 95/476 and F.O. 366/427)

		£	s.	d.
1795	North	23,000	0	0
	South	59,993	4	7
	Total	82,993	4	7
1796	North	30,736	0	0
	South	78,904	1	9
	Total	109,640	1	9
1797	North	18,656	4	8
	South	187,897	15	10
	Total	206,554	0	6
1798	North	24,181	7	6
	South	90,589	0	0
	Total	114,770	7	6
1799	North	22,179	10	5
	South	34,000	0	0
	Total	56,179	10	5
1795–9	Total North	118,753	2	7
	Total South	451,384	2	2
	Grand Total	570,137	4	9

The Treasury South Books also include accounts of funds credited to Wickham and Talbot during the same period covered in Table III. These accounts may be seen in Table IV and indicate what proportion of the total funds was made accessible to the two envoys.

---

lands. See A.O. 1/2121, Roll 5. This source notes the sum of £8,100. 0s. 0d. credited to Auckland for the period ending 24 March 1793. This accounts for three-quarters of the sum noted above.

[3] John Hookham Frere (1769–1846) succeeded Canning as under-secretary in the Foreign Office in April 1799. He remained in that post until October 1800 when he went to Lisbon as envoy extraordinary.

TABLE IV

(Source: F.O. 95/476 and F.O. 366/427)

	Total South			Wickham's and Talbot's Share			Percentage
	£	s.	d.	£	s.	d.	
1795	59,993	4	7	44,498	19	3	
1796	78,904	1	9	57,402	11	5	
1797	187,897	15	10	49,000	0	0	
1798	90,589	0	0	90,589	0	0	
1799	34,000	0	0	34,000	0	0	
Total 1795-9	£451,384	2	2	£275,490	10	8	61
Total North and South	£570,137	4	9	£275,490	10	8	48

According to other figures available from a previously cited source,[1] Wickham and Talbot expended a total of £302,994 9s. 2d. from 1795 to the time their missions came to an end. This source also discloses that during this period the total secret service funds expended by the Foreign Office amounted to £765,242 8s. 3¾d., so that the proportion expended by Wickham and his successor is some 40 per cent of the total sums devoted by the Foreign Office to the secret service, not quite as high a figure as seen in Table IV. Another source[2] reveals yet another set of statistics for 1795, the first full year of Wickham's mission. In that year, Wickham expended £94,028 10s. 2d. (See Table V.) Unfortunately Wickham did not leave similar accounts for the succeeding years of his mission, depriving us of what might perhaps have been the most reliable accounts of his actual expenditures. If Wickham's own accounts for 1795 are accepted, it is necessary to question the sum of £44,498 19s. 3d. cited in Table IV, which was credited to his account, as being too small. The other sums in Table IV can therefore not be regarded as wholly reliable. They are not consistent with the extent of his concerns, especially as they developed in the years following 1795.

Even if we assume that £302,994 9s. 2d.[3] represents the approximate rather than the exact sum which Wickham and Talbot expended, it is an impressive figure, for the total amounts made available for secret service to ministers serving abroad from

[1] A.O. 1/2121, Roll 5.   [2] F.O. 74/17.   [3] A.O. 1/2121, Roll 5.

1790 to the first two months of 1801—a period beginning earlier and ending later than the Wickham-Talbot tours—was £377,807 5s. 11¼d.[1] Thus the two men were responsible for the expenditure of 80 per cent of all the secret service funds spent by British envoys in Europe. When we also consider that the Foreign Office, through Grenville and his colleagues (see Table II) made large contributions to the same agents supported by Wickham—with Dutheil often acting as intermediary—and to the efforts of the royalists not directly under Wickham's supervision, we must conclude that the government had committed itself to a rather massive financial support of the counter-revolution. And whether we accept the total figures in Table I or Table II, they amounted to nearly £1,000,000.[2]

[1] A.O. 3/949.

[2] By comparison Portland at the Home Office made a smaller demand upon the Treasury for his secret service operations. In the period 19 September 1794 to the end of 1801, he expended £76,348 15s. 0d., A.O. 1/2122, Roll 7. Dundas's needs, as secretary of war, were naturally greater. From 11 May 1792 to 13 June 1800, the records show an expenditure of £255,093 1s. 4d., A.O. 1/2122, Roll 6.

BIBLIOGRAPHY

(I) PRIMARY SOURCES

A. MANUSCRIPT SOURCES

1. *PUBLIC RECORD OFFICE*

F.O. 27/37–52, France. 1791–7.
F.O. 28/6–17, Genoa. 1793–7.
F.O. 29/5–15, Army in Germany. 1795–7.
F.O. 67/12–29, Sardinia. 1793–1800.
F.O. 74/4–31, Switzerland. 1794–1800.
F.O. 83/12, Great Britain and General. 1773–1802. Various.
F.O. 95/2–5, Miscellanea. 1781–1837.
F.O. 95/476, Treasury (North) Letter Book. 1794–1800.
F.O. 95/605, Bouillon Papers. 1794–9. Letters to Lord Grenville.
F.O. 366/427, Government Offices. Treasury. 1792–1800.
PRO 30/8/102, 103, 119, 137, 140, 155, 334, 335. Chatham Papers.
P.C. 1/120A, P.C. 1/125–7. Bouillon Papers.
H.O. 1/1–3, General Correspondence (Émigrés, etc.). 1789–97.
H.O. 5/1–3, Correspondence. 1794–8.
W.O. 1/388–392, French Royalists, 1793–1800.
W.O. 1/663, Correspondence. 1796–9.
W.O. 1/746, Correspondence with Foreign Office. 1796–7.
A.O. 1/2121, Declared Accounts, Secret Service. 1779–1801.
A.O. 3/949, Accounts Various, Secret Service. 1779–1837.

2. *BRITISH MUSEUM*

Puisaye Papers, Add. MSS., 8055–7.
Leeds Papers, Add. MSS., 28064, 28068.
Diary of the 2nd Earl of Chichester, Add. MSS., 33629–30.
Auckland Papers, Add. MSS., 34429, 34434–5, 34438–9, 34443–6.
Bute Papers, Add. MSS., 36811.
Windham Papers, Add. MSS., 37844–6, 37859–63, 37875–6, 37903.
Liverpool Papers, Add. MSS., 38352.
Huskisson Papers, Add. MSS., 38734, 38769.
Drake Papers, Add. MSS., 46822, 46825, 46828–9, 46831–6.

3. *ARCHIVES DES AFFAIRES ÉTRANGÈRES*

Mémoires et documents, France 335. Affaires intérieures et extérieures.
Mémoires et documents, France 588–92, 609–11, 617, 624–6, 628–9, 632, 634, 636, 641. Section 'Bourbons'. Documents rélatif à l'émigration.
Correspondance politique, France 589.

BIBLIOGRAPHY

4. *ARCHIVES NATIONALES*

AFIII44, AFIII51[A], AFIII57-9, AFIII68, AFIII70, AFIII81, AFIII89. Relations extérieures.

BB³4, BB³6. Ministère de la Justice (Affaires criminelles).

F⁷3049, F⁷3688⁴, F⁷4269, F⁷4439², F⁷6259, F⁷6371. Police générale.

B. PRINTED SOURCES

1. *MEMOIRS, CORRESPONDENCE AND DIARIES*

D'ANDIGNÉ, L. M., *Mémoires* (with an introduction and notes by E. Biré, 2 vols., Paris, 1900-1).

AUCKLAND, *The Journal and Correspondence of William, Lord Auckland* (edited by the bishop of Bath and Wells, 4 vols., London, 1861-2).

BARRAS, P., *Memoirs* (edited by G. Duruy and translated by C. E. Roche, 4 vols., London, 1895-6).

BARTHÉLEMY, F., *Papiers de Barthélemy 1792-1797* (edited by J. Kaulek, 5 vols., Paris, 1886-94).

——, *Mémoires* (Paris, 1914).

BUCKINGHAM, *Memoirs of the Court and Cabinets of George the Third* (by the duke of Buckingham and Chandos, 4 vols., London, 1853-5).

BURKE, E., *The Correspondence of the Right Hon. Edmund Burke* (edited by C. William, Earl Fitzwilliam and Sir R. Bourke, 4 vols., London, 1844).

——, *The Correspondence of Edmund Burke and William Windham* (edited by J. P. Gilson, Cambridge, 1910).

CARNOT, L. N., *Mémoires* (edited by his son, 2 vols., Paris, 1893).

DELARUE, I. E., *Histoire du dix-huit fructidor* (Paris, 1821).

DUMAS, M., *Souvenirs de 1770 à 1836* (3 vols., Paris, 1839).

DUMONT, E., *Souvenirs sur Mirabeau et sur les deux premières assemblées législatives* (edited by J. Bénétruy, Paris, 1951).

DUPONT-CONSTANT, M., *Essai sur l'Institut philanthropique* (Paris, 1823).

D'HAUSSONVILLE, J. O. B. DE CLERON, COMTE, *Souvenirs et mélanges* (Paris, 1878).

LACRETELLE, C., *Dix Années d'épreuves pendant la Révolution* (Paris, 1842).

MAILLANE, DURAND DE, *Histoire de la Convention Nationale* (Paris, 1825).

MALLET DU PAN, J., *Memoirs and Correspondence of Mallet du Pan* (edited by A. Sayous, 2 vols., London, 1852).

——, *Correspondance inédite avec la cour de Vienne 1794-98* (edited by A. Michel, 2 vols., Paris, 1884).

MALMESBURY, *Diaries and Correspondence of James Harris, first Earl of Malmesbury* (edited by his grandson, the third earl, 4 vols., London, 1844).

MALOUET, P. V., *Mémoires* (published by his grandson, 2 vols., Paris, 1874).

MINTO, *Life and Letters of Sir Gilbert Elliot, first Earl of Minto from 1751 to 1806* (edited by the countess of Minto, 3 vols., London, 1874).

MONTLOSIER, R. DE, *Souvenirs d'un émigré* (edited by comte de Larouzière-Montlosier and E. d'Hauterive, Paris, 1951).

NAPOLÉON I, *Correspondance* (published by order of the emperor Napoleon III, 32 vols., Paris, 1858-70), vols. iii and vi.

BIBLIOGRAPHY

NEUVILLE, H. DE, *Mémoires et souvenirs du baron Hyde de Neuville* (3 vols., Paris, 1894).

PUISAYE, J. DE, *Mémoires qui pourront servir à l'histoire du parti royaliste* (6 vols., London, 1803–8).

REVELLIÈRE-LÉPEAUX, L. M. LA, *Mémoires* (published by his son, 3 vols., Paris, 1895).

ROCHECOTTE, *Mémoires du comte Fortuné Guyon de Rochecotte* (edited by A. de Beauchamp, Paris, 1818).

ROSE, G., *Diaries and Correspondence of the Right Hon. George Rose* (edited by L. V. Harcourt, 2 vols., London, 1860).

THIBAUDEAU, A. C., *Mémoires sur la Convention et le Directoire* (2 vols., Paris, 1824).

VAUBLANC, V. DE, *Mémoires sur la Révolution de France* (2 vols., Paris, 1833).

VAUDREUIL, J. H. F., *Correspondance intime du comte de Vaudreuil et du comte d'Artois pendant l'émigration 1789–1815* (edited by L. Pingaud, 2 vols., Paris, 1889).

LA VILLEURNOY, *Coup d'état du 18 fructidor an V d'après le journal inédit de la Villeurnoy* (edited by H. Bonhomme, Paris, 1873).

WICKHAM, W., *Correspondence of William Wickham* (2 vols., London, 1870).

WINDHAM, W., *The Diary of the Right Hon. William Windham 1784–1810* (edited by Mrs. Henry Baring, London, 1866).

2. JOURNALS

Accusateur public
Censeur des journaux
Éclair
Gazette française
Journal de Paris
Journal de Perlet
Journal des rieurs
Journal général de France
Mémorial
Messager du soir
Nouvelles politiques
Paris pendant l'année . . .
Précurseur
Quotidienne
Républicain française
Tableau de la France
Ventriloque
Véridique

3. OTHER PRINTED SOURCES

AULARD, A., *Paris pendant la réaction thermidorienne et sous le Directoire* (5 vols., Paris, 1898–1902), vols. iii–iv.

BALLOT, C., *Le Coup d'état du 18 fructidor* (Paris, 1906).

BROWNING, O. (ed.), *Despatches of Earl Gower* (Cambridge, 1885).

——, *Despatches from Paris, 1784–90* (2 vols., London, 1909–10).

BIBLIOGRAPHY

Conseil des Cinq-Cents, seconde suite des pièces rélatives à la conspiration découverte le 12 pluviôse, Brit. Mus. Pamphlet, R. 168.

Débats du procès instruit par le Conseil de Guerre Permanent de la xviiième Division Militaire, Brit. Mus. Pamphlet, F. 1134.

Déclarations de Duverne de Presle ou Dunan, annexées au régistre secret du Directoire Exécutif, le 11 ventôse an V, Brit. Mus. Pamphlet, R. 168.

Deuxième déclaration de Dunant, annexée au régistre secret du Directoire Exécutif, le 17 ventôse an V, Brit. Mus. Pamphlet, R. 168.

Historical Manuscripts Commission, *Report on the Manuscripts of J. B. Fortescue, Preserved at Dropmore* (10 vols., London, 1892–1927), vols. ii–vi.

Papiers saisies à Bareuth et à Mende, département de la Lozère (Paris, an X).

Parliamentary History of England (edited by William Cobbett, 36 vols., London, 1806–20), vol. xxx.

PIERRE, V., *18 Fructidor. Documents pour la pluparte inédits* (Paris, 1893).

Procès-Verbaux des séances des Conseils des Cinq-Cents et des Anciens.

Recueil de la correspondance saisie chez Lemaître et dont la Convention a ordonné l'impression, Brit. Mus. Pamphlet F. 570 (27).

Réimpression de l'ancien Moniteur (31 vols., Paris, 1850–4), vols. xxviii–xxix.

STEWART, J. H., *A Documentary Survey of the French Revolution* (New York, 1951).

VEYRAT, P. H., *Précis historique, rélatif à la journée du 18 fructidor*, Brit. Mus. Pamphlet, F. 1199 (9).

(II) SECONDARY WORKS

ANTOINE (DE SAINT-GERVAIS), A., *Histoire des émigrés français depuis 1789 jusqu'en 1828* (3 vols., Paris, 1828).

AUBIN, T., 'Le Rôle politique de Carnot depuis les élections de germinal an V jusqu'au coup d'état du 18 fructidor', *Annales historiques de la Révolution française*, ix (1932), 37–51.

AULARD, F. A., 'Les Bulletins d'un espion royaliste dans les papiers de Lord Grenville', *La Révolution française*, xxxii (1897), 121–8.

——, *Histoire politique de la Révolution française 1789–1804* (Paris, 1901).

BALDENSPERGER, F., *Le Mouvement des idées dans l'émigration française 1789–1815* (2 vols., Paris, 1924).

BALLOT, C., *Les Négociations de Lille* (Paris, 1910).

BARRUOL, J., *La Contre-Révolution en Provence et dans le Comtat* (Cavaillon, 1928).

BEIK, P. H., *The French Revolution Seen from the Right* (Philadelphia, 1956).

BESSAND-MASSENET, P., *La Vie de conspirateur* (Paris, 1956).

BLANC, L., *Histoire de la Révolution française* (Docks edition, 2 vols., Paris, n.d.).

BOIS, P., *Paysans de l'Ouest* (Le Mans, 1960).

——, *Cahier de doléances du tiers état de la Sénéchaussée de Château-du-Loir pour les États-généraux de 1789* (Gap, 1960).

——, 'Réflexions sur les survivances de la Révolution dans l'Ouest', *Annales historiques de la Révolution française*, xxxiii (1961), 177–86.

BIBLIOGRAPHY

BORD, G., *Études sur la question Louis XVII. Autour du Temple 1792–95* (4 vols., Paris, 1912).

BOULOISEAU, M., *Liste des émigrés, déportés et condamnés pour cause révolutionnaire dans le district de Rouen* (Paris, 1937).

——, 'L'Émigration et les milieux populaires. Émigrations, paniques, embauchages (1791–1794)', *Annales historiques de la Révolution française*, xxxi (1959), 110–26.

BROWNING, O., 'The Comité de Salut-Public in the Light of Recent Documents', *Cosmopolis*, iii (1896), 374–90.

BRUGERETTE, J., *Le comte de Montlosier et son temps (1755–1838)* (Aurillac, 1931).

CARRÉ, H., *La Fin des parlements, 1788–90* (Paris, 1912).

CASSAGNE, A., *La Vie politique de François de Chateaubriand* (Paris, 1911).

CASTRIES, (DUC DE), *Le Testament de la monarchie* (3 vols., Paris, 1958–62).

CAUDRILLIER, G., *L'Association royaliste de l'Institut philanthropique à Bordeaux et la conspiration anglaise en France pendant la seconde coalition* (Paris, 1908).

——, *La Trahison de Pichegru et les intrigues royalistes dans l'est avant fructidor* (Paris, 1908).

CHASSIN, C. L., *La Préparation de la guerre de Vendée 1789–93* (3 vols., Paris, 1892).

——, *La Vendée patriote 1793–1800* (4 vols., Paris, 1893–5).

——, *Les Pacifications de l'Ouest 1794–1800* (3 vols., Paris, 1896–9).

——, 'La Trahison de général Willot', *La Révolution française*, xxxii (1897), 403–14.

CLAPHAM, J. H., 'A Royalist Spy during the Reign of Terror', *English Historical Review*, xii (1897), 67–84.

COBB, R., 'Le Témoinage de Ruhl sur les divisions au sein des comités à la veille du 9 thermidor', *Annales historiques de la Révolution française*, xxvii (1955), 110–14.

COBBAN, A. B., *The Debate on the French Revolution* (London, 1950).

——, *Ambassadors and Secret Agents* (London, 1954).

——, 'British Secret Service in France, 1784–1792', *English Historical Review*, lxix (1954), 226–61.

——, 'The French Revolution', *London Times Literary Supplement*, 6 January 1956.

——, *Edmund Burke and the Revolt against the Eighteenth Century* (London, 2nd edition, 1960).

——, 'The Beginnings of the Channel Isles Correspondence', *English Historical Review*, lxxvii (1962), 38–52.

COGORDAN, G., *Joseph de Maistre* (Paris, 1894).

COTTIN, P., *Toulon et les anglais en 1793* (Paris, 1898).

COURCELLE, E., 'La Réaction thermidorienne dans le district de Melun', *Annales historiques de la Révolution française*, vii (1930), 112–28, 252–61, 329–50, 443–53.

DAUDET, E., *La Conjuration de Pichegru et les complots royalistes du Midi et de l'est, 1795–97* (Paris, 1901).

——, *Histoire de l'émigration pendant la Révolution française* (3 vols., Paris, 1904–7).

DELCAMBRE, E., *La Vie dans la Haute-Loire sous le Directoire* (Rodez, 1943).
DESCOSTES, F., *Joseph de Maistre pendant la Révolution* (Tours, 1895).
——, *La Révolution française vue de l'étranger 1789–99* (Tours, 1897).
DODU, G., *Le Parlementarisme et les parlementaires sous la Révolution (1789–1799)* (Paris, 1911).
DOUCET, R., *L'Esprit public dans les départements de la Vienne pendant la Révolution* (Poitiers, 1909).
DUBOIS, L., and F. DUTACQ, *Histoire de Lyon de 1595 à 1814* (Lyons, 1948), vol. ii of KLEINCLAUSZ, A. J., *Histoire de Lyon* (3 vols., Lyons, 1939– in progress).
DUBREUIL, L., *Histoire des insurrections de l'Ouest* (2 vols., Paris, 1929–30).
EGRET, J., *Le Parlement du Dauphiné et les affaires publiques dans la seconde moitié du xviiie siècle* (2 vols., Grenoble, 1942).
——, *La Révolution des notables: Mounier et les monarchiens (1789)* (Paris, 1950).
——, 'L'Aristocratie parlementaire à la fin de l'ancien régime', *Revue historique*, ccvii (1952), 1–14.
——, *La Pré-Révolution française (1787–1788)* (Paris, 1962).
FAY, B., *La Grande Révolution* (Paris, 1959).
FERRERO, G., *Les Deux Révolutions françaises* (Neuchâtel and Paris, 1951).
FORNERON, H., *Histoire générale des émigrés pendant la Révolution française* (3 vols., Paris, 1884–90).
FUNK-BRENTANO, F., *The Old Régime in France* (Trans., London, 1929).
FUOC, R., *La Réaction thermidorienne à Lyon* (Lyons, 1957).
GABORY, E., *Napoléon et la Vendée* (Paris, 1914).
——, *La Révolution et la Vendée* (3 vols., Paris, 1925–8).
——, *L'Angleterre et la Vendée* (2 vols., Paris, 1930–1).
GAIN, A., *Liste des émigrés déportés et condamnés pour cause révolutionnaire du département de la Moselle* (2 vols., Metz, 1925–32).
GAUTHEROT, G., *Un Gentilhomme de grand chemin, le maréchal de Bourmont* (Paris, 1926).
GILLOT, H., *Chateaubriand, ses idées-son action-son oeuvre* (Paris, 1924).
GLAGAU, H., 'Achtundzwanzig Bulletins über den Wohlfahrtsausschuss', *Historische Zeitschrift*, lxxviii (1897), 217–37.
GODECHOT, J., 'Moreau et les papiers de Klinglin', *Annales historiques de la Révolution française*, ix (1932), 309–24.
——, 'Les Insurrections militaires sous le Directoire', ibid., x (1933), 129–52, 193–221.
——, *Les Institutions de la France sous la Révolution et l'Empire* (Paris, 1951).
——, 'Le Directoire vu de Londres', *Annales historiques de la Révolution française*, xxi (1949) 311–36; xxii (1950), 1–27.
——, 'Carnot au 18 fructidor', ibid., xxii (1950), 160–2.
——, 'À Propos de Vannelet: Deprez et Daru', ibid., xxx (Oct.–Dec. 1958), 1–12.
——, 'Essai d'identification de quelques correspondants du comte d'Antraigues', *Bulletin de la société d'histoire moderne*, 11th series, n. 10 (1959), 5–9.
——, *La Contre-Révolution, doctrine et action 1789–1804* (Paris, 1961).
GOODWIN, A., 'The French Executive Directory: a Revaluation', *History*, xxii (1937), 201–18.

——, 'Calonne, the Assembly of French Notables and the Origins of the Révolte Nobiliaire', *English Historical Review*, lxi (1946), 202–34, 329–77.

——, 'Counter-Revolution in Brittany: The Royalist Conspiracy of the Marquis de la Roüerie, 1791–1793', *Bulletin of the John Rylands Library*, xxxix (1957), 326–55.

GRANDSAIGNES, R. de, 'Enquête sur les bulletins de Dropmore', *Annales historiques de la Révolution française*, xxix (1957), 214–37.

——, 'L'affaire du portefeuille d'Antraigues', ibid., xxxiv (1962), 54–69.

GREER, D., 'A Guide to Source Materials on the Émigrés of the French Revolution', *Journal of Modern History*, xv (1943), 39–46.

——, *The Incidence of the Emigration during the French Revolution* (Cambridge, Mass., 1951).

GUYOT, R., *Documents biographiques sur J. F. Reubell, membre du Directoire exécutif* (Paris, 1911).

——, *Le Directoire et la paix de l'Europe 1795–99* (Paris, 1911).

HALL, J., *General Pichegru's Treason* (London, 1915).

D'HAUTERIVE, E., *La Police secrète du premier Empire* (4 vols., Paris, 1908— in progress).

HEROLD, J. C., *Mistress to an Age* (London, 1959).

HOLLAND ROSE, J., *The Life of William Pitt* (2 vols., London, 1923).

HOMAN, G. D., 'Jean-François Reubell', *French Historical Studies*, i (1960), 416–35.

HUTT, M., 'The British Government's Responsibility for the Divided Command of the Expedition to Quiberon', *English Historical Review*, lxxvi (1961), 479–89.

——, 'Spies in France 1793–1808', *History Today*, xii (1962), 158–67.

——, 'Puisaye, principalement d'après les archives anglaises', *Annales historiques de la Révolution française*, xxxvi (1964), 1–21.

JACOB, L., 'L'Esprit public dans le Nord au début du Directoire', *Revue du Nord*, xvii (1944), 33–45.

JOHNSON, J. A., 'Calonne and the Counter-Revolution 1787–92', Ph.D. thesis, University of London, 1955.

JOLIVET, C., *L'Agitation contre-révolutionnaire dans l'Ardèche sous le Directoire* (Lyons, 1930).

KING, A., 'The Relations of the British Government with the Émigrés and Royalists of Western France, 1793–95', Ph.D. thesis, University of London, 1931.

KOYRÉ, A., 'Bonald', *Journal of the History of Ideas*, vii (1946), 56–73.

LAC, R. DU, *Le Général comte de Précy* (Paris, 1908).

LACOUR-GAYET, R., *Calonne financier, réformateur, contrerévolutionnaire (1734–1802)* (Paris, 1963).

LACOUTURE, J., *Le Mouvement royaliste dans le sud-ouest 1797–1800* (Hossegor, 1932).

LASKI, H. J., *Studies in the Problems of Sovereignty* (New Haven, 1917).

——, *Authority in the Modern State* (New Haven, 1917).

LEBON, A., *L'Angleterre et l'émigration française de 1794 à 1801* (Paris, 1882).

LE BRETON, A., *Rivarol, sa vie, ses idées, son talent, d'après des documents nouveaux* (Paris, 1895).

LEDRÉ, C., *Le Culte caché sous la Révolution. Les missions de l'abbé Linsolas* (Paris, 1949).

LEFEBVRE, G., 'Réponse à M. Meynier', *Annales de la Faculté des Lettres de Strasbourg*, x (1931), 49–52.

——, *Les Thermidoriens* (Paris, 1937).

——, *Quatre-vingt-neuf* (Paris, 1939).

——, *Le Directoire* (Paris, 1946).

——, *La Révolution aristocratique* (Les Cours de Sorbonne, Paris, 1946).

——, *Le Directoire* (Les Cours de Sorbonne, Paris, 1947).

——, *Napoléon* (Paris, 4th edition, 1953).

——, *La Révolution française* (Paris, 2nd edition, 1956).

LOMENIE, E. BEAU DE, *La Carrière politique de Chateaubriand de 1814 à 1830* (2 vols., Paris, 1929).

MACCUNN, J., *The Political Philosophy of Burke* (London, 1913).

MADELIN, L., *La Contre-Révolution sous la Révolution* (Paris, 1935).

MAGNUS, P., *Edmund Burke* (London, 1939).

MALLET, B., *Mallet du Pan and the French Revolution* (London, 1902).

MASSON, F., *Le Département des affaires étrangères pendant la Révolution 1784–1804* (Paris, 1877).

MATHESON, C., *Life of Henry Dundas, first Viscount Melville, 1743–1811* (London, 1933).

MATHIEZ, A., 'Les Divisions dans les comités à la veille de thermidor', *Revue historique*, cxviii (1915), 70–87.

——, *La Révolution et les étrangers* (Paris, 1918).

——, *La Conspiration de l'étranger* (Paris, 1918).

——, *La Révolution française* (3 vols., Paris, 1922–7).

——, 'Les Séances du 4 et 5 thermidor aux deux comités de salut public et de sûreté générale', *Annales historiques de la Révolution française*, iv (1927), 193–222.

——, *La Réaction thermidorienne* (Paris, 1929).

——, *Le Directoire* (Paris, 1934).

MATTEUCCI, N., *Jacques Mallet du Pan* (Naples, 1957).

MAUDUIT, R., *Les Conceptions politiques et sociales de Bonald* (Paris, 1913).

MEYNIER, A., *Le Dix-huit fructidor an V* (Paris, 1927).

MITCHELL, H., 'Francis Drake and the comte d'Antraigues: a Study of the Dropmore Bulletins, 1793–1796', *Bulletin of the Institute of Historical Research*, xxix (1956), 123–44.

——, 'Vendémiaire, a Revaluation', *Journal of Modern History*, xxx (1958), 191–202.

MONTARLOT, P., 'Un Agent de la police secrète 1800–17, Jean Marie François', *Revue des questions historiques*, xciv (1913), 94–119.

MOULINIÉ, H., *De Bonald* (Paris, 1915).

MOUSSET, A., *Le comte de Fernan Nûnes* (Paris, 1923).

OLLIVIER, A., *Saint-Just et la force des choses* (Paris, 1954).

——, *Le Dix-huit brumaire* (Paris, 1959).

PALLAIN, G., *La Mission de Talleyrand à Londres en 1792* (Paris, 1889).

PALMER, R. R., *The Age of the Democratic Revolution* (2 vols., Princeton, 1959–64).

BIBLIOGRAPHY

PARISET, G., *La Révolution française 1792–99* (Paris, 1920).

PHIPPS, R. W., *The Armies of the First French Republic* (5 vols., London, 1926–39).

PINGAUD, L., 'Le Président de Vezet', *Revue historique*, xx (1882), 282–326.

——, *Un Agent secret sous la Révolution et l'Empire, le comte d'Antraigues* (Paris, 2nd edition, 1894).

POIDEBARD, R., *La Vie agitée d'Imbert-Colomès* (Lyons, 1942).

POMMERET, H., *L'Esprit public dans le département des Côtes-du-Nord pendant la Révolution 1789–99* (Saint-Brieuc, 1921).

POUJOULAT, J. J. F., *Le cardinal Maury: sa vie et ses œuvres* (Paris, 1855).

REINHARD, M., *Le Département de la Sarthe sous le régime directorial* (Saint-Brieuc, 1936).

——, *Le Grand Carnot* (2 vols., Paris, 1950–2).

——, 'Dropmore Papers et méthode historique', *Annales historiques de la Révolution française*, xxx (Oct.–Dec. 1958), 13–16.

——, 'Les Négociations de Lille et la crise du 18 fructidor d'après la correspondance inédite de Colchen', *Revue d'histoire moderne et contemporaine*, v (1958), 38–56.

RICHARDS, N. F., 'British Policy and the Problem of Monarchy in France, 1789–1802', Ph.D. thesis, University of London, 1954.

RIFFATERRE, C., *Le Mouvement anti-jacobin et anti-parisien à Lyon et dans le Rhône-et-Loire en 1793* (2 vols., Lyons, 1912, 1928).

ROBISON, G., *Revellière-Lépeaux, Citizen Director 1753–1824* (New York, 1938).

ROCHE, A. V., *Les Idées traditionalistes en France de Rivarol à Charles Maurras* (Urbana, Illinois, 1937).

RUDÉ, G., *The Crowd in the French Revolution* (Oxford, 1959).

RUFER, A., 'En Complement des Dropmore Papers', *Annales historiques de la Révolution française*, xxx (July–Sept. 1958), 14–43.

SAGNAC, P., *La Fin de l'ancien régime et la Révolution américaine (1763–1789)* (Paris, 3rd edition, 1952).

SANGNIER, G., *Les Émigrés de Pas-de-Calais pendant la Révolution* (Blangermont, 1959).

SAUZAY, J., *Histoire de la persecution révolutionnaire dans le département de Doubs de 1789 à 1801* (10 vols., Besançon, 1871), vol. viii.

SCIOUT, L., *Le Directoire* (4 vols., Paris, 1895–7).

SICOTIÈRE, L. DE LA, *Louis de Frotté et les insurrections normandes 1793–1832* (2 vols., Paris, 1889).

SOREL, A., *L'Europe et la Révolution française* (8 vols., 21st and 23rd editions, Paris, 1927, 1942) vols. ii, iv, v.

STANLIS, P. J., *Edmund Burke and the Natural Law* (Ann Arbor, 1958).

SURATTEAU, J., 'Les Élections de l'an IV', *Annales historiques de la Révolution française*, xxiii (1951), 374–93; xxiv (1952) 32–62.

——, 'Les Élections de l'an V', ibid., xxx (Oct.–Dec. 1958), 21–63.

THUREAU-DANGIN, P., *Royalistes et républicains* (Paris, 1874).

TILLY, C., 'Civil Constitution and Counter-Revolution in Southern Anjou', *French Historical Studies*, i (1959), 172–99.

——, 'Local Conflicts in the Vendée before the Rebellion of 1793', ibid., ii (1961), 209–31.

BIBLIOGRAPHY

TILLY, C., 'Some Problems in the History of the Vendée', *American Historical Review*, lxvii (1961), 19–33.

——, 'The Analysis of a Counter-Revolution', *History and Theory*, iii (1963), 30–58.

TOCQUEVILLE, A. DE, *The European Revolution and Correspondence with Gobineau* (New York, 1959).

TÖNNESSON, K. D., *La Défaite des sans-culottes* (Paris and Oslo, 1959).

VAILLANDET, P., 'Les Débuts de la terreur blanche en Vaucluse', *Annales historiques de la Révolution française*, v (1928), 109–27.

——, 'Le Procès des juges de la commission populaire d'Orange', ibid., vi (1929), 137–63.

VINGTRINIER, E., *La Contre-Révolution. Première période 1789–91* (2 vols., Paris, 1924).

WALTER, G., *Le Comte de Provence* (Paris, 1950).

——, *La Guerre de Vendée, sociologie d'une contre-révolution* (Paris, 1953).

WARD, A. W. and G. P. GOOCH, (eds.), *The Cambridge History of British Foreign Policy 1783–1919* (3 vols., Cambridge, 1922–3), vol. i.

WEIL, M. H., *Un Agent inconnu de la Coalition, le général de Stamford* (Paris, 1923).

WILLIAMSON, A., 'Jersey, centre d'espionnage au début de la période révolutionnaire', *Revue d'histoire moderne*, ix (1934), 423–34.

ZIVY, H., *Le Treize vendémiaire an IV* (Paris, 1898).

(III) WORKS OF REFERENCE

BALTEAU, J., BARROUX, M., and M. PREVOST, *Dictionnaire de biographie française* (9 vols., Paris, 1933– in progress).

Biographie moderne ou dictionnaire biographique de tous les hommes morts et vivants (4 vols., Leipzig, 1807).

Biographie nouvelle des contemporains (20 vols., Paris, 1820–9).

Biographie universelle et portative des contemporains (5 vols., Paris and Strasbourg, 1834).

BOUCHEZ, P. J. B., and P. C. ROUX, *Histoire parlementaire de la Révolution française* (40 vols., Paris, 1834–8), vol. xxxvii.

CARON, P., *Manuel pratique pour l'étude de la Révolution française* (Paris, 1947).

Dictionary of National Biography.

Dictionnaire des Parlementaires français (5 vols., Paris, 1891).

HATIN, E., *Histoire politique et littéraire de la press en France* (8 vols., Paris, 1859–61).

——, *Bibliographie historique et critique de la presse périodique française* (Paris, 1866).

KUSCINSKI, A., *Dictionnaire des Conventionnels* (Paris, 1920).

——, *Les Députés au Corps législatif de l'an IV à l'an VII* (Paris, 1905).

ROBINET, DR., ROBERT A., and J. LE CHAPLAIN, *Dictionnaire historique et biographique de la Révolution et de l'Empire 1789–1815* (2 vols., Paris, n.d. [1899]).

SIX, G., *Dictionnaire biographique des généraux et amiraux français de la Révolution et de l'Empire 1792–1814* (2 vols., Paris, 1934).

BIBLIOGRAPHY

TEISSIER, O., *Biographie des députés de la Provence à l'assemblée nationale de 1789* (Marseilles, 1897).

TOURNEUX, M., *Bibliographie de l'histoire de Paris pendant la Révolution française,* (5 vols., Paris, 1894), vol. ii.

INDEX

Dubreuil, Jean Julien, 185
Dubreuil, L., 6, 6n.
Dufresne de Saint-Léon, Louis César Alexandre, 156
Dumas, Mathieu, comte, Lafayette's former aide-de-camp, 41; requests release of Lafayette, 46; alleged Orléanist, 127; his followers, 132, 133; members of group supporting his policies, 137; goals of, 151–2, 174–6; conferences with Carnot and Barras, 186, 187; in crisis caused by Directory's appeal to Hoche, 193–4; plans to strengthen Legislative Guard, 201; essentially moderate, 203; wavers at the end, 215
Dumolard, Joseph Vincent, 133, 138, 139, 159, 174, 177
Dumont de la Charnaye, 177
Dumont, Étienne, 130, 131
Dumouriez, Charles François, general, 28, 257n.
Duncan, Adam, 1st viscount Duncan of Camperdown, 233
Dundas, Henry (later viscount Melville), secretary of war, receives memoir from Richard Burke, 23; considers nature of future French government, 26; believes West Indies to be Britain's chief target, 31, 37; differs with Grenville, 33; has little faith in royalists, 231; points to weakness of British land forces, 234, 235; views of Bonaparte, 238–9; sides with Pitt against Grenville's conception of 1800 operations, 242–3; his secret service expenditures, 260n.
Duplantier, Jacques Paul Fronton, 138, 139, 174
Dupont Constant, 153
Dupont de Nemours, Pierre Samuel, 132, 148, 149
Duport, Adrien, 41, 126, 138
Duprat, Pierre Louis, 212
Durand de Maillane, Pierre Toussaint, 132, 138, 147, 174
Durand-Molard, 213
Dusaulx, Jean Joseph, 177
Dussault, Jean Joseph François, 213
Dutheil, Jean François, 67, 67n., 83, 89, 114, 210n., 260; and Grenville, 67,

83, 110, 163–5, 169–70; and Paris agency, 92–4, 98, 99, 105, 107, 108, 115–16, 163–5
Duverne de Presle, Thomas Laurent Madeleine, member of Paris agency, distorts meaning of Paris crisis, 66–7; his background, 72; his code name, 75n.; Dutheil's attempt to make him head of agency, 92–3; obtains news from Vendée, 94; his rôle in Louis XVIII's plans, 98–9; makes overtures to royalist deputies, 100; Louis refuses to sanction overtures, 102, 135; requests funds from Wickham, 105; requests and obtains funds from Grenville, 107, 109–10, 171; attitude towards peace, 108–9; his arrest, 111; his trial, 112–13; his confession, 113–114; his reports to Dutheil, 115; d'Antraigues' assessment of, 116; informs Grenville of true state of agency, 169; his release, 211
Du Vernegues, royalist agent in Genoa, 188–89

Éclair, 144, 148
Eden, Sir Morton, British ambassador to Vienna, 51, 54, 57, 63, 223, 230
Eden, William (later Lord Auckland), 13, 19, 20, 21, 22, 25, 26, 27, 28, 31, 36, 257n., 258n.
Egret, J., 3n.
elections of 1795, 59–60, 65, 66, 67, 96, 132, 156
elections of 1797, 11, 104, 105, 106, 107, 114, 115, 134, 136–7, 138, 163, 165, 166, 174, 177, 180, 184, 187; Institut's rôle in, 109, 152–3, 163, 164, 181; expectations from, 140, 142–3, 164, 245, 247; press campaign and, 144–9; church and, 154–6; studied by Suratteau, 157–8; Directory's alarm over, 160; significance of 160–1, 248; partial annulment of, by Directory, 212; royalists and, ch. 8, passim
elections of 1798, 184, 199, 219, 222
Elgin, Thomas Bruce, Lord, 32, 41
Elliot, Sir Gilbert, (later Lord Minto), 32n., 35, 230, 234
Elliott, Hugh, 18

INDEX

INDEX

INDEX